Pitch Battles
Sport, Racism and Resistance

decided that a meeting would be held...
competition between...
such...
their...

Or...

...

Leaving aside...
international bodies, it was to...
This was something of more of a declaration to...
Exclusion...
idea was formed...

Step: The Save My Soul boycott of sanctions cricket

The militant rugby issues... that differentiated it in principle from calls along
the movement as it reinforced... stepped out from what was always such means
to stop anti-cricket boycott to later as well in an attempt... have to...

By now, apparatus, as influence by the Anti-Apartheid Movement
went much wider. Countries led to try harder on board to boycott mix and
Bangor in South rich, Dennis also hard-urged cancellation. The Commonwealth Games, due to take place in Edinburgh, became more aware of the
important leverage over's own international expertise and contacts were put to
good use as it was pointed out to African and Asian countries that they
would be an intolerable contradiction... being so... to live in a world
now as in apartheid cricket or having to over over as a well structure.

Meanwhile, Apartheid leaders, in their own manner, were the belief
envisage, as two more gifts. The black American sports stars... who
was banned from entering South Africa to play and in international
Caribbean cricket team was also blocked to ensure... ominous non-white
prominent...

While all this was going on, there was a third ominous planned and came

Pitch Battles

Sport, Racism and Resistance

Peter Hain and André Odendaal

ROWMAN & LITTLEFIELD
Lanham · Boulder · New York · London

Published by Rowman & Littlefield

An imprint of The Rowman & Littlefield
Publishing Group, Inc.
4501 Forbes Boulevard, Suite 200,
Lanham, Maryland 20706
www.rowman.com

6 Tinworth Street, London SE11 5AL,
United Kingdom

British Library Cataloguing in Publication
Information Available

Library of Congress Control Number:
2020949467

ISBN: 978-1-78661-522-0 (cloth)
ISBN: 978-1-78661-523-7 (pbk)
ISBN: 978-1-78661-524-4 (electronic)

Edited by Gurdeep Mattu

Copy-edited by Dorothy Feaver
Indexed by Christine Shuttleworth

Designed by Mark Thomson
Typeset in Garamond Premier and Söhne
by International Design UK

The paper used in this publication meets the
minimum requirements of American
National Standard for Information
Sciences—Permanence of Paper for Printed
Library Materials, ANSI/NISO Z39.48-1992

Preface

In 2020 two seismic global events overtook and enhanced the relevance of this book. Dramatic Black Lives Matter movement protests sparked by the callous killing by an American police officer on 25 May in Minneapolis of a black man, George Floyd, sent shockwaves reverberating around the world.

In a filmed horror lynching that lasted eight minutes and forty-six seconds, officer Derek Chauvin clamped his knee over Floyd's windpipe, ignoring his anguished plea, 'I can't breathe'. The protests quickly spread from the United States to other parts of the world, shedding light on the depth of systemic racism throughout societies globally, sport included, still persisting despite official policies opposed to it. The impact of this terrible killing was heightened by the fact that it took place in the middle of the unprecedented Covid-19 global pandemic – which, at the time of writing, has infected more than 35 million people, and killed over one million.

More than half of humanity, some four billion people, were put into a state of lockdown, and whole economies ground to a halt – eerily pictured by ghost airports, deserted streets and empty sports stadia. Every major sports competition on the planet was suspended. The virus has caused a rethink about our world, politically, socially, environmentally, technologically and economically; the 'normal' propounded by global elites and monopolies is not an unchangeable reality, and sport is no exception.

The tragedy of human beings expiring while separated from loved ones, often attached to ventilators as space-suited medical staff bravely tried to help, and then that single public killing, has led to an upswell of solidarity.

The Black Lives Matter movement emphasises how black and indigenous people all over the world remain subject to oppressive structures and power relations shaped during 500 years of Western conquest – taking in colonialism, slavery and the development of an exploitative global economic system – leading to a chasm between rich and poor.

As the first comprehensive single-volume account of the making of the most racist sports system in the world – South African sports apartheid – and the ensuing six-decade-long struggle to overthrow that iniquitous system and its effects, *Pitch Battles* offers lessons that link directly to the ferment of energy and ideas in the Black Lives Matter movement.

While this publication is released to mark the fiftieth anniversary of the militant protests that stopped the all-white South African cricket tour to Britain in May 1970, the events of 2020 reinforce the interconnected themes dealt with over the following pages. From the Western DNA of systemic racism in modern sport to the agents of change – black sportspeople and their allies who spoke up against the odds, often at great cost to themselves – this book traces how sport is inseparable from societal issues.

The issues raised by the pandemic and Black Lives Matter resonate closely with many of those that have emerged in South Africa over the past few decades as it has moved from apartheid and the liberation struggle to becoming a democratic country, though with the expectations of that transition in many ways unfulfilled.

Many rugby and cricket fans were horrified by the direct-action protests that caused widespread disruption of the all-white 1969–70 Springbok rugby tour and the subsequent stopping of the 1970 cricket tour to Britain. Yet, with fifty years' hindsight, that presaged the end of apartheid sport.

Former cabinet minister Lord Peter Hain led militant direct-action demonstrations against those tours and, with one of South Africa's foremost sports historians and fellow anti-apartheid activist André Odendaal, shows how decades of international campaigns and the rise of the 'nonracial' movement inside South Africa helped change a country and led to a Springbok team captained by a township kid, Siya Kolisi, winning the 2019 World Cup.

This is a riveting story of vision, sacrifice, complex contestation, struggle and hard-earned change, full of human drama. Those opposing the system faced trial, torture, hardship and hanging. *Pitch Battles* rests on little-known contextual detail stretching from early colonialism to the coronavirus to explain the deep connections between the nineteenth-century British origins of globalisation, racism and gender discrimination in sport, and contemporary developments – and why sport can never be divorced from politics or society's values.

Sportsmen and women who had rarely stood against injustice or inequality have started speaking out. Powerful sports establishments – including the richest sports league in the world, the US National Football League, were compelled to apologise and respond. For generations, sportspeople had been in denial about the racism ubiquitous in global sport. The mantra to 'keep politics out of sport' is fervently contested in this book.

In 2016 Colin Kaepernick led with his protest against racism. In June and July 2020 Britain's Premier League footballers also bent down to 'take the knee' when the season resumed after being halted for over three months by the Covid-19 pandemic. So did most Formula One drivers when their race season began belatedly in Austria, led by six-time world champion Lewis Hamilton, the only black driver in Formula One, who eloquently demanded diversity in motor sport and gave the black power salute on the podium after his first victory. Bubba Wallace, the only black driver in NASCAR's highest level of motor sport echoed Hamilton's pleas.

Other sports – also in South Africa – followed as officials and competitors, who had for generations resisted taking a stand on issues of human rights and injustice, have found themselves swept up in the tide for change. The question remains: Will that change be fundamental? This depends on whether the pressure endures once the sense of outrage subsides. Meanwhile *Pitch Battles* illuminates and reinforces the case for sport to acknowledge and act upon its social responsibilities in a way it has rarely ever done.

Peter Hain, Neath, Wales
André Odendaal, Cape Town, South Africa

October 2020

Introduction

Sport had never experienced anything like this before.

Five decades ago, in the British winter of 1969–70, mass demonstrations and field invasions during the whites-only South African Springbok rugby tour disrupted the cosy relationship between elites from the two nations and shone global attention on apartheid in sport and, more broadly, the iniquitous system itself.

Thousands of protestors invaded rugby pitches, cricket grounds and tennis courts to disrupt whites-only teams touring from apartheid South Africa, provoking furious reaction from fans, administrators, conservative politicians and conservative media, but leading to the unprecedented stopping in May 1970 of a scheduled South African cricket tour.

A year later, the new, headline-grabbing, direct-action form of sports protest spread from Britain to former white-run British colony Australia, and then to New Zealand.

Before that, anti-apartheid protesters holding up placards outside sports venues had been tolerated with patronising disdain. But when demonstrators used direct action to disrupt games and stop tours, they could never be ignored.

Occurring at the end of the 'sixties' decade of youth revolt, cultural change and decolonisation, these spectacular protests introduced a new dimension to global sport, rupturing long-held class-based Victorian narratives about the sanctity of sport and 'fair play' as something happening apart from politics and the ups and downs of everyday life.

The protestors helped popularise a broader, burgeoning international anti-apartheid movement, which – together with the nuclear disarmament movement – would become one of the two biggest single-issue campaigns in global politics in the second half of the twentieth century. They also helped trigger a process of fundamental change in the racist nature of sport in South Africa, which would lead, two decades later, to a new, non-racial sport set-up from school through club to national level in democratic South Africa. Many argued that these and succeeding struggles for non-racial sport inside South Africa even played a role in the country's transformation under Nelson Mandela's leadership from apartheid to non-racial democracy.

Commemorating the fiftieth anniversary of the historic 1969–70 'demo tour', the cricket tour cancellation and white South Africa's expulsion from the Olympics, *Pitch Battles* explores the themes of sport, globalisation and resistance from the deep past to the present.

A key figure in those campaigns over half a century ago, Peter Hain became 'public enemy number one' to sports-mad white South Africans, an ogre to other sports fans. André Odendaal is a former first-class cricketer, anti-apartheid sports activist and historian. They have written some thirty books between them and here, from an intimate angle, they tell a remarkable story of how struggles in sport helped change South African society.

While focussed on British/South African issues and relations, Peter and André draw on their unusual personal journeys to explore and illuminate global themes in sport. These range from the formative years of modern sport to the social roots of amateurism, the impact of global economic systems, and the deeply rooted history of racism in sport. Contemporary topics include the massive commercialisation of sport, reflected by Peter's favourite club, Chelsea; US football star, Megan Rapinoe, speaking out on gender; controversy around the sex of dynamic South African athlete Caster Semenya; President Trump and the American footballers 'taking a knee' during the singing of the anthem; dribbling wizard, Eniola Aluko, protesting against racism in the England women's football team's coaching; athletes taking the knee and disrupting sport play-offs to bring attention to injustice in Donald Trump's America; as well as the seismic impact of the global coronavirus pandemic in shutting down sport completely.

Peter and André embark from the same vantage point as the historian Johan Huizinga, who explained that play is an essential part of our humanity, both as individuals and communities. Huizinga observed, 'The spirit of playful competition is, as a social impulse, older than culture itself and per-vades all life like a veritable ferment.'[1] Moreover, he noted, 'Ritual grew up in play; poetry was born in play and nourished on play; music and dancing were pure play'. He noted also that play influenced philosophy and even the rules of warfare, which were based on 'patterns of play'. He ends, 'We have to conclude, therefore, that civilisation is, in its earliest phases, played.

16

It does not come from play like a babe detaching itself from the womb: it arises in and as play and never leaves it.'[2]

Sport as we know it today emerged as a distinctly organised form of play in the nineteenth century. Starting with an early phase of rapid globalisation via the spread of empire, the Industrial Revolution and the beginnings of international sporting contests – such as Wimbledon, the British Open golf championships, the first football and rugby internationals and the Olympic Games – the book explores key themes which have underlined the social relevance of sport from that time to the present.

In the modern age, sport has come to assume huge social, political and commercial significance. Billions of people around the world are avid sports followers and the global sports industry is now worth hundreds of billions of dollars per year. Over time, the nature and meaning of sport has changed as it has evolved from an export accompanying political conquest to a commodity produced for consumption in every corner of the world, in hundreds of millions of houses and rickety shacks that people call home – and, now too, on the ever-present mobile phones we carry around.

Fifty years after the controversial demonstrations that shocked apartheid South Africa and created ructions in Britain and other members of the old boys' club of empire, Australia and New Zealand, *Pitch Battles* explores the changing face of global sport. When those demonstrations took place in 1969–70, Dr Danie Craven, head of the South African Rugby Board declared that the Springbok rugby jersey was for whites only and vowed that 'over my dead body' would black players wear it. Half a century later the world watched in awe as a Springbok team with a wholly different complexion won the gripping Rugby World Cup 2019 final in Japan, and inspirational captain Siya Kolisi, who grew up in the impoverished township of Zwide, lifted the Webb Ellis Cup joyously above his head.

The book is dedicated to the tens of thousands of courageous and mostly unheralded sports lovers inside apartheid South Africa who made the transition to that 2019 moment in Yokohama possible via the freedom struggle and a resilient non-racial sports movement. This was guided in repressive times by organisations such as the South African Sports Association (SASA), South African Non-Racial Olympic Committee (SANROC), South African Council on Sport (SACOS) and the National Sports Congress (NSC). The pages that follow offer an overview of these path-breaking groups and the vision and value of 'non-racialism' and inclusive humanity they stood for in the toughest of times.

Pitch Battles is also dedicated to the millions of people throughout the world who reached out in solidarity across boundaries to bring a violent political system and twisted sports set-up to its knees, serving as an example for us today, too, in a world where hundreds of millions of ordinary people continue to be weighed down by the climate change emergency, autocracy, repression, systemic racism, war, gender violence, bigotry, human rights abuses and appalling poverty.

Both Peter and André lived and breathed games as youngsters growing up in South Africa. Although theirs was apparently a normal sporting childhood, neither could play with, or against, anybody who wasn't classified 'white' by a controlling apartheid state.

Not only was school sport whites-only but also club sport. And that went all the way up through provincial to national levels. Under apartheid, sport was rigidly segregated on racial grounds, and for generations, 'national' teams labelled from 'South Africa' really meant from the minority 'white South Africa'.

Both are political activists and therefore approach this book from a simultaneous standpoint as sports and political participants.

Their experiences complement each other. André was involved in the sports and political resistance to apartheid inside South Africa; Peter, forced into exile as a teenager in 1966, operated outside the country.

André participated in small ways through sport and the heritage sector in the broader micro-negotiations that led to the abolition of apartheid. Subsequently he was appointed by Nelson Mandela's first democratic government to run Robben Island and turn the notorious maximum security prison into a national museum and UNESCO World Heritage site, becoming its founding director.

Peter, initially a militant British anti-apartheid leader, subsequently served as a British member of parliament for a quarter of a century, half of this time as a government and cabinet minister, and is now a member of the House of Lords.

However, Peter and André do not make any claims to the book being definitive or comprehensive. Instead, following sport passionately like any avid fan and narrating human experiences that sometimes reach moments of profoundness, they seek to understand and explain its context in a readable way, believing that sport can no more be insulated from the ideological and political trajectories of society and globalisation than can people from the air and daily life around them.

1

'Hain Stopped Play'

Direct-action protests disrupt apartheid rugby and almost accidentally become part of the 1960s revolutions

The sportsman who gave early oxygen to the protestors did so rather unwittingly and reluctantly.

During the late 1960s, Basil D'Oliveira had become an established member of the England cricket team – an all-rounder, both free-scoring batsman and medium-paced swing bowler. But what made him unique was that he hailed from Cape Town, born to parents classified as 'coloured' in South Africa, and therefore barred from playing for Western Province or his country because apartheid laws allowed only white cricketers that opportunity.

So his community raised funds for him to travel to England, where the legendary cricket journalist and commentator John Arlott took him under his wing. Soon he graduated from the Lancashire League to the Worcestershire County team and thence to become an automatic choice and star performer for England's test match team.

But in 1968 came the selection for the English cricket tour to South Africa that year. Following weeks of seedy manoeuvring and high drama, D'Oliveira was initially offered £40,000 to declare himself unavailable by a South Africa-based representative of the cigarette company Rothmans. Upon the shock news that he was omitted from the touring party, John Arlott wrote: 'No one of open mind will believe that he was left out for valid cricketing reasons.'

And he wasn't. Decades later, it transpired that the chairman of the selectors, Doug Insole, had been in touch with the South Africans beforehand to be told D'Oliveira would not be welcome and decided therefore to exclude him.[3] Even middle opinion, not previously sympathetic to anti-apartheid protests, was outraged at the transparently political exclusion. Mike Brearley – who alone amongst England internationals opposed the 1970 tour and would later be England cricket captain – provides a fascinating insider insight into the shenanigans involved in what he describes as the 'fishy business'. Based upon conversations with key figures and readings of the MCC Committee minutes, he describes how 'many or all' of the senior officers of the MCC 'were keen to keep cricketing contacts alive through mutual tours between England and South Africa, with its apartheid laws and policy that affected every area of life, including sport.'[4] Controversy raged and the pressure built.

Then, dramatically, D'Oliveira was selected when the Warwickshire swing bowler Tom Cartwright withdrew with a shoulder injury; he later explained privately to Peter that this was a pretext for his own uneasiness about the tour.

The South African government was decidedly unimpressed. In a dramatic new twist, Pretoria refused to accept D'Oliveira's selection. 'It's not the England team. It's the team of the anti-apartheid movement,' Prime Minister Vorster absurdly fulminated at a ruling party rally, abruptly cancelling the tour. So much for 'not mixing politics with sport', the habitual charge levelled at anti-apartheid protesters.

Yet just a few months later, it was business as usual for the English cricket authorities, apparently unperturbed by the apartheid government's unprecedented veto of their tour. As if nothing had happened, in January 1969 they simply announced that they would proceed with the scheduled 1970 cricket tour to Britain by a white South African team.

About to turn nineteen, Peter was outraged though hardly surprised. This was because the English cricket chiefs headquartered at Lords Cricket Ground were unapologetically head-in-the-sand about the racialised social and political environment in which cricket unavoidably found itself. Known as 'the Conservative Party at play', they were by origin, culture and ideology deeply reactionary and indifferent to moral appeals, let alone political ones – not even from cricket legends like John Arlott or the former England captain, Bishop David Sheppard, still less anti-apartheid protestors, who they saw through a prism of 'communist agitators destroying English civilisation'.

Frustrated with this obduracy, Peter (who was by then an activist in the radical Young Liberal Movement) drafted a motion and press statement for the Young Liberals in January 1969, pledging 'ourselves to take direct action to prevent scheduled matches from taking place unless the 1970 tour is cancelled'. Although the statement got a small mention in *The Times*, the cricket authorities ignored it. This was the first time that militant action had been proposed; cricket protests were previously orderly, as when the British Anti-Apartheid Movement (AAM) organised placard-carrying pickets outside each ground during the 1965 South African cricket tour to Britain.

Peter had meanwhile met those in exile in London running the South African Non-Racial Olympic Committee (SANROC), which had been successful in getting white South Africa suspended from the Olympics for the first time in 1964. Its then chair was the former Robben Island prisoner and poet Dennis Brutus, its secretary the former South African weightlifting champion Chris de Broglio. The two had already built a worldwide network of sympathetic sports officials whom they lobbied increasingly effectively.

SANROC had been forced into exile because its leaders had been banned and harassed to such an extent that, like the ANC of Chief Albert Luthuli and Nelson Mandela, it could no longer operate legally inside the country. Brutus was successively banned, put under house arrest and finally sentenced to hard labour on Robben Island. During an attempt to escape his ban and attend an International Olympic Committee (IOC) meeting in Europe in 1963, he was arrested on the Mozambique–Swaziland border and taken back to Johannesburg police headquarters. Trying to escape again, he was shot in the back on his left side, the bullet passing through his body and exiting through his chest. An ambulance for whites arrived, found he was classified as 'coloured' and drove off; he waited bleeding on the pavement for a vehicle that could take 'non-whites'.

In May 1969 SANROC held a public meeting in London where Peter raised from the floor the question of direct action to stop the cricket tour now due to start a year later. Brutus was in the chair and was very supportive, as was his colleague de Broglio.[5]

Peter had been the first to advocate a national campaign of non-violent direct action against sports apartheid teams – by physically disrupting matches, laying siege to team hotels and harassing the tourists wherever they went – which could not be ignored by the sports elites previously impervious to moral appeals and symbolic protests (though there had been some localised militancy in Europe and England). He had become involved in the late-1960s era of student sit-ins, factory occupations and squats in empty houses. Enthused by the 1968 Paris uprising and student agitation throughout Europe and the United States, joining opposition to the 1968 Soviet invasion of Czechoslovakia and participating in anti-Vietnam War protests, Peter felt part of an iconoclastic 'new left', explicitly opposed to both capitalism and Stalinism: 'Neither Washington nor Moscow' was the socialist slogan chanted at demonstrations and conferences he joined. Aged eighteen going on nineteen, he became immersed in an exciting ferment of new ideas shaped by teach-ins, conferences, demonstrations and sit-ins, and saw the opportunity to apply similar tactics to block whites-only South African tours.

*

Peter's experience of sports apartheid was personal. He played for Arcadia Shepherds youth and on Saturday afternoons watched first team matches from the whites-only part of Pretoria's Caledonian stadium. Partitioned off on the other side were black spectators, some personal friends with whom his family sometimes mingled before the match, then separated unable to use the same entrances, toilets or facilities. Although Arcadia was a white team in an all-white league, black spectators were amongst its noisiest and most partisan supporters. Then a government proclamation restricted such major sports events to whites alone. But crowds of black Arcadia fans still gathered outside to catch sounds of the match, some of the keenest shinning up overlooking trees – until angry white neighbours complained and police dogs pulled them down bloodied and screaming. And one day Peter arrived home from school in the middle of a Security Police raid to find a young policeman actually checking whether his personally chosen 'World XI' cricket team, including famous West Indians Gary Sobers and Wes Hall, as well as Australia's Richie Benaud and South Africa's Graeme Pollock – their names listed randomly with batting order numbers attached – was a coded list.

Some of the vocal left in those radical times asserted sports apartheid protests to be peripheral, at worst eccentric, when the real issue was confronting the economic and military underpinning of the Pretoria government by Western nations.

But they expressed a fundamental misunderstanding of the white South African psyche under apartheid. Because Peter originated from South Africa's 'white tribe', he intimately understood their psyche: like him, they were sports-mad. Afrikaners were especially fanatical about rugby and saw the then invincible Springboks both as an expression of their white supremacy and a break-out from the siege imposed upon them, first by British colonialists, then by world in its disapproval of apartheid.

Whether it was participation in the Olympics or a cricket tour, international sport gripped the white population as nothing else – and, importantly, granted them the international respectability and legitimacy they increasingly craved as the evil reality of apartheid began to be exposed by horrors such as the 1960 Sharpeville massacre. Leaders of white Commonwealth nations might speak of their distaste for apartheid but welcomed the Springboks and gave them generous hospitality and admiring recognition.

Peter always believed it would be easier to achieve success through militant protest against sports links than to take on the might of either international capital or military alliances, both of which underpinned the white supremacist state. He was, however, also active in anti-apartheid campaigns against those links, including the successful student protests to drive Barclays Bank off their campuses, thereafter to withdraw from South Africa.

Moreover, the sports boycott successes came at a time when resistance inside the country had been suppressed: Mandela and his comrades were imprisoned on Robben Island, the ANC, PAC and most other anti-apartheid parties had been outlawed, their leaders banned, harassed and imprisoned. Victories in sport were crucial during this period when the freedom struggle was extremely hard. And these victories soon started to be achieved.

*

Peter hadn't the faintest idea that by the end of 1969, he would be catapulted into the headlines as the notorious leader of a new militant movement.

If the movement's genesis was through the D'Oliveira affair and the radical political renewal of 1968, it began in small ways. This was despite uneasiness amongst leaders of the British Anti-Apartheid Movement (the biggest and most successful in any country) that militant (bordering upon or actually illegal) demonstrations might undermine the broad support they had been so effectively mobilising. They feared disruptive protests might tarnish the cause. Indeed, one of the AAM's leaders, former member of the South African Communist Party (SACP) Alan Brooks, close to the ANC, tried to dissuade Peter from pressing ahead. The sense Peter got from him was that the AAM wouldn't otherwise be able to exert the control it wanted and was accustomed to.

Their conversation was polite and friendly, but Peter resolved to press ahead anyway, albeit respecting the AAM's authority and necessarily more

25

conventional role, as it maintained a discreet yet cooperative and friendly distance.

And very soon immediate targets presented themselves.

Peter and other anti-apartheid activists were alerted to a private tour by an all-white South African invitation side sponsored by a wealthy business-man, Wilf Isaacs. This tour became the first to be targeted by direct action disruption. The opening match was in the Essex town of Basildon, to the east of London, in July 1969. There seemed to be no plans to do anything about it, so, encouraged by Brutus and de Broglio, Peter roped in half a dozen Young Liberal colleagues and borrowed his parents' Volkswagen Beetle to drive across London from Putney, where the Hain family lived. As well as being chair of Putney YLs, Peter was by then press officer for the South East England YLs, and alerted a number of media outlets about his plan to disrupt the match.

The group gathered near the small club ground to discuss tactics, and then joined spectators, the sun shining, the grass beautifully green, the atmosphere tranquil – a typical Saturday for a typical English club match. The young protesters were tense yet excited, Peter included. Suddenly they jumped up, ran onto the pitch and sat down, unfurling banners as they did so. Play was interrupted for over ten minutes as players, club officials and spectators reacted with dumfounded frustration and anger at this unprece-dented and unseemly strike at England's cricketing soul. The local police were summoned and dragged Peter's gang, hanging limp but not resisting, off the field; they were instructed to get the hell out of there or be arrested. Over the next twenty-four hours, various national media outlets reported this novel occurrence, with photographs of the sit-down and quotes from Peter and a club official, embarrassed at the discourtesy shown to the tourists.

Local groups of the Anti-Apartheid Movement organised even greater and more successful disruptions at subsequent Wilf Isaacs tour matches in Oxford and at the Oval, south London. Isaacs himself denounced the pro-testers for 'behaving unlawfully' and for being 'anti-cricket' and 'bringing politics into sport', presenting himself as a philanthropic businessman, not a politician and honorary colonel in the South African military. On his return to South Africa, Isaacs said that the demonstrators were well organ-ised and had a big following, adding in language and attitude typical of his ilk at the time:

Some of them are definitely paid. Their tactics were usually to insult the biggest player in the team in the hope that we would retaliate. Their behaviour was disgusting. I was spat on. They were very rude and their language was filthy. Some of them are drug takers.[6]

None involved in the demonstrations could recognise his fanciful accusations – except perhaps that some might have taken cannabis occasionally – as volunteers to a person wondering when they might be paid, and by whom.

Peter, delighted at the impact and hoping that the publicity generated by the protests would build momentum, was soon presented with a new target. In Bristol later that July, there was a Davis Cup tennis match between white South Africa and Britain, and he persuaded three Young Liberal friends to join him in protest on the opening day. Again borrowing the family car, he travelled down with two Putney YL activists, Helen Tovey and Maree Pocklington, like him in their late teens. They discussed plans on the drive down, not knowing quite what to expect, and were joined by a third YL in Bristol. The four purchased tickets, tense and worried, and took their seats separately amongst the large crowd.

On Peter's signal, they leapt up and ran onto the court, disrupting white South Africa for the first time in an international sports event in front of live television coverage, causing consternation and wide-spread media reports. The four were carried off and taken to the local police station before being released after several hours which included perfunctory questioning. It was Peter's first taste of a police cell – ironic, his parents later remarked, that it was in Britain, rather than the South African cell they had experienced for two weeks. Over the three-day tournament, play was further disrupted by an invasion and flour bombs were thrown onto the court in protests organised by the Bristol Anti-Apartheid group.

As Peter had intended, the direct-action protests were highly newsworthy – and on the sports pages not simply the news pages – thereby reaching a much wider audience than anti-apartheid campaigning had previously managed or expected.

When Peter was later asked why he had focused so specifically on sport in the battle against apartheid, he recalled a vivid memory as a ten-year-old in South Africa during the 1960 state of emergency. With the ANC, together with others, now banned as an unlawful organisation, Nelson Mandela and some of his colleagues decided they had no alternative but to go underground.

Many activists were arrested in police swoops and Peter's mother was warned she might be too. So, at very short notice, her four young children were packed into their Volkswagen minibus for an unscheduled holiday to their grandparents' house in Port Alfred, on the banks of the Kowie River, where Peter's father joined them. They drove back to Pretoria via the home of Liberal Party president and renowned author Alan Paton, called 'The Long View', high up overlooking the hills north of Durban. Paton was kindly, though a little gruff, and something he said made a big impact: 'I'm not an all-or-nothing person, Peter. I'm an all-or-something person.' Nearly ten years later, this was to become Peter's activist watchword: to focus on achieving concrete goals. Just such an achievable goal, he was determined, would be stopping the 1970 cricket tour.

As direct-action protests against South African sports events gathered pace across Britain, they gave birth to an emerging movement, albeit one with considerable local autonomy and spontaneity. A national network began falling into place and an idea of a broad-based coordinating committee reaching well beyond Young Liberal activists began to crystallise in Peter's mind, who at the time was working with all sorts of left-wing and radical groups on such issues as forming a 'New Left' to apartheid to the Vietnam War and world poverty.

With the help and advice of Brutus, he was introduced to Reading University student Hugh Geach and the three convened a meeting in London on 12 August 1969 to discuss forming a campaign group. But with disagreements on tactics or whether there was any need at all for a new campaign on sport – Anti-Apartheid Movement representatives arguing against its formation – the meeting proved frustratingly unproductive to Peter, Brutus and Geach.

They resolved to go ahead on their own, and the next day decided to set up the campaign Stop The Seventy Tour (STST). Brutus and de Broglio of SANROC, with their greater experience and credibility, were indispensable in this venture, giving advice and encouragement to the young enthusiasts Peter and Geach.

Collectively, they sent out a circular to around fifty organisations announcing STST's formation and inviting support, and on 22 August, Peter wrote a letter to the *Guardian* saying:

> The consequences of another refusal to cancel the tour should not be underestimated. The token disruptions during the recent tour of the

28

Wilf Isaacs XI to Britain and the Davis Cup match at Bristol demonstrated the seriousness of threats to massively disrupt the 1970 tour:
next summer could see a season consisting of an endless series of protests
and disruptions.

The launch of STST went ahead on 10 September 1969, despite further
attempts by AAM/SACP representatives to block it. Peter's Young Liberal
media training proved useful and there was wide newspaper coverage
including in South Africa. The campaign gathered broad support, including
from the Anti-Apartheid Movement, whose leaders resolved to swing
behind it, joining with United Nations Youth, the National Union of
Students, Christian groups and young communists, Trotskyites and Young
Liberals.

Geach was made secretary and, aged nineteen, Peter was pressed by
Brutus, de Broglio and others into a leadership role, finding himself acting
as press officer and convenor of the new STST committee and propelled into
chair of the group. Although Peter was excited and determined to do his
best, he felt daunted. He may have conceived and initiated the campaign,
but he had anticipated being more of a foot soldier, supporting experienced
and illustrious figures.

Having organised a press conference in The White Swan pub in London's
famous Fleet Street, where pretty well all Britain's national newspapers were
based, Peter stood alongside Brutus before a packed room of journalists,
including South African ones. He promised 'mass demonstrations and disruptions throughout the 1970 cricket tour' – more out of hope and a determination to lead from the front, since there was no national organisation as
such in place to deliver this. But he felt confident it would emerge on the
back of local activity. His public threat to wreck the tour was deliberately
pitched to be newsworthy and therefore to capture the sense of interest
needed to galvanise a big movement.[7]

There was one other critical component to his public threat. The cricket
tour was due to begin the following May. Rather belatedly, it was realised
that there was a Springbok rugby tour beginning just six weeks later. The
focus on cricket following the D'Oliveira affair meant rugby had slipped by
almost unnoticed. Peter and his colleagues resolved to use the tour as a
dummy run; with twenty-five rugby matches to disrupt, they could build
a campaign that would be capable of stopping the more vulnerable cricket
tour.

In retrospect, a certain innocence drove Peter and Geach onward. Peter was determined to win a decisive battle against the evil of apartheid he had experienced as a boy and was maybe more convinced than anybody else involved of the real possibility to achieve that through non-violent direct action.

*

Now Peter found himself in the limelight. His photograph appeared in national newspapers in September when he spoke for the first time at the Liberal Party's annual conference in Brighton, urging support for direct action – a nerve-racking experience as he'd never been a natural orator.

He was invited by the then producer of the Thames Television popular evening news show, Frank Keating (later a noted sports journalist), to travel to London for his first television interview. Taking it step by step, uncertain he could manage the next one, but then finding indeed that he could, Peter found himself thrust into the public eye, his South African roots giving him an authority to advocate the anti-apartheid cause.

Almost daily reports by London-based South African journalists rapidly elevated him to the status of a 'hate' figure in his old home. He was called 'public enemy number one' – the gist was a betrayal by 'one of our own' who was 'taking revenge' for the repressive treatment of his parents. Not surprisingly perhaps, and a sign of the early impact of the nascent STST campaign, was the arrival of a registered letter, date-marked 'Pretoria October 1969', from the South African minister for the interior. It informed Peter that his right as a British citizen to enter South Africa without an 'alien's temporary permit' or visa had been withdrawn (ironic, since he had no intention of going back to the country of his childhood, where he would have been arrested or worse).

Around the same time, the headmaster of Pretoria Boys High School, Desmond Abernethy, arrived in London and sought out his former student, asking courteously (but not that forcefully) that Peter call a halt to his troublesome activities, which Peter politely declined to do. Abernethy's mission was reported by the South African media.

With growing momentum, the Stop The Seventy Tour campaign took off. The headquarters address and 'office' were based in the modest flat in Gwendolen Avenue, Putney that Peter's parents had rented from a friend since their exile to London in 1966. His mother, Adelaine, assumed the crucial if unofficial role of secretary, fielding media and activist phone calls, coordinating information and helping with correspondence – all skills well developed in her Pretoria activist days. His father, Walter, came home from work to write leaflets and background briefs. In a sudden reversal of roles, Peter had become the front person, his parents providing invaluable and constant background support as he had tried to do for them as a teenager in Pretoria. Lunch breaks between his London University lectures were spent with homemade sandwiches in a phone box talking to journalists and local organisers through messages relayed from his mother at home, where the phone rang incessantly.

*

Support for the movement was by now swelling largely spontaneously. Local branches were formed, often around university student unions, involving also trade unions, local groups of the Anti-Apartheid Movement, socialists, radicals, liberals, Marxists, independents, trade unionists and the churches. The Stop The Seventy Tour campaign was predominantly, though by no means exclusively, young, and soon took the Springbok rugby tour by storm.

The campaign received an early boost when the Wales and British Lions forward John Taylor announced in a newspaper interview that he could not play against the Springboks for reasons of conscience. Like others of his generation, he had toured South Africa, but unlike every one of them was horrified at what he experienced and resolved to make a stand, attracting extreme hostility from the rest of the rugby world.

When the Springbok team arrived for their twenty-five-match tour on 30 October 1969, the Reading Anti-Apartheid group was waiting for them at the airport with banners, shouting 'Don't Scrum with a Racist Bum!'

Two weeks before the opening match against Oxford University, activists used weedkiller to spray a huge slogan, 'Oxford Rejects Apartheid', on the pitch. The venue was switched after strong opposition from both the university authorities and especially students, who threatened to wreck the match. Adding to the drama, the new venue was kept secret to try to avoid demonstrations. But that proved impossible, and a friendly rugby journalist, Bob Trevor of the *London Evening News*, promised to tip Peter off as soon as the media were informed. Late the night before the match, the phone at the family home rang and his familiar voice said, 'Twickenham, 3 p.m.'

Peter immediately phoned the Oxford Committee Against Apartheid and as many organisers around the country as he could. They had pre-booked coaches to bring over a thousand demonstrators to the match. Now they had a destination. Mingling with rugby fans, activists purchased tickets, grouping together in the main stand, Peter was tense as he made his way to the spectator fence surrounding the pitch. The match took place under siege, with pitch invasions and the constant din of hostile chanting. Spotting an opening in the police cordon, Peter tried to jump over the fence, but was grabbed by the police, carted out and dumped on the pavement. Sensationally, the Springboks lost, clearly unnerved by the atmosphere – humiliating at the hands of a mere university side.

It proved a perfect springboard for what was to follow. The drama of switching the first fixture from Oxford at the last minute attracted front-page lead stories on the morning of the match and set the scene for the remaining games of the tour. Local organisers realised they were part of a mass movement and each of the matches saw demonstrations of varying sizes.

At the next match against Midlands Counties East at Leicester on 8 November, 3,000 demonstrators tried to burst through police lines of 1,000 officers. Some did get inside: one group with insulated bolt cutters temporarily switched off the floodlights, while a few others ran onto the pitch.

As Brutus – who, like Peter, campaigned tirelessly around the country – put it: 'Our strategy was based on letting the local people choose their own strategy. We never told them what to do. We just said, the "Springboks will be here next, do what you have to do."'

In late November the Springboks came back to Twickenham, the home of the Rugby Football Union; within easy reach of central London, the heat was truly on the beleaguered tourists. Some 2,000 protesters bought tickets for the match – some 'disguised' by cutting their hair or wearing Springbok rosettes – while a similar number gathered outside. Peter was one of over a hundred demonstrators who outwitted the police by jumping the fence and stopping play for more than ten minutes until they were carried off and summarily ejected from the stadium.

At Swansea the week before, there was the most brutal confrontation of the entire tour. Inside the ground some seventy demonstrators made it onto the pitch and stopped the match for twenty minutes. Two hundred demonstrators were treated for injuries. A Wales Rejects Apartheid Committee had been formed with support from all walks of life. But in south Wales – a socialist and trade union stronghold with an honourable tradition of international solidarity going back at least to the Spanish Civil War – rugby fanaticism came first. Reflecting on this many years later, the captain of the Swansea team, Stuart Davies, wrote in the club's programme: 'It would be true to say that I, as captain, the rest of the team, the club and indeed rugby in general chose to ignore the moral issue, a stance which my daughters would not be happy with, if it happened today!'

There were ugly scenes as police threw over a hundred peaceful demonstrators back from the pitch and deliberately into the clutches of 'stewards', who handed out severe beatings. One demonstrator's jaw was broken and he nearly lost an eye. Others, including women, were badly assaulted. Journalists from papers that were not supportive of the demonstrations, such as *The Times*, nevertheless condemned the 'viciousness' of the police and stewards. The atmosphere in and around the Springbok games had become akin to a mini-civil war, alarming the government, which after consultation with chief constables made the matches all-ticket and banned 'stewards' (dubbed 'suede jacketed toffs acting like thugs' by one disgusted former Swansea rugby player).

At the Aberdeen match in early December, John Lennon of the Beatles sent a cheque for £1,500 to pay all the fines of arrested protesters. In Cardiff on 13 December, all pretence at a normal rugby match was abandoned as a ten-foot-high barbed wire fence was put up around the field: it resembled an internment camp. Two thousand demonstrators besieged the venue.

The biggest and best demonstration of the whole tour was in Dublin in early January 1970 at the international against Ireland. Taking part was the radical new republican MP to the British Parliament, Bernadette Devlin, who came as part of a Northern Ireland delegation from the civil rights group People's Democracy. Action was led by the Irish Anti-Apartheid Movement, which exiled ANC activist Kader Asmal (later a minister in Mandela's government) and Louise Asmal helped found. An all-night vigil was staged outside the Springboks' hotel. Irish trade unions acted in solidarity. Post Office workers attempted a boycott of telephones and mail to the Springboks' hotel, and journalists were urged to boycott reporting of the match though not the protests. Irish president Éamon de Valera and government ministers refused to attend and the Taoiseach refused to give the usual hospitality to the team. Anti-apartheid slogans were painted on the Irish Rugby Football Union's headquarters, the home of its secretary was picketed, and goal posts at the University College Dublin rugby ground were sawn down in protest against its pitch being used for training by the Irish team.

Viewing these events fifty years later, the STST demonstrators seemed possessed of a fearless idealism. Peter never worried overly about potential repercussions – personal threats of violence or prosecution, or the fury he increasingly attracted from sports fans and British right-wingers. Like his colleagues, he felt strongly that their cause was just and their militancy essential.

The forces of apartheid were becoming increasingly apoplectic. The Afrikaans government-supporting paper, *Beeld*, stated in an editorial:

> We have become accustomed to Britain becoming a haven for all sorts of undesirables from other countries. Nevertheless, it is degrading to see how a nation can allow itself to be dictated to by this bunch of left-wing, workshy, refugee, long-hairs who in a society of any other country would be rejects.

By then the Springbok tour was becoming a parody. In Northern Ireland, the match was cancelled for security reasons amidst gathering turmoil, about to slip into armed violence by Irish paramilitaries following the bludgeoning of civil rights protesters. In Britain, Labour government ministers banned all armed services grounds from hosting matches. Elsewhere, matches were made all-ticket, and security inside was massively increased so that police stood shoulder to shoulder around the pitch facing spectators. In blue-rinse conservative Bournemouth, the match had to be abandoned because the open ground could not be defended.

Protestor tactics therefore changed too. To circumvent suspected infiltrators and the tapping of Peter's home telephone number – déjà vu for those from Pretoria – an 'inner group' was formed of trusted and older activists who years before participated in nuclear disarmament direct action demonstrations. Called the Special Action Group, it worked on clandestine projects.

One was booking a vivacious young woman, Rosemary Chester, into the team's London hotel in Park Lane, flitting through the corridors in the early hours gumming up the players' door locks with solidifying agent so they had to break down the doors to get out on the morning of the pre-Christmas international match at Twickenham.

On top of that, as the team's coach waited outside their London hotel, STST activist Michael Deeny, who worked in the City, turned up in a smart suit and politely told the driver that he was wanted inside; he slipped into the driving seat, chained himself to the steering wheel and drove the coach off to crash it nearby as he was grappled by some of the Springbok players who had already boarded. In an interview with the *Daily Telegraph* in 2006, the Springbok vice-captain Tommy Bedford recalled what he saw from his seat:

> He started the ignition and pulled away from the hotel . . . And then all hell broke loose. The police outriders had been caught by surprise. Half the team weren't even on the bus. And where on earth were they going? As they sped past Green Park underground station one of the players managed to get his hands round the driver's neck. The bus crashed into half a dozen cars. The police arrived. Chaos. The guy had tried to hijack the Springbok rugby team. And all this only four hours before kick-off.[8]

Over the Christmas break, an STST activist managed to attach the flag of the ANC to the flagpole of the Springboks' London hotel. Another attractive young woman became a 'Mata Hari', deputed to chat up the players. She struck up a friendship with one Springbok at Bristol and back in London they met again. He and some colleagues agreed to go with her to a 'reception party', although unaware it would be attended by Peter and STST colleagues. But when she went to collect them from the post-match festivities she found her Springbok was completely drunk and inter-ested only in groping her.

Tickets had been bought from agencies for the England international in December and Peter had 400 hidden in his bedroom to be distributed to protesters. Two of Peter's friends evaded the heavy police cordon – they had practised their plan in the family garden. Unlike other protesters, they dressed neatly in jacket and tie, and sat in front of the security cordon in special ringside seats purchased from the embassy in Trafalgar Square by Peter's South-African accented Aunt Jo. At a pre-arranged moment, they burst out, sprinting to evade furious pursuers, one just managing to chain himself to the goalposts. Play was interrupted until he was cut free. Orange smoke pellets were also thrown among the players, which, as well as disrupting play, produced dramatic television and newspaper pictures.

For the final Twickenham match in late January 1970, packets of powdered dye were distributed to selected protesters which turned black on contact with dampness. These were thrown onto the pitch so that the Springboks, rolling on the wet grass, were smeared with black stains to chants from protesters on the terraces of 'paint them black and send them back'.

Wherever the team went, resting, training or playing, it was under siege. Over Christmas, two months into the tour, the players had taken a step inconceivable in the annals of Springbok history and voted to go home. But the management, under political pressure, ordered them to stay. The tour finally staggered to an end, with the players bitter and unsettled.

For the first time, the Springboks, accustomed to being lionised as perhaps the leading national rugby team in the world, had instead been treated as pariahs. They no longer faced the mere spluttering of 'misguided liberals and leftists' while they retreated to the hospitality of their hosts. This was something of quite a different order. Anti-apartheid opponents had shown a physical capacity to stop the Springboks touring – either in the old way, or at all.

Stop The Seventy Tour: Isolating apartheid cricket

The militant rugby protesters had achieved their original purpose: providing the movement with a perfect springboard from which to plan direct action to stop the cricket tour, due to start at the beginning of May 1970.

By now, opposition, coordinated by the Anti-Apartheid Movement, went much wider. Churches, led by the former England cricket captain and Bishop of Woolwich, David Sheppard, urged cancellation. The Commonwealth Games, due to take place in Edinburgh that summer, also became an important lever. SANROC's international expertise and contacts were put to good use as it was pointed out to African and Asian countries that they would be in an intolerable position participating in the Games at the same time as an apartheid cricket tour was under siege elsewhere in Britain.

Meanwhile, Apartheid's leaders, in their inimitable way, handed the campaigners two more gifts. The black American tennis star, Arthur Ashe, was banned from entering South Africa to play, and an International Cavaliers cricket team was also blocked because it contained 'non-white personnel'.

While all this was going on, there was a meticulously planned and carefully timed detonation. Late at night on 19 January 1970, demonstrators simultaneously raided fourteen of the seventeen county cricket club grounds. All were daubed with slogans. A small patch in the outfield of Glamorgan's Cardiff ground was dug up and weed killer was sprayed on Warwickshire's Birmingham ground.

Pre-planned telephone reports from each small, tight group poured in throughout the night to the Press Association news agency and to Peter's home. In the morning, the coordinated protest dominated the broadcast bulletins, and there were screaming headlines with photos in the evening papers and television programmes and the following day's national newspapers.

The protests were a devastating shock to the cricket authorities and a surprise to virtually everyone else. The strength and extent of the movement had been starkly revealed in an operation carried out with seemingly military precision. More than this, the fear at the back of the cricket authorities' minds had been realised: the spectre of a cricket tour collapsing amid damaged pitches and weedkiller.

After the January attack on all county grounds, the Cricket Council launched the 1970 Cricket Fund to help cover extra security costs around the tour; thousands of small donations poured into Lords Cricket Ground and were handed over to bank branches all over the country or to individual county clubs. In the flood of mail, one letter typified the attitude of donors: 'Great pleasure to counter the objectionable and unwarranted intrusion of politics into sport.'

In similar vein, a memorandum on 4 February 1970, written by Jack Bailey, assistant secretary of the Test and County Cricket Board (TCCB), for a meeting of the Cricket Council in five days' time, summarised its stance on the planned South African tour:

(a) They are traditional opponents; (b) We are satisfied that SACA [the all-white South African Cricket Association] are making every possible effort to further the cause of multi-racial cricket; (c) No minority group should be able to dictate to the majority in this country. No amount of blackmail or pressure should influence this decision; (d) the Tour is practicable and profitable within the terms of the revised itinerary; (e) the ultimate good of all cricketers in South Africa is best served by the Tour taking place; (f) in the interest of world cricket in the long term, expediency, however desirable it might seem in the short term,

37

should not be a consideration; (g) public opinion is on our side and therefore the majority of people would be disappointed if the Tour did not take place. Furthermore, it would be difficult for them to reconcile our constantly stated intent with any change of heart.

Speculation and outrage were rife, especially as it was not clear who was responsible for the actions at the fourteen cricket grounds. The Anti-Apartheid Movement denied all knowledge. People inevitably accused STST – as it alone had the organisational capacity necessary to mount the raids – but Peter said (accurately) that the STST national committee had neither authorised nor approved the action, thereby maintaining a distance from it. It was in fact a covert operation by key STST activists in its clandestine Special Action Group, executed with deadly planning, efficiency and effect.

Within weeks, 300 reels of barbed wire were installed at Lords and most county grounds introduced guard dogs and security. The pressure on the cricket authorities grew. There was speculation that African, Asian and Caribbean countries would withdraw from the Edinburgh Commonwealth Games. One by one, a range of public bodies came out against the tour and there was talk of trade unions taking industrial action. Labour MPs, including the AAM's vice-chair Peter Jackson, said they would join sit-down pitch invasions. The chair of the government-sponsored Community Relations Commission, former trade union leader Frank Cousins, told the home secretary that the tour would do 'untold damage' to race relations.

On 12 February, a snowy night, the Cricket Council met at Lords, the pitch surrounded by barbed wire, eerily silhouetted against the whiteness. Lords, the magisterial home of international cricket, looked for all the world like a concentration camp, symbolising the torment which had torn asunder this most dignified and graceful of games. It was announced that, on security grounds, the tour had been cut drastically to twelve matches from its original schedule of twenty-eight and would take place on just eight grounds instead of twenty-two; artificial all-weather pitches would be installed as an additional security precaution.

The shadow attorney general, Conservative politician Sir Peter Rawlinson, attacked the Labour home secretary, James Callaghan, for remaining 'neutral' and thereby 'acknowledging the licence to riot'. Rawlinson also called for an injunction to be taken out against Peter, insisting his public statements threatening to stop the tour constituted a direct incitement to illegal action. When cabinet documents were made public thirty years later (ironically, when Peter was a Labour government minister), it was revealed that ministers had discussed whether or not to prosecute him, with Callaghan in favour.[9]

Even before then, Peter had been warned by a friendly solicitor that his open advocacy of disruptive protests made him extremely vulnerable to a charge of conspiring unlawfully because the then conspiracy laws provided a catch-all basis for curbing radical political action. Although thankful for the warning, Peter pressed on, regardless of the risk of prosecution and likely prison sentence. There was no question of doing anything else in his mind. His whole strategy was predicated upon being open about STST's disruptive plans because it was public knowledge of the planned direct action that constituted the prime tactical weapon. The threat of direct action was the key to the strategy to get the tour stopped in advance, and as its author, Peter was determined to carry it out.

*

The campaign soon snowballed. Action groups to complement those established during the rugby tour sprang up throughout the country. The AAM was deluged with offers of help, its membership trebled and its local activists joined the campaign sometimes forming the backbone in their areas.

Christabel Gurney, a prominent AAM activist and the editor of *Anti-Apartheid News*, reported:

> Throughout the campaign there were tensions between the AAM and STST. The AAM was not opposed to direct action – it was the subject of vigorous internal debate between those who ... stressed that the Movement should not itself organise disruption and a radical young group on the Executive Committee who joined in alternative forms of protest. A resolution passed at the AAM's 1969 annual meeting applauded the pitch invasions during the Wilfred Isaacs tour and warned the cricket authorities that the Springboks' matches would 'inevitably be disrupted'. But it held back from organising direct action, from fear both of legal action and of alienating its more sedate supporters. The main problem between the AAM and STST was over the

39

latter's high media profile. The AAM was concerned that the concentration of media attention on STST would detract from its own ability to build a stronger organisation. It always faced the problem – like all single-issue campaigns – of how to translate the interest it attracted during action peaks into a base which it could use to take pre-emptive action in quieter times. And although it understood that exclusion from world sport was a psychological blow to white South Africans, it still felt that this was of minor significance compared with breaking Britain's economic ties with South Africa. The stopping of the 1970 cricket tour was the AAM's biggest victory since its formation ten years before. The campaign had tapped into a deep – and unexpected – vein of public support and was fuelled by growing polarisation over the issue of race in Britain. The rugby and cricket campaigns received huge media coverage, and apartheid became a talking point on a scale that was not repeated until the sanctions campaign of the mid-1980s.[10]

About a hundred enquiries a day by phone and letter poured into Peter's family home, which remained the STST headquarters. His mother, Ad, was almost permanently on the phone and the flat was filled with volunteers, callers and correspondence.

The Labour prime minister, Harold Wilson, publicly opposed the tour for the first time; with the Conservative Party actively supporting it and a general election imminent, STST's controversial campaign had become a hot political matter. The *Observer* newspaper chapter of the National Union of Journalists proposed a media ban on reporting the sports aspect of the tour. That was followed by the Association of Cinematograph, Television and Allied Technicians urging its members not to broadcast the tour on television, in turn deepening a debate about media freedom and illustrating how the STST campaign had triggered profound questions about British society going well beyond accepting apartheid-selected teams. The West Indian Campaign Against Apartheid in Cricket was launched after leading black activist Jeff Crawford contacted Peter, who welcomed this as a way of fusing the campaign with the battle against racism in British society.

Meanwhile, Dennis Brutus and Chris de Broglio of SANROC, through the Supreme Council for Sport in Africa, consolidated the basis for a Commonwealth Games boycott. Trade unions came out against the tour: television workers and journalists threatened a media blackout, and radio's 'voice of cricket', John Arlott, announced he would not do the ball-by-ball commentaries for which he was internationally renowned. Exceptional amongst his peers, cricketer Mike Brearley took the courageous step of speaking out at STST's national conference against the tour.

Opposition was by now reaching right into the establishment. Leading public figures formed the Fair Cricket Campaign (FCC), whose vice-chairman was the senior Conservative politician, Sir Edward Boyle. Former England captain David Sheppard, by then the Bishop of Woolwich, was an influential FCC voice, arguing: 'I do not regard cricket in South Africa as a non-political game.'

Though explicitly committed to lawful methods, in private the FCC was friendly. Through a mutual contact Peter was invited for a confidential meeting with its leaders. They found common ground when Peter said he was relaxed if they felt it necessary to criticise STST's militancy, but it would be best if both refrained from arguing publicly with each other since they shared a common objective (to stop the tour) and a common enemy (cricket apartheid). Arguing between each other would merely play into the hands of their opponents, he suggested. They agreed to stay in touch and keep this and any contact confidential.

Peter was enthusiastic, believing in the importance of having a 'spectrum of protest', from STST's militancy, through the AAM's conventional, highly effective pressure group profile and its very good links with the labour movement, and SANROC's expert international lobbying, to the FCC's im-peccable respectability: there was now a broad-based opposition to the tour, which Peter knew was essential for victory. It also reflected his anti-pathy to the debilitating sectarianism he had witnessed over his previous couple of years of youthful radical activism. Although STST's direct action powered the whole campaign, it could have been isolated without a hinter-land of broad public support, and Peter was at pains to stake out a non-sectarian position, refusing to criticise the more moderate groups and understanding their concerns about militancy and potential illegality.

Barbed wire now surrounded the grounds and especially the pitches, policed 24-hourly by guard dogs and security teams. With the much-reduced tour due to begin in early June, the campaign's momentum was still accelerating during April. Prime Minister Harold Wilson said that people 'should feel free to demonstrate against the tour', though he specifically criticised plans for disruptive protests. The British Council of Churches also called for peaceful demonstrations, and the Trades Union Congress called for a complete boycott of the tour by all workers. The Queen announced that neither she nor any member of the royal family would make the traditional visit to the Lord's test match, and the South Africans would not receive the traditional invitation to Buckingham Palace.

Then, with the tour just six weeks away, the Supreme Council for Sport in Africa announced that thirteen African countries would boycott the Commonwealth Games if the tour went ahead; Asian and Caribbean countries soon followed, raising the prospect of a whites-only Games in Edinburgh running alongside a whites-only cricket tour. Sparked by local direct action, the campaign had provoked an international diplomatic and political furore.

Despite early reservations, the Anti-Apartheid Movement played a crucial organisational role, both as a participant in STST and in its own right. Its indefatigable executive secretary, Ethel de Keyser, always comradely to Peter, worked herself into the ground. An AAM poster caught the public's imagination and was widely published in the press. Under the caption, 'If you could see their national sport you might be less keen to see their cricket', it showed a policeman beating defenceless black township dwellers in Cato Manor outside Durban.

Plans went ahead to blockade the team in at Heathrow Airport. Thousands of tickets were bought up by local groups (the games had been made all-ticket). Secret plans were being executed by the tightly run STST Special Action Group, which privately consulted Peter throughout. Its members had ingeniously discovered the existence of an old underground train tunnel running right underneath Lord's cricket ground, with a disused but still functional airshaft which could facilitate a dramatic entry – potentially by hundreds of activists.

Although activity was coordinated nationally by STST, local groups operated quite independently. This was partly by design – to avoid acting like a conspiracy – and partly as a product of the way the movement had evolved. There was also a considerable degree of individualistic autonomy in the campaign. People were quite literally doing their own thing. Peter opened his front door one day to be faced by two bright-eyed if somewhat zany youths who were model aeroplane buffs. They spoke excitedly of plans to buzz the pitch during play from their aunt's flat, which overlooked Lord's. There were reports from all over the country of other novel protest methods. Some individuals were breeding armies of locusts, which they planned to let free on the turf. A London University biology student said he already had 50,000 insects at home and would breed another 500,000 by the time the tourists arrived; *The Times* quoted him on 11 May: 'Anything up to 100,000 locusts will be let loose at a particular ground . . . They will ravage every blade of grass . . . It takes 70,000 hoppers twelve minutes to consume 1 cwt of grass'. Others acquired small mirrors with which they intended to distract the batsmen. Newspapers had a field day reporting a series of such stories, and Peter was blamed for just about everything, whether he had any involvement or not.

Peter was at the eye of a huge political storm. Learning all the time while leading, and having to play daily media demands by instinct, he was only too aware that saying the wrong thing could be calamitous but was equally resolved to stick to his chosen course, come what may. He was increasingly the target of hate mail and threats to his safety – something familiar to the family from his parents' anti-apartheid activism in Pretoria during the early 1960s, when the danger had been very real and constant.

Peter sent a letter (drafted, as often, with the help of his father, Wal) to the *Guardian* and *The Times*, which was published simultaneously on 30 April:

As the barricades go up, the demonstrators prepare, and the massive public opposition grows, perhaps it is time that we stopped to consider what this white South African tour is all about.

It is certainly not about cricket. And it is becoming increasingly obvious that the issue of racialism is losing out to the 'law and order' controversy.

Ever since the Test and County Cricket Board's statement last December, it was clear that the cricket authorities were intent on switching public debate on the issue of apartheid sports tours (perhaps because even they recognise that their position is untenable) to the tactics of demonstrating.

The tour has become a Conservative Party showpiece. And we have a right to ask what the Cricket Council hopes to gain out of it and at what cost?

Lords is in the dock right now. Is cricket prepared to bear responsibility for poisoning race relations in this country; for intensifying a politically motivated absurdity about 'law and order'; for precipitating a split in international sport; for sacrificing the Commonwealth Games; and, above all, for capitulating to racialism? All this in order to protect an apartheid regime which will be laughing at Britain's discomfiture?

This is a time for courage, not for retreat. In cancelling the racialist cricket tour, even at this late stage, the Cricket Council will have shown a dignity worthy of the game itself.

On 5 May India announced it was joining the Edinburgh Commonwealth Games boycott alongside African and Caribbean countries. On the advice of Brutus and de Broglio (whose expert lobbying of African, Asian and Caribbean Commonwealth country sports leaders on behalf of SANROC was bearing fruit), Peter predicted a mass withdrawal in a media statement:

The white tour in the South will be complemented by white Games in the North, making a sorry picture of racial sport in Britain. The multi-racialism of the Games is in direct conflict with the racialist cricket tour. Unless British sport as a whole is prepared to stand up and be counted against racialist sport, the Games could be sacrificed – so making a grand slam for apartheid.

The combination of sport, race and direct action had a toxic potency for Middle England. For some, a cricket tour to England stopped by 'radical agitators' seemed equivalent to the loss of empire, as revealed in letters from members of Marylebone Cricket Club (MCC).[11] One labelled Peter and STST as a 'complete negation of all this country stands for'; another saw the MCC as 'the last bastion of what remains of the British way of life'. Peter was denounced as a 'dangerous anarchist and communist'; the writer – blissfully unaware that the two ideologies were at loggerheads – noted that if they can 'smash this tour they will turn to other things'. Another described the STST campaign as 'persistent mob pressure and an attempt at neo-communist rule'. The anti-apartheid struggle was caricatured through a distorted Cold War prism, which the apartheid government fomented with its deliberate portrayal of all resistance as 'communist'.

In that mindset, the cricket establishment held firm against all the pressure, even though the serious consequences had by then become very evident, including Pakistan's decision to cancel its Under-25 summer cricket tour to Britain and, together with India, threatening also to cancel their 1971 Test tours. In mid-May, with the first match just three weeks away, the Cricket Council was invited to meet the home secretary James Callaghan who was concerned at the likely threat to public order, and the government was also deeply embarrassed by the impending collapse of the Commonwealth Games. After an unfruitful exchange in which he urged cancellation, Callaghan said he 'detected a lurking belief that they are a lonely band of heroes standing out against the darkening tide of lawlessness'. Certainly, the Cricket Council's members reflected old-worldly, far-right political beliefs. And both they and other critics were now making a stand on defending the rule of law against STST's alleged illegality.

A week after the meeting, events scrambled to a climax. It became clear that the prime minister was about to call a general election, and there was a notable shift in opinion. E. W. Swanton, cricket correspondent of the conservative *Daily Telegraph*, and Ted Dexter, the former England captain and one-time Conservative Party parliamentary candidate, urged cancellation. The Cricket Council met in emergency session, amid predictions in the media that the tour would be off.

Although hopeful, Peter was sceptical that they would cave in. And, indeed, the Council meeting ended defiantly, even though, perversely, they effectively conceded STST's case by announcing a new policy against future tours until South African teams were selected on a multiracial basis. It was as if they hoped this switch would sugar the pill of their stubborn refusal to be 'bullied', as many of their diehard members saw it.

But still the drama was not over. The Home Secretary asked to see cricket's chiefs again and now formally requested cancellation. Another hurried meeting was arranged at Lord's and, on this occasion, the decision was final. At long last, the tour was off. Cricket's leaders complained bitterly that they had no option but to accede to what they interpreted as a government instruction – in reality a face-saving excuse for their humiliation.

From their sordid manoeuvrings over Basil D'Oliveira to their astonishing decision to proceed with the 1970 invitation to the South Africans, the cricket leaders seemed impervious to the modern world and to the values of equality, justice and anti-racism shared by tens of millions beyond the protesters' ranks. It was as if Lords remained a relic of a bygone age of Britain's imperial grandeur.

Peter's own delight was tempered by intense relief that what would have become an ugly series of skirmishes had thankfully been avoided. In the weeks leading up to the cancellation he had become increasingly worried about the dangers of violence. For him, the direct-action strategy was designed to succeed because of the *threat* it posed. Although he would have

45

carried it through, he would have taken no pleasure in doing so. Others involved, however, saw things differently; some were even a little disappointed at his announcement the same evening that since the tour had been stopped, STST would wind up and encourage its supporters to join the AAM. Leadership, Peter had learnt, required taking decisions which might not be universally popular within the ranks, but proved correct in the longer term.

'Hain stopped play' was the headline in a sympathetic feature in the *Guardian*. But the right-wing press trumpeted darkly about 'anarchy', 'lawlessness' and the threat to England's civilisation. The Conservative Monday Club called him 'Führer Hain'. A campaign whose nine-month gestation was originated by Peter and taken forward by a handful of people including Brutus and de Broglio of SANROC had now won with mass support. STST had emerged as one of the few British protest groups to have achieved its singular objective.

It had always been the contention of apologists that maintaining sports contact provided a channel for encouraging whites to see how the rest of the world lived and so breed more liberal attitudes. This was pure fantasy, for during all the decades of so-called 'bridge building', apartheid in sport had actually become more entrenched, and Peter was always convinced that an effective sports boycott would deliver a decisive blow. And so this proved. Hardly had the cricket tour been stopped than top South African cricketers, one after the other, tumbled out to condemn apartheid in sport. Never before had they spoken out like this. Peter Pollock, the fast bowler who had been due to tour and who hadn't previously opposed apartheid in sport, was forthright. A week after the cancellation he told the Johannesburg *Sunday Times*: 'Sports isolation stares South Africa in the face, and to creep back into the laager is no answer. Sportsmen who genuinely feel there should be multi-racial sport should say so.' (The *laager* means a safe space encircled by ox waggons during the great trek into the hinterland by Afrikaners escaping dominance by the British colonialists.)

Twenty-five years later, the captain of the ill-fated tour, Ali Bacher, told Peter: 'There is no doubt the cancellation forced us to change. We wouldn't have done so otherwise. It was the turning point. There was no way back for us. You were right – we were wrong.' Around the same time, the brilliant South African left-handed batsman Graeme Pollock – whom Peter, a left-handed batsman himself, had idolised as a boy – described his reaction to the termination of his international career:

We didn't give too much thought to the people who weren't given the opportunities. In hindsight we certainly could have done a lot more in trying to get change . . . I was still a young guy . . . and we probably at that stage had our best side ever. Mike Procter, Barry Richards, Eddie Barlow, my brother Peter – there were really classy cricketers. Poor old Barry played just four Tests, Mike Procter seven. But at the same time Peter Hain and his guys got it absolutely right that the way to bring about change in South Africa was through the sport. It was difficult for twenty-two years and lots of careers were affected, but in hindsight it was needed and I'm delighted it did achieve change in South Africa.

Shortly after the cricket tour was stopped, the *Financial Times* reported: 'Is it purely coincidental that the stepping up of the anti-apartheid campaign in Britain and America during the past year or so has been accompanied by a sharp falling off in the inflow of capital into the country? Those who follow these matters are convinced it is not.'

For the Springbok's vice-captain, Tommy Bedford, the ill-fated rugby tour proved cathartic. Within a year, he publicly stated that Peter should be listened to, not vilified, and praised STST's objectives. Although his response, like Peter Pollock's, was a relatively isolated one in white South Africa, it signalled the huge and destabilising impact of the Stop The Seventy Tour campaign.

Nineteen seventy proved a cathartic year. It saw South Africa's expulsion from the Olympics, and from Davis Cup tennis, international athletics, swimming, cycling, wrestling and gymnastics. This followed on from an expulsion from boxing in 1968 and judo, pentathlon and weightlifting in 1969. One by one, they got the push in team sports. And neither the Springboks nor the cricketers toured Britain again until after the fall of apartheid.

Stop the Tours goes international:
Australia picks up the direct-action baton, 1971

Encouraged by STST's success, in Australia the Campaign Against Racism in Sport (CARIS) teamed up with its more militant sister organisation, the Stop the Tours campaign, to focus on the mid-1971 Springbok rugby tour to Australia and, in an uncanny repeat, a cricket tour due to start in October.

47

Meredith Burgmann, one of the organisers, explained: 'We were very influenced by the Stop the Springbok Campaign in England led by the exiled South African activist Peter Hain. We used to rush home to watch the news on telly and see how the protesters climbed up the goalposts and stormed the rugby fields.'[12]

Peter was invited over and, arriving in Sydney two days before the Springboks on 24 June 1971, he met Peter McGregor, one of the leaders of the Stop the Tours campaign, and they went straight into a packed press conference. Thereafter he embarked upon a frantic two-week schedule of flights across the huge country, media appearances, public-speaking engagements and private tactical briefings on direct action lessons from the STST campaign.

The two main Australian anti-apartheid organisations employed very different strategies. CARIS, led by John Myrtle, did not endorse direct action but supported the protests with intense propaganda campaigns which were hugely effective. The Sydney-based Anti-Apartheid Movement, which quickly morphed into the national Stop the Tours campaign, consisted mainly of students and trade unionists impressed by the success of the British protesters and determined to physically stop the matches. They had sharpened their protesting skills in the previous months by campaigning against South African tennis players, women basketballers and surf life-savers.

Australian students generally were in the middle of a tumultuous period of protest and resistance. Theirs was one of the few countries which had young men, including conscripts, fighting and dying in the American war in Vietnam, and universities around the country had been radicalised from the mid-1960s onwards. It was a far more all-encompassing experience than in Britain, and for radical young Australians, the anti-apartheid struggle was an easy fit into their worldview.

This general radicalisation of the student population goes some way to explaining the third important element of the campaign. This was something STST had not been able to achieve: support from international rugby stars. Seven current and former Wallabies (Australian rugby internationals) – bravely and publicly made themselves unavailable for selection. Six of the seven had been university students and had played for the Sydney University rugby club. Most of them had participated in the 1969 tour of South Africa and were appalled by what they had seen of apartheid and, led by Anthony Abrahams, James Roxburgh and Jim Boyce, they campaigned vigorously against the tour.[13]

Boyce had toured South Africa with the Wallabies in 1963. When they played a test match against the Springboks in Port Elizabeth, as was customary, black spectators cheered the visiting team. Their vociferous support provoked a riot. White spectators – some drunk – vented their frustration, supported by white police, by viciously attacking black spectators chanting for the Wallabies, injuring several. The visiting winger Jim Boyce – subsequently a vocal opponent of protests against the 1971 tour – was horrified: 'I'd never seen brutality of that kind before . . . South African whites treated blacks like non-persons.' Hearing this news at home, another Wallaby felt fully vindicated. He was Lloyd McDermott, the first indigenous rugby player ever to represent Australia, who had asked not to be selected for that 1963 tour.

Another crucial element of Stop the Tours was the participation, especially in Sydney, of young Aboriginal activists led by Gary Foley, Paul Coe and Gary Williams – and in Brisbane by Denis Walker.[14] With growing awareness of the injustice and oppression suffered by Australian indigenous communities from the arrival of white settlers on the continent to the present day, their participation gave a powerful extra moral legitimacy to the often unruly protests. It also triggered the beginnings of young white radicals' involvement in Aboriginal rights issues, particularly land rights – yet another example of the interconnection between sport and politics.

The international anti-apartheid movement, especially in sport, 'had dramatic implications for white Australia . . . encouraging constitutional reforms that belatedly granted Indigenous people political equality under Federal law', argued Roger Bell.[15] He added of Australia that 'Sporting success was a metaphor for a small country's wider achievements. In this nationalist narrative, race and culture were implicitly linked. Individual sporting prowess . . . displayed physical attributes and athletic achievement unique to the people of a white nation.' That in turn masked a reality that 'barriers commonly denied Indigenous Australians opportunities to participate fully in virtually any sporting code, at virtually any level. Most Australians who denied the connections between sport and politics, equally ignored the brutal reflections of racism and discrimination evident throughout every level of sport and recreation.' Indigenous Australians had for decades been denied equal access to recreational facilities or educational institutions.

On Peter's return to Britain, horrified by what he had seen and read of

49

Australia's blatantly racist discrimination against Aboriginals, he wrote a paper widely covered in the media which, Bell recorded, 'aroused a storm of debate . . . When Hain spoke of the plight of the Aboriginals in Australia he introduced an international audience to a bleak situation well-known but seldom acknowledged in white Australia.'

Bell further explained: 'At the 1956 Olympics Australia welcomed South Africa's participation free from any reservations about apartheid or its own deep culture of racism.' Many talented Aboriginals had been excluded from Olympic selection and only in 1968 was an Indigenous Australian selected. As Bell observed: 'Blind to racism in sport in their own society, most Australians were untroubled by the insinuation of racial politics into sporting competition against white South Africa.' During the campaign against the 1971 Springbok tour, Peter said: 'Australia openly constitutes itself in the eyes of the sporting world as South Africa's white friend and greatest ally.'

Australia had been one of white South Africa's staunchest supporters in the 1950s and 1960s, from its conservative prime ministers right down through sports officials, fighting hardest to keep the country within the Olympics. A cabinet decision on 10 September 1963 typified the Australian government's stance: 'Our attitude to all . . . moves against South Africa is to deprecate apartheid', while trying 'to limit pressure and actions against' the South African government. On 2 June 1971 the Australian prime minister William McMahon echoed this in a letter to the trade union leader Bob Hawke over the 1971 Springbok tour with the familiar platitude that a 'great deal of good can flow from international sporting exchanges'.

Australia, with Britain and New Zealand, had formed a white Commonwealth triumvirate backing white South Africa's global sports participation, broken only during the 1965 white South African cricket tour to Britain, when Labour prime minister Harold Wilson, joined by the Queen, refused to attend the opening day of England playing South Africa at Lords.

*

Soon after arriving in Australia for the 1971 campaign, Peter was flown to Brisbane and taken to the field where the match was due to be played. He was struck that it was completely open with no visible defences. Standing on the boundary, he gave a television interview – which was repeated for days afterwards – in which he said that it would be 'a piece of cake' to stop the match. A few days later the match was switched to a more secure venue – a first victory for the campaign.

A formidable opponent was the bellicose right-wing premier of Queensland, Sir Joh Bjelke-Petersen, who promptly called a state of emergency to deal with the expected demonstrations. He commandeered the match venue, outlawed labour strikes and gave the police unlimited powers of arrest, publicly telling them they 'would not be penalised for any actions they took to suppress the demonstrators', Bjelke-Petersen was determined to stop what he denounced as 'all this going soft on all these demonstrations'. He could see it leading to 'complete anarchy'. Decades later, it was revealed that in order to get the police on side, he promised the police trade union a pay rise, a superannuation fund and carte blanche to deal with demonstrators.

Perhaps unsurprisingly therefore, the demonstration outside the Springboks' Brisbane hotel was violently attacked by police. One of the protesters, seventeen-year-old Peter Beattie, was so badly beaten up at a rally that he became politically radicalised and ended up being elected Labor Party premier of the state for many years. He was quoted as saying the experience was not something he could ever forgive or forget.

The Springboks began their tour in conservative Perth, where the hard man of the Australian Rugby Union, its president Charles Blunt, walked on to the field and made a point of formally welcoming each Springbok with a handshake.

But the campaign was immediately able to achieve something that had eluded STST in Britain when trade unionists, led by the charismatic Bob Hawke, president of the Australian Council of Trade Unions, promised to boycott the servicing of planes, and both the major domestic airlines decided they would not carry them. The team had to fly 1,700 miles from Perth to the next match in Adelaide, cramped into a series of chartered light aircraft, the seven-hour journey three times longer than the regular flight. Australia's Conservative prime minister, William McMahon, even promised the Springboks the use of the Royal Australian Air Force if they needed it, underlining the deep ideological divide in the country, which had been echoed a year earlier in Britain, albeit where the Labour government was supportive of the anti-apartheid cause.

Peter meanwhile flew into Adelaide on a scheduled flight from Brisbane to speak at a huge meeting in the Central Methodist Church, finding an excellent response reminiscent of the days of STST. His message was clear:

just as in Britain, the cricket tour would be stopped and the rugby one so badly disrupted that it would be the last by a whites-only team.

Over a thousand demonstrators besieged the Adelaide match, with interruptions to play and smoke flares let off under the floodlights. The police and stewards lashed out indiscriminately, even arresting the mild-mannered correspondent from *The Times*, Englishman Stuart Harris, who was so enraged by the police tactics that he recorded his observations in a book, *Political Football* (1972).[16]

The campaign generated front-page headlines and gathered pace. At packed student union meetings, Peter described some of the tactics STST had deployed and encouraged activists to follow suit, delighting them with amusing tales of ingenuity and of sports apartheid's incongruity.

In Melbourne, armed guards with dogs patrolled the venue. At a rally attended by 5,000, Peter was greeted enthusiastically, saying that the campaign was 'well on the way to emulating the success that we achieved in Britain'. He went on: 'We are seeing a concentration camp-type atmosphere building up and I welcome that. It strips this tour of all its pretensions.' The demonstrators then set off to the ground, where 650 policemen with truncheons started to wade into them, police on horseback charging as people fled terrified in all directions. The next day, the *Sydney Morning Herald* reported: 'Many policemen took the law into their own hands.'

That morning, calls had been made to the media purportedly from a right-wing assassin threatening to shoot Peter, causing him to peer around constantly, knowing all too well, however, that there would be no way of preventing such an attempt – if indeed it was for real, rather than the hoax he suspected but could not ignore. Nothing transpired and by the time he left after a frenetic fortnight dogging the Springboks, the campaign was in full swing.

One of the British tactics that the Australian demonstrators were determined to re-enact was taking over the playing areas and climbing the goal posts. They were never able to achieve this because of the massive police presence at the grounds, but they did have a moment of anarchic joy when two well-known trade union officials were arrested and charged with cutting down the goal posts at the Sydney Sports Ground, one of the proposed Sydney venues. This was one of the reasons why the matches were all moved to the easier-to-barricade Sydney Cricket Ground.

The first of the matches played in Sydney, the heart of rugby in Australia, was a dramatic affair, with 20,000 protesters confronted by 600 police drafted from all over the state, twenty-foot-high barricades topped with barbed wire protecting the field and smoke bombs. There were fifty-nine arrests. Four protesters actually made it onto the field. Activist Verity Burgmann – whose older sister Meredith was one of the campaign's leaders – delighted the crowd of demonstrators by grabbing the ball and kicking it high into the air. *The Bulletin* called it 'the best kick of the season'. Protesters successfully disrupted play for some minutes, engendering huge animosity from the crowd. Meredith Burgmann received a two-month jail sentence for her simple charge of 'offensive behaviour' (on appeal amended to a suspended sentence).[17]

Five more matches in New South Wales were almost as chaotic. There were 142 arrests at the second Sydney game and even rural Orange and sleepy Canberra saw massive demonstrations. Four hundred Sydney police were drafted into the nearby Australian Capital Territory for the match in Canberra. With still more games to play, the New South Wales Police announced there had already been 600 arrests.

As in New Zealand a decade later, Australian society was divided, families were split and the sports bodies were forced to confront the issue of continued interaction with racially selected teams. Evidence of tension within the rugby community itself was demonstrated when an internal Australian Rugby Union document detailing the team's itinerary for the following week was leaked to the leaders of the protest campaign in Sydney. This resulted in the team being greeted with noisy demonstrators even on their days off, as they were trying to enjoy Sydney's famous restaurant scene.

Another extremely effective part of the trade union boycott was imposed by the hotel workers' union who put food and alcohol bans on all the hotels used by the team. This ban was so effective that the Sydney-based Squire Inn Motel was forced out of business.

One month after the battered Springboks had departed, on 8 September 1971, the legendary cricketer Sir Donald Bradman, as chairman of the Australian Cricket Board, announced 'with great regret' that the cricket tour had been cancelled. Instead of blaming the fact that they could not guarantee the players' safety, Bradman urged the South Africans to 'relax the Apartheid laws' so that cricketers could once again take their place 'as full participants in the international field'. How different to the stubborn refusal of the English cricket hierarchy to cancel the tour until ordered to by the Labour government. Bradman told his son John that his lengthy correspondence with the Stop the Tours leaders Meredith Burgmann and

Peter McGregor had helped him come to this conclusion. 'He came to trust their judgment,' said John Bradman.

The Australian campaigners were jubilant – job done, like STST.

'Public Enemy Number One!'

The direct-action protests in Britain and Australia against apartheid sport in the late 1960s and early 1970s led to a reactive frenzy on the part of white South Africans towards Peter. For a whole generation he came to personify the threat from 'outside' to their 'traditional' way of living. In short, 'public enemy number one', as he was labelled in the local media.

From their colonially rooted Calvinist and McCarthyite perspectives, they, like the regime, saw the actions of Peter and the demonstrators as part of a communist onslaught on Western civilisation in South Africa. For Afrikaner nationalists, it was another reminder of how the British couldn't be trusted.

The 1960s counterculture roots of the demonstrations in Britain and the inter-generational conflict they represented also reinforced the idea of a permissive Western society that had become soft and decadent. Colin Bundy in his delightful summary of that decade and what it meant, started with a poem by Philip Larkin:

> Sexual intercourse began
> In nineteen sixty-three
> (which was rather late for me) –
> Between the end of the *Chatterley* ban
> And the Beatles' first LP.[18]

Bundy continues:

The sixties were years of pop music, fashion, youth culture and consumerism; 80 per cent of British homes had television sets and the Mini and Cortina brought cheap car ownership to the masses. Social change accelerated: abortion and homosexuality became legal, capital punishment was abolished, and measures were taken to improve the position of women. More generally, the authority of age and experience were drastically weakened by an emphasis on youth and novelty. Old patterns of deference were under threat, symbolised by the popularity of satire. The 1960s also marked a post-imperial moment: the independence of India and Pakistan was now followed by the end of colonial rule in the Caribbean and in Africa. The Suez fiasco dealt a lasting blow to Britain's self-image as a world power.[19]

These new influences blowing in from abroad were seen as *volksvreemd* (alien to the nation) by the Afrikaner establishment. Pop culture, long hair, changing sexual mores and the impending arrival of television were greeted with shock and horror. Therefore, Afrikaners needed to withdraw into the *laager* to protect 'standards' and Christian civilisation.

Never mind the demonstrations: the state-controlled South African Broadcasting Corporation (SABC) cancelled the radio broadcast of the Springboks match against Combined Services at Aldershot because it fell on 16 December, the Day of the Covenant, a public holiday celebrating the victory of the Voortrekkers over the Zulu armies in 1838. This was after the Dutch Reformed Church (NGK)'s journal, *Kerkbode*, expressed dissatisfaction on behalf of 'tens of thousands of shocked Christian consciences' that the Springboks agreed to play on a day that 'was promised as a Sabbath to the Almighty by the forefathers of the Afrikaners'. A *dominee* (priest) from Potchefstroom warned of the 'judgment of God' if the Springboks played.[20]

The South African press became overwhelmingly preoccupied with the anti-apartheid protests. Scarcely a piece appeared without some hint of the elephant in the room: thus, in the victory against Munster in Limerick, the heading was 'Boks demonstrate – just how to score'. But the first line of the report mentioned that 400 demonstrators 'paraded' outside the ground. After the big demonstrations at Lansdowne Road in Dublin, two large photographs filled a newspaper page. The top one, showing rugby action, had the bold heading 'Piet Greyling druk . . .' (Piet Greyling scores). And, headlining the crowd scenes picture below: '. . . en betogers druk' (and demonstrators push). There were often two reports of big games, one dealing with the play and the other with the demonstrations. In Dublin, the latter covered the eggs and rotten vegetables being thrown at the tour bus and the mile-long protest which wound its way to the ground, with many of the 4,000 demonstrators present giving Nazi salutes to characterise the all-white team as they sang 'Springboks go home'. Reporting on Coventry, a headline (in Afrikaans) read, 'Boks experience shock day', after a bomb threat and backline star Mannetjies Roux chasing and kicking a demonstrator on the field, which earned him disapproval in the British press but made him an instant hero in the white South African media.[21]

The off-field pressures seeped into every conversation and report, and into the consciousness of white South Africans. Mere reference to the 'demo tour' would be sufficient for people to know exactly what was being referred to. A headline in *Beeld* quoted captain Dawie de Villiers: 'Breekpunt was baie naby' (Breaking point was very close). He said the team had been under extreme pressure, with some nightmare moments, and they had done well to complete a tour in which twenty-four of twenty-five matches had been disrupted in some way. The *Sunday Tribune* quoted him as saying: '"I think the general feeling among the players is one of disgust and I think a sense that we've had it up to here" – he held his hand up to the level of his throat'.

The demonstrations had pushed the apartheid team to the limits. But, despite having the worst playing record of any Springbok touring team until then, the previously invincible Springboks arrived back at Johannesburg's Jan Smuts Airport (today O. R. Tambo International) to a greeting from 5,000 white South Africans. It was 'the biggest welcome ever accorded a returning touring team'. The minister of sport was on hand to welcome them; to their surprise, the players were carried shoulder high through the airport and the team was awarded the state president's award for sport. Apartheid South Africa was closing ranks behind its traditional policy.

The rugby commentator Gerhard Viviers, who became part of white South African folklore, wrote a book on the tour titled *Rugby agter doring-draad* (Rugby Behind Barbed Wire), in which he expressed the universal opprobrium felt by white South Africans towards the demonstrators. In his book and in his distinctive broadcasts, they were at best *langhaar gedrogtes* (long-haired apparitions). The images of *betogers* – meaning the anti-tour demonstrators but conveying something unspeakably distasteful at the same time – became fused with all the negative stereotypes and prejudices about the threats posed by 'liberals and communists' to the narrow re-actionary apartheid worldview. Those opposing the tour became fixed in the popular imagination and narratives of white South Africa as sewer rats, scum in need of a bath, a 'vociferous minority', effete hippies, 'unruly ruffians bent on anarchy' and the almost untranslatable '*beginsinlose liepelappers*' – the meaning of which could range from unprincipled good-for-nothings, loafers, ne'er-do-wells to rotters and rogues.[22]

This virulent propaganda quickly coalesced into an attack on one person, Peter. Because of his campaign's outrageous departure from hypocritical 'fair play' traditions, and his South African and anti-apartheid background, he became the epitome of the 'external threat' to South Africa. The lightning rod for the anger of white South Africans – a hate figure.

The evolution of this anger towards opponents of apartheid, was already well established in lurid colonial *swart gevaar* (black peril) and Cold War *rooi gevaar* (red danger) stereotypes, but the flames were fanned in the 1970s as international pressure and internal resistance increased, leading by the end of that decade to the notion of 'total onslaught'. Backed by the might of the security forces, total onslaught became a formal part of the apartheid government strategy to silence critics, justifying a retreat into the *laager* and the increased use of repression. Anyone who wasn't with you was against you. They were part of the evil 'communist onslaught' against Christianity and Western civilisation, the reasoning went. This would have very negative consequences for South Africa in the violent 1980s as a National Security Management System was put in place, leading to a range of state-sanctioned extra-judicial actions, including the South American-style murder, assassination and disappearance of anti-apartheid activists.

*

André was just seven years old when Prime Minister Hendrik Verwoerd – the apartheid ideologue – declared South Africa a republic independent of Britain in 1961. Boarding with his aunt, he grew up in an environment of church, rugby and apartheid in segregated, small-town 1960s South Africa, a world away from the experience of Peter and the Hain family, both in Pretoria and in exile.

His father, K. P. Odendaal, supported apartheid and coached the Queenstown rugby club, Villagers, comprised mainly of Afrikaners, most of whom would have supported the governing National Party (NP). The latter's traditional rivals were the Pirates, the more English-speaking club, who would probably have been inclined to support the opposition (and only marginally less reactionary) United Party (UP), which under Jan Smuts had ruled South Africa before, during and immediately after the Second World War until it was eclipsed by the NP in 1948. But they played together for the all-white Queenstown team, the Swifts, who K. P. had also repre-sented. The first Christmas present André remembers was a new Springbok-branded rugby ball; at eight, his Dad took him to watch his first rugby test match in Bloemfontein. At the conference to discuss one hundred years of Springbok rugby at Twickenham in 2006, André recalled how on one winter's morning in 1962, his father woke him up at five o'clock, and said, 'It's time to go, boetie.'

> We were on our way to Bloemfontein to watch the Springboks play the British Lions. It was going to be my first test, something exceptional for an eight-year-old from a country town, where test tickets were as rare as biltong in Birmingham. An early start was necessary if we were to cover the 220 kilometres in time for the curtain-raisers which commonly kicked off mid-morning in those days. I remember vividly how we packed the *padkos* (trip food) and hit the road in a 1950s American sedan. Shortly after the sunrise, we reached the Orange River and stopped for a picnic breakfast on its banks – leg of lamb, with my mom's homemade peach pickle, and other farm food – before crossing over into the Free State, another first for me.
>
> At this time of the morning, another contingent from Queenstown, travelling by overnight train, were steaming into Bloemfontein station. This was a notorious party excursion where some, like [family friend and] respectable local lawyer Cedric Fiveash, failed to make it to the match, remaining on the train until it departed for home again in the evening.[23]

South Africa won 34–14 and among the images recalled by eight-year-old André were the giant Scot, Mike Campbell-Lamerton, barging over for a try, the elegance of Keith Oxlee at fly-half and the mercurial energy of Mannetjies Roux.

As this cameo indicates, André was one of those born into the rugby tradition that white South Africans are known for. Starting with that 1962 Lions tour, he made over a hundred rugby scrapbooks as a schoolchild and could boast 150 letters from ex-Springboks or their families. Indeed, from a widow of one of legendary Springbok brothers, the Morkels, he received an original 1906 Springbok badge. Like tens of thousands of other fans, he lived and breathed the tradition and history of the Springboks. From scrapbooks inherited from a cousin, he learnt about Basil Kenyon's great 1951–52 team and 'Murrayfield', the 44–00 thrashing of Scotland, which stood out in rugby folklore like Bob Beamon's long jump record in athletics for many years. And then came the 1955 Lions, the electrifying Cliff Morgan and the unforgettable photo of the Springbok fullback, Johnny Buchler, captured with his shoulders stooped and head bowed, as his match-deciding kick swerved past the uprights in the last minute. André credits the scrapbooks with encouraging a young addiction for reading newspapers and started him on his journey as a historian.

Then came the 'demo' tour of 1969–70, which indelibly imprinted itself on South African psyches and brought home the realisation that things could not stay the same in apartheid South Africa. While his father was vehement in his criticism of the *betogers*, fifteen-year-old André was at the age where he could start reflecting on these messages from outside his narrow world. Still at school, he carefully cut out and glued into his rugby scrapbook some of the dramas of the 1969–70 rugby tour. And in them are indications of how the 'fightback' against Peter by the pro-apartheid forces would begin. Within hours of the 1970 cricket tour being cancelled, the Bureau of State Security (BOSS) asked Gordon Winter in London to prepare a detailed report on Peter and on each one of the activities undertaken by the STST campaign.

The route chosen was via an eccentric English barrister and parliamentary draughtsman, Francis Bennion, who the day the 1970 tour was stopped announced he was launching a private prosecution for criminal conspiracy against Peter. Bennion's initiative was soon backed by the right-wing Society for Individual Freedom (then with close links to British Intelligence). Gordon Winter was instructed by BOSS to help and pass over his material on Peter. This he did, liaising initially with the pro-Pretoria general secretary of the Society, Gerald Howarth (who entered Parliament in 1983 as a hard-right Conservative close to Margaret Thatcher).

On 27 May 1970 Bennion printed and published a thousand-word statement entitled 'Why I Am Prosecuting Peter Hain'. He argued: 'Agitators must not be allowed, however good or bad their cause may be, to stop the lawful activities of others . . . it is a dangerous impertinence for the Hains of this world to take the law into their own hands. What a nerve they have, what a colossal cheek!' Elsewhere in the statement he wrote: 'I agree with the Cricket Council's view that cricket is a wonderful improver of racial harmony and the South Africans would have benefited from playing multiracial teams here.' Declaring he was 'opposed to apartheid', he nevertheless actively sought funds for his prosecution from the apartheid state during fundraising inside South Africa.

In June 1971 the 'Hain Prosecution Fund' was launched to raise £20,000 for Bennion's venture, the equivalent at the time of R65,000. Howarth was its treasurer and Ross McWhirter its chairman. These two, together with Winter, respectively provided links with the hard right, MI5 and BOSS. Bennion was soon in South Africa to raise money, embarking on an early version of today's online crowd funding, and BOSS circulated subscription lists through the South African civil service. Among the many reports in André's scrapbooks, there is a full-page feature in the Johannesburg-based *Sunday Times*, proclaiming 'Crusader Lawyer takes on Demo King'. The newspaper reported that 'sickened by activities of demos, people have opened collection lists to lighten his financial load'. Bennion had sold his '14-room Georgian mansion in Surrey home and was clearly in campaign mode when he declared, "It's my home or Hain". He said he wanted to "fix" Hain "in much the same way as [heavyweight boxer] Joe Frazier zipped the loud mouth of Cassius Clay"' (aka Muhammad Ali).[24]

Danie Craven and his executive committed the whites-only South African Rugby Board (SARB) to supporting Bennion. Craven said, 'People in this country who want to destroy sport should also be destroyed ... just as we want to destroy Hain'. He advised people to send donations to the Rugby Board, giving its PO Box address, saying it would 'centralise collection'. Provincial affiliates reported a 'regular flow' of money coming in. Explaining his attitude, white South Africa's rugby supremo said, 'Look, if someone attacks you with a knife and you flatten him, then you have of course not assaulted him. It is of course self-defence'. Craven declared himself ready to testify at the trial.

Opposition MP Vause Raw chaired a meeting of support in the Durban City Hall with 'leading sportsmen, officials and administrators' sharing the platform. Bennion also met with various rugby and cricket personalities such as tour captain Dawie de Villiers, manager Corrie Bornman, Mike Lawless, H.O. de Villiers, Wilf Isaacs and white South African Cricket Association (SACA) president Jack Cheetham. On the highveld, Bennion was hosted by the Mayor of Benoni and 'Vrystaat [Free State] aid', in a bid to 'halt Hain', was also forthcoming from farmers in Bethlehem who 'gave an ox to the cause'. There were also collection boxes in bars and other venues for what was described in the South African media as the 'Pain for Hain' campaign – a title that caught on among right-wing circles in Britain where donations were also solicited.

The case became something of a cause célèbre, and friends of Peter's organised a 'Peter Hain Defence Fund' to assist with legal costs. His lawyers, reading his recent book about the STST campaign, *Don't Play with Apartheid* (1971), explained it could be construed as an admission of guilt; they said grimly that they faced a battle to prevent him going to prison.

*

The fundamental problem remained apartheid and the laws that barred mixed clubs and mixed school sport as well as preventing teams from one racial group playing in an area designated for another. Even black-only teams playing away required special permission to be entered in their 'pass books' – the identity document restricting blacks to their designated residential areas unless they had jobs in a white area signed for by a white employer.

But apologists of apartheid made all sorts of excuses to sugar-coat the discrimination that underpinned apartheid in sport. Speaking as late as 1980, Dawie de Villiers, the Springbok captain during the demo tour and by then a National Party MP, could confidently state, 'Don't forget that the Blacks have only really known Western sports for the last ten years.'[25] His successor as captain, Hannes Marais, suggested: 'The Coloured population do not seem very interested in sport. They do not play much rugby and cricket.'

In one short sentence, they validated and made 'natural' or normal deep-seated discrimination, even though their claims of black South Africans not playing or being interested in sport were way off the mark, as we will see below. It is as far removed from the truth as it could be.

Firmly entrenched in power through whites-only elections, the governing National Party's official sports policy was explained by Senator Jan de Klerk (father of subsequent president F. W. de Klerk, who over two decades later released Mandela and his comrades). It was accepted with hardly a murmur by white South Africans: 'The South African custom, which is traditional, finds expression in the policy that there should be no competition in sport between the races, within our borders, and that the mixing of races in teams taking part in sports meetings within the Republic of South Africa and abroad should be avoided.'

On 3 March 1967 the minister of sport added: 'If Whites and non-Whites start competing against each other there will be viciousness as has never been seen before.'

That sport was an issue absolutely central to the ideology of white domination was demonstrated with devastating clarity by the mouthpiece of the apartheid government, *Die Transvaler*, on 7 September 1965. Pointing out that 'the white race has hitherto maintained itself in the southern part of Africa' because 'there has been no miscegenation', its editorial continued:

> The absence of miscegenation was because there was no social mixing between White and non-White . . . In South Africa the races do not mix on the sports field. If they mix on the sports field then the road to other forms of social mixing is wide open . . . With an eye to upholding the white race and its civilisation, not one single compromise can be entered into – not even when it comes to a visiting rugby team.

Countless statements could be quoted by top rugby, cricket, sports or government figures justifying racism in sport on the most spurious and blatant basis. Some resorted to extraordinary sophistry, almost word for word the kind of thing which Hitler and his fellow Nazis used to exclude Jews from pre-war German teams and as a means of asserting Aryan supremacy. The following two quotes are telling. In the Johannesburg *Sunday Times*, 3 August 1969, a white South African tennis official justifies why their Davis Cup teams were always white: 'The standards of non-white South African tennis players are very low. None could rank amongst our first 52 players.' Similarly, Karl Ritter von Halt, the Nazi sports minister justified why the 1936 German Olympic team was all Aryan: 'The reason that no Jew was selected to participate in the Games was always because of the fact that no Jew was able to qualify by his ability for the Olympic team. Heil Hitler.'

Others resorted to plain fantasy. Attempting to justify the omission of blacks, a South African Olympics swimming official told the US magazine *Sports Illustrated* in June 1968: 'Some sports the African is not suited for. In swimming the water closes their pores and they cannot get rid of carbon dioxide, so they tire quickly.'

Respected Welsh journalist John Morgan wrote with perception in the London *Sunday Times* in November 1969:

> Of all the curious experiences in observing South African rugby and talking to its leaders and followers, none was more astonishing than that

none of them raised the question of African or Coloured players. The matter did not appear to exist in their minds. The African and coloured rugby federations might have been in another physical continent, not merely a separate continent of the spirit. Old Springbok players would talk earnestly, even with passion, about the virtue of rugby in 'uniting the races' ... but for them the races were Afrikaner and English, the religions Dutch Reformed and Anglican. The blankness with which they responded to the idea that rugby might bring together other races with Whites would be a useful spectacle for those to contemplate who believe that 'tours build bridges'.

There was a kind of cognitive dissonance operating amongst white South Africans on the apartheid issue. The habitual cry against the anti-apartheid protesters – that 'sport and politics should not mix' – simply ignored the facts. Sport was intrinsic to the very fabric of apartheid and sport's maintenance on a racist basis was important to the continuation of apartheid.

*

An important point to make about the sports politics of the late 1960s and early 1970s in South Africa is that it wasn't only deeply reactionary apartheid-supporting Afrikaners who were in favour of white domination and fervently against Peter and his fellow anti-apartheid campaigners. While leading sportsmen and women and the English-speaking white cricket establishment, who started meeting as members of the Imperial Cricket Conference until 1961 by toasting the Queen, often self-righteously protested that they were against apartheid and what the 'dour, uncouth Afrikaner Calvinists' were doing, they were actually comfortably part of the apartheid system, and always had been prior to apartheid from 1948.

Sport in South Africa had for generations been run by the English-speaking establishment and the country's national teams had from the start of international competition in the 1880s been all-white. The whole South African sports system had been riddled with British and European ideas of social Darwinism and racism from its beginnings.

It was actually the arch-imperialist and empire builder, Cecil John Rhodes, who formalised the colour bar in South African sport. And, until well into the twentieth century, sport was very much the domain of the English-speaking establishment. Those cricketers with Afrikaner surnames who played for South Africa were generally anglicised, educated at the elite Bishops and other boys high schools modelled on the English public-school ethos, for example, the Van der Bijls and Van Rynevelds, who had Oxford pedigrees.

While Afrikaners had enjoyed privileges in British colonial society on the basis of their skin colour, they also had long experienced being looked down upon by the British in a cultural sense. It is no secret, for example, that until as late as the 1970s, Afrikaners, Jews and black South Africans were told they were not welcome in certain prominent clubs. Writing in the nineteenth century, John Buchan summed up old prejudices when said the Afrikaners had none of the 'qualities of courage, honour and self-control' that defined sportsmen and the British national character. The Boer was 'seen at his worst' in sport. He was 'without tradition of fair play' and he was 'soured and harassed by want and disaster'.[26] The South African War (1899–1902), between the British Empire and the two Boer states, exacerbated what were at the time called the 'race' differences. André's father, KP, was one of those who grew up with a keen sense of the unjustness of the *Boere-oorlog* (Boer War), its concentration camps and the prejudice and cultural superiority the British displayed. Thousands of Afrikaner women and their children died in these concentration camps – the British, not the Nazis, first created them. His mother had to wear a board around her neck with 'I AM A DONKEY' written on it because she dared speak Afrikaans at school – after the Anglo-Boer War, as it was then known, Lord Milner dictated that only English was allowed. (In the 1990s, while representing and living in a Welsh parliamentary constituency, Peter learnt from local people that the same applied to Welsh speakers for many decades, who had to wear 'WELSH NOT' signs if they dared speak their native tongue at school.) André recalls his father taking him back to the village of Tylden where he grew up, and specifically pointing out the village commonage. Here he'd won one of the biggest races of his life. It was a village sports day and he'd heard a parent tell one of the children who was studying at the prestigious English-speaking St Andrew's College, 'If you beat that Dutchman, I'll give you half a crown.' That day, he said, he gritted his teeth and ran like he'd never run before. English speakers, as Peter recalled from his own Pretoria schooldays, gave the label 'Dutchmen' to Afrikaners as a derogatory term.

Nevertheless, the British and the Afrikaners had united as a racial aristocracy to create the new Union of South Africa in 1910, making it clear to the majority of its population that they could not become citizens and that their role was effectively to service the 'white' economy through cheap labour. Under General Jan Smuts (later Chancellor of Cambridge University), the United Party represented this uncomfortable alliance between white English- and Afrikaans-speaking interests. When the more separatist-oriented Afrikaner National Party won the whites-only elections in 1948 on the programme of a still little-known word – apartheid – South Africa moved into the era of rigid, institutionalised apartheid, hardening long-standing discriminatory practices already in place. The explicit aim of Prime Minister D. F. Malan and the new rulers was also to become a republic and to use the levers of power in a calculated way to improve the political, economic and social status of Afrikaners.

There were some important outcomes for sport. Starting with rugby, Afrikaners deliberately sought more influence in sport, which they soon achieved. For example, Sandy Sanderson, the English establishment head of Transvaal rugby for several decades, was ousted in a coup meant to get Afrikaners at the helm, supported by the influential secret brotherhood, the Broederbond. This opened the way for the long reigns of Jannie le Roux and Louis Luyt in later years. Gert Kotzé describes these manoeuvres in detail in his 1978 book, *Sport en Politiek* (Sport and Politics). Among the new National Party Members of Parliament in 1948 was Paul Roos, who had captained the first Springbok team to Britain in 1906. He was succeeded as MP for Stellenbosch by his 1906 teammate, Bob Loubser, part of the famous thin red line of Stellenbosch backline players.

Political power was used to ensure the economic upliftment of Afrikaners. By the 1960s, the economic gap between the English and Afrikaner had been more or less equalised. In that decade the economy grew at a rate second only to Japan. White children of both languages increasingly began to share the same middle-class interests, such as pop music, shopping mall fashions and games, including cricket.[27]

This economic growth for whites, however, came on the back of increasing repression of black South Africans. When the Beatles hit the scene, and South African folk singer Jeremy Taylor was singing 'Ag Pleez, Deddy' – about the good life of drive-in cinemas, chewing gum, candy floss and Eskimo Pie – Nelson Mandela was settling down on Robben Island with its taste of salt and stone for a spell of twenty-seven years in prison.

As the national struggle for freedom and international opinion against apartheid intensified, English- and Afrikaans-speaking white South Africans increasingly shared the same political viewpoints and retreated into the same *laager* to protect racial privilege. Dissidents and supporters of the liberation struggle, such as Bram Fischer, Rev. Beyers Naudé, Ruth First, Joe Slovo and the Bernstein and Hain families, were the screaming exception rather than the rule in white society. This was reflected in the 1966 elections. With apartheid at its pinnacle, more English-speaking white voters put their crosses for rather than against the 'Nats' for the first time. This date has, not without an element of truth, been jokingly referred to as the real end of the South African War between 'Boer' and 'Brit'.

It was against this background of the consolidation of apartheid power by the National Party that the formerly British game of cricket grew in popularity amongst Afrikaners and that the Springbok rugby team's travails garnered universal sympathy in the white communities in the 1960s and 1970s. It was also in this context that the white Springboks threw away the colonial gentlemen image of the past and with a muscular energy (typified by the charismatic Eddie Barlow) started thumping the 'Poms' and 'Aussies' to whom they had shown so much deference before. In cricket, South Africa won the series in England in 1965 and whitewashed Australia 4–0 and 5–0 in 1966–67 and 1969–70 respectively. After the disaster of the demo-plagued 1969–70 tour, the Springbok rugby team also restored white South Africa's battered pride with a series win against the mighty All Blacks. Faced by an increasingly hostile outside world, English and Afrikaans-speaking white South Africans started going on their own against the stream.

As Christopher Merrett said of sports apartheid: 'International contact was interpreted as approval; victories were regarded as vindication of the white South African way of life, and defeat was akin to national tragedy.'[28]

An editorial in the Afrikaans newspaper *Volksblad* on 28 October 1969 stated bluntly, 'every international sporting success . . . is a blow against our political enemies'. Anti-apartheid activist Joan Brickhill argued that 'defeat in the sports field is treated as a national humiliation for whites; success confirms their worldview of the master race, the heroic image of themselves, and justifies to themselves the position of superiority they claim and hold.'[29] As white South Africa became increasingly isolated, whites closed ranks behind their national sports teams.

English-speaking national sports icons such as cricket captain Jackie McGlew and batsman Eric Rowan were among the active supporters of the National Party and South Africa's 'traditional way of life'. When Prime

Minister Vorster declared in September 1968 that he would not accept the
MCC team with D'Oliveira in it because it 'is not the team of the MCC but
the team of the Anti-Apartheid Movement', McGlew commented, 'England
were aware of the politics of this country and it does seem a shame that they
saw fit to put a man in the Prime Minister's position to the test on his
already clearly defined positions.'[30] Similarly, Ernie McKay, president of the
Western Province Cricket Union, declared, 'I am disappointed, but I
support Mr Vorster on this.'[31] Another strong response by the English-
speaking sporting establishment came from the doyen of South African
cricket writers, Louis Duffus. Christopher Merrett has quoted him as
making the strange claim that 'those who selected D'Oliveira were attempting to break the law'. He said apartheid segregation was 'as much a part of
South African tradition as grass at Wimbledon and eight-ball overs in Australia' and, therefore, 'When you visit a country that drives on the left side
of the road, you do not drive on the right.'[32]

Even opposition-party English-speakers supported Bennion in his court
case against Peter. David Dalling, later a parliamentary colleague of Helen
Suzman in the 'liberal' Progressive Federal Party, acted as Bennion's legal
advisor when he visited South Africa. Liberal newspaper editor Donald
Woods and the iconic Suzman herself were among those who strongly
criticised Peter for his militant demonstrations. The newspaper reports of
Bennion's well-publicised visits specifically stressed that 'English-speaking
South Africans' were contributing to the Peter Hain Prosecution Fund, like
the five young people from the East Rand who donated a thousand rand.

Johnny Waite, wicket-keeper batsman for the SACA Springbok test team
from 1951 to 1965, asserted that 'the black and coloured public of South
Africa is not equipped or ready for multiracial sport any more than the
black and coloured public of the Union is ready to govern South Africa or
to manage its industries.' In his 1961 book, he stated with blind confidence
that 'There is no non-white South African cricket player who could earn a
place in a Springbok team.' Waite justified his assertion: 'Outstandingly the
best such player is Basil D'Oliviera [*sic*] and his value as a cricketer is considerably reduced when he plays on turf instead of matting.'[33] Forced to go
abroad in search of opportunity, and making his debut in his thirties,
D'Oliveira went on to score 2,484 runs in forty-four test matches for
England at an average of 40.06; Waite scored 2,405 runs in fifty test matches
for South Africa SACA at an average of 30.44.

Gary Player, voted the top South African sportsmen of the twentieth century, was another who openly supported the 'traditional' way of life in South Africa. Undoubtedly a superstar with a famously disciplined approach to the game, the 'Black Knight' also had a dark side to him. In the 1960s and 1970s he was an avid supporter of apartheid. In his first auto-biography, *Grand Slam Golf*, published by Cassell in London shortly after he became the fourth golfer in history to win a Grand Slam, he openly supported the system and its prime architect, Hendrik Verwoerd, saying 'I am South African. And I must say now, and clearly, that I am of the South Africa of Verwoerd and apartheid.' In a virtual treatise on racist paternalism, Player went further, saying that his country was 'the product of its instinct and ability to maintain civilised standards amongst the alien barbarians because to have abandoned them would have meant its disappearance.' Going on with the grittiness for which he is known, Player said, 'So little, so very little that is good is written about my country in the West that it really makes my blood boil.'[34] Then the last word: 'I have no evidence that I live in a police state, a "Hitler" state . . . But our government is totally determined that there shall not be another Belgian Congo situation here . . . and I have to approve of that.' And a rider: 'A good deal of nonsense is talked of, and indeed thought about, "segregation" . . . We in South Africa . . . believe that our races should develop separately, but in parallel.'[35]

Player never acknowledged or apologised for his open support for apartheid. To add salt to the wound, he was allowed after 1994 to reinvent and sell himself as one of the builders and ambassadors of the new South Africa. A simple 'I am sorry' or 'I was wrong' is all it would have taken to redress a fundamental dishonesty underpinning the elaborately constructed image of one of the greatest golfers in history.[36]

In contrast to Player stood Papwa Sewgolum, the caddy from Durban with a back-to-front grip. His story is the stuff of legend that sport has a habit of so often producing. An illiterate caddie from an impoverished background, he became the best black golfer in South Africa in the 1950s and 1960s, winning close to twenty titles under the unrecognised non-racial South African golf body. He was never allowed to test his skills against whites because of apartheid conventions – until, one day, complete chance brought an unexpected benefactor. Graham Wulff, the wealthy entrepreneur behind Oil of Olay skincare saw him play and was impressed. He personally air-hopped him through Africa in a small plane via Beira, Dar es Salaam, Nairobi, Khartoum and so on to compete in Europe. Against the odds, Sewgolum won the Dutch Open and qualified for the British Open. The white golfing establishment was then embarrassed into allowing him to play in the Natal Open, which he promptly won twice, in 1963 and 1965. Not allowed into the whites-only clubhouses, Sewgolum had to change in a minivan and eat with the caddies. He was at times also forbidden to play in practice rounds as his permit was for the tournaments only. When he won in 1963, he was handed his trophy outside in the rain, then the rest of the participants withdrew into the clubhouse to complete the prize-giving and start their festivities without him. In the 1965 tournament, Sewgolum beat the selfsame Player in a play-off watched by a supercharged crowd of thousands. Player was an ungracious loser, but for that one day, Sewgolum and his fans were his equals.

Chris Nicholson, the judge who was to cause Thabo Mbeki's downfall through a flawed judgement which paved the way for the corrupt presidency of Jacob Zuma, wrote a book about Sewgolum, in which he contrasts Player's support for apartheid and his journey to fame with the rise and fall into alcoholism of this golfing untouchable.[37]

In the 1970s, Player became a member of the Committee for Fairness in Sport (CFS), chaired by a former journalist of the pro-apartheid newspaper, *Die Vaderland*. Funded in the name of wealthy white South African businessmen (including rugby legend Louis Luyt) using money laundered through the Information Department, its mandate was to promote an image of 'change' in order to appeal for international sports readmission. Player was primed to invite rich American business chiefs for games of golf in South Africa, their expenses and Player's fees laundered through the Information Department's secret account. Sometimes these sanctions-breaking initiatives would include rounds of golf with the club-swinging apartheid ironman John Vorster, who had refused to allow D'Oliveira to tour with the MCC. After these lavish hospitality trips, they were encouraged to write letters to the US government praising South Africa and urging a supportive attitude to the apartheid government. 'A personal letter from Gary Player was worth ten invitations from the foreign minister,' the top Information Department chief boasted.[38]

The complicity of English-speaking white South Africa with apartheid was reflected when Peter attended the Franschhoek Literary Festival in 2019 to talk on his biography *Mandela: His Essential Life*. One after another of his generation of white attendees came to speak to him and they almost inevitably mentioned in an animated way how they had 'hated' him in the 1970s, how for them he had been 'public enemy number one', but today everything was 'forgiven'.

Thus, political power, increasing wealth and greater social opportunities and confidence after the electoral victory of the National Party both broadened the base of Afrikaner involvement and leadership in South African sport and brought increasing convergence in the social and political viewpoints of English- and Afrikaans-speaking white South Africans. Besides a brief, walk-off and a petition by cricketers at Newlands in 1970, aimed last minute at saving that year's Springbok tour to Australia, the white sports establishment abided by government policy and stood by the regime throughout the apartheid period to counter the 'onslaught' against their South Africa. White sportspeople benefitted from the system in which they were embedded throughout the long years of colonialism and apartheid.

Furthermore as Peter and his fellow campaigners discovered, the apartheid-grounded perspectives of the Afrikaans- and English-speaking white South African sportspeople and administrators were very close to the basic worldview and attitudes to apartheid in sport held by the rugby and cricket establishment and the conservative ruling classes in Britain at the time. During the 1969–70 demonstrations, the rugby and cricketing icon Wilfred Wooller had told Peter in no uncertain terms that he looked forward to seeing him 'behind bars'. Referring to the MCC, Lord Monckton once remarked, 'I have been a member of the Committee of the MCC and of a Conservative cabinet, and by comparison with the cricketers, the Tories seemed like a bunch of Commies.'[39] Letters to MCC from its members urged it to stand firm, giving a sense of the atmosphere of crisis of the time: one labelled the STST a 'complete negation of all this country stands for' and felt the MCC were defending 'the last bastion of what remains of the British way of life'. Peter was seen as a 'dangerous anarchist and communist', and it was noted that if the STST can 'smash this tour they will turn to other things'. Another described the STST campaign as 'persistent mob pressure and an attempt at neo-communist rule'.[40] Representatives of county clubs were often landed gentry, and as one secretary said of them on 14 December 1969, 'this was their opportunity to apply all their dislike and loathing of permissiveness, demonstrators and long hair. Staging matches is their chance to make a stand against these things.'[41]

The Chief Constable of Leicester and Rutland Constabulary wrote to Lords: 'The country has to face a situation which, if it slides much further, will lead to complete anarchy.' A letter, sent on 14 December 1969 to the chairman of the MCC, drew its attention to a newspaper quote from Peter,

'We don't want to have to drag the MCC kicking and screaming into the twentieth century', and protested:

> I could scarcely believe my eyes when I read this. Are you going to take this from a 19 year old boy who, I understand, was not even born in this country and only came to Britain four years ago. How dare this young fellow speak in that way of the MCC? Dammit, you are grown-up men like me and you should make it crystal clear that you are not going to allow a 19 year old boy and his followers to disrupt the tour. For heaven's sake what have we come to if a fellow like this can be allowed to hold our cricket to hostage.

The writer would doubtless have approved when Sir John Junor, editor of the *Sunday Express*, castigated Peter and wrote: 'It would be a mercy for humanity if this unpleasant little creep were dropped into a sewerage tank. Up to his ankles. Head first.'

Another letter to the MCC asserted: 'I am sure that time will tell that the present SA government are treading on the right lines. Whilst segregation is not the best method of dealing with the matter I have it on the highest authority that the SA native is better off to-day than ever before.'

A further letter protested against the possible cancellation of the tour through 'the efforts of the African and Asian and the nigger loving scum of this fair land'. In a similar vein came a missive from Taunton protesting, 'one immigrant student [Peter] has started this campaign and our nigger loving bishops and MPs will have made England the laughing stock of the world.'[42]

As Colin Bundy has noted, the MCC, which first excluded and then included D'Oliveira in 1968, and which several months later issued the invitation to the white South African cricket team to tour in 1970, was a bastion of class snobbery run by the conservative British elite, and thus it had always been:

> The MCC presidents held office for one year – and between 1919 and 1939 only six were not aristocrats: they compensated for this inadequacy by including a Tory MP who became governor of Bengal; the chairman of Midland Bank; the proprietor of the Times newspaper, and a baronet who became Lord Mayor of London. The decision-making body of the MCC was its 16-member Committee elected each year. Of 67 men who served on the committee between the wars, all had been to public school, 23 to Eton alone. Twenty were MPs, including the Prime

Minister Baldwin, the Home Secretary, a Governor-General of Australia
– and so on.[43]

There were good reasons why the opinions of the apartheid sports establishment and conservative opinion in Britain coincided in many ways with
regard to the direct-action demonstrations in 1969–70. Their worldviews
and attitudes towards the South African question were rooted in a deep,
shared history going back some 170 years. 'All in all,' Bundy concluded, 'the
sixties [and the Hain-led demonstrations] disrupted a cultural continuity
largely intact since the Victorian period.' Therefore, to understand apartheid
in sport and the sports cultures in both South Africa and Britain in the late
1960s and early 1970s, it is also important to understand Britain's role in
spreading sport to South African and its other colonies at a time when the
sun never set on the British empire in the eighteenth and nineteenth centuries. For it was in this process of British conquest and colonialism that the
roots of apartheid and racism in twentieth century sport lay, as well as the
crusted old mentalities that Peter and the anti-apartheid lobby had to
confront.

2

Empire and the British roots of sports apartheid

Africa's version of 'The Demon' Spofforth: Cecil John Rhodes and the introduction of the colour bar in South African sport

A fast bowler of exceptional ability in 1890s Cape Town exemplified the on-field racism under British colonial rule. His name was William Henry 'Krom' Hendricks and he was someone who came to life on the cricket field. His hostile and skilful bowling was a thrilling sight. He delivered high-speed yorkers that burst through defences and electrified big crowds who queued to see their hero bowl. Week after week he turned in exceptional performances. Hendricks was in constant demand and played for more than a dozen teams in his long career.[44]

Early in 1892 he was one of eighteen cricketers who played a serendipitous match against the English touring team to South Africa. In those days of steamships, the English team was due to play the last test in Cape Town before taking the boat back home. But the visitors quickly overwhelmed the South African Cricket Association side in a mere day and a half, and some local cricketers, sensing an opportunity, challenged the English to an extra game. The professionals in the team saw this as a chance to earn some money and agreed. Thus, the *Cape Times* reported, 'On the conclusion of the Test . . . a match was commenced by the professionals for their own benefit, against a picked team of eighteen Malay cricketers of the district.' The contest took place at Newlands from 22 to 23 March 1892 and, the newspaper added, it 'caused great interest among the Mohammedan community, who showed their appreciation of the great honour accorded them by attending the match in large numbers, as did many Europeans who were wishful of contributing to the benefit'.[45]

Hendricks was one of those who stood out in the match, making a lasting impression on his opponents. Opening batsman, William Chatterton of Derbyshire (who also played football for Derby County) recalled that he had 'played at home against Richardson, Lockwood and Mold, and against the greatest of Australian genius, Spofforth and Turner'. Yet the very ablest bowler he had ever met he believed to be 'not Spofforth, but a South African black, Hendricks'. He added: 'The memory of this man's pace from the pitch, his quick swing away, alternating with a fine break, stirred a cold and critical nature to enthusiasm.'[46] W. W. Read, the English tour captain, advised, 'If you send a team [to England], send Hendricks; he will be a drawcard and is to my mind the Spofforth of South Africa.'[47] F. R. Spofforth, known as 'The Demon Bowler', was the first great Australian quickie to wreak havoc against English teams.[48] The vastly experienced George Hearne, who played 252 times for Kent between 1875 and 1895, confirmed that the parallel was not exaggerated: 'A Malay named Hendricks was very fast indeed. In our last match against the Malays, the wicket was very bad and we didn't like facing the man at all. I was captain during the match and everyone began to ask me to let somebody else go in his place ... The balls flew over our heads in all directions.'[49] The Surrey wicketkeeper Henry Wood, who had just scored an unbeaten 134 in the test at Newlands, had to retire hurt after a 'bumping ball' hit him on the finger. The Surrey and England great, George Lohmann, and the English-born professional, Charles Mills, who had represented Surrey, played for South Africa in the 1892 'Test' and toured England in 1894, confirmed that Hendricks 'was by far the finest fast-bowler in South Africa'.

There could not have been higher praise than that provided by this range of vastly experienced English professional cricketers who saw Hendricks play. But these views were for a long time unknown because until comparatively recently, you had to look hard to find the name of William Henry 'Krom' Hendricks in the official records of South African cricket. In the massive 848-page history of South African cricket written by Maurice Luckin in 1915, he appears as 'the Cape coloured boy, Hendriks [*sic*]' whose selection for the 1894 tour would have been 'impolitic' and is listed in a single scorecard hidden away on pages 517 and 518.

Hendricks and his teammates were lucky even to be included in Luckin's history because they were described as 'non-Europeans' and later 'non-whites' under the terminology of the time. And they are the only eighteen players so defined who made it into the 'official' record of South African cricket for the eighty-five years from the beginnings of competitive cricket there in the mid-1870s to 1960. No other person not classified white was included in the four dense volumes written by Luckin, Louis Duffus and Brian Bassano covering that period. Save for the one-off opportunity to play in this unusual match, they would have been invisible.

The clear implication arising from Luckin and other histories like his was that cricket was a 'white man's game', and that 'the natives' never played it or showed an interest. The exclusions and silences in the history books mirrored the horrible real-life discrimination that people suffered under the violent and exclusionary systems of colonialism and apartheid. The ruling classes assumed for generations that others who did not look like them were somehow less human – 'savages' was an epithet both writers recall being thrown at black people by disdainful whites – and did not have the same capabilities or deserve the same opportunities.

Recent research on Hendricks has brought out a truth stranger than fiction. It turned out that he suffered cruelly for his temerity in being both black and better than the British Empire at its own game, and that no less a person than the prime minister of the Cape Colony decided that his face literally did not fit with their notion of cricket as an essentially British pastime. Therefore, though good enough, it was decided that under no circumstances should he be selected to play cricket for South Africa.

At the heart of the plot were arch-imperialist Cecil John Rhodes, and his right-hand man, Sir William Milton, a former England rugby player and South African cricket captain. Working together with their acolytes in the Western Province Cricket Club – which styled itself as the MCC of the Cape Colony – and the Western Province Cricket Union of local clubs, these die-hard, high-society British racists set out to systematically hound Hendricks out of the game. A panoply of exclusion followed as grand empire intersected with virulent social racism.

Although Hendricks was nominated by Transvaal for the first tour to England in 1894, a certainty for selection, the Cape cabal ensured he was banned from playing for South Africa, Western Province and the Colonial-Born team in what was then the annual cricket showpiece versus the British 'Home-Born' XI. He was further prohibited from plying his trade as a professional playing in the Cape Town club 'Championship' and the second-tier 'Peninsula league', and forced into the subservient status of 'net bowler' for whites. For more than a decade, the bigoted and incompetent Club and Union officials obfuscated and held the line about Hendricks's status despite being forced to consider his eligibility on several occasions in the period between 1894 and 1905. On every occasion they failed to revisit, let alone change their original decision, frustrating Hendricks's career step by mean step until he was past his prime and irrevocably denied the opportunities he so deserved. This was cruel, systematic discrimination carried out over a long time by poker-faced bigots parading as society's leaders upholding 'civilisation' and standards.

When the journalist and founding secretary of the South African Cricket Association, Harry Cadwallader championed Hendricks's inclusion in the team for England, he too was unceremoniously dumped by Milton as manager for the tour. Having been virtually assured of the position because he had been the tour's main organiser, he was held responsible for the 'Hendricks affair' and subsequently lost several influential positions in national rugby and cricket. Shunned by the system, he relocated to the Transvaal where he died in 1897 in 'such grievous need' that a public fund was set up to assist his wife and children. Incredibly, his name does not even appear in Luckin's history. For challenging those in power upholding British values, he too was purged and made invisible.

As a bowler, Hendricks's pace and aggression viscerally challenged white batsmen and the social order they inhabited. The better he was, the more threatening he became. He regularly demolished senior clubs when he had the opportunity to play against them, making a point of dismissing those who had been selected for the provincial or test teams. Whether or not leading Cape batsmen were frightened of his pace, they were certainly unhappy at being shown up by a coloured player. White supremacy required white control. A humiliation on the pitch was intolerable for it confounded all the racist superiority stereotypes and mythology upon which white South Africa's domination rested. When Peter pointed out to school friends in the 1960s the great black cricketers such as Barbados's Garfield Sobers – arguably the best all-rounder in the world at the time – or Muhammad Ali, the world heavyweight boxing champion, a familiar retort was, 'Ah, but they are not like *our* blacks.'

The whole white psyche rested upon such mythology, and the Hendricks affair showed that cricket in South Africa, and globally, was not simply a game – it was a vehicle for culture, ideology and politics. And Hendricks was not alone, but the first in a catalogue of hundreds of black cricketers, up to Basil D'Oliveira and beyond, who despite their talent were denied the opportunity to represent their country. His contemporaries Ebrahim Ariefdien, Robert Grendon, Armien Hendricks and Lamarah Samsodien would all have been certainties for representative honours in a fair, non-racial system. Hendricks was the key to a non-racial sporting door. That was the real threat to the colonialists. So they closed that door in 1894.

Had Hendricks gone to England with the first South African touring team in line with the relatively inclusive Cape Colony constitution of the time, as he should have on merit, South Africa would have preceded the route subsequently followed by West Indies cricket. Lebrun Constantine, father of the great Sir Learie Constantine, became the first black cricketer 'allowed to play for Trinidad' in 1895, and he was one of five black players included in the first West Indies tour to England in 1900. As Charles Lister has pointed out in *Fire in Babylon* (2016), one of the five, Charles Olliveirre, was persuaded to stay behind and play for Derbyshire in county cricket, starting a tradition of West Indian stars in the English leagues and county cricket. Seven decades before a man with a similar-sounding name – D'Oliveira – led an exodus of black talent from South Africa to England in the 1960s, South Africa's top five of the 1890s, in the shape of the two Hendrickses, Ariefdien, Grendon and Samsodien, and the talented players who followed them, could have been sharing the same roadway as the Constantines, the legendary George Headley and Sir Frank Worrell. South Africa was scheduled to meet the West Indians in England in the early 1900s, but, in an ominous portent of what the future would hold, the match never took place.

The decisions taken by Rhodes, Milton and their jingoistic and racist allies formalised segregation and apartheid as official policy and took South African cricket on a hundred-year journey down a dead-end street. Wasted opportunity and the deliberate suppression of human potential were the biggest outcomes of their folly. That meme was to become the destructive legacy of the tragedy that was apartheid.

Instead of South African cricket and rugby following an inclusionary path, both went in the opposite direction. Both refused to allow black players to play in their club leagues and Currie Cup provincial competitions and, in a hundred years of test matches, the cricketers played only against the white countries of empire, England, Australia and New Zealand.

Black sportspeople, though present from the start, were removed from the stage and from the record books. They became invisible. This reflected the political system, which locked them out of citizenship. The ruling classes, both in South Africa and England, both English- and Afrikaans-speaking, could now carry on as 'normal'. Which is why at the height of apartheid in the 1960s and 1970s they could claim that black South Africans had 'no interest or inclination' to play British sports such as cricket and rugby, or that they 'weren't good enough'.

Cricket and conquest: British Army origins of sport in South Africa

Four days after the New Year celebrations in 1806, 'Sentries on Signal Hill saw the horizon begin to fill with sails and by afternoon a British fleet, awesome in its magnitude, had moved into Table Bay.'[50] The invasion force, headed by the sixty-four-gun man-o'-war *Diomede*, consisted of more than sixty ships and several thousand soldiers. It turned out to be one of the biggest sea-based invasions in the history of the British Empire until D-Day in 1944.

That 1806 display of 'shock and awe' started a century and a half of colonial rule administered from Whitehall in London. As one historian has noted, the British added 'a new element . . . to an already complex mix of people at the Cape', and 'Motivated by imperialism, deceit, greed, prejudice and humanitarianism, the colony's new rulers would play a leading role in constructing one of the world's most troubled societies.'[51]

Cricket and its spread through southern Africa were extremely closely linked to the process of military and political conquest in the nineteenth and early twentieth centuries. Starting off as a garrison game, it was at first confined to barracks, only gradually spreading to involve civilians and schoolchildren among both the indigenous people and settlers arriving from Europe.

Cricket was played on a regular basis almost immediately after the intimidating, if not accident-free, entry of the British fleet. A Dutch observer noted: 'With the English officers at the Cape I was on the best of friendly terms. With a number of them serving in the artillery and light dragoons I twice a week played a game of ball-casting, called cricket by the English, on the level ground by the sea at the Lion's Tail.'[52]

The level ground by the sea at the Lion's Tail where the first matches were played is today's Green Point Common, and why Rowland Bowen, in his pioneering account of cricket history, has described the Green Point Common as 'probably the oldest surviving cricket ground but one outside the British Isles'.[53] The first detail of a match is from a newspaper advert notifying locals that 'A grand match at cricket will be played for 1,000 [rix] dollars a side on Tuesday, January 5, 1808, between the officers of the artillery mess, having Colonel Austen of the 60th regiment, and the officers of the Colony, with General Clavering. The wickets are to be pitched at 10 o'clock.'[54] Who were the two principals in this early match on the local scene, the notice of which has for so long been rehashed without any context? Lieutenant-Colonel Thomas Austen was commander of the 4th Battalion of the 60th Regiment, which had been sent to the Cape after a long tour in Jamaica and Martinique, while the forty-seven-year-old Brigadier-General Henry Mordaunt Clavering belonged to a distinguished aristocratic and military line. His grandfather Sir James married Lady Augusta Campbell, daughter of the fifth Duke of Argyll – also a field marshal – and his father, Lieutenant General John Clavering, led the attack on Guadeloupe in 1772 and became commander-in-chief in India in 1774.

A distinguishing aspect of colonial cricket in the first decades of the nineteenth century that jumps to the fore is the leading role played by class-conscious 'gentlemen' officers, who brought pomp and pageantry to the play, and would give the game an elite character in Africa. Imperial nations, whose status is inevitably based on force, glorify their military. This was as true of Britain in the nineteenth century as it is of America today. The image of the officer and gentleman became a central part of cricket's self-image as it spread through southern Africa.[55]

It is also worth noting that this early cricket also marked the beginning of the globalisation of the game. An intimate connection developed via the military between cricket in Cape Town and the colonial project in India and other colonies, such as Barbados, the next posting for Colonel Austen. Troops being transported by ship to and from India played regularly at the Cape. The so-called 'Indians' – officers, troops and officials who served in India and came to rest and recuperate at the Cape because returning to England took too long – later also directly influenced the development of local cricket.

During the course of the nineteenth century, tens of thousands of British soldiers came to be stationed in South Africa. Their influence was strongest in Cape Town, the seat of British power in the Cape Colony. But cricket spread throughout modern-day South Africa as the British military presence expanded from the 1810s to 1850s, firstly into Xhosaland (today's Eastern Cape), then Zululand (KwaZulu-Natal) and finally to the central interior. Rather than spreading out systematically overland from Cape Town, to Swellendam, Oudtshoorn and so on, cricket followed the seaward movements of the soldiers and officials, making big jumps along the east coast to Port Elizabeth, and later to Durban, and from these ports into their hinterlands. In those wagon-and-cart days, inland travel and communication were difficult: the first (short) railway line in southern Africa was opened only in 1860 and the telegraph line and telephone were to come later.

The British population in the Cape Colony was at first very small, so there was no immediate large-scale take-up of the game by the locals. At first it was really the military playing among themselves who participated. It was only in the 1840s and 1850s that the first clubs and schools were set up.

In the eastern Cape, ten wars over one hundred years between the British and the indigenous isiXhosa-speaking people brought both conflict and co-operation not experienced anywhere else, which had a distinct impact on the development of cricket in South Africa.

The tough resistance put up by the African chiefdoms in the eastern Cape deterred the British from wholesale annexation. In fact, the risks and costs were a restraining factor and by mid-century, Britain showed no great appetite to expand its colonial boundaries. But that all changed with the discovery of diamonds in the late 1860s, followed by the discovery of gold in the 1880s: South Africa had one of the richest mineral deposits in the world. A wholesale process of violent conquest and incorporation in the subcontinent now followed. Britain and its proxies set out to pacify, re-organise and unify southern Africa, and succeeded within a few decades in doing so. All this was in the service of the new mining economy under the British flag, which required for its efficient operation political stability, geographical unity and a cheap, controlled labour force. Previously in-dependent societies were steamrolled into submission, generally with the aid of British troops. African territories fell one by one. The pattern of settlement, and of identity and state formation in the interior of southern Africa, which had been extremely fluid and undefined up to the 1860s, became fixed.

Year by year between 1868 and 1902 the dominoes fell, enabling Brit-ain to consolidate various fragmented political entities into a single Union of South Africa by 1910. Precolonial entities collapsed one after the other in the wake of the mineral discoveries and lost their independence.[56] Many submitted 'voluntarily' to their pacification, but this process can be fully understood only against the background of a century of conflict and the systematic use of force.[57] Annexation merely legalised a gradual process of expanding British rule. Those who refused to bend the knee were conquered militarily. Thabo Mbeki, a spokesperson in the liberation struggle years, and later president of South Africa, explained in the 1980s that:

South Africa was conquered by force and is today ruled by force. At moments when White autocracy feels itself threatened, it does not hesitate to use the gun. When the gun is not in use, legal and administrative terror, fear, social and economic pressures, complacency and confusion generated by propaganda and 'education', are the devices brought into play in an attempt to harness the people's opposition. Behind these devices hovers force. Whether in reserve or in actual employment, force is ever present and this has been so since the White man came to Africa.[58]

He continued:

The British brought new dimensions to the whole process of conquest in the nineteenth century. They modernised the petrified and outdated Boer economy and subjugated the indigenous workers and peasants in a much more systematic, sophisticated and brutally exploitative manner. In the end it was the British armies which defeated the African people, the British which drove us off our lands, broke up the natural economy and social system of the indigenous people. It was they who imposed the taxes on the African peasants and . . . laid down labour laws which govern the black workers in South Africa today.[59]

In parallel, the first competitive cricket in South Africa was an inter-town tournament for the Champion Bat Tournament started in 1876, and it underlined the key role played by the military in the development of South African cricket. The mayor of Port Elizabeth challenged other towns in the Cape Colony and a start was made in the slow process of building organised competitions. The thinking was that this should become a colonial version of the 'Canterbury week', the oldest cricket festival in England. Organised by the Kent County Cricket Club since 1842 at the St Lawrence Ground 'with its tents and famous lime tree, unchanging in a changing world', it is still going more than 160 years later.[60] Four centres accepted invitations, Cape Town, Port Elizabeth, Grahamstown (today named Makhanda) and King William's Town.[61] The 'redoubtable kaffrarians' from King William's Town were the first winners, heading the table with three wins out of three. The *Eastern Province Herald* generously conceded, 'Their physique, pluck, athletic training and fine discipline bore down all opposition.'[62]

It was no accident that King William's Town won. Its attack revolved around a 'good pair of soldier bowlers', Phillips and Gillman of the 32nd Regiment, who took twenty-nine wickets between them. There were four British regiments in southern Africa in the late 1870s, and most of these troops were stationed in King William's Town on what the colonists would come to call 'the Border', with the others mainly at the capital, Cape Town. The town also hosted the headquarters of the 1,200-strong Cape Mounted Rifles (CMR), who were frontier police recruited and paid for by the Cape government. The CMR was the main fighting force on the frontier and its men were said to be 'much more efficacious' than the ordinary British soldiers. Most of the recruits were from England, and not only were they all mounted, but most of 'the men themselves come from a much higher class than that from which our soldiers are enlisted'.[63]

An 'extraneous match' on the final day pitting Civilians against the Military Past and Present brought this then popular tournament to a close and underlined the prominence of the military; these kinds of contests were described as 'a favourite in those warlike times', a reference to the fact that ninth war of dispossession in the eastern Cape was imminent,[64] These military/civilian contests were clearly meant to deepen colonial solidarity in the process of military conquest, which was then entering a particularly expansive phase; in the next quarter of a century Britain would complete the forceful subjugation of the entire vast area known today as South Africa and Zimbabwe.

With that kind of pool available to it, King William's Town also won the second Champion Bat four years later in the 1879–80 season. Copying the ruling classes, the local black cricketers duly also won the first Native Inter-Town Tournament held in 1884–85. They sometimes challenged the local white teams and it was not unusual for the Africans to win. Sir Derek Birley noted in his classic social history of English cricket that representatives of the mother country thought in such cases that 'it was an inversion of the natural order of things if they did not win' and that it was 'not entirely necessary always to behave well towards colonials.'[65] Indeed, this seemed to have been the case when the King William's Town Africans challenged the Cape Mounted Rifles – who had pushed a CMR XXII into the field for two games against the English tourists in the previous season and lost badly – to a match in preparation for the 1892–93 Native Inter-Town Tournament. The Africans fell one run short of the soldiers' 119, 'kodwa singati baqatwa yi Umpire yecala lama CMR' (but it seems they were cheated by the umpire of the CMR side).[66] Even if it was only a game and umpires were expected to be fair, by beating the 'Europeans', the King William's Town black players would have inverted the basic message of colonialism, driven home through the barrel of a gun – that the dispossessed were weaker and should be subservient. Mihir Bose has commented on similar circumstances in India in the encounters between the British and the Parsis in Mumbai, which were known to lead to 'displays of feeling'. The British objected to Parsi umpires, although they were agreeable to the Parsis appointing their own white umpires – otherwise, said Bose, this would have meant 'an Indian, a subject race, giving decisions on an Englishman, the master race'.[67]

These kinds of contests were therefore cricket with an epic dimension reflecting the underlying tensions of a racist colonialism with all its sporting contortions.

From the 1880s onwards, British attention shifted more to Zululand and the interior highveld and by the end of that decade Kimberley was the strongest cricket centre in the country, winner of the Champion Bat for inter-town cricket in 1888 and first winners of the new Currie Cup for inter-state (later inter-provincial) cricket in the following season. The Diamond City was a place that attracted both money and migrants, facilities were upgraded and first national bodies in cricket and rugby were formed there, for both white and black sportspeople. By 1890 it was described as a 'supremely British place' and cricket became an integral part of the project to make the subcontinent British. This conflation of interests was reflected in April 1890 when both the Pioneer Column established by Cecil John Rhodes to 'open up' a new colony to the north and the cricketers playing in the inter-regional Currie Cup competition were in the town at the same time. By the time the Column set out after a week of socialising, it had in its ranks as a celebrity participant England's youngest test captain, Monty Bowden, who had just played in the Currie Cup contest, and various other top cricketers. They were moving directly from the cricket pitch to taking a piece of Africa.

The direct link between the development of South African cricket and violent conquest in the nineteenth century was nowhere better illustrated than in the subsequent subjugation of Zimbabwe. Thanks to Jonty Winch's pioneering research, we know that no fewer than six of South Africa's first ten cricket captains became involved in helping to set up the new colonial administration in what became known as Rhodesia. Besides Rhodes's right-hand man, William Milton, who succeeded Rhodes's confidant Dr Leander

Starr Jameson as administrator of the territory, after the former had been arrested for the attempted coup d'état in the South African Republic, they included Alfred Richards, Murray Bisset, Henry Taberer, Percy Sherwell, and Hubert Castens and Godfrey Cripps, the captain and vice-captain on the 1894 tour to England. It was observed that cricket was the principal qualification of his civil service appointees.

Several of them had been part of Rhodes's lobby to stop Krom Hendricks from playing for South Africa. For example, Murray Bisset, captain of Western Province Cricket Club and of the second South African team to England in 1901 became chief justice of the country (as did a brother of the SACA test player Charlie Vintcent). Hubert Castens became Milton's chief secretary,[68] and was acting public prosecutor in the case of Mbuya Nehanda, the famous Shona spirit-medium and leader in the first *Chimurenga* (war of resistance) in what is today Zimbabwe in 1896–97. Castens secured a death sentence, and there was drama at Nehanda's hanging, which confirmed to her followers her spiritual powers: 'Two unsuccessful attempts were made to hang her. An African prisoner present at her hanging then suggested that the hangman should remove from her belt a tobacco pouch. This was done and on the third attempt she was successfully hanged.'[69] Rejecting attempts to convert her to Christianity at the gallows, Nehanda's dying words were, 'My bones will rise again.' She became one of the inspirations in the later liberation struggle which brought independence to Zimbabwe. A shocking photograph of the hanging tree in Salisbury (Harare) made infamous by the great novelist Olive Schreiner in her book *Trooper Peter Halkett of Mashonaland* shows Castens watching on, nakedly exposing the connection between cricket, European 'progress' and inhuman colonial brutality.

Recent in-depth research has also revealed that Brigadier General Robert Poore, the epitome of the late-nineteenth-century soldier and sportsman, who represented South Africa in 1895–96, was one of those who played cricket between military excursions against the Ndebele and Shona. Winner of the Matabeleland tennis championships and scorer of a century for the 7th Hussars in one of the many games he played during his stint in the north, Poore was in joint command of the troops that led attacks on Shona homesteads and 'forced the Shona into caves, from where they were eventually evicted with dynamite'. In his long military career, this outstanding cricketer served under senior British commanders such as Haig, Kitchener, Roberts and Baden-Powell, and he was in charge during the controversial execution of the Australian soldier 'Breaker' Morant in the South African War.

While the traditional literature romanticises the gentleman and officer and both cricket and military derring-do in the colonies, the realities on the ground do not provide a pretty picture of 'fair play', illustrating instead how the game was spread in a discriminatory way directly through war and conquest by the British in southern Africa. The cricket establishment in South Africa became indistinguishable from the imperial venture and its accompanying violence and fundamental disrespect for African people.[70]

'The Club' and the unadmitted millions:
'Traditional' British and South African sports cultures

Going with the notion of British 'gentlemen's game' is the idea (still widely held without much critical reflection in cricket circles) that cricket has somehow been neutral, 'above politics' and marked by 'fair play'. It is one of cricket's founding myths, passed down uncritically for generations in South Africa and in England where it was largely shaped. In this narrative cricket in southern Africa was an innocent pastime played under sunny skies on the African veld in the spirit of fair play by quirky Englishmen and the few locals who understood its peculiarities and the delightfully eccentric nature of English culture.[71] The fact that cricket's much trumpeted 'traditional culture' at different stages featured only white men in colonial contexts in Africa, Asia and the Caribbean is generally politely and conveniently glossed over. This conceals the biased history of the game and further reproduced, in different times and different contexts, the ugly exclusions that lay at cricket's core in the past.

But, as André, Jonty Winch, Christopher Merrett and Krish Reddy show in Cricket and Conquest (2016), cricket arrived in Africa as part of the baggage of invading British military forces and accompanied the invading soldiers every step of the way through the subcontinent in a hundred-year process of systematic and violent conquest. The inherent violence that underpinned cricket's growth in southern Africa also shaped its character. It was impossible for the archetypal British game, with its close military associations, to remain innocent against the long background of conquest and dispossession in southern Africa. British and settler militarism directly shaped attitudes and mindsets that became entrenched in the game. Far from innocence and fair play, cricket's 'culture' in southern Africa became infused with notions of racism, narrow masculinity, social Darwinism and imperial superiority.

The breeding grounds for these colonial, patriarchal and racist values which cricket was drenched in for generations were the army, the school and the club. The historian Jan Morris explained that for the British in the colonies:

> The club, in the highly class-conscious nineteenth century British society, was based on the notion of hierarchy and exclusion. In the African and Asian colonies of Britain this notion of exclusivity, going far beyond the sports field, was taken to even greater extremes. Here the club served as a symbol, not only of social status, but also of political domination. It was developed as an enclave of power and privilege in an alien setting. Its members were patently different from the unadmitted millions. Not only in colour and status, but also in place. More than anywhere else, it was the place where the imperialists celebrated their Britishness, authority and imperial lifestyle.[72]

Using the example of India, Ramachandra Guha added to Morris's observations as follows:

> Places such as the Calcutta Cricket Club and the Madras Cricket Club provided English food and English entertainments . . . cricket was collective, longer lasting and rather more ceremonial [than the other games]. The slow stateliness of the walk to the wicket, the interruptions between balls and overs, the graceful clothes that the players wore, the greenness of the grass, the understated gaiety of the lunch and tea intervals – all these made cricket an extended escape from India, from its chatter, its dirt, its smells and its peoples.[73]

Across the Indian Ocean, the Western Province Cricket Club (WPCC) in Cape Town fitted this bill to a tee. It was where the local elite celebrated their Britishness. The key figure at the club for more than a decade in the late 1800s was William Milton himself. He arrived in 1877 in the company of the well-known Victorian author and family member, Anthony Trollope, who described Cape Town as 'a poor, niggery, yellow-faced, half-bred sort of place, with an ugly Dutch flavor about it'.[74] The local Africans he called 'much more of a Savage than the ordinary negro' encountered elsewhere.[75] The pair were received by the governor and within weeks Milton was appointed WPCC secretary. In his doctoral dissertation on Milton, Jonty Winch (drawing on Brian Stoddart) wrote: 'As an ex-Marlborough schoolboy, Milton was deeply conscious of the ethics and values of cricket. Yet his and his colleagues' sense of "fair play" were shaped by prevailing assumptions of the moral and physical superiority of the white English race; views reinforced through the argument that "social distances were considered an important and integral part of maintaining order."'[76]

As the local cricket supremo, he and the club assumed the right to 'commandeer' top visiting cricketers passing through Cape Town, kept the prestigious annual Home- versus Colonial-Born match restricted to WPCC members, controlled the local fixture lists and despite personal pleas from the mayor of Port Elizabeth was part of the decision when Cape Town twice declined to play in the inter-town tournament for the Champion Bat. At a time when 'gentlemen' and professional cricketers in England entered grounds through separate entrances, had separate dressings rooms though playing in the same team and stayed separately at different hotels on tour, Milton and his colleagues insisted on the same class snobbishness in Cape Town. For example, Private Edward Beech of the Garrison Club, the first player in southern Africa to score two centuries in the same match, was forced to travel separately in third class from his Cape Town teammates when they went by train to play Kimberley, much to the mirthful disgust of the local 'diggers' who hosted him. Other clubs expressed dissatisfaction about the way the mini-African MCC ran local cricket and set up the Western Province Cricket Union as a balance to its influence. Milton nevertheless became first president of the Union and, as co-organiser of the first English cricket tour to South Africa (and captain in the second test), an influential national cricket figure.

Milton's career – sportsman, administrator, private secretary to the prime minister, and political head of the colony of Rhodesia – was one of those that personified the close connections between sport, colonialism and conquest in Britain and South Africa during the nineteenth century. Indeed, as has been well recorded, the 'MCC of the Cape Colony' and its long-standing secretary/treasurer became the fathers of apartheid in sport when they systematically hounded Krom Hendricks out of the game and firmly established the colour line in cricket in the 1890s. As with the famous clubs in India, which stayed mostly all-white until independence in 1947, the venerable WPCC club would remain a bastion of unreconstructed jingo-istic WASP values, excluding Afrikaners, Jews and black people as members until deep into the twentieth century.[77]

Can one deduce anything else but that the much-vaunted traditions and 'culture' of cricket that developed in British South Africa stood for nothing other than a reactionary worldview and support for systemic violence and discrimination? Therefore, those who reify the 'traditional culture of the game' today are consciously or subconsciously also endorsing an early British cricket culture rooted in imperialist notions of Social Darwinism, colonialism and conquest. This is something that those who even today endlessly bemoan transformation in South African sport and what they see as a disregard for 'merit' would do well to understand.

*

If the club was the place where social discrimination and imperial power in sport in the colonies was exercised, then the school was where these values and visions were taught. As Kathleen McCrone has pointed out:

> a new definition of what constituted the British gentleman emerged.
> From Rugby and other public schools came the notion that exercise
> and sport were essential in shaping young British boys into muscular
> Christians and imperialists, destined to lead the world in an age
> of Empire and expansion. Sport toughened them up for the job.
> It cultivated respect for rules, a subordination of the self in service of
> the greater whole. It taught young boys skills and restraint and imbued
> them with a sense of gentlemanly 'honour'. The popularisation of these
> ideas coincided with the rise of modern organised sport. Cricket
> especially was regarded as the sport par excellence where this new
> masculinity could be played out.[78]

The industrial revolution and the expansion of empire created great change, stress and fluidity in British society. Under these pressures, very specific constructions of what constituted British 'ladies' and British 'gentle-men' took place during the Victorian period. As a defensive reaction to change, the patriarchal notion that 'man' was the provider and leader and women, the 'weaker sex', the nurturers and procreators, responsible for childcare and the household, became fixed. Cricket, strictly defined as a so-called 'gentlemen's game', became a metaphor for these gendered identities and power relations in ways other sports such as hockey, golf and tennis did not. The game's deep class history and close connections with the British aristocracy and the officer ranks of the British army during a century of unparalleled British expansion and empire surely contributed to this.

Christopher Merrett has elaborated in *Cricket and Conquest* on how the muscular Christianity of the boys' public school in Britain was transplanted to a South African whites-only context. To start with, he referenced Robert Morrell who has made the point that elite white boys' schools in colonial South Africa were built on structural violence. The actions of staff and prefects were often brutal and, matched by pupil bravado, created a culture of violent masculinity. Some of the powerful people at white schools were severely damaged characters and, more commonly, simply jingoistic racists, he concludes. It was accepted that the route to male adulthood was marked by bullying, beatings and humiliation. At the same time, conventional masculine values concerning physical and mental toughness were articulated through team sport and reinforced by the cadet corps, which prepared colonial white men for the wars they were often called out to fight in. Those who did not subscribe to this ethos, the non-sportsmen for example, were openly disparaged and stigmatised even in the school magazine.[79] Sexism also became deeply inculcated into the culture of sport in these environments.

When the First World War broke out in 1914, dubbed 'The Great War for Civilisation', the cheerleaders included the cricket and rugby establishments in England and South Africa, and it was expected of the most athletic young men in the land that they would be willing to die for 'King and Country'. The cricket-loving arch-imperialist Sir Arthur Conan Doyle, who had been based in Bloemfontein during the South African War, summed up the mentalities and propaganda of the age perfectly when he declared in 1914: 'There was a time for games, there was a time for business, and there was a time for domestic life. There was a time for everything, but there is only time for one thing now, and that thing is war. If the cricketer has a straight eye let him look along the barrel of a rifle. If a footballer had strength of limb let them serve and march in the field of battle.'[80]

Not for the sports establishment the doubts and pain experienced by the poet Wilfred Owen, who warned in his immortal lines about 'The old Lie: *Dulce et decorum est / Pro patria mori*', the Latin adage that 'it is sweet and honourable to die for your country'. More than 230,000 South Africans enlisted, a high percentage for a country with a total population of only 6.4 million people in 1914. At least 12,452 of these South Africans died, including many sportsmen, like the South African international batsman Reginald Hands who was among those who expired with 'froth-corrupted lungs' from poison gas in the horror that Wilfred Owen railed against at Boulogne in France in April 1918, aged only twenty-nine. South African troops were involved in some of the most vicious battles in a vicious war. For example, only 142 of the 3,153 who went into battle at Delville Wood in France in July 1916 emerged alive and uninjured.[81] It was one of the fiercest engagements in the grisly long-running Battle of the Somme on the Western Front, which resulted in nearly one million Allied casualties. On day one alone, 1 July 1916, 57,470 Allied soldiers were injured, of whom 19,240 died in what was described as 'the bloodiest day in the history of the British army'. Survivors called Delville Wood 'easily the worst place on earth'. For six days and five nights, amid ceaseless shelling, which stripped and destroyed the surrounding forest, a soldier died every minute – one South African every three minutes – as they stumbled over their comrades' bodies and carried out the order to 'take and hold the wood at all costs'. Among those who did not make it out of the hell that was Delville Wood were no fewer than forty-three staff and pupils from Michaelhouse, and mercifully a smaller number – nine – from the nearby Hilton School.[82] South Africa's premier boys' cricket schools were among the main recruiting grounds for the war. Drill and musketry were a routine part of life at these schools, and the rhetoric of sport was used to justify both colonial domination at home in South Africa and this war further afield. The fact that so many cricketers and other sportsmen failed to return did not seem to temper these militaristic attitudes. As the historian Bill Nasson points out, the 'blooded brambles and barbed wire' of the Western Front contributed to the further development of a growing white South African nationalism.[83]

A relatively few traditional boys' sports schools, still actively celebrating nineteenth century public schoolboy cultures, have produced the overwhelming majority of South Africa's international cricketers up to today, although the percentages have diminished slightly since democracy as the opportunity pool has widened. Among the top schools on the list are Grey College, Bloemfontein; Grey High School, Port Elizabeth, where 2019 Springbok captain Siya Kolisi studied; King Edward VII School, Johannesburg, alma mater of Graeme Smith; Durban Boys' High, where Hashim

Amla was educated; Pretoria Boys High, where Peter studied; and Queens College, Queenstown, which André attended. The leading twenty-five boys' schools in South Africa continue to meet regularly under the Annual Conference of Traditional Public Boys' Schools, and they mostly still have sport and 'tradition' as a core part of their value system and marketing. They pride themselves on their adherence to the 'culture' of sport. School masters and players alike still often emerge here unquestioning about the roots of these cultures of masculinity and play that are given such prominence. And the system continues happily to perpetuate itself, inter alia through the bursary-driven incorporation of talented black children and the creation of new multiracial elites. The poor standards and underperformance in the general post-democracy school system has meant that these old values have not received the critical scrutiny they deserve. However, educational psychologists have warned that the 'particular history' of local boys' schools has left them with explicit challenges in the democratic dispensation: how to honour their pasts, preserve their culture and celebrate masculinity without reproducing unhealthy ideas, practices, power relations and exclusions.[84]

British sports and the quest for citizenship

Despite the exclusions and harsh realities of conquest and colonialism, the indigenous people and descendants of slaves from the beginning became ardent followers of the British sports introduced into South Africa, especially in the early areas of British expansion, namely Cape Town and the frontier regions of the eastern Cape.

At the mission schools set up by the British, recreation became a matter of supreme importance. Many of the traditional pastimes of Africans were deemed 'incompatible with Christian purity of life' and had to be abandoned by those embracing the new religion of the missionaries. Provision was therefore made in the school programme for 'healthy exercise and the profitable employment of leisure'. Drill became a regular feature on time-tables and sports like cricket and football were introduced.[85]

And cricket, with its 'gentlemanly' connotations, was particularly important. Love of the game, it was believed by the teachers and their students, would demonstrate the ability of the 'native people' to assimilate European culture and behave 'like gentlemen', and, by extension, show their fitness to be accepted as fellow citizens in the evolving Cape society. By this means the school people could pay homage to the leading ideas of 'civil-isation', 'progress', Christianity and empire, which were so important to the Victorian-era colonists.[86]

At the Anglican Institution in Grahamstown as early as 1869, Rev. Robert Mullins coached 'his native boys every afternoon, and they beat the white St Andrew's boys by an innings and four runs'. Moreover, 'Three of the four return matches were all won by the natives.' The mission schools of St Matthews, Lovedale and Healdtown (where Nelson Mandela went to school) not only produced generations of political leaders but also became the main nurseries for African cricket over the years. Inter-college matches came to assume the same importance as they did at British public schools and the local whites-only boys' schools. In fact, in 1891 Lovedale played Dale College from King William's Town, another of the top sports schools in the country today, and beat them by 15 runs.[87] At the time there were no less than five clubs centred on the small hamlet where Lovedale was based. From schools like Lovedale and Healdtown, thousands of departing students took with them skills and talents, setting up or joining clubs and becoming involved in spreading the game wherever they settled. In Port Elizabeth, for example, ex-Lovedalians challenged the rest in 1883 and easily beat them.[88]

The development of organised cricket in black communities closely followed in the footsteps of the segregated white cricket establishment in many respects. From the introduction of the game into schools (in the 1850s), the growth of clubs (1860s), and the introduction of inter-town competitions (1870s and 1880s), to leagues, provincial competitions and the formation of a national controlling body (1890s), black cricketers soon followed step by step. Nowhere was this enthusiastic growth more evident than in the eastern Cape. Following white precedent, there were thriving clubs and regular competi-tions in almost all areas in the region by the 1880s.[89] As in politics, a distinct tradition of sport developed in the eastern Cape and cricket clubs soon became an integral part of the new community networks and activities.[90]

The first regular reports of Africans playing cricket can be found in *Isigidimi Sama-Xosa*. This missionary newspaper reported, for instance, on the first inter-town match between Champions CC of King William's Town and Gaika [Ngqika] CC from East London on the Queen's birthday, 24 May 1883. The King William's Town team won, but when they went by train to East London for the return match in September the tables were turned.[91] From then on, matches between teams from these towns became regular features, played mainly on public holidays. In the 1883 East London game, Walter Rubusana, a respected community leader and translator of the bible, was one of the umpires; special mention was made in the newspaper report of how well he did the job.[92] The captain of the King William's Town was Nathaniel Umhalla, a grandson of Ndlambe of the Xhosa royal house, who had excelled at school and been sent to study at St Augustine's College in Canterbury, but who had only recently emerged from the traumatic experience of losing his job and being charged with treason for refusing to take up arms against his countrymen.

Cricket was placed on a more coordinated footing in the mid-1880s. In 1884 teams from the main eastern Cape centres of East London, King William's Town, Queenstown, Grahamstown and Port Elizabeth organised the first official inter-town tournament, based on similar inter-town tournaments for the best white sides in South Africa.[93] This was a remarkable achievement, because white cricketers were holding only their third inter-town tournament in nearby Port Elizabeth in the same month.[94] From this time on, tournaments of all sorts became commonplace.

The King William's Town Champion Cricket Club under Umhalla, which won the first tournament, gave an indication of the proficiency of Africans at the game when they subsequently defeated one of the white King William's Town club sides, which included several players who had participated in the white tournament.[95] At about the same time, the Port Elizabeth Africans twice beat the white Cradock side.[96] These victories were by no means the exception.[97] No wonder that the *Port Elizabeth Telegraph* observed that the game 'seems quite to hit the *Kaffir* fancy' (our italics).[98]

Commenting on the King William's Town match, the *Cape Mercury* remarked that it was significant 'to all those who take an intelligent interest in the progress of the country'. Evoking images of peace less than a decade after the last of the wars of dispossession, the newspaper said that the game reminded it of an old song:

And men learn't wisdom from the past,
In friendship joined their hands;
Hung the sword in the hall;
the spear on the wall,
And ploughed the willing lands.

The newspaper added: 'those who play together will not object to work together, and the manly fellows who donned the flannels last week will have a heartier feeling of respect for their dusky conquerors than they had before.'[99] Delighted, the newspaper *Imvo Zabantsundu* commented that such cricket matches were 'calculated to make the Europeans and Natives have more mutual trust and confidence than all the coercive and repressive legislation in the world'.[100] When the Port Elizabeth Africans followed by beating the white Cradock town club early in 1885, *Imvo* exclaimed: 'It is enough to say that the contest shows that the native is a rough diamond that needs to be polished to exhibit the same qualities that are to be found in the civilised being, and that he is not to be dismissed as a mere "schepsel" [creature], as it has been the habit of the pioneers to do so hereto.'[101]

The launch of *Imvo* in November 1884 revealed just how popular cricket had become among eastern Cape Africans. In the very first edition, the bright twenty-three-year-old editor, J. T. Jabavu, devoted his editorial notes to the game:

To our Colonial English contemporaries, the playing of the of the game of cricket by natives would seem to be regarded as a strange phenom-enum [*sic*]; and already all sorts of guesses are indulged in as to the probable motives of the sons of Ham in taking to this English time-honoured pastime. 'Mimicry', 'travesty of civilization' and expletives of a like character have been hinted as the possible causes, but our country-men have gone on the even tenor of their way without noticing their critics . . . the natives do not only mean to persevere in playing at cricket, but are resolved to proceed from conquering to conquest so far as the cricket world is concerned.[102]

Over the years, hundreds of cricket reports appeared in *Imvo* (even during winter), under the title *Ibala labadlali* (sports field or 'patch of the players'). By 1887 the paper had appointed a sporting editor.[103] The Dyer & Dyer merchant house soon began placing advertisements in *Imvo*, directed spe-cifically at African cricketers and clubs, offering cricket kit of every variety.[104] *Isigidimi Sama-Xosa* noted that the educated and Christianised school people had left behind the old tribal ways, but had not yet also adopted the new, in particular the leisure activities of cricket, lawn tennis, croquet, hunting and dancing of the English. The paper fostered interest by, for instance, placing news of a century by 'Dr Grace' against Australia,[105] and giving advice on how cricketers could best protect their bats in hot climates, where they broke easily. The suggested remedy: 'Uyifake kunye namafuta embizeni, uyibilise ke yonke lonto kunye' (You put it together with fat [oil] into a pot and bring everything to a boil together).[106] In time, cricket became not only the favourite sport in the African communities of the eastern Cape, but an integral part of their lifestyles.

*

Sport served an explicitly political function for these missionary-educated Africans from the beginning. They saw it as an important part of a self-conscious process of modernisation in which they were involved. Early political leaders were almost invariably also leaders and members of the first sports clubs. This showed their commitment to community development, at a time when black people were organising at every level and starting to build a whole new framework of interrelated activities based on Western and colonial models.

Sport was also one of the ways in which they could celebrate lofty British notions over colonial prejudice. In shaping their vision for the future, the new elite idealised British values. This was partly tactical, so as to win support for British intervention, and partly aspirational, so that their own visions for the future of the colony could be held up publicly as a goal. Despite the many contradictions, they glorified things British. When the first English cricket side under Major Wharton toured South Africa in 1888–89, black spectators cheered them on against the local white sides in an obvious political commentary. In the report on the match by the tourists against the King William's Town-based Cape Mounted Rifles team, *Imvo* noted, 'It is singular that the sympathies of the Native spectators were with the English.'[107]

As important as the games were, the social activities connected with cricket. Sports on public holidays such as Empire Day and Christmas were almost inevitably followed by social functions. Here the aspiring black middle class could display their elegance and accomplishments. These events differed little from those that catered for white society. Often, functions were held in the local town hall, with the mayor or other dignitaries in attendance. At one typical event in Kimberley, a splendid dinner was put before the guests, followed by a programme of musical entertainment and speeches. It started off with a toast to the Queen and ended with a rendering of 'God Save the Queen'. Finally, the proceedings were brought to a close with speeches, hymns and a benediction.[108]

Sport, as well as the related social activities, provided the school people with a training ground for participation in the new society. In typical Victorian fashion it offered both a personal and political lesson. As a member of the African Political Organisation emphasised, when speaking on the topic of a sound mind in a social body, sport and politics were closely linked:

> Great lessons can be learned . . . on the cricket and football fields – two forms of sport of which our people are passionately fond. No one who is not punctual, patient, accurate and vigilant, can ever expect to become a consistently good batsman. Both batsman and spectators know that; and yet do we carry those moral lessons into our private or public life? Patient, of course we are: but are we punctual and vigilant? . . . are we as watchful of our public welfare as the batsman is of every ball – even those which the umpire declares to be wide? If we were, much of our present trouble would have been forestalled.[109]

Membership and rank in sports clubs were signs of social success: they enhanced the respectability and status of political figures. Besides being a pillar of middle-class respectability as an editor, politician, long-serving Wesleyan church steward and Templar, J. T. Jabavu was president of two of the sports clubs in King William's Town, the Frontier Cricket Club and the Oriental Lawn Tennis Club.[110] In the 1890s he presented the Jabavu Cup for inter-town cricket competition in the eastern Cape.[111] Committee members of the Frontier Cricket Club at the time included leaders of the emerging proto-nationalist political groupings such as Paul Xiniwe, W. D. Soga, Nathaniel Umhalla, John Knox Bokwe and James Dwane.[112] Political differences do not seem to have been a major factor here. Sol Plaatje's newspaper, *Tsala ea Becoana*, seemed to corroborate this when it declared that despite historical antagonisms between the Mfengu and Xhosa they should learn to cooperate in politics in the same way they did in sport.[113]

*

While cricket was by far the most popular sport, the aspiring black middle class also took, to a lesser extent, to sports such as tennis, croquet, football and rugby. According to Rev. Elijah Makiwane, writing in 1888, in 'almost all the towns [of the eastern Cape] there are cricket clubs which are in a more or less thriving state, and at Port Elizabeth and a few other towns, there are also croquet and lawn tennis clubs', which generally included both men and women.[114] Football among Africans took root in the 1890s, also initially in Port Elizabeth.[115] Rugby, or *mboxo* (the thing that is not round), followed later in the decade and became the next most popular game in the eastern Cape after cricket. Today, the eastern Cape is still the only region in the country where rugby has a popularity rivalling football among Africans.[116] One indication of this is that captain Siya Kolisi and two of his colleagues from South Africa's 2019 World Cup winning team, Makazole Mapimpi and Lukhanyo Am, learnt their rugby there.

As in cricket, the first black teams were probably institutional, based at Lovedale, Healdtown and the Anglican Institution in Grahamstown. According to one source, it was the headmaster of the last-mentioned school, Rev. Mullins, who introduced rugby to black players.[117] The first adult rugby club was the Union Rugby Football Club, formed in Port Elizabeth in 1887. Among those involved were leading figures in the local Native Vigilance Association. At first, Union's opponents were the town's coloured rugby teams, which formed themselves into a Port Elizabeth Coloured Rugby Union in 1892; but in 1894 a second African club, Orientals, was established, followed by the Morning Star, Rovers, Frontier and Spring Rose clubs.[118] Union and Orientals became the strongest teams, and their matches and colours were modelled on the rivalry between the main white clubs, Crusaders and Olympics.

Rugby contests between different towns in the eastern Cape took place well before the turn of the century. By 1904 the level of organisation and enthusiasm had reached the stage where the first inter-town tournament could be organised in Port Elizabeth. Teams from Grahamstown and East London participated. Following the inauguration of the tournament, an Eastern Province Native Rugby Union was formed in 1905. Its first president was Tobias Mvula, a delegate from Port Elizabeth to many South African Native Congress conferences.

*

With the opening up of the diamond and gold fields in the last quarter of the nineteenth century, the new sports began to take root in the interior as well, mimicking the process of economic and political integration that the mineral discoveries had unleashed. Cape migrants in these new centres were prominent in organising clubs and events there and they reported on these developments in the pages of *Imvo*. In Kimberley, cricket and rugby flourished, with local Africans playing with and against 'Malays' and coloured sportsmen who had carried the games with them from Cape Town. Kimberley became the new sports capital of southern Africa.

Contests began across territorial boundaries. In 1888 a Kimberley team travelled down to the coast to play Port Elizabeth at cricket for the first time.[119] From 1890 onwards, teams from the South African Republic took on Kroonstad and other towns in the Orange Free State. By 1898 there were around ten 'native' cricket clubs in Johannesburg.[120] Regular contests now occurred between teams from the two republics and sides from the eastern Cape and the diamond fields.[121] The new railway spread sport, as it did politics.

In Natal, Edendale (and, later, Adams College) became the main base for cricket.[122] The team lists were full of prominent *kholwa* or 'believers' with surnames like Msimang, Mtimkulu, Xaba and Kumalo, who played a large role in the politics and social life of that colony.[123] Richard Msimang, one of the first black lawyers in South Africa and an early ANC leader, made a name for himself playing rugby while studying at Taunton School, England. Cricket was also played at the Ohlange Institute, founded by John Dube, but football became more popular here and, indeed, throughout Natal.

In Bloemfontein there were seven cricket clubs by 1907. Oriental, captained by Joseph Twayi, was reported to be the strongest club in the city. Matches with white teams apparently also occurred.[124] Tennis, golf and football were played, too. Describing life in Bethulie in the southern Free State in 1911, the magistrate wrote that 'Natives go in for tennis, football and cricket whilst nearly all the younger population attend school. Nearly all are church goers.'[125] Cricket was also played in the Rolong enclave of Thaba Nchu and in neighbouring Basutoland. At Thaba Nchu in the 1900s, teams drawn from the prosperous, highly politicised landowning elite played against their white neighbours, perhaps former British soldiers who had been granted land in the area after the South African War. Commenting on these matches, which the Africans won more than once, *Tsala ea Becoana* remarked that whites held themselves socially aloof in order to command respect from blacks, but 'the fact is no Natives respect their European neighbours as much as the Barolongs at Thaba Nchu who twice beat the whites in fair games of cricket. In other parts, where the whites will not play them, the coloureds boast that the whites are afraid of them.'[126]

*

Running parallel to the process of political mobilisation and unification, the spread of sport throughout southern Africa led to the formation of the first regional and national bodies for black sportspeople.

In 1897 the South African Coloured Rugby Football Board was formed, and in 1903 the South African Coloured Cricket Board (SACCB). Remarkably, the latter was only the second national cricket association to be established in the world, predating the Australian Cricket Board and – by several decades – the West Indian, New Zealand and Indian controlling bodies. The black cricketers also started inter-state competitions for the Barnato Trophy in 1899, replicating the launch of the white Currie Cup (on which they were based), the Sheffield Shield in Australia and official County Championships in the same decade. The involvement of both African and coloured sportsmen in these new national boards also predated formal co-operation between African and coloured organisations in the political arena. Though political union was still nearly a decade away, emerging black leaders were already defining themselves as South African and seeking to cross assumed boundaries in more ways than one. By basing organisations on accepted international rules and structures they were showing, too, that they wished to become global sporting citizens as well, part of the wider sporting world.

Thus, black cricketers were active participants in the unfolding history of the game in South Africa from the start. In fact, looking back in retrospect, their early vision had a defining long-term impact on South African cricket. The new SACCB declared in clause 25 of its founding constitution in 1903 that 'this Board does not recognise any distinction amongst the various sporting peoples of South Africa, whether by Creed, Nationality or otherwise'.[127] The SACCB formed by excluded black cricketers in the first decade of the twentieth century thus became the first repository of a vision of unity in cricket across class and colour divides that would finally be realised when democracy arrived in the last decade of that century.

The new histories now being written show that the cricketing dramas that unfolded in the nineteenth and early twentieth centuries were part of a truly remarkable, rich multihued sporting tapestry. The whole new set of sporting characters who emerged – known up to now by only a select few working in the basements of archives – deserve their rightful places in history.

Sports racism as part of a wider process

In the decade before 1894, as South Africa readied itself for and entered test rugby and cricket, a door opened. A multi-ethnic sports community sharing many similarities and interacting in significant ways emerged in the Cape Colony. This made possible the emergence of an inclusive South African sports culture based on the small but energetic Cape liberal tradition (rooted in a pre-diamonds and gold era), which included an emerging, enfranchised, talented, sports-loving (especially cricket) black middle class in Cape Town, Kimberley and the eastern Cape; these qualified black voters alone reached a figure of over 10,000.

But then Cecil John Rhodes and his influential cabals in sport and politics, linked to rapacious imperialist interests and hard-line 'native policy', closed the door on black sportspeople. They introduced legislation which would set the pattern for the future in politics, and in a very public way established the formal colour bar in sport through the patently unfair exclusion of Krom Hendricks from the first South African cricket tour abroad in 1894 – and by vindictively rebuffing his attempts to play 'official' cricket for a decade after that.

The developments in cricket at the turn of the century were part of a broader pattern and process. The war that Britain fought against the Boer republics brought the whole of South Africa under British rule for the first time and set in motion a process of unification. This led to the birth of the Union of South Africa in 1910. The Union was founded on a constitution, drawn up by white colonial leaders in constant consultation with British administrators, which largely excluded black South Africans from participation in the political life of the country, contrary to pre-war British promises.

When the terms of the constitution became known, Africans protested strongly. For the first time a national conference of black organisations from the different colonies was held in Bloemfontein in 1909. It dispatched a special delegation to London in an attempt to persuade the British government not to ratify the constitution of the new state before amendments to the colour bar clauses were made. The so-called Coloured and Native Delegation was filled with sports personalities. Six of the nine members were cricketing as well as political leaders. One of the most prominent was Dr Walter Rubusana, president of the South African Native Congress and the new South African Native Convention formed at the Bloemfontein conference to unite African opinion throughout southern Africa. This respected church minister was first president of the Border Native Cricket Union. J. T. Jabavu, the renowned editor of *Imvo*, was Rubusana's political rival but shared his love for the game. Besides publishing thousands of cricket reports in his newspaper, he donated the Jabavu Cup for the Inter-Town Tournaments and was president of the Frontier CC in King William's Town. Dr Abdullah Abdurahman, leader of the African Political Organisation, the mouthpiece for coloured opinion, was president of the Western Province Coloured Cricket Union. One of his APO co-delegates was Daniel Lenders, president of both the Diamond Fields Colonial Cricket Union and the South African Coloured Rugby Football Board. The other was Matt Fredericks, president of the Cape District Cricket Union. Finally, Thomas Mtobi Mapikela of the Orange River Colony Native Congress was a patron of cricket in Bloemfontein and had played for Queenstown in the regular Native Inter-Town Tournaments. Nothing could have shown more the convergence of the political and cricket struggles of the time.

But the delegation found that Britain's economic and strategic interests far outweighed any concern it might have felt for black South Africans; it chose to go into an alliance with the recently vanquished Afrikaners instead of the colonised majority, even if it meant contradicting its own professed political ideals and legitimising institutionalised racism in South Africa. This was, after all, the logical outcome of its century-long process of conquest and colonialism. So, the British parliament passed the South Africa Act, which made for union, leaving African leaders and intellectuals feeling betrayed.

After diamonds and gold, a free black citizenry with access to the political machinery and markets was not conducive to the formation of a cheap, controlled labour force, so the trend in the following decades was for the British and colonial whites to place statutory restrictions on African economic advancement and to restrict their political and social rights.

The failure of political liberalism in South African – symbolised by Union in 1910 – took the early black activists and leaders into a cul de sac. Instead of gaining for themselves an extended role in a non-racial political system, similar to the gradual incorporation of the working classes and women in Britain, for example, they were to come under increasing pressure in a system that institutionalised racial discrimination, until they were eventually deprived completely of the limited voting rights they had enjoyed for nearly a century in the Cape Colony. The tremendous progress black cricketers had made from the 1880s onwards would be reversed in a similar way. The influential liberal parliamentarian Saul Solomon had once rhetorically questioned whether the Colony would 'ever degrade itself to prevent by law any Coloured man from having the right to vote for members of the legislature or to hold an acre of land'.[128] Rhodes and the imperialists were determined to do exactly that. They simply sidelined the small Cape liberal tradition and, with it, the aspirations of black middle-class voters and cricketers in favour of creating a cheap labour system and a voteless working class that could service the mining industry and maximise profits. The fact that the legendary Lord Harris was at the same time an MCC notable and long-time chairman in the giant Consolidated Gold Fields company, served only to highlight the link between a violent, exploitative system and the British cricket and financial establishment.

This link of British complicity with institutionalised racism in South Africa continued right up until the time of high apartheid and the militant British demonstrations of 1969–70. Just as nineteenth century strands of progressive Christian and liberal British opinion supported the struggles of the sports-loving black cricketers for greater rights in colonial South Africa, so the likes of former England captain Bishop David Sheppard and commentator John Arlott now supported Peter and the anti-apartheid demonstrations. Pitted against them were the inheritors of the ideas and ill-gained wealth and privilege of the likes of Rhodes and Harris in the MCC and Conservative Party establishments, who stood solidly in favour of 'traditional' ties with whites-only sport. This would have come as no surprise to those who understood history: a central figure in the D'Oliveira Affair, Lord Cobham, whose grandfather and father were MCC presidents before him, had 'extensive business interests' in South Africa. It was reported in 1980 that one in four Tory MPs (seventy-one all told, compared to only five opposition members) had interests as 'directors, shareholders, parliamentary consultants or advisers' in eighty-three companies with a financial stake in apartheid South Africa.[129] They were merely conducting business – and cricket – as usual.

Jesse Owens and the 1936 Nazi Olympics

Similar themes underpinned a spectacular sporting spectacle with 5,000 athletes from fifty-three nations in August 1936 – the Berlin Olympics. The Games both echoed the elements of earlier South African colonial racism and uncannily foreshadowed the prejudices, practices and contorted justifications decades later used to justify sports apartheid's place in international competition.

Although we have become accustomed in modern times to governments of all stripes hosting the Olympics to showcase their nations, even their ideologies, and certainly to boost their global reputations, nothing compares with the way the Nazis used the 1936 Games staged over sixteen days in the German capital.

'Nothing was spared to intoxicate the visitors; to lead them, like the Germans, into a state of mindless optimism . . . Besides being a success, the 1936 Olympics were also a vast razzle-dazzle that blurred the outlines of a threat to Western civilisation.'[130] While Hitler eyed up intervening militarily in Austria and Czechoslovakia and the looming Spanish Civil War, and put on hold his baiting, vilification and oppression of Jews, the Nazis staged an extravaganza of pageantry, festivity and warmth.

It became a case study in the way politics is indelibly imprinted upon sport, perhaps the supreme example of exploiting the noble pursuit of athletic excellence for political objectives, in this case evil ones. Comparisons with South Africa are perhaps unsurprising, because many of apartheid's architects supported the Nazis, and in the South African Parliament voted against backing the Allies in the Second World War. John Vorster, an apartheid prime minister from the mid-1960s to mid-1970s, was amongst those interned for sabotage against allied troop trains.

The Nazis saw sport and physical exercise as a vehicle for increasing Aryan prowess: 'physical education develops and forms body and soul . . . through physical exercises rooted in *Volkdom*', insisted one of their edicts. So much so that members of the elite SS[131] were only allowed to marry women with Reich sports medals. Nazism was not simply a political project but a cultural one too: its task to give the German people nothing less than a 'purist' renaissance in which sport was intrinsically integral.

By December 1933, nearly three years before the Games, virtually all Jewish sports organisations had been forced to disband. Jewish teams were forbidden to compete with Aryan teams. Non-Aryans could not be life-guards and some ski resorts to be used for the Winter Olympics had signs stating, 'Jews forbidden'. Jews were also banned from using swimming baths, gyms, youth clubs and other places for training, thereby depriving them of competitive facilities and paving the way for Nazi leaders to assure the IOC that Jews would not be excluded as a matter of principle, 'only' on merit.

Notorious Nazi propagandist Julius Streicher, editor of *Der Stürmer*, stated bluntly: 'Jews are Jews and there is no place for them in German sports.' Bruno Malitz, sports leader of the SA (*Sturmabteilung*, or storm-troopers, a crack Nazi assault force), wrote in 1933: 'Jewish sports leaders . . . have absolutely no place in German sport. They are all worse than . . . fam-ine, floods, drought, locusts and poison gas – worse than all these horrors.' By 1935, all fields (private as well as public) were required to bar Jewish sportsmen and women from practicing.

Unsurprisingly top Jewish athletes were forced to emigrate, including world-record sprinter Alex Natan and Germany's best tennis player Daniel Prenn, who both fled to England. The nation's best hockey player, Rudi Ball, went to France.

Amidst rising concern about the plight of German Jews, in January 1936 one quote from Nazi chiefs was widely reported: 'We can see no possible value for our people in permitting dirty Jews and Negroes to travel through our country and compete in athletics with our best.' The *Guardian*, then the *Manchester Guardian*, strongly supported a boycott, and asked: 'Who thrust politics into sport in the first place?' The *New York Times* similarly advocated a boycott amidst campaigns in many countries to do so.

Britain's Conservative government resisted such pressure, as did ruling elites across Europe and America. The guest speaker at the British Olympic Association's annual dinner in May 1936 argued that Hitler was a 'firm believer in the peace-creating influence of sport'. Supporting this view, the government's defence minister Sir Thomas Inskip added: 'Germany can count on many warm hearts in this country.'

The boycott movement – largely spurred by Jewish, trade union and left-wing groups – campaigned across Europe and America. In Britain, the National Workers' Sports Association – renamed the British Workers'

Sports Association – led the fight. Under pressure, the National Convention of the American Olympic Committee voted narrowly (by just sixty-one to fifty-five) to participate. Rival Olympics were staged in many countries. A 'Peoples Olympiad' planned in Barcelona in July 1936 was widely supported as a 'final gesture of protest against the Hitler Nazi Games in Berlin'. And 6,000 athletes from twenty-two nations registered to participate. But it never progressed beyond the opening ceremony, cut short by the outbreak of the Spanish Civil War, after Franco's fascist forces attacked it.

Protest movements had been formed in America and Britain, demanding to know of the Nazi regime whether German Jewish athletes would be allowed to take part in the Berlin Olympics. They also demanded the international community boycott the Games if not. But the IOC, just as they steadfastly did for decades over South Africa's whites-only policy, shunned these pressures. Their president, Count Henri de Baillet-Latour, insisted the IOC never 'interfered in the internal affairs' of member countries' – exactly the specious phrase trotted out by apartheid's rulers, its apologists and indeed the IOC itself over white South Africa's international sports participation. The fact that Nazi policy 'interfered' directly in sport and therefore the Olympics was conveniently ignored.

But the pressure built. In America, the Amateur Athletic Union continued to be under pressure to boycott the Games unless the Nazis granted equal opportunities to Jewish athletes. Eventually, the American Olympic Committee grudgingly sent their president and IOC luminary, billionaire Avery Brundage, on a fact-finding mission to the Third Reich for six days.

After a cursory tour of Berlin enjoying local hospitality, Brundage reported back to the American Olympic Committee that he had mounted 'thorough investigations', and that no German athlete was being discriminated against – even though apartheid-like restrictions had been placed upon Jewish athletes to train, compete and be selected for German national teams. He hardly left any time to converse with Jewish athletes or their representatives. But when some told him Jews were now barred from membership of German sports clubs, he retorted that his club in Chicago barred Jews as well. All was well under the Nazis, Brundage reported. He 'knew of no racial or religious reasons why America should withdraw'. Later he wrote in Kafkaesque terms: 'Certain Jews must now understand that they cannot use these Games as a weapon in their boycott against the Nazis.'

Such was the outcry however, that the American Olympic Committee was obliged to send a further delegation, led by Charles Hitchcock Sherrill, a veteran IOC member and former general. It was a convenient choice, for Sherrill was a declared Hitler admirer and was granted a personal audience with the Führer, who duly charmed him. However, Hitler did insist that German Jews were not suffering from discrimination: they were merely being treated in a different category from other citizens, and therefore were ineligible for the German Olympic team. A discomforted Sherrill then told him the IOC would be under pressure to exclude Germany and switch the venue away from Berlin. To avoid that calamity, Sherrill and a grumpily reluctant Hitler hatched a face-saving formula involving 'token' Jewish athletes.

The main one chosen was Helene Mayer, a fencing gold medallist who had competed for Germany in the 1932 Olympics in Los Angeles and decided to remain living and teaching in California. Blonde with green eyes – in appearance the epitome of Aryan womanhood (indeed Nazi sports officials declared her 'an Aryan') – Mayer was also a public favourite. But she was also half-Jewish and after the Nazis came to power, the fencing club in her hometown Offenbach expelled her.

Mayer was asked to re-join the German team, her invitation sent by registered mail as advised by Sherrill so that, even if she refused, Germany could show proof of respect for IOC principles. Despite being pressed not to by American Jewish groups, Mayer duly accepted, though insisting she was granted full German citizenship from which Jews were barred by the Nazis.

Her agreement effectively spiked the boycott movement. But top Olympic standard high jumper Gretel Bergmann was less fortunate than 'half-Jew' Mayer. German sports officials informed her she would not be selected because she was a 'full Jew'; the same bar applied to Jewish sprinter Werner Schattmann, who was denied the opportunity to participate in Olympic selection trials.

Meanwhile Sherrill, having returned home, said all was well and insisted that the treatment of German Jews was no more his business than was the 'lynching of Negroes in the American South'. Not content with that brazenly racist dismissal, he added a veiled threat to American Jews, saying around 5 million Jews out of a total American population of 120 million should not be allowed to spoil things for the vast majority.

He was backed by the secretary of the American Olympic Committee Frederick Rubien who was reported as saying in the *New York Times*: 'Germans are not discriminating against Jews in their Olympic try-outs. The

Jews are eliminated because they are not good enough as athletes. Why are there not a dozen Jews in the world of Olympic calibre?'

No matter, the IOC was relieved. Job done by Brundage and then Sherrill. The Games proceeded, despite a warning from the US Ambassador to Austria, George S. Messersmith that the Berlin Olympics would make war more likely by encouraging Hitler's sense of omnipotence in the face of craven Western sycophancy. He also argued that by its participation in Berlin, the United States was breaching the ideals of 'fair-play and the non-political character of sport'.

The British were hardly less compliant. The head of the Foreign Office, Sir Robert Vansittart, attended the Games on a 'private holiday', arriving suspicious of the Third Reich. But after being lavishly entertained and talked to by leading Nazis, including chief propagandist Joseph Goebbels, he ended up revising his assessment. Hitler's ideological adviser, Alfred Rosenberg, claimed both that Vansittart expressed his anger that the US 'negroes were putting the English to shame' in the Games, and that Vansittart's wife agreed there was a danger Jews would 'finance communist revolt'.

The Nazis also rolled out the red carpet for leading British Conservative MP Sir Henry 'Chips' Channon, like many of his fellow Tories a Nazi appeasement advocate. Around fifty years later, Tory MPs were similarly feted by the South African government with lavish hospitality, including John Carlisle dubbed 'the Member for Pretoria' for his apartheid apologism.

*

Just as the International Olympic Committee (IOC) connived with apartheid South Africa over its whites-only teams, so it effectively allowed Hitler to hijack the Berlin Games from the very outset. It was 'abundantly clear that politics and sport were made inseparable by Hitler.'[132] That however was turned on its head by apologists for the Games: they actually accused Jews of 'bringing politics into sport' after Jewish groups across the world, joined by others especially on the political left, protested against the Berlin Games; the very same accusation directed at anti-apartheid protesters in the 1970s.

Goebbels arbitrarily insisted on changing the lyrics of the Olympic hymn in a special composition by Richard Strauss, insisting they didn't reflect the spirit of the Third Reich.[133] Goebbels objected to the phrase 'Peace shall be the battle cry', replacing it with 'Honour shall be the battle cry'. Against precedent, the IOC meekly complied.

Hitler attended every day in his VIP box, not always enjoying what he saw, though ultimately hailing Germany's medal-winning triumph, at his side his right-hand man and architect of the Nazi police state, Hermann Göring, festooned with military regalia.

On the second day, German athlete Tilly Fleischer broke the world javelin record, winning her country's first gold medal, and Hitler broke IOC protocol by inviting her and the two other medallists to his VIP box for a photo. 'I almost burst into tears in front of the Führer,' said Fleischer, the photos carried widely in both German and foreign media.

The opening ceremony had been preceded by a 30,000-strong Hitler Youth rally, and giant swastikas fluttered alongside the Olympic flag on the entire route to the stadium. The Austrian athletes, who gave a *Sieg Heil* marching into the stadium, and the French, their arms held high in a Nazi-like salute, were greeted raucously, while the British group, giving only an 'eyes-right' salute, was sullenly snubbed.

However, Goebbels also devised a sophisticated strategy to downplay Nazi practices and he left no stone unturned to put on hold the regime's persecution of Germany's Jewish citizens. The Nazi journal *Der Angriff* told its readers to be 'more charming than the Parisians, more easy-going than the Viennese, more vivacious than the Romans, more cosmopolitan than Lon-don, and more practical than New York.'

Publication of the viciously anti-Semitic newspaper *Der Stürmer* with its virulent anti-Jewish cartoons, was suspended for weeks over the Games, its 700 public collection boxes empty. Park signs in Berlin carried two plaques at the time. The top one asked people to keep their dogs on a leash; the bottom one instructed that Jews were restricted to using yellow benches. But these and other anti-Jewish signs across the city were removed for the duration of the Games on Hitler's express orders.

Rather like apartheid defined whiteness in its 1950 Population Regis-tration Act – 'A white person means a person who is ... not in appearance obviously not a white person' – the 1933 Nuremberg Laws defined non-Jewishness and contained a raft of anti-Semitic regulations effectively ex-punging Germany's Jews and part-Jews from society, barring them from citizenship and removing all their rights. But during the Games these were by edict put in cold storage and harassment of Berlin's Jews halted – to be resumed with a vengeance afterwards.

The objective was to project an external image of normality, peace and generosity. Internally preparations for war meanwhile continued. Goebbels recorded in his diary: 'The Führer would like to intervene in Spain. But the situation's not ripe . . . First we need to bring the Olympics to a happy conclusion.' Eight months after the Olympic closing ceremony, German bombers blasted the Basque town of Guernica almost to smithereens in support of Franco's fascist forces during the Spanish Civil War.

*

Despite contortions by Nazi leaders to keep their anti-Semitic virulence at bay, all manner of sports controversies surfaced untidily.

All along, the elephant in the room for Hitler was the humble Jesse Owens, then America's supreme black athlete. In the final of the 100-metre race, he was up against Germany's Erich Borchmeyer, one of Europe's top athletes who held the regime's superiority hopes. But Owens won and Borchmeyer trailed in fifth out of six finalists. Hitler's hopes were dashed and when it was suggested he have his photo taken with the winner Owens, Hitler replied: 'The Americans should be ashamed of letting Negroes win their medals. I'm not shaking hands with them.'

Foreshadowing apartheid myths again, Hitler remarked to his Nazi friend Albert Speer: 'People whose forefathers come from the jungle are primitive – more athletically built than civilised white people . . . They're not fair competition, they should be excluded from future Games and other sporting competitions.'

But that was not all the pain Hitler had to endure. Owens also triumphed in the 200 metres with a new Olympic record under the eyes of a glaring, sulking Hitler. Then again in the long jump, beating the favourite, Germany's Carl Ludwig Long, a tall blonde symbol of the Aryan race. The Nazis were livid at this eclipse of white supremacy, especially when the two athletes embraced. Later on, Long was visited by Deputy Führer Rudolf Hess and given a command never again to 'embrace a Negro'. Two black Americans, Cornelius Johnson and David Albritton, further dashed Nazi hopes by coming first and second in the high jump and were also snubbed by Hitler, who scuttled quickly out of his VIP box.

However, the Jesse Owens legend masked racism at home. Black American sportspeople suffered from blatant discrimination, especially in the South, which then barred blacks from representing their states. Only certain Afro-Americans broke through, including Owens and world boxing champion Joe Louis who, famously, defeated blonde Nazi idol Max Schmeling in a New York bout in 1938. But Owens and Louis conformed to certain norms. Owens was regarded as a dutiful, amiable, polite 'Negro' who knew his place. 'Their performances were viewed not as those of exceptionally gifted, handsome individuals, but as those of good Negroes and – better still – good Americans', wrote Richard D. Mandell.

*

There were other telling asides to the obnoxious politics infesting the Berlin Games.

Two Jewish American athletes suspected foul play when they were unexpectedly excluded from the relay team. But their coach vehemently insisted this was for purely competitive reasons; and there were several Jews in the US team.

There was a bizarre football match between Hitler's native Austria and the unknown Peru team. To the shock of all, Peru won 4–2, but only after a pitch fracas involving its fans. Football's governing body FIFA promptly ordered a rematch and furious Peru stormed out of the Olympics, protesting that the real reason was that their team included five black players. In a gesture of solidarity, Colombia left with them.

The Wehrmacht captain Wolfgang Fürstner was widely praised for his stewardship of the Olympic Village. But he was also one-quarter Jewish and posters were hung in the Village stating, 'Down with the Jew Fürstner'. Those posters were quickly removed as were anti-Semitic posters adorning German highways until the Games were concluded. But within days of the Games ending, and wearing full uniform and medals, Captain Fürstner committed suicide by shooting himself in the head.

As Oliver Hilmes concludes: 'Most of the foreign visitors enjoyed their trips and came away overwhelmed by what Nazi Berlin had to offer. Hitler and his regime were able to present themselves as peace-loving reliable members of the family of nations . . . [giving] . . . new hope that . . . Hitler can be trusted to keep his promises of peace. The sporting spectacle . . . helped pull the wool over their eyes.'[134]

At the end of the Games, 100,000 SS and SA officers lined the stadium route. As Hitler entered the stadium 100,000 people leapt to their feet for the closing ceremony to salute their country's winning haul of medals by saluting *Sieg Heil! Sieg Heil* in a crescendo of fervour at their Führer standing erect above them.

But the real hero of the Berlin Olympics was four-time gold medallist Jesse Owens, who spoiled Hitler's party, exploding the Nazi myth of Aryan supremacy.

Moreover, the Olympics themselves would continue to prove the point made by the commentator Garry Linnell that 'playing games is always political' and that 'games are not just sporting contests; they never have been' and 'they never will be'.[135] For example, he points out, 'the politics of de-colonisation and Cold War One brought division to the Olympic Games' in 1956 in Melbourne, over the Suez crisis, the Soviet Union's invasion of Hungary and the China-Taiwan impasse'. Then South Africa would be banned from attending Tokyo in 1964 because of apartheid. Mexico City in 1968 saw the famous black power salutes by world 200-metre record-holder, Tommie Smith and John Carlos in solidarity with the Black Power and civil rights movements. (Australian runner Peter Norman gave his support and was never again selected to run for Australia because of this.) And in 1980, Cold War politics led to a boycott of Moscow's games by some Western countries.

South Africans start reaching for the stars as well

If the 1936 Olympics were a sign of the deep discrimination that existed globally in sport before the Second World War, Jesse Owens's achievements also signalled that athletes from Africa and the diaspora wanted the opportunity to participate in what had been a white-dominated Anglo-Saxon closed shop of international sport, ranging all the way through from the Olympics, to tennis, cricket, rugby, football, athletics and other minor sports.

Racial discrimination in sport followed a remarkably consistent pattern throughout the world, not surprising given the interconnected experiences of slavery and colonisation. For example, it was only in the 1950s that the first black basketball and ice hockey players were signed up in the United States and only in the second half of the 1960s that Marlin Briscoe of the

Broncos became the first African-American quarterback to make the starting line-up in major league football. Moreover, it took another fifty years before every one of the thirty-two NFL teams had played black quarterbacks. Like South Africa, African-American sportspeople were for decades contained in segregated leagues. Similarly, in Brazil, the 1958 Brazilian World Cup winning team was predominantly white, though a young Pele announced the beginning of a new era. And only around that time did Frank Worrell became the first black captain of the West Indian cricket team. Before that the West Indies had always had a white captain and a team where the majority of players were white. On the other side of the globe, the appalling treatment of the aboriginal population was reflected in their almost total exclusion from Australian sport, the discrimination experienced by the talented cricketer Jack Marsh providing a ready case study. And Māori were, of course, omitted from New Zealand rugby teams to South Africa in order to appease the colonial cousins there.

In all these cases – the Olympics, American football, Brazilian football, West Indian cricket and antipodean rugby – it is almost impossible today to conceive of these sports without a preponderance of superstars from the ranks of the previously excluded. Contextually, it is therefore important to understand that Europe's classical inheritance – the ideas of Greece, Rome and the Enlightenment – has for the last five centuries gone along with violent conquest, racism and othering and that the old power relations still remain globally entrenched in many ways, including sporting inequality and never-ending wars (vide North Africa and the Middle East) and the particular kind of schizophrenic logic and politics required to justify them. It has, indeed been a long and painful journey to equal opportunity for many generations of black sportsmen and women.

Black South Africans who took up the sports imported by the British in the nineteenth century naturally aspired to be part of national and international competition as well, particularly those in cosmopolitan cities such as Cape Town and Kimberley, and those emerging from the mission stations in the eastern Cape. This point is emphasised by the fact that the South African Coloured Cricket Board was older than the Australian Cricket Board and predated – by several decades – the West Indian, New Zealand and Indian national controlling bodies, as well as the fact that it started its inter-state competitions in the same decade as the white Currie Cup, the Sheffield Shield in Australia and the official County Championships in England.

Hundreds of Africans had travelled abroad to study and work by 1910, when South Africa came into existence as a country, including no less than four of the first five ANC presidents. Many of them thrived as sportsmen. Examples included cricketers Nathaniel Umhalla and Josiah Benekazi who were sent to St Augustine's College in Canterbury in England at the time when overarm bowling was being legalised in the 1860s, coming back competent in technique; Richard Msimang, who starred at rugby in Taunton in Somerset while studying to become one of the first black lawyers in South Africa in the early 1900s; and the two young men from the eastern Cape, Harry Mantenga and Livingstone Mzimba, who played college football for Lincoln University in Pennsylvania, the oldest degree-granting black institution in the United States, started by African-American veterans of the civil war in 1866.[136]

The first football tour from South Africa to England in 1899 was by a team of black players from Bloemfontein, captained by Joseph Twayi, one of the leaders of the Orange River Colony Native Vigilance Association. His team was described as 'a gentlemanly lot, well conducted' and 'of no mean intelligence'; 'They can all speak English fluently – some of them are capable of writing and conversing in four different languages, including English and Dutch. They all have a trade – some are clerks, others grocer's assistants, tailors and carpenters.'[137] Organised by impresarios out to make money, the Free Staters rushed through forty matches in a crowded itinerary, which from the perspective of the globalisation of sport and the mega football leagues of today, was astonishing. It included fixtures against teams that are top names in English and World football. The first match was against Newcastle United at St James' Park and the South Africans lost 6–3 in front of a crowd of 6,000. Their other opponents included Liverpool, Manchester United, Aston Villa, Tottenham Hotspur, Arsenal, Sunderland, Nottingham Forest, Derby County, Sheffield United and West Bromwich Albion in England, Glasgow Celtic and Hibernian in Scotland, and Belfast Celtic in Ireland. The matches were watched by large crowds. However, it soon became apparent that the South African footballers were woefully mismatched. As with an earlier cricket tour by Aboriginals from Australia – who were expected to give displays of boomerang-throwing during breaks – and a rugby tour by Māori from New Zealand, the sport became a sideshow. [138]

In 1904 South Africans participated in the Olympic Games for the first time in St Louis in the United States; no South African team was chosen but three athletes competed unofficially, two of whom, Jan Mashiane and Len Taunyane, worked at the South Africa exhibition at the accompanying World's Fair, playing the part of Zulu warriors in crude enactments of battles from the recent South African War. The two took part in the marathon and 'ran with ordinary working shirts, the sleeves rolled up, and knee-length trousers'. While Mashiane had 'shoes and socks', Taunyane decided to tackle the course barefoot and came ninth, three places ahead of his countryman. The race was the most bizarre in Olympic marathon history. The two South Africans were chased off course by a 'large dog'. Another runner was found unconscious next to the road, a victim of the thirty-two-degree Celsius heat and total lack of support for the runners, the only watering point being at the twelve-mile mark. Yet another took a lift in a car after developing cramps and, when the car broke down, he resumed running, entering the stadium first to be greeted as the winner by the daughter of the American president. But the charade was soon discovered, and he was disqualified. The official winner, Thomas Hicks, was lucky to survive, never mind finish, having re-portedly lost twenty kilograms during the race. At one stage, he was 'having hallucinations' and 'moving mechanically' in the heat. The solution of his back-up team was to mix him a supplement of strychnine, egg and brandy, which would definitely not have passed modern doping regulations.[139]

Carrying on in this vein, Andrew Jeptha from Cape Town became the first black boxer to win a British title when he knocked out Army and Royal Navy champion, Curley Watson, in London in March 1907 to lift the welterweight crown and a purse of £550. A few years earlier, Jeptha had taken the boat to Britain to try his luck there, boxed for good purses as far afield as Paris (where he was billed as *le nègre*) and married a British woman. Tragically, when he knocked out Watson, he was already virtually blind, following a brutal twenty-rounder with the same opponent a few months earlier. After receiving 'medieval' medical treatment, including 'two leeches on my eyes to draw the bad blood', he left his family behind and returned home with 'the hope that the magnificent climate of my native land might do much to restore me to complete health'. It was not to be, and he ended his days selling a one-shilling booklet on his career alongside the flower sellers at the bottom of Adderley Street.[140]

Jeptha became British champion in the same period that Jack Johnson become the first black world heavyweight boxing champion and successfully defended it against the great white hope Jim Jeffries. The champion out-raged white America with his flamboyant personality and open liaisons with women, mostly white, and the grudge fight gave rise to 'black peril' fears of black subjects rising up against their white overlords in Britain's colonies. For this reason, the showing of the fight in the new media of film was banned in South Africa, the first case of film censorship in what would in later decades become a highly censored society.[141]

In the early twentieth century, it was not the place of black athletes to beat whites, so the achievements of Jack Johnson and Jesse Owens were powerful statements in a racist, white-dominated sports world. Their coun-terparts in South African wanted to be part of the action too, regularly making calls for more opportunities, including against international teams. In the First World War, the coloured Cape Corps soldiers, stationed near Alexandria in Egypt for nine months, won the army divisional cricket championships in 1919 after beating the 158 Brigade HQ and 436 Company RE in the semi-finals and finals respectively. The Corps showed little respect for their opponents from abroad, also beating the 34th Division Signallers, the personnel of the British transit camp, the Somerset Light Infantry and the El-Barud Detachment team. Two of their players were selected for a combined team that played in Alexandria. When the Australian Services touring team visited South Africa after the war, captained by Herby 'Horseshoe' Collins, an all-rounder who bowled slow-medium with a two-step run-up, and had become a 'habitual' gambler during the conflict, the local ex-servicemen asked for a match against them, but this was refused. Not even the fact that the local community had contributed to the governor-general's fund for returning servicemen counted. Black sportsmen were reminded that fighting for the King did not mean an exemption from racial discrimination in Britain's Empire.[142]

Nevertheless, black sportspeople persisted with their calls. In the 1930s, cricketers on more than one occasion asked for matches against the MCC, and in 1939, three years after Owens had won his four golds in Berlin, the South African Coloured Rugby Board selected its first national rugby team. Captained by fly-half John Niels, it called itself the Springboks, had the Springbok on its badge, and stitched under it '1ST NATIONAL TEAM 1939'. The team embarked on an internal tour in preparation for a planned tour to Britain, but the Second World War intervened and the plan was aborted.[143]

Having once again fought on the side of the Allies, and encouraged by the international acceptance of the Atlantic Charter and the Universal Declaration of Human Rights in the wake of the Second World War fight against fascism, black South Africans intensified their political and sporting demands. Segregated African, coloured and Indian bodies in football, rugby and cricket started selecting national teams and working together to organise joint 'inter-race' tournaments, mimicking the co-operation between the militant African, Indian, Coloured and white Congresses, which formed the new Congress Alliance at the time. The African rugby team's badge was a map of Africa with a jumping Springbok in it. The badge of cricket's SACBOC eleven was a direct imitation of the white SACA's Springbok head. The inter-race bodies also started seeking international tours for their combined teams – rugby in Fiji, football in India, and cricket in that country as well as Pakistan and Kenya.

A distinct trend of individual sportsmen going abroad to look for opportunities to compete internationally in the absence of such opportunity at home also emerged. Several met with success from 1948 onwards. The best known of these were the weightlifter, Ron Eland, who represented Britain at the Olympics, and Jake Ntuli (Tuli), who made history when he won the Empire flyweight boxing title in 1952.[144] Given the chance to travel by his brother's employer at American Express, Ntuli defeated the experienced British and Empire champion, Teddy Gardner, in a bout in Newcastle. He campaigned overseas until 1958 before returning permanently to South Africa and settling down as a respected member of the Orlando community in Soweto.[145]

Many sportspeople were to follow successfully in the footsteps of Eland and Ntuli, among them footballers Albert Johanneson (Leeds United FA Cup finalist) and Steve 'Kalamazoo' Mokone (Coventry City and Barcelona); the Samaai brothers (tennis at Wimbledon); 1939 coloured rugby Springbok, Louis Neumann, also going to Leeds, followed by David Barends, Winty Pandle, Goolam Abed and Green Vigo (rugby league); Cecil Abrahams and Basil D'Oliveira (cricket); Precious McKenzie (British Olympic weightlifting); and Papwa Sewgolum (golf).

These movements were signs of political and sport struggles evolving in parallel, as the 1950s also marked the rise of the ANC as a militant mass movement, launching the Defiance Campaign against unjust laws and other militant protests. In 1956 the non-racial South African Table Tennis Board became the first black organisation to be recognised ahead of the whites-only body when it was made a member of the International Table Tennis Federation. This was thanks to the support and initiative of the ITTF's president, the filmmaker and British Communist Party member Ivor Montagu. This move caused a sensation and led to the apartheid government issuing its first formal sports policy forbidding inter-racial contests.[146]

All over the world, black athletes were starting to make their voices heard. South Africans wanted to be part of this new wave, leading directly to the rise of the non-racial sports movement whose struggles against apartheid in sport are the main focus of this book.

'Neither ladies nor cricketers': Women and the gender ghetto in sport

The struggles for fairness in South African and world sport in the twentieth century centred largely on race, as Jesse Owens's epic performances remind us. In time, discrimination against black athletes, largely men, came to be seen as a key sporting anomaly. But racism and class snobbishness in sport went hand in hand with another aspect of deep-seated institutionalised discrimination – sexism, which has only in the past few decades started to be regarded as a major obstacle to levelling playing fields.

The same power relations and socially constructed conventions that made sports such as cricket white imperial games also reinforced patriarchal control over the female body, on and off the field. Black sportswomen – understood to be triple oppressed in South Africa, according to race, gender and class – faced the biggest discrimination. But white women as well; some sports were so exclusionary that the very sexuality of those who sought to play them was questioned and turned into a source of ridicule.[147]

The depth of the prejudices faced by women in sport was well illustrated by a remark by W. G. Grace, iconic cricket figure of the Victorian era, when he said of some players who in the 1880s played before large crowds as aspirant professionals, 'They might be original and English, but they are neither cricketers nor ladies.'[148]

Grace was not alone in his thinking. The founder of the modern Olympics, Pierre de Coubertin, believed that it was 'against the laws of nature for women to do athletics'. Women's participation in the Olympics before the First World War was restricted mainly to figure-skating and swimming.[149] Women's athletics was not allowed. It was regarded as a common pursuit for women of a lower class.

The exclusions of the so-called fairer sex were institutionalised. Cricket, most prominently, gave itself the title of 'The Gentleman's Game', a consciously created social construction which continues to define it even in the twenty-first century. In a male-dominated world there was not the space to challenge this 'gentlemen's game' notion. It underpinned the very notion of masculinity and empire in the Victorian age. Thus, ingrained sexism has been at the core of the 'traditions' and 'culture' of cricket since the start. This was largely the case in global sport as well until very recently – again games reflected the social norms of deeply patriarchal societies worldwide.

Yet, going back to the 1700s, women have been part of cricket and other sports from the beginning – and not only as social adornments, partners in socially constructed mating rituals, and makers of tea and servers of sandwiches. The first known report of women playing cricket was in July 1745, when 'eleven maids of Bramley and eleven maids of Hambleton, dressed all in white', took each other on. It was described as 'the greatest cricket match that ever was played in the South part of England'. Guildford was the venue. The reporter observed, 'There was of both sexes the greatest number that ever was seen on such an occasion.' And, 'The girls bowled, batted, ran and catched as well as most men could do in that game.'[150]

The games of the eighteenth and early nineteenth centuries seemed to cater for the whole social spectrum, from popular contests at alehouses, which offered the chances for betting, gambling and other passions, to private matches organised by aristocrats. Matches between married and single were common for both women and men. These were typical of the pick-up sides that provided betting opportunities for spectators – such as handsome versus ugly, or 'beauties' versus 'beasts', whisky drinkers versus teetotallers, gentry versus commoners and (in one bizarre case watched by 5,000 people in 1796) those with wooden legs against those with one arm. In September 1835, two teams of women married versus single played at Parsons Green and earned twenty pounds and a 'hot supper' for their efforts. A report of a similar encounter in 1838 conveys the lively atmosphere:

> A somewhat novel match of cricket was played on Wednesday between two female parties (married and single), in a field in the rear of the newly-erected public house near Westend, kept by Mr J. Vare. The fineness of the weather and the novelty of the scene drew together an immense concourse of spectators, who signified their delight by repeated rounds of applause. Vehicles of almost every description were also in attendance, from the dashing phaeton and pair down to the humble donkey tandem; on the whole, there could not have been less than 3,000 persons present.

The report concluded that the women

may be safely backed against any three boys under 18. The bowling of
Mrs Carter on the married side was also very good. The peculiar manner
of the ladies in stopping and catching, or attempting to catch, the ball
was highly amusing. When the game was over they all sat down to a
comfortable tea provided by the landlady, and concluded the day's sport
by a dance in the evening.[151]

At another game around this time, women cricketers apparently enjoyed
themselves so much afterwards that by their 'applications to the tankard,
they rendered themselves objects such as no husband, brother, parent, or
lover could contemplate with any degree of satisfaction'.[152]

These contests revealed a reality different from the world of the 'lady'
and 'gentleman' idealised in the literature of cricket. Women cricketers
offered novel alternatives to the usual betting and gambling on games,
which were so popular before sport was codified and made 'decent' by
educationists, clergymen and the middle and upper classes in the second
half of the nineteenth century. Even late in the 1800s, when entrepreneurs
put together two teams of women cricketers who earned money playing at
various county grounds, one observer noted, 'The sporting men found that
[they] were a nice change from the usual fare of dogfights and fisticuffs.'[153]

The historian Keith Sandiford has explained that 'A significant feature
of the Georgian legacy [before the start of Queen Victoria's long reign in
1843] was the remarkable growth of women's cricket.' But he notes, too, that
this trend of women's cricket stopped during the Victorian era. Part of the
answer lies in the different cultures that surrounded the game in the two
periods: 'Georgian enthusiasm gave way to Victorian earnestness.' Whereas
the Georgians were (in the words of Sandiford) noted for their laxity,
licentiousness and gambling, the Victorians were 'earnest, prim and evan-
gelical', and they 'cleansed' the game and turned it into a kind of morality
play. In fact, according to Sandiford, 'different notions of femininity persuaded the Victorians to abandon female cricket for about fifty years'.[154] As
Kathleen McCrone, Jennifer Hargreaves and other scholars have pointed
out, the industrial revolution and the expansion of empire created great
change, stress and fluidity in British society. Under these pressures, very
specific constructions of what constituted British 'ladies' and British
'gentlemen' took place. Thus, during the mid-nineteenth century, partly as

a defensive reaction to change, the patriarchal notions that men were the providers and leaders and women, the 'weaker sex', the nurturers and procreators, responsible for child care and the household, became fixed in the Christian and capitalist societies of western Europe, including Britain, and this flowed over to South Africa. Patriarchal norms were redefined and 'scientifically' rationalised during the Victorian period. Cricket was almost a metaphor for these identities.

McCrone explains that alongside the new ideal of muscular Christianity, came ideas about the 'passive ideal' woman: 'traditional Victorians summoned all the power of custom, religion and science at their disposal in defence of existing social arrangements. They insisted that God and nature had imbued women with qualities of mind and body that destined her for specific tasks such, such as being man's helpmate, nurturing his children, and protecting the sanctity of his home. Their ideal woman was antithetical to sport. Passive, gentle, emotional and delicate, she had neither the strength nor the inclination to undertake strenuous exercises and competitive games.'[155]

It was expected of women to be childbearers and mothers and sport was declared to be detrimental to the performance of these duties. Girls were not encouraged to do exercise in school. Science was roped in to support this thesis. 'Specialists' such as the physicians Clarke and Maudsley, whose views became very influential, maintained that women were biologically weaker. If they exercised, their health would be ruined: 'if women and girls behaved abnormally by acquiring a masculine type of education, their vital energy would be sapped and their health ruined . . . they would lose their natural grace and gentility and be turned into coarse, imperfectly developed creatures who would produce degenerate off-spring or none at all.'[156]

This view remained the orthodoxy for many years. Unchallenged, it 'represented a potentially fatal blow to the ambitions of women in every direction except the domestic', scholars have pointed out. Women's participation became frowned upon during the Victorian age when cricket and other sports (such as rugby, football, tennis and athletics) took on their current forms.

Parents, doctors, teachers and ministers of religion warned that athletics was 'a corrupting influence for a "properly brought up girl"'. While for boys, exercise, and cricket in particular, bred 'a healthy mind in a healthy body' – and prepared young men to be leaders in life – for women, 'rude health . . . was considered quite vulgar'. It is difficult to credit such views today, but the prim and proper moralists of the time believed that sport, generally, was 'likely to do irreparable damage to the adolescent girl'.[157]

Women who played sport were regarded as almost deviant. The result was to marginalise them – sport, the professions and politics were not for them, it was decided. They were needed as supporting organisers and social adornments, but they could not play. In polite society, girls were expected to do only the lightest exercise, such as gentle walks. A survey of one hundred private schools in 1868 found that almost without exception they insisted on nothing more strenuous than crocodile walks, calisthenics, croquet and social dance, all done according to self-conscious protocols.

Some horrendous stereotypes about sport took root. Horse-riding was said to lead to 'an unnatural consolidation of the lower part of the body, ensuring a frightful impediment to future functions'. Hockey could 'disable women from breastfeeding'. Athletics was said to 'produce an unnatural race of amazons', unproductive breeders who would contribute to the 'deterioration of the human race'. Cycling was 'an indolent and indecent practice which would even transport girls to prostitution'. Sport, generally, was 'likely to do irreparable damage to the adolescent girl'. Swimming, if allowed at all, had to happen in segregated enclosures, with women often fashionably wrapped in costumes made from seven yards of 'twilled' cloth. The notion of the naturally frail women was turned into a virtuous stereotype – and an industry. So-called scientific facts about women's frailty led to an excessive belief in the benefits of spas, prescriptions and treatments. Women's conditions became medicalised. Doctors and moralists thrived as women's complaints were turned into a 'medical-business-complex'.[158]

Even at Oxford and Cambridge, where young women experienced greater freedom than usual, some colleges banned cricket and hockey and had strict rules for bicycle riding as late as the 1880s. These exclusions from the male domain of sport and vigorous exercise began to be challenged only slowly. As the women's emancipation movement grew, and the success of the boys' public school system manifested itself, women educational reformers started fighting to extend sport at girls' schools. The movement was led by first-generation Oxbridge women graduates who had come into contact with the public school 'games' culture at university.

They turned the old argument around and said that far from hampering girls' education, exercise enhanced their effectiveness. If they were fit, girls could 'endure, without damage, the solid strain of learning'.[159] They countered with the ideas of the Swedish educational reformer, Madame Bergman-

Österberg, who argued that far from impeding childbirth, gym-nastics was 'the best training for motherhood': 'Remember, it is not "hips firm" or "arms upwards stretch", it is *not* "drill", but it is moulding and reshaping and reforming the most beautiful and plastic material in the world, the human body itself.'[160]

Penelope Lawrence from the elite Roedean School for girls – which established a sister school in Johannesburg – contended that cricket was a game that 'admitted girls to a world wider than their own' and, with practice, they could 'produce quite a respectable standard of performance'. By the end of the nineteenth century, as in other spheres of life such as university studies, the medical profession and municipal politics, British women were beginning to break through old barriers and stifling taboos in sport.

In the 1880s cricket started following the new pattern of organised sport for women. The first women's cricket club in England was the White Heather Club formed in 1887. With aristocrats such as the Marchioness of Willingdon, Lady Milner, the Countess of Brassey, Lady de la Warr and Lady Abergavenny at its head, it soon grew to fifty members. Several other clubs followed. *Athletic News* commented in 1887, 'Ladies cricket in the north seems to be rather popular, judging from the reports of the various matches that have crept into the papers of late.' Various public schools by now also had teams. By 1890 around 2,000 women were members at the Lancashire County Cricket Club, fully a quarter of the total. Throughout the Victorian period, women were enthusiastic spectators, particularly at the Oxford–Cambridge and Eton–Harrow games, and the festivals held in the counties. In 1871 Ladies Day at the Canterbury Week in Kent drew 7,000 spectators, of which more than half were women.[161] In 1890 entrepreneurs trading under the title of the English Cricket and Athletic Association Limited set up an early kind of professional women's circuit. They contracted two teams of women players, put them through a stiff training programme and for two years moved from place to place playing exhibition games. The players were known as 'The Original English Lady Cricketers'. For some reason, they were required to play under assumed names. They played at county grounds, including the famous Headingley in Leeds, and drew large crowds. It was these players that W. G. Grace so mercilessly derided.[162]

But women's cricket in England struggled to grow. It never really spread beyond upper-class women and ex-public-schoolgirls. According to Holt, there were not many more than fifty women's clubs by the 1920s – women's cricket and football clubs 'were laughed at, scoffed out of existence'.[163] It became established that women could play golf, tennis and hockey but not the 'gentleman's game'. Nevertheless, despite the slow process, women had 'come out of the closet' as far as sport was concerned by the time Europe exploded into war in 1914. They were slowly breaking old boundaries and taboos and opening up more spaces for themselves in public life, including the professions and politics. As historians have shown:

> Whereas a little walking, croquet and gentle calisthenics was thought
> sufficient exercise for the young lady of the 1860s, her grand-daughter
> could run, bicycle, climb mountains, play tennis at Wimbledon, golf
> at St Andrew's, hockey for England, and any number of team and
> individual games at college and school, and then she could read about
> so doing in features on 'The Sportswoman' or 'The Outdoor Girl' in
> respectable periodicals and newspapers.[164]

*

Women's cricket developed along similar lines in South Africa. Women were part of the game of cricket from the very beginning, at least the social side of it, from the first regimental games played by the British army in Cape Town from 1806 onwards, and they started playing actively from the late 1880s onwards.

The first known report of women playing cricket is from 1888, when the first British touring team came to South Africa. Harry Cadwallader, first secretary of South African Cricket Association, commented on 'a number of the fair sex indulging in practice with the willow on the Pirates' Ground [in Kimberley] and they showed they are possessed of not inconsiderable talent. It surely will not be long before we shall have a ladies' match at Kimberley'. During that historic English tour, around 4,000 people attended the first day of the first match at Newlands and 'a very large proportion of the crowd were ladies'. The visiting captain, Charles Aubrey Smith (later a famous Hollywood actor), said: 'Newlands Cricket Ground was a picture to be remembered, with its surrounding mass of pines, over-topped by the great Table Mountain on the one side, the new stand covered with red cloth on the other ... The picturesque effect given to our grounds being enhanced by the bright and varied colours of many Malay women in their holiday attire'. Later, he noted: 'we saw as quaint a site as ever cricketers saw at Mowbray. Two or three cricket matches were being played by Malays and [Africans] and hundreds of Malay women in their many coloured costumes were there to do honour to the friends.'

In 1893 a proposal was put to the annual general meeting of the Western Province Cricket Club that women be admitted as members, but it was quickly quashed. However, by the early years of the twentieth century there were women's teams at two of the best-known clubs in South Africa, the Wanderers Club in Johannesburg and the Ramblers Club in Bloemfontein. They were reported to have played against each other.

Nurses attached to the British forces played during the South African War, and in April 1902 the Wanderers was hired for a match between 'Ladies' and 'Gentlemen' in order to collect funds to buy literature for soldiers 'garrisoning lonely block-houses'. The women in the forefront were linked to the strong, very British cultures flourishing at the main cricket clubs in South Africa. Some of them, like Winifred Kingswell, described as the pioneer of women's cricket in South Africa, strongly believed in the value of sport for women and were influenced by growing struggles for political rights to be extended to women. But, of course, at that time she was talking only about white women. She resigned in protest from the Wanderers after women players were told to make way for men to practice.

From the 1880s black sportsmen excluded from the clubs and competitions of the colonial establishment, started becoming involved in these new sports as well, as noted above Among the thousands of students at the church-run British mission schools in the eastern Cape by the 1880s and the educated aspiring middle class that emerged from them were many women. They, too, soon showed an interest in the British games. When the King William's Town Champion club played Ngqika CC from East London at home on Boxing Day in 1883 in one of the first inter-town matches, *Imvo Zabantsundu* reported that 'lingathi liphume lonke iQonce' (it was as if the whole of King William's Town turned out). It was a hot day and, we are told, the ladies and old men brought along umbrellas to shade themselves. In January 1885, when Champions CC became the first inter-town champions after a tournament in Grahamstown, a prominent local woman handed over the bat awarded to the best player.

When Port Elizabeth played cricket against Kimberley in 1888, the black community turned out in force for the fixture played at the white Union CC grounds in St George's Park. Entrance to the pavilion was sixpence, and the local reporter, *Nkosi* (Chief), noted, 'For the first time in the history of matches in the area married men brought their wives and single men brought their partners'. He said this needed to be applauded 'as it is a symbol of change in our communities'. The wives and partners of the leaders of Port Elizabeth's black community set up a tennis and croquet club to go with their church, education and choir activities, and promptly advertised this fact (and the croquet constitution written in Xhosa) in the missionary-controlled *Isigidimi Sama-Xosa* newspaper. These were amongst the earliest women's sports clubs in South Africa.

The first known black women's cricket clubs were formed in Kimberley in 1909. Women from the coloured community there 'set the pace in a highly commendable way' by forming The Daisies, The Ivies and Perseverance clubs, and grouping themselves into a union under prominent local sports administrator, J. S. Lackey.

By the early 1900s cricket was being introduced into schools such as Roedean in Johannesburg and Wynberg and Rustenburg in Cape Town. Roedean was staffed by teachers from its sister institution in England, known for its pioneering role in girls' sport in the 'mother country'. The South African school immediately made sport one of its educational priorities. A highlight of the first term at the new school was a cricket match against Jeppestown High School, and one of the school songs – titled 'The First Eleven' – was specifically about the cricket team. It would have made Kipling proud: 'It doesn't matter where your place may be / Or if batting or if bowling be your forte / If in the Eleven you are playing; / Then of you we will be saying: / "Well stopped!" "Well hit!" "Well bowled!" / "Well tried!" "Well caught!"

For the next sixty years, the school magazine faithfully recorded the progress of cricket at the African Roedean, listing the school teams, publishing poems about the game and commenting critically on each player's shortcomings and strengths.[165] In 1908, when Mr McGregor and Miss Rankin laid a new pitch and nets, it was observed that 'overhand [bowling] is weak and has not been practised sufficiently', while the fielding 'is neater and more scientific, but only a few can throw long distances'.[166] In true cricket fashion, the coaches stressed the importance of a correct technique and using 'a straight bat'. Following the tradition at boys' schools, the most outstanding cricketers were awarded colours.[167]

Winfred Kingswell was 'instigator and first president' of the Peninsula Girls' School Games Union. Regular inter-school sports events began to be held in Cape Town and the annual Cavanagh Cup for inter-school competition was started in 1921, with the Kenilworth Racecourse a popular venue. One observer noted that 'almost the whole school – children and staff included – would turn out to support the competitors'. Schools cricket started growing in this environment and soon there was a time 'when all the girls schools played competitive inter-schools cricket'. The appointment of the first qualified physical education teacher from Britain and the introduction of 'Games and Sports Trophies' at Wynberg in the 1920s reflected this new emphasis on sport in girls' schools.[168]

*

In the male-dominated world of that time there was not the space in either Britain or its colonies in southern Africa to challenge the notion of cricket as a man's game. The exclusions of women from sport only slowly began to be addressed. As the women's emancipation movement grew, British suffragettes demanding the vote and other rights, and the success of the boys' public-school system of a 'healthy mind in a healthy body' showed itself, women educational reformers started fighting to extend sport at girls' schools too. They turned the old arguments around and said that far from hampering girls' education, exercise was good for learning and 'the best training for motherhood'.

Today we take it for granted that exercise is an essential part of a healthy all-round lifestyle, and can safely say that jibes about women playing the so-called 'gentleman's game' come from the dinosaur days and fossilised thinking. But it took a long time to get to this point, and the past still casts its shadows over us in this respect.

The first national cricket organisations, test matches and international tours for women took place in the decade and a half after the First World War, when the vote was extended to women in Britain. Political rights brought women greater social freedom, assertiveness and mobility and this also resulted in a notable expansion of international sport for women, for example, increased participation at the Olympics and the formation of the first international women's cricket body. This was the Women's Cricket Association, established in England on 4 October 1926. The Australian Women's Cricket Council was formed in 1931 and the New Zealand Women's Cricket Council and the Nederlandse-Dames Cricket Bond in

1934. At the end of 1934 an English team embarked on the first ever international tour, visiting Australia and New Zealand under the captaincy of Betty Archdale. England beat Australia by nine wickets in the first women's test match held in Brisbane in December 1934.

South Africa tried to come in line as well. In 1932 the irrepressible Winifred Kingswell started the Cape Town-based Peninsula Ladies Cricket Club and two years later it affiliated to the Women's Cricket Association in England, to all intents and purposes the international governing body or women's MCC. The aim of the Peninsula Ladies CC was to build on affiliation by sending teams to play the Ramblers Club in Bloemfontein and the Wanderers Club in Johannesburg – 'the pioneers of women's cricket in South Africa' – and, thereafter, to form a South African Women's Cricket Association 'after which international games in England, Scotland and Australia will be possible'.[169]

The few South African cricket bodies mentioned here were for white women only, but there is ample evidence to show black women continued to share many of their cricket interests and aspirations, even though segregation and discrimination were on the rise. For example, a photograph from *Umteteli wa Bantu* in December 1933 shows fashionably dressed women spectators at the first inter-provincial tournament of the South African Bantu Cricket Board in Johannesburg.

During the 1930s and 1940s black sports clubs had well established 'Ladies Sections'. A life-long cricket and rugby fan recalled, 'We were very smart, we even had blazers. Ours had one button and the men two buttons'.[170] These were specially made. Tailored blazers. And then 'you had your caps, you know, with pom poms'. 'We were strong, very, very strong.' At the famous *macal' egusha* (sides of a sheep) tournaments in the rural areas – where a sheep was the prize to play for and the source of the festivities to follow – women were cheerleaders and vocal supporters, escorting successful batters and bowlers off the field.

The affiliation of the Peninsula Ladies Cricket Club to the Women's Cricket Association in 1934 raised the prospect of a national association and international cricket, but it took nearly two decades before the South Africa and Rhodesia Women's Cricket Association (SARWCA) was finally formed in 1952. In keeping with apartheid thinking at the time, SARWCA was for white cricketers only. The first of over thirty official annual inter-provincial tournaments for the Simon Trophy followed in Bloemfontein in December 1952. The first inter-provincial century was scored by

Johannesburg-based Eileen Hurley in 1953–54 and Sheelagh Nefdt from Western Province took a double hat trick with her leg-spin, and later became the first South Africa captain.

At the Durban tournament in 1955, a *Daily News* women's reporter noted that the cricketers were not the type to stoop to flirtatious 'Gorgeous Gussy' tricks, that they 'spurned the use of make-up' and 'clean-bowled' glamour, on the field at least: 'These are the sort of girls, one imagines, who led the suffragette campaigns of half a century ago: feminists who believe that anything men can do they can do better – and very often can.'

The new SARWCA finally joined the small test circuit (with England, Australia, New Zealand and Holland) when England toured in the 1960–61 season. This was only the eighth international test series in just over a quarter of a century of international women's cricket, during which time twenty-four test matches had been played.

Bowled over by these details emanating from his broader cricket research, André made it a point to promote women's cricket after becoming Chief Executive Officer at Cape Town's Newlands Cricket Ground in 2004, stating in a tournament brochure for a girl's tournament, 'Go out there and live out your cricket dreams, like any other cricketer.' And he drew on his work and the views of some of the women's players from these earlier years, who had 'to deal with much more prejudice than you to keep playing', to give intellectual ammunition against the 'rugger buggers' and bigots.

Responding to the stock imputations that women cricketers were 'unfeminine' and acting in opposition to their destined roles as wives and mothers, Dr Muriel Ritchie from Southern Transvaal explained during the 1956 women's inter-provincial tournament (of the then segregated SARWCA): 'I have never had the time to get married – but have had it to play cricket . . . It is the best game that a woman can play. It gives you excellent exercise, without over exerting one. It is a physically and emotionally healthy recreation. It teaches you to concentrate, and it develops the co-ordination between brain and body . . . it has no negative effects.'[171]

Another simple piece of logic women's players applied in relation to the irrational 'gentleman's game' argument was to point to comparative examples. Provincial cricketer Christine Bald said 'I see nothing unfeminine about cricket; it is no different from women playing tennis or golf'.[172] Vicky Valentine-Brown (thirty-three times Western Province captain in the 1950s and a Wimbledon quarter-finalist in tennis) said that for her, cricket was not 'light-hearted and social' like tennis, but 'an intelligent game' that

'demands teamwork, enthusiasm, patience, knowledge and years of practising'. She concluded, 'It is my whole life'.

Thus, from the beginning of organised sport in the nineteenth century,
black sportspeople and women of all shades showed a desire to participate,
also in the colonies, but were generally excluded on the basis of their race
and gender. From the 1960s onwards, this discrimination, and the power
relations which maintained it, would be increasingly challenged, both in
South Africa and the wider world. Global anti-apartheid campaigns and the
rise of what was designated as the 'non-racial sports movement' inside
South Africa became a distinctive feature of this struggle.

3

A matter of life and death: Sport and rebellion

John Harris and the emergence of SANROC, 1962–65

As he tried to board a flight to attend a meeting of International Olympic Committee (IOC) Executive Board session in Baden-Baden in October 1963, an idealistic twenty-six-year-old married teacher, John Harris, was unexpectedly turned back and had his passport confiscated by Special Branch officers.

South Africa's race policies in sport were on the agenda at Baden-Baden, and Harris was desperate to be there so that he could appeal for white South Africa's exclusion from the 1964 Tokyo Olympics. Not only was his passport seized, but the following year in February 1964, he was issued with a banning order and received death threats – and terrifying gunshots were even aimed at his living-room window.

Highly intelligent (formerly a national radio 'Quiz Kid') and an experienced debater, Harris was a good choice to argue the case for expulsion before a hundred and more IOC delegates. Many were rooted in the days of empire, though newly independent countries in Africa, Asia, Latin America and the Caribbean were slowly beginning to change the IOC's composition of hitherto elderly, white, conservative, male aristocrats, gentry and businessmen.

Harris was representing the South African Non-Racial Olympic Committee (SANROC), having recently been elected its chairman. He succeeded poet and activist Dennis Brutus, who had also been blocked from this leading sports role by a banning order, and then shot, prosecuted for leaving the country illegally and despatched to Robben Island, joining Nelson Mandela and others from the liberation struggle.

The Special Branch officers who officiously confronted Harris were on a clear mission: to suppress his role as a sports official in the resistance to sports apartheid. But they were also propelling him away from peaceful idealism and activism, and down a road of increasing desperation as the apartheid police state crushed all resistance, whether sporting or political. That road would eventually lead to his arrest in July 1964, and the following April he was the only white person (joining over a hundred black people) to be hanged by the neck for his role in the anti-apartheid struggle.

Harris's treatment, coupled with the banning or imprisonment of other SANROC officers, gave the lie to habitual pleas from officers of the IOC-affiliated white South African Olympic Committee (SAONGA) 'not to mix politics with sport'.

*

SANROC's story went back to the 1950s, when pressure against whites-only South African participation in international sport first began to develop.

Various black sports bodies started actively opposing apartheid in sport by joining together to play what was called 'inter-race', and later 'non-racial' sport, and seeking international opportunities. In 1955 a teacher and poet from Port Elizabeth, Dennis Brutus, helped to set up the Coordinating Committee for International Relations in Sport (CCIRS) in an attempt to give momentum to this process.

This emerging movement secured a singular success with the previously mentioned expulsion of the all-white South African Table Tennis Association in 1956 by the International Table Tennis Federation (ITTF). ITTF instead gave affiliation to the non-racial body. However, three years later, the government would seize the passports of black players from that non-racial affiliate as they were about to depart for the world table tennis championships.

In October 1958 Brutus and other campaigners met in East London to discuss the formation of a stronger new umbrella South African Sports Association (SASA) to coordinate the battle for non-racial sport and replace the short-lived CCIS. The launch of SASA took place in Durban in January 1959. Some twenty national organisations representing 70,000 sportsmen and women came out in support. The weightlifting president G. K. Rangasamy was elected to lead SASA. Rugby's V. C. Qunta was his vice and the up-and-coming Brutus the secretary. The Liberal Party president and renowned novelist Alan Paton became its patron and vice-president. Two of the specific aims in SASA's constitution were 'to work for the removal of all race discrimination in sport' and 'to coordinate the work of various bodies for international recognition'.[173]

SASA successfully opposed a proposal by local black cricketers to bring a West Indies cricket tour to South Africa in 1959 because it would be racially confined to only black players, within the parameters of the government's new apartheid sports policy. SASA started campaigning against the establishment's whites-only tours as well. In 1960 soon after Sharpeville, the homes of its leaders were raided by the security policy ahead of the International Olympic Committee meeting in Rome and they were refused passports to attend. SASA launched several more campaigns in 1961 and 1962, including a call to FIFA to suspend the whites-only affiliate from South Africa. But the target remained the IOC. SASA pressed for the inclusion of black athletes in the country's Olympic team at the 1964 Olympics in Tokyo. Brutus was banned for his activities and in July 1962 he was among the 102 writers whose work the government decreed could no longer be quoted or published in the country.

Having been rebuffed by officials of the white South African Olympic Committee, Brutus told them he was left with no alternative but to form a truly non-racial Olympic Committee in order to challenge their membership of the International Olympic Committee. 'Go right ahead,' they told him, laughing at his suggestion, oblivious to what lay ahead for them.

So SASA agreed to the launch of SANROC in October 1962, with the banned Brutus its chairman and weightlifter Reg Hlongwane as secretary, the latter promptly called in front of a judge and given a warning that he was contravening the Suppression of Communism Act, as Peter's mother, Adelaine, found a year later. Like her, he was no communist but that was the habitual method of intimidating apartheid's opponents. Former weightlifting champion and non-racial sports activist Chris de Broglio also became involved, subsequently to become a key SANROC leader.

The SANROC campaign gathered pace, and in February 1963 John Harris attended an IOC meeting in Lausanne to lobby ahead of the 1964 Tokyo Olympics against SAONGA's continuing racial policies. He also visited London during the trip, where he did broadcast and newspaper interviews and appealed to MPs.

In May 1963 SANROC's acting chair, N. Rathinasamy, wrote to National Olympic Committees and Olympic sportspeople across the world, appealing for support. As well as contacting national sports bodies, SANROC wrote to Pepsi-Cola Africa and to Tottenham Hotspur captain Danny Blanchflower, asking them to condemn racial segregation in South African sport.[174]

Across the course of the year, statements of support for the campaign were received from far and wide, including the Italian, Egyptian and Bolivian Olympic Committees and the Weightlifting Federation of the USSR.

The increasing impact of SANROC's campaign obviously jangled IOC establishment sensitivities. Its chancellor, Otto Mayer, wrote informing SANROC that it was not legally entitled to use the word 'Olympic' in its name – a minor setback quickly overcome by replacing 'Olympic' with 'Open', meaning the SANROC acronym was unaffected by the IOC's attempts to hamper the campaign, and its Olympics label continued to be used colloquially.

In an effort to coordinate a joint declaration by National Olympic Committees, in July 1963 Harris wrote to the Ghanaian and Nigerian Olympic Committees. He explained that 'our work for non-racialism in the Olympics becomes increasingly difficult as a result of various pressures, such as those of the security police. It is possible that it will be completely stopped in the near future.' With heightening surveillance from the South African security police, SANROC also appointed Neville Rubin as its London representative. Rubin, already involved in the Anti-Apartheid Movement in Britain, was asked to set up a Committee in London and attend the upcoming meeting of the IOC on behalf of SANROC, were its South African delegation unable to do so.

Preparations for the IOC meeting which would determine white South Africa's fate were further complicated by a declaration by the government of newly independent Kenya that it would not issue visas to any Olympic delegations from South Africa (or the still colonial power Portugal, which was suppressing independence movements in its territories of Angola and Mozambique). Kenya refused to host white South African delegates, stating that to do so would be to condone apartheid in sport, standing firm despite threats from IOC leaders to suspend Kenya from the next Olympics. 'They argue that our position is political while the Olympic charter doesn't allow politics', wrote Tom Mboya (Kenyan minister for justice and constitutional affairs) to Harris, adding, 'this is an amusing argument coming from the same group who have allowed to South Africa to delay non-European participation purely on political grounds.'

Although Mboya's arguments reflected SANROC's, in a letter to Brutus, Harris expressed frustration that Nairobi would have been an ideal place to make SANROC's case, both because of its physical proximity to South Africa, and the likelihood of gaining a more supportive reception within Africa.

SANROC quickly tried to convince the Kenyan government to rethink their position. But President Jomo Kenyatta did not retract his refusal to host any South Africans, insisting that to do so would be a concession to IOC pressure, rather than an act of support for SANROC. In retribution, the IOC leadership summarily resolved to change the venue of the meeting. It was moved to Baden-Baden in West Germany and the date was set for October 1963.

Meanwhile Dennis Brutus, who had been served with stricter banning orders in March 1963 expressly to restrict his ability to act for SANROC, was playing an important role in the background. Harris warned him that he should leave the country as the security police were showing increasing interest in him. So he left illegally, crossing the border into first Swaziland and then the Portuguese colony of Mozambique in September 1963 with the important IOC meeting as his destination. But he was promptly arrested by the Portu-guese security police, detained and interrogated, before being handed over to South African Security who drove him back to its Johannesburg headquarters, by then becoming notorious for intimidation and torture. Realising that he was extremely vulnerable because his family and fellow sports activists were completely unaware of his predicament, Brutus resolved somehow to escape. As the vehicle pulled up in front of the security head-quarters in John Vorster Square, he was instructed to collect his bag from the boot and quickly ducked away, running onto a nearby bus with the police giving chase. The bus conductor pushed him off and Brutus was shot at point-blank range by a policeman, the bullet entering his back and passing out of his chest.

Lying on the pavement bleeding, someone called an ambulance but failed to specify for which racial group. When it arrived, the driver refused to pick him up as it was for whites only. Still bleeding, he was finally taken to a hospital for black people for treatment, subsequently to be sentenced to eighteen months on Robben Island.

*

John Harris was amongst those who visited his wounded comrade in hospital in September 1963, by which time he had become Brutus's successor as chairperson of SANROC. Brutus and Harris expressed concern about the actions of Ahmed Gora Ebrahim, an ex-SANROC committee member who was in Dar es Salaam, claiming to act on its behalf.

Ebrahim had asked for documentation and money so he could make appeals to the Tanganyika Olympic Committee for support. To them, the speed with which Ebrahim had been granted a passport to leave South Africa was suspicious. While Brutus had been struggling to escape South Africa covertly, Ebrahim had left the country and reached Tanganyika with ease. Harris contacted the IOC to warn that SANROC believed Ebrahim to be 'an agent of the South African government, deliberately attempting to sabotage SANROC's campaign'.

Following his trip to the IOC meeting in Lausanne that February and given these complications, it was decided that Harris should go to the IOC meeting in Baden-Baden in October 1963. As he was prevented by his passport confiscation from attending, he submitted a tape recording.

Characteristically eloquent and logical, Harris opened by explaining why he was delivering the appeal, describing how Brutus was in prison at the time, after being banned and having his passport withdrawn. 'He is not allowed to attend any meetings; he is not allowed to belong to any organisation; he is not allowed to have any statement of his published. Again, when I was on the point of openly and legally leaving South Africa and was prevented from doing so, the South African Olympic Committee made no comment on the matter, and the South African government had again interfered in sport.' He emphasised that neither of them had been convicted of any criminal act, instead drawing attention to the Olympic Charter:

> The very first clause of Olympic Charter forbids racial discrimination on grounds of race, religion or political affiliation, yet the South African Olympic Committee maintains strict racial segregation in its administration of sport. White and non-white athletes are not allowed to compete together, to train together, do not take part in trials together. The Olympic Charter forbids any form of discrimination. Segregation or apartheid in sport is discrimination and that is precisely what the South African Olympic Committee is doing.[175]

Dealing with the devious attempt by SAONGA 'to offer opportunities to non-white sportsmen', he cited the case of champion black weightlifter Precious McKenzie in order 'to clarify the situation'. McKenzie, a member of the non-racial national weightlifting body affiliated to SANROC

happens to be by far the best bantam-weight weightlifter in the country and he ranks fifth or sixth in the world. He was recently offered the chance to go to the World Weightlifting Games in Stockholm by the Weightlifting Union under the control of the South African Olympic Committee. But he was offered this opportunity – and obviously it was a magnificent opportunity – on the condition that he joined an all non-white body. In other words, Mr McKenzie had to choose between his principles of non-racialism and a very large opportunity. Mr McKenzie remained faithful to his principles and turned down this opportunity [subsequently leaving the country and representing Britain at the Olympics].[176] It seems inconceivable to us in SANROC that the IOC can condone behaviour of this sort by the South African Olympic Committee which is using its position as the officially recognised body to force racialism on all those South African sportsmen, whatever their race may be, who are against racialism.

Harris continued by quoting the then most recent official South Africa government policy statement issued on 4 February 1963:

Whites and non-whites must play sport separately; whites and non-whites must not compete against one another whether on individual events, or as teams or as part of teams; whites should compete against whites and non-whites against non-whites; participation in international sports tournaments or competitions of mixed teams as representatives of South Africa could not be approved; for example if whites took part individually in such tournaments they must do as representatives of the whites in this country and the non-whites must take part as representatives of non-white South Africans. In other words, should the South African Olympic Committee select a contingent of individuals and say 'these are the South Africans who are going to the Olympic Games', should there be for argument's sake thirty whites and ten non-whites, the Government's policy is that the thirty whites represent the whites of South Africa and the ten non-whites represent the non-whites of South Africa. No one apparently, according to the Government, represents South Africa. Non-white sports associations could exist and develop alongside the corresponding white associations. The white executive committees could serve on a higher level as co-ordinating bodies between the different associations and as representatives in the corresponding world organisations. In other words, this is merely the application in sport of the overall Government policy of the South African Government of 'separate development', of apartheid, of segregation. This policy has hardened as regards sport over the last few months. Consequently, in terms of the resolution passed by the IOC in Moscow in June 1962, the South African Olympic Committee must be suspended. There is a flagrant and increasing violation of the Olympic Charter as regards racial discrimination. It must also be suspended because of the political interference in sport by the South Africa Government.

Harris concluded:

We offered to merge with SAOC [South African Olympic Committee] on the basis of complete compliance with the Olympic Charter and they rejected it. We ask that South Africa be suspended until all the sports bodies affiliated to the South African Olympic Committee can prove that they are non-racial as regards, training, competition, trials and administration. And when racialism has been eliminated then we will welcome the lifting of the suspension. But that is for the future. We now urge the IOC to act unequivocally, to act decisively and we ask our allies to press the case for us. Please ensure that the 1963 IOC conference delivers a smashing blow against racialism in South African sport.

Meanwhile, Ebrahim had made it to Baden-Baden after the switch from Nairobi, as a self-appointed representative of South African sportspeople. At the conference, he stated that 'he opposed the policy of Mr Harris and Mr Dennis Brutus of bringing politics into the Olympics argument', undermining the consistent case made by SANROC that it was the racism of the South African Olympic Committee, not SANROC, that had brought politics into sport.

Nonetheless, the conference at Baden-Baden was a victory for SANROC. The IOC ruled that if the South African Olympic Committee did not eradicate racism from its constituent sports, it would be banned. Coming on top of SANROC's wider lobbying together with that of the British Anti-Apartheid Movement (whose secretary, Abdul Minty, attended the meeting after writing to 118 national Olympic committees), Harris's cogent appeal to the Baden-Baden IOC was successful. South Africa was indeed suspended from the 1964 Tokyo Games, and instructed to fully implement non-racialism and eliminate all discrimination or face expulsion.

The international press picked up on both SANROC's success and the injustice of its treatment by the South African security police. On 10 October 1963 the *Daily Mirror* published an open letter from its sports correspondent Peter Wilson to the Marquess of Exeter, the senior British member of the IOC who had ostentatiously walked out of Harris's testimony to the IOC in Lausanne. Referring to the shooting of Brutus, Wilson wrote, 'you cannot shoot or wrench away ideas of freedom', and he placed SANROC's campaign in a tradition of anti-racism in the Olympics dating back to Jesse Owens's success at the 1936 Berlin Olympics orchestrated by Hitler. In the *Observer*, Christopher Brasher, British Olympic athlete and co-founder of the London Marathon, praised the IOC suspension as 'adhering strictly to the Olympic Charter and by steadfastly keeping politics out of sports'. Brasher specifically highlighted the irony of South Africa's apologists who claimed that banning would be a 'political' action, pointing out it was the apartheid regime that applied politics to the qualification criteria for the Olympic team.

In February 1964 Harris was slapped with a banning order that prevented him from openly continuing with his public leadership of SANROC. By then SANROC's leaders had been banned and harassed to such an extent that, like the ANC, it could in effect no longer operate legally inside the country.

Harris's wife Ann took over as acting secretary. On 26 May 1964 she wrote to a letter to the Johannesburg *Rand Daily Mail* demanding that the South African Olympic Committee stop 'deliberately leaving its position on Apartheid in sport obscure', in order to qualify for the Olympics without ending segregation.

Harris's journey from articulate, law-abiding sports official tragically ended at Pretoria's notorious gallows.[177] Banned from all sports or political activity, he had, like the suppressed ANC, grown increasingly frustrated by the inability to accomplish anything against a police state that remorselessly crushed all peaceful opposition. So, with other similarly frustrated young white radicals, many of whom were also members of the South African Liberal Party, he was attracted to the sabotage strategy of the African Resistance Movement (ARM).

With his close colleague, fellow ARM and Liberal Party member John Lloyd, Harris planned to place a bomb in Johannesburg's Park Station on 24 July 1964, the day before a rugby test match between the Springboks and France in nearby Springs. But Harris never intended to harm anybody. He had meant it as a spectacular demonstration of resistance to tightening state oppression. Indeed, he planned a fifteen-minute warning: police testimony at his trial confirmed that he had telephoned a warning to the railway police and two newspapers, urging that the station concourse be cleared with calm and precise instructions:

> This is the African Resistance Movement. We have planted a bomb in
> a large brown suitcase twenty feet from the cubicle above platforms five
> and six on the concourse of the new Johannesburg Railway Station.
> On the handle of the suitcase is tied a label bearing the words 'Back in
> Ten Minutes'. It is not our intention to harm anyone. This is a symbolic
> protest against the inhumanity and injustices of apartheid. The bomb
> is timed to explode at 4:33 p.m. Clear the concourse by using the public
> address system at once. Do not try to defuse the bomb as the suitcase
> is triggered to explode if it is opened.

The authorities ignored the demand and the bomb exploded on the whites-only concourse of Johannesburg railway station, mortally injuring a seventy-seven-year-old woman, Ethel Rhys, and severely injuring her twelve-year-old granddaughter, Glynnis, who was maimed for life; twenty-two others were injured, five suffering terrible burns. According to former South African spy and journalist Gordon Winter,[178] the head of the security police, Hendrik van den Bergh, confirmed to him that the Railway Police had alerted him at 4:20 p.m. to an anonymous phone call two minutes earlier warning that the bomb had been planted. He had immediately used his hotline to talk to the security minister, John Vorster. But they calculated that it was better to exploit the subsequent and inevitable furore than to use the station loudspeaker system to clear travellers from the concourse.

A fellow Liberal Party activist and close family friend of Peter's parents, Harris had tried, unsuccessfully, to persuade them to join him in the ARM. Ad and Wal argued strongly against its violent tactics, insisting that these would be counter-productive and invite greater repression. Although horrified at Harris's action, they remained convinced that he had never intended to kill or injure anyone.

They also believed that they had a duty to assist John, his wife Ann and baby son David. Their values of loyalty and solidarity came before their family's predicament – which became increasingly dire. They carefully explained to fourteen-year-old Peter that, despite deploring his action, they would be standing by Ann and giving what help they could to John in prison.

To their shock, Ad and Wal discovered that Harris's co-conspirator John Lloyd – also a friend of theirs – was to be the main prosecution witness. Harris would have been liable for a life sentence for manslaughter had Lloyd not turned state witness and insisted – against all other evidence – that the act was premeditated murder. His version was accepted by the judge, who passed the death sentence.

A legal appeal on 1 March 1965 was rejected, and Ad and Wal helped with other activist friends to organise clemency appeals. Desperate personal pleas were made to Lloyd, by then living safely in England, to retract the damning part of his evidence, but he refused. Ann Harris paid a warder R 1,000 (a considerable amount at the time) to help him escape, but as the family suspected, this offer was a cruel joke on the part of the security police.

In Pretoria Prison, Harris started preparing for the grisly, medieval ritual of being hanged by the neck that awaited at 5 a.m. on 1 April 1965. Scarcely recovered from his jaw having been broken by a running rugby kick to his face by the notorious 'Rooi Rus' ('Red Russion') Swanepoel during his interrogation, he was determined to go to his end singing the anthem from the American civil rights struggles, 'We Shall Overcome'. He requested a sympathetic Catholic priest to help him rehearse the words so that he didn't get them wrong. Used to comforting condemned prisoners before executions, Father McGuinness found Harris, an atheist right to the end, markedly and admirably different. He recounted that whereas most prisoners 'went into a state of grace' at the point of their execution, Harris remained calm and determined – as he had planned, singing 'We Shall Overcome' until the moment he died. These were his last words of defiance – the family learnt later from Father McGuinness – right up to the brutal violence of the act: trapdoor opening below his feet, the sudden jerk of the body, jack-knifing as the neck bore all the weight and broke, blood spouting, and the last breath was torn from him.

The hangman, Chris Barnard was the longest serving in South Africa, responsible for 1,500 judicial murders between 1964 and 1986. He later described John Harris as 'very brave'.

'Maintain the human and social within you':
Sharpeville, Robben Island Maximum Security Prison
and sport in the early 1960s

Dennis Brutus, the public face of the struggle for non-racial sport in the early 1960s, was put on trial in January 1964 after recuperating from being shot in the back by police and sentenced to eighteen months hard labour on Robben Island Maximum Security Prison. His crime was breaking his banning order. In March that year, he and some sixty others convicted for political offences in the crackdown at the time were handcuffed, put into leg irons and loaded into two large police vans for the thousand-mile journey from Leeuwkop prison down to Cape Town. His journey and the experiences he and other prisoners encountered could be read as a metaphor for the imprisoned society that apartheid South Africa had become by the mid-1960s.

The island – or *Siqithini* as it was called in isiXhosa – opened in April 1961 as a maximum-security prison, following hasty preparations in the wake of Sharpeville, but had by then already earned a reputation as apartheid's 'hell-hole'. Like Goree, Alcatraz and Devil's Island, it became fixed in the popular imagination the world over as a place of institutional brutality reflecting a harsh system. This was not an undeserved title. For three centuries, the island had been a place of banning, 'othering', pain and marginalisation. The people sent there by those in power during the colonial years included women and men of the original Khoisan people who fell out of favour with the Dutch; the Muslim religious leaders from Indonesia banished to the Cape, who brought Islam to South Africa; lepers taken from their verandas during a time of harsh ignorance and held there against their will; and nineteenth-century anti-colonial resistance heroes from the various African chiefdoms.

The duty of those who ran the new prison was to isolate opponents of apartheid and to break their morale. The prisoners – all so-called 'non-Europeans' – were subjected to spartan treatment by warders who were all white, after black warders were removed because some developed empathy towards the intelligent and highly disciplined people put in their care. The warders were abusive and quick to punish. Steve Tshwete, a rugby fan from the eastern Cape who later became the first minister of sport in a democratic South Africa, recalled that he was constantly reminded that he was a 'kaffir' and a 'dog'. In one infamous case, the PAC's Johnson Mlambo suffered the vile treatment of a warder urinating on his face, while buried up to his neck in the ground in full view of his fellows.[179] Food was sparse – and differentiated according to race in keeping with the logic of apartheid. While Indian and coloured prisoners received a quarter loaf of bread per day, Africans were given only porridge – for breakfast and supper. They were allowed to buy one loaf of bread once a year at Christmas time. Unlike their comrades, Africans had to make do with short pants and sandals – no shoes, socks, underpants or long trousers, even in the wet Cape winters. Until 1973, the prisoners had to wash in cold water. They slept on a concrete floor with a thin mat and two blankets. They were allowed one letter of 500 words every six months. Even though these letters had to be confined to family matters, they were often censored, some looking like gate-grills with multiple paragraphs cut out of the pages. Prisoners were permitted one visit every six months. Newspapers were forbidden. Day in, day out, the prisoners were subjected to hard labour.[180] On top of this came unspeakable psychological deprivation, like the many Robben Islanders who were not allowed to hear, talk to or touch children, even their own, for ten, sixteen, twenty or twenty-three years, the testimonies show.[181]

This was the prospect that Dennis Brutus faced as he was loaded, manacled, onto a large police truck with sixty others for the long journey by road from Leeuwkop prison in Johannesburg to Cape Town. In *Dennis Brutus: The South African Years* (2020), Tyrone August leaves us a graphic picture of the trauma Brutus suffered when he entered Robben Island, which this account draws on extensively. It was so severe that it led to a nervous breakdown of sorts. Fellow prisoners noted that as an educated intellectual, Brutus appeared to be singled out for specific attention by the predatory bullies wearing uniforms at the time.

In his poem, 'Strains', Brutus wrote: 'I have sat in one place in a prison truck / gritting my teeth to keep from moving / and bracing myself to keep from bobbing / to ease the pressure of the manacles / that cut into my wrists and ankles / for a thousand miles.'[182]

Still 'tied together in pairs at their wrists and ankles', the large batch of prisoners finally arrived on the island. They were made to strip naked, given blankets and sleep on the floor in a cold, still unfinished cell without toilets or showers. As an initiation for what awaited, they were moved the following morning to the administration block 'from where they could witness a group of prisoners about to be punished' in a brutal attack by warders using 'batons and sticks' and even 'pick handles from a nearby shed'. Brutus recalled: 'It was an indescribable kind of fury unleashed, and when we came out of our section a while later, there were still splashes of bright red blood, almost vermilion in contrast, on the grey broken flint that formed the gravel of the ground.'[183]

Now it was their turn. For several days Brutus and his group were the target of a particularly hard initiation. The playing field was the notorious stone quarry where they were made to work in ill-fitting sandals, sometimes barefoot, on sharp rocks half submerged by the ebb and flow of Cape Town's cold Atlantic tides:

> The catch was, first, that we had to carry these stones at a run to the pole where they had to be deposited. Second, as we ran, we were beaten by guards to hurry us along. Third, they also attempted to trip us, and sometimes succeeded, so that we fell heavily, and were then beaten while we lay on the ground, or as we got up and gathered our stone and made off with it. As the work went on, the tempo increased – we were required to run ever faster – the beatings increased, and the number of guards who were beating us was augmented by other guards who were off-duty, and who came along to join in the fun.[184]

Brutus was appalled by what he described as 'the arbitrary and almost limitless brutality, the sadism, the malicious glee with which the guards saw people fall and beat them and forced them to their feet again'.[185] The treatment was repeated several times. August continues:

> A senior prison officer informed the guards of Brutus's application to study while in prison, and sarcastically instructed them to give him special treatment in future. Perhaps in direct response, the still-injured and weak Brutus was ordered the next day, 17 March 1964, to push a wheelbarrow loaded with rocks. In itself, this was extremely strenuous; pushing a heavily loaded wheelbarrow on sea sand was near impossible. He tried to cope as best he could, yet still the guards were not satisfied; they felt his loads were too light and constantly instructed the common-law prisoners to put more rocks in his wheelbarrow. Again, Brutus persevered. Yet the beatings continued relentlessly; one prisoner, wearing boots, even leapt into the air and kicked him in his stomach.[186]

August narrates how a 'semiconscious Brutus' was brought to the hospital section and 'flung onto the concrete floor' where fellow prisoner Indres Naidoo witnessed the scene. 'He lay curled up on the floor and when I lifted his shirt I got a terrible shock. His whole back was red and black and there was a deep gash right across his stomach.'[187] Brutus could barely speak. Naidoo described how 'with his [pre-prison, gunshot and operation] wounds freshly stitched and scarcely healed', Brutus – 'one of the most articulate of us all' – lay in his bed in deep distress: 'he could barely get the words together, they came out in a groaning whisper, broken up and harsh, hardly making sense'.[188]

The poet and sportsman himself wrote that 'I do not think I will ever be able to erase from my mind the images of that day of terror and violence by the sea with the bright water and the bright sunlight, and the men struggling with slimy masses of seaweed and on the sharp slippery rocks.' And he painfully recalled the humiliation that followed. His feet were torn, 'trailing grimy bandages'. And, as he 'puttered' through the prison, his fellow pris-oners 'gaped', 'wondering how they had managed to make of me / a thing / of bruises, rags, contempt and mockery.[189]

These vivid first-person accounts by Brutus and eyewitnesses, deftly put together by his biographer Tyrone August, are mirrors into the private pain that he and John Harris, two of the best-known leaders of the non-racial sports movement in the early 1960s, had to endure and shed light on the high costs of resisting apartheid at its height. And the trauma that came to be built into the psychological fabric of South African society as a repressive state went to extreme lengths to assert white control and implement its mad, chessboard designs. Over a quarter of a century after democracy arrived in 1994, this undealt-with trauma is still revealing itself in many disturbing ways in a society still full of dissonances, such as high rates of crime, rape and the domestic abuse of women. To highlight this is not to excuse these horrors, but to explain their roots in the trauma and terror of apartheid.

The cinematic intensity of the treatment meted out to prominent sports activists like Harris and early Robben Islanders like Brutus was exceptional, but their experiences should not be separated from those of tens of thousands of sportspeople and citizens in the imprisoned society that was wider South Africa of the early 1960s. Countless ordinary South African (non)citizens and sports lovers were quiet participants in a struggle to maintain their human dignity and right to play. And they too were affected in many ways. For example, among the 15,000 people detained in swoops after the government imposed a state of emergency were South African Bantu Cricket Board (SABCB) secretary, Lennox Mlonzi, a Pan Africanist Congress (PAC) supporter. Despite still being in detention when the SABCB AGM was held, he was voted back into his position by his colleagues. His rugby counterpart, Louis Mtshizana, president of the South African African Rugby Board (SAARB), was not so fortunate. When he was banned in 1963, he was asked to stand down as president and the SAARB became a sweetheart body that worked with and was co-opted by the sports apartheid system. Mtshizana, a supporter of the African People's Democratic Union of Southern Africa (APDUSA), an offshoot of the New Unity Movement, also ended up serving time on the island.

During the 1960s apartheid social engineering on a grand scale affected hundreds of thousands of South Africans in adverse ways. The Group Areas Act was particularly harmful to many sportspeople and their clubs. In Cape Town alone well over 60,000 people were forced to move out of the homes they had occupied for generations in the city because the government declared that henceforth only whites could live in these areas. People went through unspeakable pain, even committing suicide rather than leave their home; long-settled communities with their churches, mosques, schools, sports clubs, cinemas and distinct cultural life were broken up and scattered to bare patches of land which have become today's depressed, gang-infested Cape Flats townships. The black sporting community had to totally reorganise itself in spatial terms and many long-established clubs went out of existence or had to merge with others.

The club that André joined when he moved to non-racial cricket was called United Cricket Club because it was an amalgam of what remained from thirteen previous clubs in Cape Town's city centre. Many of his new teammates and friends had stories of heartache to tell.[190] Nazeem Smith grew up at 6 Dreyer Street, Claremont, and had to watch as the landmark Cavendish Square retail complex was built where his home had been. The entrance is on the exact spot, so every time he went into this high-end shopping mall in what became an exclusive white suburb under apartheid, he would be reminded of the childhood home his family was forced from. He later moved to New Zealand.

The Conrad family were among many who had to move from the streets right next to the Newlands rugby stadium. The famous Magiet brothers,

Rushdie and Saaiet, brought up in Stegman Road, a few hundred yards from the Newlands cricket stadium, had to pack their bags and the taste it left was bitter. The young Rushdie decided not to watch again at Newlands until he was recognised as a human being with the same rights as everyone else – and he stuck to his word for fully thirty-two years, until non-racial cricket unity happened in 1991. Angelo Carollisen from Paarl remembers how the bulldozers came to break down the family home, with the furniture still inside; he recounted the dramatic image fresh in his mind of the warm Welcome Dover stove of his childhood plucked high in the air in the jaws of front-end loader with the blue sky as background behind it. Salie Green, who André played with at United CC, told him with tears in his eyes how he and his mother went around to say goodbye to old neighbours when they had to leave: 'I can still see the pain in my mother's face as if it were yesterday. That pain also went into my body. She was never the same again and soon got sick out there in the sticks at Grassy Park.'

Countless South Africans were affected like this by apartheid legislation. Like left-arm spin bowler Owen Williams, who was offered a contract by Warwickshire in the 1960s. His family was split up by the Population Registration Act, which introduced humiliating forms of racial classification. One half of the family was declared white and the other half coloured. Children on the wrong side of the line and therefore wrenched out of their family had to sneak in after dark to visit their mother, for fear of being caught out. Tragically some of the family members became alienated, and later as 'whites' wanted nothing to do with Owen and their once unified family.

Day-to-day apartheid could kill as well. Nicholas van Oordt, father of the sporting Van Oordts from Tygerberg, expired on a street one rainy day in the 1960s after he was hit by a car. As when Dennis Brutus was shot by the police, an ambulance arrived believing he was white, but turned back because, according to instructions, a different one would have to be used for 'coloureds' like him. By the time a second ambulance arrived it was too late, and a mother had to bring up her seven children on her own with the smallest of pay packages – and she made sure they became good sportsmen.

The stories of the systemic and overt violence of apartheid go on and on. In a brain drain, thousands of people classified 'Non-European', held back by racist restrictions, streamed out of the country for greener pastures abroad in the 1960s and 1970s. Amongst them were D'Oliveira and four other members of his SACBOC eleven of the 1950s – the first national cricket team open to all South Africans. His teammates Owen Williams, Basil

Witten, Sidney Solomon and John Abrahams, followed by the younger Dik and Goolam Abed, ended up in Australia, New Zealand, Canada, Britain and the Netherlands respectively, part of the incalculable loss that South Africa suffered because of its apartheid.

Most socially aware black South Africans did not have these choices and had to retreat into submission, but they did not accept passively the immense indignities visited on them. The anger remained and years later the flame of internal protests in sport and politics would be lit again.

In myriad ways, disenfranchised sportspeople operating in generations-old social networks continued playing their sport every weekend, determined to defend their humanity and counter the apartheid narratives that only whites played so-called 'Western' sports.

The iron-fisted response of the state and its overt smashing of opposition to apartheid in the years after Sharpeville, including in sport, might have given the apartheid rulers a sense of control, but they did not foresee that they were planting the seeds for uncompromising future internal resistance and a powerful global anti-apartheid movement centred around high profile sports protests which would expose the soft underbelly of the apartheid rulers and, indeed, lead to the eventual collapse of apartheid rule.

*

The genius of the South African struggle was that despite the huge indignities visited on the oppressed, and the narrow racialised mindsets of the power structure under which the majority of South Africans lived during apartheid, they still managed to assert their humanity and imaginations of an inclusive future based on respect, inclusivity and universal values in powerful ways that ultimately changed the country.

Many lives were destroyed by the Robben Island experience, but somehow most political prisoners came out fortified and strengthened. The key to survival was their political commitment and approach to incarceration, promoting collective solidarity and mutual support and enabling them to dig deep into their own sense of humanity.

Sport on Robben Island was very important in building these strategies for resilience. To understand some of these transcendent aspects of survival on the island, begin with the observations by the Dutch historian Johann Huizinga (as outlined in the introduction) that play is an essential part of our humanity, both as individuals and communities. And that 'The spirit of playful competition is, as a social impulse, older than culture itself and pervades all life like a veritable ferment.' So that 'civilisation is, in its earliest phases, played [and] does not come from play like a babe detaching itself from the womb: it arises in and as play and never leaves it.'[191]

Not surprisingly, the first prisoners brought to Robben Island after the prison was opened in 1961 sought to relieve their hardships and tap into their deepest yearnings and needs through culture – through music, dance, art, learning and play – and through this form bonds of solidarity, teamwork and companionship in extremely trying circumstances. They rolled up socks to fashioned footballs for silent mini cell games after lock up, for in-stance. They did ballroom dancing and performed dramatic pieces; the prisoners would 'brush' their hands together to show appreciation rather than clapping, which would alert the warders to the forbidden pleasures underway. One of their staggering achievements was the saxophone that Vusi Nkumane built from flotsam and jetsam he gathered on the island, with which he made music. Drawing on his own imagination and humanity, his specially named 'Nkumanephone' was something majestic created out of nothing.

Sport was an important part of this creative imagination prisoners developed on the island to help them survive and look forward. The African intellectuals and activists held there understood its inherently affirming human dimension and meaningfulness to them as political prisoners. Steve Tshwete elegantly explains: 'Sport was an important element in our ability to cope on the island. It helped to relieve anxieties about families and home, to ease the burden of prison life, to relieve tension with prison authorities, [it] kept us mentally alert and provided us with good poise to look into the future.'[192]

As Tshwete's fellow prisoner Nelson Mandela explained, 'prison consti-tutes its own society even if inmates are coerced into membership' and, therefore, to maintain their dignity and beliefs, individually and organ-isationally, the prisoners set out to create their own 'world within a world'. This famous ex-Robben Islander also observed:

> The prison is above all punitive, it operates to break the human spirit,
> to exploit human weakness, undermine human strength, destroy initia-
> tive, individuality, negate intelligence and process an amorphous
> robot-like mass. The great challenge is how to resist, not how to adjust,

to keep intact the knowledge of society outside and live by its rules, for that is the only way to maintain the human and social within you . . .

In the course of time we had to build our own social life and we modelled it in terms of the life we lived outside the prison walls. We encouraged, above all, study . . . In that constricted, deprived environment, we placed the highest value on sharing, sharing everything, every resource, material and intellectual, and on the whole we succeeded.[193]

This notion of maintaining the human and social within your very being is a profound philosophical point and explanation for the resilience and visionary thinking that emerged on Robben Island and in the resistance struggle. Sport not only became one of the welcome distractions and survival mechanisms for those who were incarcerated, it also helped them from deep within to develop new ideas and strategies of struggle, including negotiation.

The prisoners tried to organise and structure their own lives as far as possible and to this end set up their own committees – educational, political and recreational – on an organised basis. Eventually nearly every activity in prison was run in this way, with each political organisation's members working together, across party-political lines, with teammates and fellow administrators from other organisations.

At first the prison authorities would not entertain the idea of prisoners playing sport. 'Of course, when we felt the aches and pains we began to wish for some form of recreation,' one prisoner recalled, 'this propelled us into action and hence our campaign to have recreational activities.'[194] After repeated requests, the first official games were allowed in 1967. At first this was conditional, allowing the authorities to manipulate the situation at times. When the prisoners wrote a letter asking for permission to buy a packet of sweets to present as a prize, the reply came back, scratched across the page in red: *Nie goedgekeur nie* (not approved). But they persisted, and organised sport became an increasingly important feature of prison life.

Many prisoners came from strong sporting areas or were already well known for their prowess when they arrived. Tshwete came from the village of Peelton, which was rooted in the deep, century-old sporting, political and educational traditions of the eastern Cape, discussed earlier. According to fellow prisoner Marcus Solomon, he was barely out his teens when he became recording secretary of the Border rugby union. Another example was the young Black Consciousness leader, Mosiuoa 'Terror' Lekota. He earned his nickname from his exploits as a fiery semi-professional on the football field. Prisoners with backgrounds such as these needed no encouragement to exercise on their own. The need to cope with prison restrictions, such as solitary confinement, also contributed here. Mandela, cut off in B-Section from the main body of sports-playing prisoners, was famous for his daily routine of rising as early as four in the morning, making his own bed and doing push ups and other exercises, a routine he continued after becoming president. This discipline had its source in the stick-fighting days of his youth in rural Thembuland; the lessons he learnt at Healdtown, the Methodist mission school where he was taught the manners and behaviours of an English public schoolboy and was a middle-distance runner; and his workouts in township boxing gyms in the 1950s captured in the pages of the glossy *Drum* magazine during his pre-prison struggle and celebrity years in Johannesburg. He applied the discipline and habits learnt in those days to help him survive and stay intact and as fit as possible in the prison environment and struggle.

This sports-based discipline allowed Mandela (and others) to overcome the unthinkable deprivations Robben Islanders faced and to emerge after twenty-seven years of incarceration not only with enhanced authority as a person and leader but also empowered to define the vision of a transcendent humanity that he became world-famous for.

In 1967 permission was given for games under certain conditions. The prisoners started competitions and clubs, as well as a Coordinating Recreation Committee (later the General Recreation Committee). Its aim was 'to inculcate the spirit of sportsmanship and co-operation amongst the prisoners of Robben Island, negotiate with the prison authorities in a formal way and generally encourage and oversee sport on the island'. Tshwete of the ANC became the committee's first president (and also president of the Island Rugby Board and president of the Robben Island Amateur Athletic Association). The secretary was mathematician Sedick Isaacs, known for his administrative efficiency, who was aligned with the rival PAC. Football was the most popular game. By 1972 thirty-six teams were participating in the league run by Makana Football Association, named after the legendary nineteenth-century military leader who was imprisoned on Robben Island by the British and drowned in cold waters trying to escape in 1820.

The weekend sports contests were eagerly awaited and the political prisoners recounted that 'whoever scored . . . on Saturday was the hero for the rest of the week'. The highlight of the sporting calendar was the annual summer games held over two weekends during the festive season. The games were based on the model of the Olympics, with outdoor and indoor sports and an official opening with a parade of participating teams. Inmates made cardboard cameras and videos and 'recorded' the action. The games culminated in a prize-giving function and the awarding of diplomas and trophies made by artistic-minded people in the prison workshops with the Olympic rings emblazoned on them.[195]

One political prisoner remembered, 'It was an event enjoyed by all the inmates at a time when they wished to be back home with their family and friends.' Another said, 'After our Summer Games I am sure we [could] show the Olympic guys a thing or two about being creative and organising.'[196] The imagination of those who were confined soared far beyond the prison walls to the great spectacles in sport.

Isaacs recalled: 'Athletics, when it was finally approved was a source of great fun . . . Besides the more serious events such as the one-kilometre medley relay, the shot put, discus and the triple jump, I also introduced the egg and spoon race, the sack race and the three-legged race. The problem was that the rules with judgment criteria for each event had to be carefully documented. This I did with great care.'[197]

Driven by socialist dreams of a new humanity, Marcus Solomon of the small National Liberation Front grouping explained that 'we play because we want to create friends and it's not to win, it's to create a new human relationship, a new social order and sport must in that way contribute to that.'[198]

Much has been written about the Robben Island sports experiences and the remarkable archive of the General Recreation Committee and various clubs is preserved at the UWC/RIM Mayibuye Archives at the University of the Western Cape. Professor Chuck Korr and Marvin Close have written the most comprehensive study so far. Their book, *More Than Just a Game: Football v Apartheid* (2008),[199] was marketed as 'the most important soccer story ever told' and came out with perfect timing to coincide with the FIFA World Cup football tournament held in South Africa in 2010. It was translated into various languages, including Korean and Japanese, and also formed the basis for a film documentary with the same title.

Sport, together with the special efforts to promote study via formal and informal courses, and political education curricula drawn up by inmates, as well as cultural activities like the regular music programme – relayed in later years through the prison announcement system to every cell after lock-up

– played a big role in creating a 'world within a world' in the notorious island prison. In this way, sport came to have tremendous significance for the struggle and country as a whole. All these activities were organised primarily in order to make sure that even while in captivity the political prisoners remained disciplined and united and kept promoting the broader struggle against apartheid. So, for example, when the prisoners heard the news of John Harris's hanging in Pretoria, they were busy with their gruelling daily work in the lime quarry. During their lunchbreak, Harris's ARM colleague Eddie Daniels called on them to stand and observe a minute's silence 'to a great freedom fighter'. Mandela and members of the ANC, PAC, Communist Party and other political groups paused to honour him.[200]

According to Tshwete, sport also crucially helped defuse sectarian political tendencies in the prison environment. At first the ANC and PAC organised teams by party, but 'This was very bad as it strained our relationships with each other'. Rugby led the way with mixed teams and 'relations between the ANC and PAC improved considerably'.

Eventually the authorities came to realise unofficially that order in the prison was preserved not by warders, but by the prisoners themselves. Slowly Robben Island changed from a punishment 'hell-hole', where daily life was often extreme, to a more normal prison environment. According to Ahmed Kathrada this was made possible because the prisoners responded collectively rather than individually: the individual personality was submerged in a wider social unit, 'a profoundly humbling but enormously rewarding experience'.[201]

Robben Island's dark days remind us today, in a time of great change, stress and uncertainty in South Africa and globally, that the secret is to find the human and social and the universal within us. To realise our own power. To reach out in empathy and solidarity with others throughout the world, especially during periods of challenge, stress or hardship.

The debates and experiences on Robben Island fundamentally shaped the direction of the liberation struggle and the future of a country. Mandela, confined to a six-foot-square cell for nearly twenty years (before being moved to prisons at Pollsmoor on Cape Town's outskirts and finally Victor Verster in the Cape winelands), became the international symbol of the struggle against apartheid. To use the cliché, he and his comrades of various political persuasions became not apartheid's prisoners but its jailers. They contested and eventually more or less completely subverted the aims of the state on the island. It was from prison (but not the island) that the most famous Robben Islander of all initiated the process of negotiation that broke the historical impasse in South Africa and finally led to the democratic elections in 1994 when all South Africans were allowed to vote for the first time. The long patient queues twisting away into the dawn mist that marked that April day were a deep tribute to generations who had sacrificed immensely to make that moment possible.

*

In the International Slavery Museum in Liverpool, UK, there is, amongst the exhibits, a quote by former slave William Prestcott from 1737, in lament of the way in which enslaved people are rendered invisible: 'They will remember that we were sold, but not that we were strong. They will remember that we were bought, but not that we were brave.'[202]

Like Prestcott, the Robben Island sportspeople and the thousands of disenfranchised South Africans who continued playing sport through tough times, believing that fair play should apply to all sportspeople, were not merely passive victims of an ugly system. This book aims to show that they were multidimensional characters who, through sport, affirmed that the best of humanity is possible and, therefore, should have their names inscribed in South African sports history. The novelist André Brink was able to capture these intangible aspects of the sports struggle in his observations about the colourful District Six in Cape Town before it was bulldozed and destroyed to make way for a white area under the Group Areas Act: 'This . . . is what truly spells Cape Town for me: its indomitable, raucous, rebellious way of confirming a heretic otherness, of saying no – not only to apartheid, but to everything that tried to domesticate and inhibit the human spirit and its wild, affirmative freedom, its laughter, its compassion. And also its outrageous and jubilant way of saying yes to life itself.'[203]

'Non-whites' are largely absent from the official records of South African sport, but far from being insignificant, those who played on the wrong side of the colour line in the bad old days had deep sporting cultures. They were often the ones really sowing the seeds for the future and their inclusive goals and inherited legacies and imaginations influenced and shaped the way forward after democracy. Forced for a hundred years to play the game in the margins and under the most difficult circumstances, through skill, perseverance, knowledge and an irrepressible love for life they moved beyond victimhood to lay the foundations of South Africa's post-democracy sports system.

The Robben Islanders showed what the human imagination is capable of and emerged from these hard prison experiences with new sensibilities and African-rooted ideals about politics and the unity of all of humanity. Mandela came to symbolise these notions, championing the idea of a united nation in harmony with the world – in which former oppressors and oppressed would join together to build a new nation upholding the dignity of all South Africans. It should be remembered that the rainbow-nation ideas of the founders, much criticised today, came not from a passing whim, but were the product of decades of profound struggle.

Many of the 'Islanders' went on to play a prominent role in the transition to democracy in South Africa from 1990 onwards, after the unbanning of organisations and the release of all political prisoners. Mandela, of course, became first president of democratic South Africa. Tshwete became the first minister of sport, known as 'Mr Fixit' for his vital role in facilitating sports unity. Together, they were responsible for South Africa's return to the Olympic Games in Barcelona in 1992 (even before formal democracy in 1994) and the prisoner and president-in-waiting was a special guest of the IOC president at the opening ceremony. Dikgang Moseneke, the youngest political prisoner on the island who learnt skills of administration and constitution-writing as secretary of one of the sports clubs, was appointed to the newly created constitutional court and became deputy chief justice of South Africa. (In 1963, on trial in Pretoria aged fifteen, Moseneke had been astonished to be given help, food and his favourite chocolate bar each day by Peter's mother Adelaine, the only white person he'd ever had any support from.) Stix Morewa emerged to become president of the South African Football Association. At the time of a big reunion of 4,000 ex-prisoners in 1995, the journalist and former prisoner Ace Mgxashe noted in the *Cape Argus* newspaper that over half the 300 new ANC MPs in the first democratic parliament were Islanders. Thus, the story of the Robben Islanders also became the story of the founders of democratic South Africa, with sport integral to their own remarkable evolution.

*

On 1 January 1997 André had the profound privilege of presiding over the opening of the prison doors of Robben Island after three centuries of banishment and marginalisation.

It was day one of the new Robben Island Museum and André, appointed by the first democratic government of South Africa as its head, handed over the keys of the old Robben Island Maximum Security Prison to Lizo 'Bright' Ngqungwana, one of those who had first set foot there in chains. Lizo was now helping to build the museum and reimagine the island. A child was asked to open the door with him. The absence of children's voices was one of the things that had most pained prisoners on the island. Choosing a child for this role reflected the humane future envisaged by the founders of democracy in South Africa. For Ahmed Kathrada, first RIM Council chairperson, and many islanders whose stories André had greedily absorbed, this was an important part of the ceremony.

A noisy turn of the key. Then the clanging doors were thrown open. It was a throat-constricting moment. Buzzing voices and small barefoot feet pattered into the passages. A ballet of freedom. The island entered a new phase of its history. And democratic South Africa took another small step forward.

4 SANROC in exile: Intensifying the sports boycott

Note for coming late to school

When John Harris was hanged at 5 a.m. on the morning of 1 April 1965, a lot of people across South Africa rose unusually early. The Hain household were up well before the moment came, with none of the clatter and chaos of normal mornings with school and work. His wife Ann Harris waited with them, still and silent as the darkness outside. His baby son David slumbered.

Then the phone rang, piercingly loud. The caller asked to speak to Ann. Ad refused, recognising the familiar voice of a security police officer. 'Your John is dead,' he said.

The Hains were overwhelmed by a blank hopelessness combined with deep anger. They had not condoned what John had done, but under any civilised system, he would have continued to devote his life to teaching children and would never have been involved in the sabotage which ended it so grotesquely. It had been arranged that Harris's funeral would happen at Pretoria's Rebecca Street Crematorium at seven thirty in the morning, just a few hours after his execution. The evening before, the authorities refused to allow the banned Walter Hain to give the eulogy. Ann Harris gladly accepted fifteen-year-old Peter's offer to read the two-page funeral address written both to remember key people and reflecting John's strong atheist convictions. Dignified yet uplifting, it began with John's chosen Shakespearean sonnet, and continued with John Donne: 'No man is an island, entire of itself. Every man is a piece of the continent, a part of the main . . . Any man's death diminishes me, because I am involved in mankind, and therefore send not to know for whom the bell tolls; it tolls for thee.'

From the Bible was Matthew's 'Blessed are they which are persecuted for righteousness' sake' – specially for John's very ill mother – and Ecclesiastes, 'To everything there is a season, and a time for every purpose under heaven,' which was on an album sung beautifully by Judy Collins and often played in the Hain family home during those fraught months. In their last conversation, when John and Ann discussed the funeral, they decided that the songs would be 'We Shall Overcome', which he had been rehearsing for his last political act, and the 'Battle Hymn of the Republic'. The latter, they decided, would be sung up to the verse that ended 'as he died to make men holy, let us die to make men free'. John also wanted included Shakespeare's Sonnet 116 as a memorial to their deep love, which would not change, a constant despite their horrendous predicament and his own culpability. They went over the words together: 'Let me not to the marriage of true minds / Admit impediments. Love is not love / Which alters when it alteration finds'.

Ann was astounded to find the small chapel packed. As prison warders carried the coffin in, angry that they should be discharging this solemn duty, a small, twelve-year-old Tom Hain inserted himself amidst them. His elder brother Peter, aged fifteen and dressed in his Pretoria Boys High School blazer, tie and grey trousers, went up to the raised lectern before the assembled congregation. A private, undemonstrative and rather shy boy, he had never spoken from any platform before and had avoided school plays and performances. The proximity of the coffin, containing John's body, his last breath taken only two hours earlier, made the ordeal especially distressing for those present. The congregation stood, their voices resounding through the small building, in defiance at the Special Branch outside and the system which had condemned a good man. The memorial ended with 'We Shall Overcome' which John had so courageously taken with him as his final message, and which was immortalised at the time at American civil rights and peace demonstrations by pop icon Joan Baez and thousands of marchers. Then Peter pressed the white button on a shelf immediately under the lectern marked 'push to move coffin'.

That was it. Finished. The former sports official and political activist was incinerated.

Ad and Wal dropped the children off at their schools – each with a note for lateness.

The vicious repression of the apartheid state in the years after Sharpeville and the bomb had a huge impact on the families involved and it also radically impacted on the future direction of South African sport and society.

As the Hains had feared in arguing against their comrades' switch to ARM's sabotage strategy, the station bomb was exploited to increase state repression and to discredit and destroy the Liberal Party. Ann Harris and her toddler David, together with the Hain family, cut off, left without work or prospects, were driven into exile in Britain, to find themselves playing a decisive role in the sports apartheid struggle alongside Harris's former comrades in SANROC.[204]

With Harris dead, Dennis Brutus in jail and brave sports administrators such as George Singh harassed by the security police, SASA was forced to disband and SANROC was crippled and banned the same year. Sports leaders and organisations seeking 'fair play' through non-racial sport fell into a dissonant compliance. Hassan Howa, at the forefront of raising the flag again in the next decade, commented that things got so bad that people were even scared to speak at local ratepayers' meetings. It would be years before internal protests started again, though the anger remained particularly as millions of people would soon be forced to leave their homes and relocate to fulfil the chessboard designs of the apartheid schemers under the Group Areas Act and 'homeland consolidation' legislation, destroying generations-old community cohesion and institutions in the process as people's personal space, schools, clubs, congregations and competitions were thrown into permanent dislocated chaos.

The baton of leadership in SANROC was passed on to Chris de Broglio, by then one of the few still openly active. He was finally forced to leave South Africa in March 1964, the month before Harris was hanged. The security police had frequently descended upon the office of the French airline where he worked to pressure him. He headed for London with his wife and five children and began immediately to establish the banned SANROC in exile. De Broglio later bought the small Portman Court Hotel near Marble Arch, which became the organisation's headquarters. After Brutus was released from Robben Island in 1965, he followed his comrade into exile in London. SANROC resumed its campaigns with vigour.

Harris went to his grave that year with the small comfort of knowing that the IOC had suspended white South Africa from the 1964 Olympic Games. He would have been glad to know also that the appeals he and his SANROC colleagues made to the IOC would finally end in success when apartheid sport was expelled from the Olympic movement at the IOC's meeting in Amsterdam in 1970.

A base in the city of exiles

London was historically a city of exiles. Voltaire, Marx, Lenin, Trotsky, Sun Yat-sen and Ho Chi Minh were among the revolutionaries and dissenters who at some stage found themselves on its streets, plotting and planning.[205] By the time Chris de Broglio, Dennis Brutus, Ann Harris and the Hain family joined the rollcall of exiles in the mid-1960s, the city was teeming with displaced South Africans and the anti-apartheid and boycott movements were growing stronger.

In 1958 the president of the African National Congress, Albert Luthuli, had appealed to progressive forces internationally for a boycott of apartheid South Africa. Beginning with a targeted boycott of individual products such as Outspan oranges, it gradually expanded to sports and culture, especially in Britain, Ireland, and the Scandinavian countries (who were real stalwarts in the struggle). A worldwide campaign spread through the Organisation of African Unity, the Non-Aligned Movement, the Arab League, and other international organisations. Pressure by anti-apartheid movements eventually led the United Nations to back the boycott, although not without resistance from the apartheid government's de facto Cold War allies led by the United States and the United Kingdom, both of course with vetoes on the UN Security Council. But finally, by 1977 the UN had imposed an arms embargo and the Commonwealth had committed to the Gleneagles Agreement calling for a sports boycott.

Unlike Britain's formidable Anti-Apartheid Movement, there was no single anti-apartheid organisation in the United States, instead local 'Free South Africa' groups formed in nearly every city which, under leadership of the 'Black Caucus' of African-American representatives in Congress, helped deliver vital loan sanctions legislation against South Africa in 1986. A European association of anti-apartheid movements was also established to negotiate with the European Union, enabling EU funds to be channelled through resistance organisations in South Africa for educational and humanitarian purposes. All in all, anti-apartheid forces generated pressures through what Kader Asmal in a lecture in 2000 – by then an experienced government minister – called 'globalisation from below'.

The British Anti-Apartheid Movement, formed in 1959, became the most effective and important of all the national anti-apartheid groups. And South African exiles in turn linked up with local humanitarian, church, anti-colonial and anti-racist groupings, some with roots going back a century. For example, the Campaign Against Race Discrimination in Sport (CARDS) had been formed in Britain in 1958 by Father Trevor Huddleston, one of the earliest international voices against apartheid and subsequently president of the British Anti-Apartheid Movement. His *Naught for Your Comfort* (1956)[206] is a riveting exposé of the evil indignity of apartheid and first alerted the world to what was happening in South Africa. Presciently, Huddleston wrote: 'Just because the Union [of South Africa] is so good at sport, such isolation would shake its self-assurance very severely.'

The CARDS campaign was backed by a number of public figures, church groups and organisations. They included Fenner Brockway of the Movement for Colonial Freedom (MCF) – one of the key members of the alliance which set up the AAM in 1959 – and the South Wales Miners' Federation. The latter had expressed solidarity in the 1950s for the black American actor-singer Paul Robeson – a victim of McCarthyism – as one of their leaders, Tyrone O'Sullivan recalled. In a BBC Wales interview in 2003, he described the miners' support for the anti-apartheid movement – marching in solidarity and even sending Christmas cards to Nelson Mandela on Robben Island: 'I've always said we were the black South African a hundred years ago. We were abused and mistreated [and] remember, 50 per cent of the time we were underground we were "black" anyway!'

CARDS immediately challenged South Africa's participation in the 1958 Empire and Commonwealth Games in Cardiff. It similarly began to lobby the International Olympic Committee and British sports authorities for white South Africa's isolation. On 17 July 1958 *The Times* published a letter signed by over twenty famous sportspeople condemning the white-only composition of South Africa's Commonwealth team and calling on all participating teams to endorse 'the principle of racial equality which is embodied in the Declaration of the Olympic Games'. Amongst the star signatories were leading footballers Wally Barnes, Danny Blanchflower, Johnny Haynes, Jimmy Hill, Stanley Matthews and Don Revie; the motorcycle champion Geoff Duke; athletes Geoff Elliott, Mike Ellis, Thelma Hopkins, Derek Ibbotson, Ken Norris and Frank Sando; the boxer Joe Erskine; cricketers David Sheppard and M.J.K. Smith (both subsequently England captains); and tennis player Bobby Wilson.

CARDS then appealed to British sports clubs asking them to pass resolutions demanding that their national associations press international sports federations to adopt the same Olympic principle. They got widespread support from football clubs such as Bristol Rovers, Hull City, West

Ham United, and Dundee United. The campaign next sent a letter to the International Olympics Committee meeting at Munich in May 1959 explaining that South Africa broke the Olympic principle. It was signed by world-renowned figures such as the Archbishops of York and Cape Town, French actor and singer Maurice Chevalier, the philosopher Bertrand Russell, and Olympic star athlete Emil Zatopek. At the meeting, India, Egypt and the Soviet Union strongly supported an accompanying memorandum submitted by the South African Sports Association and by CARDS. Fearing expulsion, the South African Olympic Committee responded they had 'no objection' to non-white sportsmen being included in future Olympic teams, 'if they were good enough'.[207]

In 1960 CARDS called for a boycott of the South African cricket tour to Britain. In an unprecedented stand, the England test cricketer David Sheppard (later to play a leading anti-apartheid role when he became a bishop) refused to play. The same year, the annual meeting of cricket's ruling body, the MCC, heard in icy silence a demand that links with racist cricket should be abandoned from Rowland Bowen, the editor of *Cricket Quarterly* and a cricket historian.

Faced with the news of the all-white South African cricket team arriving in May 1960 for a summer tour of England and Wales, the AAM and CARDS protested against the invitation and urged local anti-apartheid committees to take the 'strongest possible action against the touring team's fixtures'. The London Anti-Apartheid Committee, with CARDS and MCF, met the South African team with placards at London airport on 17 April and at their Park Lane Hotel. It also distributed a leaflet on the Campaign for Nuclear Disarmament's Aldermaston march with a list of the tourists' fixtures. MCF booked a coach to take demonstrators to the first match of the tour against the Duke of Norfolk's XI at Arundel.

AAM supporters held a series of poster parades at Lords that July, braving the hostility of England cricket fans. In Nottingham, Birmingham and Bristol, anti-apartheid supporters reported that they were planning action; in August members of the local Boycott Committee in Sheffield were arrested in the act of painting slogans at the ground.

Throughout the 1960s AAM supporters demonstrated at sports events involving white South Africans. Labour Party-led Cardiff and Glasgow City Councils refused to entertain a South African bowls team after representations from the AAM, and the Cardiff AAM Group protested at the venue hosting the all-white event. In 1964 the AAM organised a picket outside a match played by a white South African tennis player at Wimbledon.

During its next tour in 1965, the whites-only Springbok cricket team was met by demonstrations at every match. The AAM sent a delegation led by Labour MP David Ennals to protest to the MCC and on the advice of the Labour government, the Queen broke with tradition to stay away from the test match at Lords. Activists picketed outside the grounds at every match, the AAM therefore laying the ground for the militancy of the Stop The Seventy Tour campaign four years later.

The legendary West Indian former cricketer and civil rights campaigner Sir (later Lord) Learie Constantine spoke at campaign launch organised in June 1965 in the House of Commons on the theme, 'the campaign against apartheid in cricket'. Sir Learie said memorably: 'Must we be hosts to people whose guests we can never be?'[208]

A few days later at an AAM rally in London's Trafalgar Square, prominent speakers included Labour and Liberal MPs, the Bishop of Johannesburg, and exiled ANC activist, Ruth First, who made a passionate appeal: 'You must pass from verbal condemnation to practical action. The people of Britain must see that their government stops dragging its feet at the United Nations whenever the question of South Africa comes up. The guilty men of apartheid are not only those who make the laws in South Africa, they are among us here in Britain – those who draw the profits from apartheid.'

The AAM collected names for a mass petition in protest at the tour and produced campaign badges.' Nearly three years later in January 1968, the Shimlas, a white-only rugby team from the University of the Orange Free State, were due to play ten university teams. Sparked by the AAM, protests by student unions and anti-apartheid activists forced most matches to be cancelled, leaving just three games still scheduled. At a match against Newcastle University at Gosforth on 31 January 1968 around fifty students protested with placards but were forced by police to keep well away from the ground. So instead they spontaneously resolved to purchase tickets and some thirty invaded the pitch – the very first instance of direct action against sports apartheid in Britain. The *Daily Telegraph* reported: 'In the second half a girl dressed in green tights and jumper with a snappy red waistcoat ran onto the pitch and almost playfully, invited half a dozen young policemen to catch her. She led them a merry dance until she tripped and then was transported bodily to the sidelines.'

The second game at St Andrews University on 2 February 1968 was also disrupted for half an hour, this time by fifty student protesters despite being threatened beforehand with severe disciplinary action if they did so. Vice-principal and Tory historian Professor Norman Gash strode onto the pitch and demanded that the protestors leave, threatening them with police dogs, which left them unmoved. A group of spectators chanting 'nigger lovers' were provoked to attack the demonstrators. Some remained steadfast and later in the game there were further invasions; a dozen were arrested and charged under Scottish law with trespass and breaching the peace.

There was widespread media coverage of these novel direct-action tactics, forcing the third and final match at Lancaster University to be abandoned, leaving anti-apartheid campaigners buoyant.

Reviving SANROC in London and institutionalising the boycott, 1965–70s

Newly arrived in London, Chris de Broglio set about reviving SANROC in 1965, linking up with the growing London-based anti-apartheid networks. Both the exiled South African Communist Party and the Anti-Apartheid Movement tried to dissuade de Broglio from continuing with SANROC as a separate organisation in exile, urging instead that he swung under their umbrella, not least because Abdul Minty, secretary of the AAM, had formally represented SANROC abroad.

De Broglio nevertheless decided to press ahead with SANROC after getting agreement from Dennis Brutus, by then out of Robben Island. Canon John Collins, head of the International Defence and Aid Fund for Southern Africa, set up in the 1950s to provide support to Chief Luthuli and the 155 other treason trialists, too, overrode belated objections from the AAM, later becoming an indispensable funder of SANROC's activities, agreeing to buy de Broglio a plane ticket to attend the International Olympic Committee meeting in Rome and to give him funds to help him set up an office.

Once in Rome, de Broglio overcame various obstacles, both political and organisational, as he was not an accredited delegate to the IOC and others had been representing the non-racial South African sports case. Spotting the IOC president, Avery Brundage, in the conference hotel lobby, de Broglio asked for a word as the representative of SANROC but was rebuffed. Brundage, an American firmly in the IOC old guard was a known apologist for the whites-only Olympic affiliate.

He had form, going back to the 1936 Berlin Olympics (discussed in Chapter 2). The US Amateur Athletics Union had voted to boycott the Games unless the Nazis granted equal sport opportunities to Jews. Brundage's rebuttal was brief and dismissive: he said that he 'knew of no religious or racial reasons why America should withdraw'. He also wrote at the time: 'Certain Jews must now understand that they cannot use the Games as a weapon in their boycott against the Nazis.'

De Broglio was undeterred and went for a beer in a bar across from the hotel, where he was recognised by a reporter for the South African *Sunday Times*. The following Sunday, the paper carried a banner headline about SANROC being in Rome, Brutus, still in South Africa, thrilled when he saw the paper, especially as his friends began congratulating him.

SANROC in exile, with funding from Canon Collins, was poised for lift-off, soon to start inflicting serious damage on white South Africa. In July 1966 de Broglio was joined in London by Brutus, his prison sentence complete and having been given permission to leave on a one-way exit permit, the same terms as Peter's parents Ad and Wal. It was the Saturday of the football World Cup Final at Wembley between England and Germany and the BBC had offered him a ticket. De Broglio, having picked him up at Heathrow airport, purchased a ticket himself and they both watched the match together, afterwards meeting up with football delegates from other countries, including the General Assembly of the African Football Confederation which was also meeting there.

The Brutus–de Broglio duet soon mounted a relentless lobbying drive against white South Africa at meetings around the world of just about every conceivable sporting organisation, over the years notching up success after success. Forced exile for them rebounded dramatically on the apartheid state.

Speaking in Parliament on 8 February 1967, the minister for the interior had declared: 'We will not allow competition between Whites and non-Whites on the playing fields.' Two months later, on 3 April, the chairman of the *Broederbond* declared in a statement: 'If the price of participation in international sport is political integration, it is too high a price to pay.'

SANROC had to show huge persistence and ingenuity in its campaign because it was up against not simply white South Africa's resources and its many allies, but the rigged structure of international sports bodies. These were cast from the era of British imperialism and European colonialism before the Second World War, despite all that had happened since its high noon. Most had been formed at the turn of the twentieth century by individuals from the colonial powers who were an 'old boys' club' of upper-class men, many aristocrats, bankers and financiers. This elite ensured the constitutions of these sports bodies gave control to countries such as Britain and the United States, and even by the 1960s and 1970s, these structures remained substantially unchanged.

In that period for example, in the International Olympic Committee only fifty-six out of 130 Olympics nations had full member status; the majority had no voting or representative rights. Out of seventy-four voting members on the IOC, over fifty came from Western Europe, the white Commonwealth and the United States. For example, Britain had two voting members and Finland three, whereas over forty Black African countries had just six members.

But the undemocratic structure of the IOC in those days did not end there. It comprised individual voting members elected only after selection and nomination by the IOC Executive which defined them as its *ambassadors* rather than representatives of their countries' National Olympic Committees. That meant IOC members sometimes ended up being opposed by their own Olympic Committees, which was the case for instance with Kenya's Reg Alexander, who proved a steadfast ally of white South Africa, on occasion angrily confronting de Broglio and Brutus.

The only way therefore that Africa could exert its power to try to exclude white South African teams was to threaten boycotts. Spurred on by SANROC and the Anti-Apartheid Movement, this happened increasingly as the grip of isolation was remorselessly tightened.

However instead of being determined by the fundamental sporting principle of merit not race, the pattern of isolation still reflected the global power imbalance within sport. White South Africa clung on in minor sports such as rowing, hockey, badminton and stock-car racing where developing nation membership was almost negligible. In other international federations like tennis and athletics voting was loaded against the influence of African and Asian countries. But in football, where one-country-one-vote operated, white South Africa was excluded early on despite vehement opposition from FIFA's old-school conservative British president Sir Stanley Rous.

When in 1966 Brutus and de Broglio travelled to Budapest to attend the congress of the International Amateur Athletics Federation, they found themselves booked by the Hungarian organisers into a hunting lodge outside the city and far from the other delegates all staying at the same hotel. But they managed to contact Nigeria's Abraham Ordia, president of the Supreme Council for Sport in Africa, who introduced them to African delegates. It was agreed that the Egyptian delegate would raise the South African question at the end of the session, but the chairman, the Marquess of Exeter, refused to call him to speak and abruptly closed the meeting in order to block discussion of the South African problem.

Even within the IOC, its white hierarchy – a product of colonialism – sought desperately to maintain South Africa's participation. IOC president Avery Brundage, the Nazi collaborator in 1936, did all he could to smuggle the whites-only South African team back in.

Manipulating the IOC's voting system, Brundage managed to secure agreement at the Grenoble IOC meeting in February 1968 to invite South Africa to the 1968 Mexico Olympics, even though most countries were strongly opposed. The decision was backed by thirty-seven votes (representing just twenty-three countries including Britain and the United States) to twenty-eight (representing twenty-five countries); around seventy countries due to send teams to the Games had no say because they had no voting rights on the IOC.

The reaction was fast and furious. Every African country except Malawi (under its pliant President Hastings Banda) announced withdrawal, followed by Asian nations, in all totalling fifty withdrawals. Black American athletes threatened a boycott. The Mexican Organising Committee refused to invite South Africa. Yet Brundage remained defiant, insisting the Games would go ahead regardless, until finally Mexico declared it would no longer stage the Games without the presence of African and Asian nations.

Facing an Olympics debacle, Brundage was, through gritted teeth, forced to back-track and the IOC Executive he controlled announced that it 'could not guarantee the safety of the South African team' in Mexico and withdrew their invitation. White South Africa's supporters on the IOC did 'an about-turn without batting an eyelid' as SANROC's de Broglio, active behind the scenes, caustically put it.[209]

In defiance, the South African prime minister, John Vorster, began to organise a 'mini Olympics', the so-called South African Games, as compensation to his white electorate. It was planned for two segments: one for white athletes, the other for blacks, in Bloemfontein in March and April 1969, quickly becoming a show for white supremacy. Black spectators were at first banned, then, after anguished concern about international reaction, admitted but only in separate spectator stands, entrances and facilities in line with apartheid. National stamps using the Olympic symbols were issued and white interest started to build up. However, the use of the Olympic Rings infuriated IOC president Avery Brundage, who immediately ordered his erstwhile South African allies to stop, having been contacted and informed by Brutus, who flew specifically to Switzerland to show him South African newspaper cuttings containing photos with the Rings.

SANROC began systematically to press countries to withdraw their teams. After the news that the socialist and anti-Nazi resistance hero Willy Brandt had been elected German chancellor, de Broglio called its London Embassy, informing them a German team was going to the apartheid mini-Olympics and arguing that would damage Germany's relations with Africa. An embassy official sent a courier to pick up a SANROC file and assured de Broglio it would be on Willy Brandt's desk later that day. The next day Germany announced its withdrawal.

One by one, other invited countries began withdrawing, including the United States and countries from Western Europe, the Games quickly degenerating into a fiasco and backfiring amidst world opposition to an all-white festival. A Games staged for 'non-whites' was packed with black schoolchildren bussed in, with all black sportsmen and women participating belonging to racially constituted sports groups. Non-racial sports groups boycotted the event, with the Johannesburg-based black newspaper *The Post* observing that the venture underlined 'the tragedy and absurdity of this country'.

It certainly cut no ice with the Olympic movement because – after a detailed case had been compiled by SANROC and presented to the meeting[210] – white South Africa was finally expelled at its Amsterdam session on 15 May 1970. It was a vindication for the banned and exiled liberation movements and the growing global anti-apartheid coalition, in particular SANROC and its leaders Brutus, de Broglio and of course Harris, who tragically never saw his Olympic mission fulfilled.

By the 1970s, the South African question was jeopardising the smooth functioning of global sport as old sports elites and their patrician leaders came under attack from newly independent nations, the Supreme Council for Sport in Africa playing a crucial role in this battle. Formed in 1966, it represented thirty countries and was a key influence in the Olympics expulsion, the stopping of the 1970 cricket tour and a range of other sports events at the time. The Supreme Council's hand was strengthened by the rising success of African sportsmen, especially in athletics where some became international stars craved by event organisers. Abraham Ordia, its president, and Jean-Claude Ganga, secretary general, proved loyal allies to SANROC.

Additional pressure also came from Eastern Bloc countries and African-Americans who were protesting against racism in US society, some of whom Brutus and de Broglio linked up with to explain the sports apartheid case. Coordinated by Professor Harry Edwards of Cornell University, they focused upon the 1969 Mexico Olympics, threatening to withdraw were white South Africa invited. Tommie Smith and John Carlos raised their fists in a Black Power salute on the winner's podium, a stance which generated worldwide impact. Both were heavily censured by US officials. Australian silver medalist, Peter Norman, supported the protest by wearing a human rights badge on his tracksuit. For this gesture he was excluded from the next Olympics and cold shouldered for decades by the Australian athletics authorities. Similarly, British swimming captain Tony Jarvis was suspended for demonstrating against apartheid at the 1970 Commonwealth Games.

As in Australia over the racist plight of the Aboriginal people, these protests interacted with racism in the United States. In his 1969 book, university professor Harry Edwards explained the background to the Black Power protest at the Olympics: 'A call to arms for many black athletes has been their realisation that once their athletic abilities are impaired by age or injury, only the ghetto beckons and they are doomed once again to that faceless, hopeless, ignominious existence they had supposedly forever left behind them.'[211] Writing of the late 1960s, with black civil rights leader Martin Luther King assassinated, Edwards argued: 'More and more people have been participating in Olympic Games for the United States, yet race relations in America are worse today than at any time since slavery.' He added, 'whites may grudgingly admit a black man's prowess as an athlete, but will not acknowledge his equality as a human being.'

One by one, South Africa had been getting the push in team sports. Only individual sports such as golf and tennis still permitted white South African participation; by and large anti-apartheid campaigners decided it was tactically unwise to target individuals, even though they were undoubtedly the privileged products of a racist sports system. Attention instead focused on whites-only team sports since these glaringly reflected the apartheid system.

The system's dirty tricks

Nobel Laureate J. M. Coetzee wrote that for white South Africans 'sport is the opium of the masses'.[212] And any doubts about their anger at the impact of stopping the 1970 cricket tour were swiftly dispelled when Peter came under a three-pronged attack from apartheid forces. They sent him a letter bomb, helped prosecute him for conspiracy and in a surreal twist set him up in 1975 for a bank theft he knew nothing about.

Even during the 1969–70 demonstrations, police planted evidence on STST activists, including drugs, knives and broken bottles and Special Branch officers persistently infiltrated radical campaigns at the time: self-nicknamed 'hairies', one called 'Mike' later boasted (quite inaccurately) about being Peter's STST 'second-in-command'. Years later, amidst controversy about the use of police undercover officers in environmental and other campaigns, the *Guardian* reported:

> Special Branch had targeted the campaign after warnings that there was likely to be 'blood on the streets'. Mike has since died but his handler, Wilf, is still very much alive. 'I don't think Hain ever realised he had a hairy as his number two.' Mike provided the intelligence that enabled the police to deal with the disruption planned for a big rugby game between the Springboks and the Barbarians at Twickenham. The demonstrators planned to throw smoke bombs and metal tacks onto the pitch, but thanks to Mike the police were ready with sand and electric magnets. News film of the time clearly shows them being used. There was the inevitable inquest into how the plan had been thwarted. 'Hain felt, quite rightly, that there was a spy in their midst,' says Wilf. 'Mike looked down the room at one poor devil and said: "I think it's him!" He was thrown out and Mike survived.'[213]

Neither Peter nor his closest surviving STST comrades recall any such incident nor any such individual called Mike, and there were emphatically no metal tacks plans because violence to players was ruled out by STST. Although there is a lurid element of hyperbolic reinvention in this account – perhaps also one of self-serving self-importance – there is no doubt that such undercover agents existed. (For example, police at the final Twickenham match in January 1970 were expecting and searched obvious demonstrators like Peter for flour bombs at the turnstiles.) However, despite being centrally planned and locally delivered by leading STST activists, no undercover agent detected or stopped the midnight raids on all county cricket grounds in January 1970, which proved decisive, first in halving the number of tour venues and matches, and second in exponentially escalating the seriousness of the threat the tour faced. (Nevertheless, after he had been invited to give evidence at the official Undercover Policing Inquiry in 2020, Peter was shown police documents confidential to the Inquiry proving that he had been targeted for surveillance for over a quarter of a century, with a British police or security service officer in almost every political meeting he attended, private or public, innocuous and routine, or serious and strategic.)

In mid-1972 things turned potentially life-threatening for the Hain family. At breakfast time in their modest terraced home one Saturday morning in June 1972, Peter's fifteen-year-old sister Sally began opening a pile of campaign mail, helped excitedly by John Harris's then eight-year-old son, David. 'What's this?' she asked as Peter looked up, horrified to see an explosive device. Recessed into a thick sheet of balsa wood were hideous metal cylinders and terminals with protruding wires.

Fortunately, there was a technical fault in the letter bomb's trigger mechanism – otherwise the entire home and all in it would have been blown up, the London Metropolitan Police's anti-terrorist bomb squad reported ominously, having made the device safe and taken it away.

South Africa had one of the world's most ruthless security services and a number of anti-apartheid activists were killed by letter bombs sent by BOSS, the South African Bureau for State Security, established in 1969. BOSS's 'Z-Squad', set up explicitly to wage such terrorist attacks, took the final letter in the alphabet because it specialised in final solutions: assassination of apartheid's enemies. One of the first victims was Dr Eduardo Mondlane, the president of the Mozambique Liberation Front, FRELIMO, who was killed in Tanzania in 1969 when a letter bomb exploded as he opened it on his desk. In 1972 (the same year as the attempt on Peter's life), the Black Consciousness student leader Abraham Tiro was similarly blown up in Botswana, shortly after he delivered a powerful address at the University of the North's graduation ceremony and had then been forced to cross the border. ANC activist Ruth First was blown up ten years later in Maputo in 1982, and in that decade the regime added car bombs to its arsenal of terror: one killed ex-Robben Islander, Joe Gqabi, and another targeted leading ANC constitutional lawyer Albie Sachs, who lost his left eye and right arm.

ANC leaders were on constant alert as their leaders became targets for assassination, their offices in foreign cities bombed and burgled, their leading figures shot and their camps in the African bush attacked by fighter planes. Anti-apartheid demonstrators were harassed and the London head-quarters of the Anti-Apartheid Movement was broken into. There was also a great deal of co-operation and outright collusion between South African security services and those of Western governments such as Britain's, as was evident during the Stop The Seventy Tour campaign, in which there were several instances of agents provocateurs deliberately inciting violence, one of whom was followed back to the South African Embassy.

Before the 1969–70 rugby tour started, BOSS printed a leaflet signed 'The Vigilantes' stating that 'counter protest cells' had been established all over the country. It appeared to come from loyalist rugby supporters and warned that any left-wing protesters who interrupted play would be 'carried off and walloped'. The leaflet was distributed to national newspapers and *The Times*, among others, reported it. During the rugby tour, BOSS distributed a press release from a hoax group, the 'Democratic Anti-Demo Organisation', which threatened to spray demonstrators with red paint and cover them with feathers, later confirmed in book by the former South African agent and journalist, Gordon Winter.[214] Winter's BOSS handler in London asked him to prepare a detailed report on Peter and on each one of the activities undertaken by the STST campaign in order to 'pin Hain to the wall'. And after his South African tour to drum up support for his private prosecution of Peter, Francis Bennion succeeded in getting him charged for criminal conspiracy on the basis that Peter's book, *Don't Play with Apartheid*, provided ready evidence of his guilt on this very unusual charge.

*

The conspiracy trial took place in August 1972 and Peter's book was triumphantly produced in court as the equivalent of a confession of guilt on the four counts of conspiracy levelled against him: covering the sit-down at Bristol tennis court, the interruption of the Wilf Isaacs cricket match, disruption of the rugby tour and the stopping of the cricket tour. Peter was charged with conspiring with 'others unknown' – even though many were well known, or could at least have been easily identified. Laid at his door were nearly a thousand individual actions, including trespass, breaches of the peace, intimidation, violence against people and property, and the antique offence of 'watching and besetting' which had centuries before been directed at highway robbers and vagrants.

Although some of these individual actions were not criminal offences, when prefixed with 'conspiracy', they were transformed into serious crimes, Peter finding himself in an Alice in Wonderland world where the law on conspiracy dating from 1304 could be manipulated as an instrument of political repression. Prosecutors backed by judges were effectively declaring: We don't like what Peter Hain was up to, interfering with our enjoyment of cricket, tennis and rugby, and we shall find a way of reinterpreting the law to stop him doing it.

The trial lasted four weeks, the court clerk taking fully seven minutes to read out the lengthy list of charges against him.[215] Soon the portentous prosecutor was launching into a day-and-a-half-long opening speech, referring to Peter's 'fertile, trouble-making propensities' and insisting that the 'very future of English civilisation' was at stake.

Precedent from a judge in an earlier conspiracy trial meant that 'conspiracy can be affected by a wink or a nod without a word being spoken', and since Peter had openly advocated direct action and played a leading role in STST, the law meant he was guilty of conspiracy from the outset, reversing the normal presumption of being innocent until proved guilty. The only way he could prove he was *not* responsible was by calling some of those who *were*. For example, a schoolteacher who on 31 December 1969 ran onto the pitch in Bristol and sprinkled tin-tacks. Although Peter had nothing to do with it and strongly disapproved because of likely injuries to players, he had been charged with conspiracy for this action too.

Various South African luminaries including the 1969–70 Springbok captain, Dawie de Villiers and 1969 cricket tour patron Wilf Isaacs, were flown over as witnesses to give evidence. The last prosecution witness was Wilf Wooller, the right-wing Welsh rugby and cricket official whose opening greeting when Peter and he first met at an Oxford Union debate during the STST campaign was: 'I hope to see you behind bars before the tour is out. And I really mean that.'

Given the oppressive, catch-all nature of the law on conspiracy, Peter's lawyers advised him it was almost impossible to prove his innocence and recommended he should not go into the witness box, because he would in all probability have convicted himself. Although certainly not guilty of over 90 per cent of the particulars charged, he was nevertheless guilty of coordinating and organising action to disrupt and stop the various sports events and tours. Michael Sherrard, Peter's experienced Queen's Counsel, thought that the judge, Bernard Gillis, was after an exemplary prison sentence, and was especially concerned about a likely question from the judge as to what 'exactly was his client's defence in law'. It appeared there was none, in which case Peter's defence would collapse instantly. However, Peter could not be asked that question because he was not a lawyer. Once Sherrard and his deputy, Brian Capstick, had cross-examined prosecution witnesses, it was decided that Peter should effectively 'sack' his barristers and defend himself. By conducting his own case he could appeal directly to the jury on a basis of justice. Through his opening and closing speeches for the defence and by examining witnesses, he would be talking to the jury without being cross-examined in the witness box.

It was a daunting task as Peter had no legal training, though he was by then an experienced public speaker and saw it as part of fighting the anti-apartheid cause, as a conviction could open the way for other such prosecutions. In summary, Peter told the court that he 'stood broadly by' what he had written in *Don't Play with Apartheid*, but insisted that it had not been written 'as a confession'. There had been no lawyer vetting every sentence in anticipation that it could be transformed from something written for readability into a legal document in which the interpretation of even the most casual sentence was liable to land him up in prison. Clearly exasperating an openly hostile Judge Gillis, Peter's mention of 'prison' was premeditated in order to alert the jury to that outcome.

He emphasised his opposition to violent protest and insisted that he had been honest and open about his role and objectives. He had never hidden his commitment to non-violent direct action – indeed had publicly proclaimed it. It was no sinister, covert conspiracy. STST was disarmingly open and candid. Furthermore, Peter pointed out: 'The campaign was a loose movement. It was not a rigid organisation. We had no generals. We had no apparatus through which to conspire.' It was quite ludicrous to charge him with nearly a thousand offences committed the length and breadth of the British Isles. Moreover, it was oppressive to frame the conspiracy charge in such a way that, if he was found guilty of one particular offence, he was guilty of the lot. The jury's verdict would be given only on each of the four counts rather than their contents.

This was iniquitous, Peter argued, because, even if the jury found him not guilty of hundreds of offences in the four counts of conspiracy, there was no way of the judge knowing this when he passed sentence. The jury might decide he was guilty only of the trivial offences or those which were strictly non-violent. But the judge could not know this and might assume guilt for the most serious or violent offences. However, the iniquities of the then law on conspiracy meant that it was the *conspiracy* that mattered, rather than the particular actions or offences. And since STST was clearly an organisation of which Peter was the leading public figure, this made his defence an uphill battle.

Archbishop Trevor Huddleston, president of the Anti-Apartheid Movement, appeared in his clerical clothes to give evidence about non-violent direct action and the evil of apartheid. A series of activists were lined up to testify that they had organised local protests – from scattering tin-tacks and digging up cricket pitches, to demonstrations outside the grounds – quite independently of Peter. The prosecution objected and Judge Gillis became increasingly testy, until eventually Peter was stopped from putting questions.

The defence witness subject to the most hostile cross-examination was Ethel de Keyser, the indomitable executive secretary of the Anti-Apartheid Movement, herself a South African exile and friend of Peter's. Over two days she was asked 218 questions by the prosecution and, despite being on the receiving end of a QC skilled at tying witnesses in knots, she never flinched. With almost uncanny precision, she skipped deftly between his barbs, her composure never ruffled. She looked carefully at several STST campaign bulletins giving details of upcoming demonstrations and said she had never seen one before, which meant they could not be presented as evidence before the jury. So effective was her performance that the prosecuting QC was unable to make any use of her evidence in his final address to the jury. But when he questioned her about the Anti-Apartheid Movement's annual general meeting in October 1969, it became apparent he was working from a transcript of a secret tape recording made by either a South African or British security agent. It contained a potential trump card because Peter had spoken of STST's direct action plans at that meeting. But that was thwarted because de Keyser was unable to confirm the prosecutor's detailed account of that meeting held three years before.

Although de Keyser emerged unscathed from her two-day ordeal in the witness box, it was salutary for Peter and his small team. With a hostile judge and the now obvious danger of inadvertently revealing such ricochet ammunition for the prosecution, there was a danger that new evidence would be uncovered against Peter. Other than his book, the prosecution had little if any evidence of his direct culpability. Peter and his solicitor decided not to call a queue of other witnesses, some of them outside waiting to give evidence, his mother Adelaine included.

Instead they proceeded to a pre-planned but unannounced conclusion to the defence case. Labour MP Peter Jackson and the imposing, robed Colin Winter, bishop-in-exile of Damaraland, South West Africa, were both stopped by the judge from answering questions confirming their publicly stated intention to run onto cricket pitches – quite independently of Peter. Anticipating this, Peter protested that legal procedures were being used to stop him from mounting his defence properly. He abruptly announced that, although he had plenty of witnesses ready to be called, he had no alternative but to close his case.

The judge was furious, seeing perfectly well how the jury would view Peter as a victim. So was the prosecutor, forced to stumble immediately into what transpired was a long, boring closing statement to the jury over two days with the nightmare of a weekend break intervening and the jury forgetting what his arguments were. He concluded with a flourish: if Peter were let off, it would be 'an incitement to politically inspired law breaking' on such a massive scale that England's green and pleasant civilisation faced the terrible threat of anarchy – with, for example, homeless families occupying empty properties, Jews protesting at the Russian ballet, Palestinians disrupting performances by Israeli artists. All that stood in the path of that appalling prospect was the jury.

In his closing speech, Peter took two days to dissect the evidence and insist that his was an open, honest campaign in which he had never sought to hide his role or anti-apartheid objectives. This was a 'scapegoat prosecution' in a 'politically motivated' trial. He reminded jurors of the honourable tradition of non-violent direct action – from Chartists and Suffragettes demanding the vote in Britain, to Gandhi over independence for India and black Americans demanding civil rights in the United States. Every sentence, every word had to be judged carefully for he knew too well that only the jury stood between him and imprisonment.

Repeatedly interrupted by Judge Gillis – another departure from the court convention that allows closing speeches to be delivered without challenge – it was transparent he was in a political trial. Furthermore, Judge Gillis's laborious, three-day summing up was, legal observers believed, so biased as to constitute a basis for appeal should Peter be convicted.

After a weekend break, the jury retired to consider their verdict at 10:35

a.m. on Monday 22 August 1972. Conscious he could face prison, Peter had packed a few clothes and toiletries, and was taken down and confined to the cells below the court to await his fate alongside other inmates mystified about his presence amongst the criminal classes.

Six long hours later there was a jangle of keys and a warder said the court was reconvening, Peter shown ominously into the dock instead of the well of the court where he had previously sat. The twelve jurors all looked strained, the foreman nervously announcing that they could not agree on any of the four conspiracy counts. A frisson swept through the by now packed court room, the press section bulging, Peter's spirits rising at this unexpected development.

The judge informed them solemnly that he would now accept a majority verdict 'if ten of you are in agreement' and Peter was taken back down and locked up, tense and wondering what fate awaited him. Finally, at 5:57 p.m. the jury trooped back in all looking glum. The foreman announced 'yes', that Peter was guilty on the third count, the peaceful Davis Cup tennis court sit-down at Bristol – by far the least serious.

But then came a dramatic twist. Pressed hard by the judge, the foreman stated that they could not agree on any of the remaining three counts. There were gasps of relief from spectators and smiles all round, Peter overcome with both elation and vindication, the judge and prosecutors looking thunderous. As *The Sunday Times* reported: 'It was evident that Hain had succeeded in going over the heads of the prosecution and the judge and influencing the majority of the jury with his political philosophy.' It was confirmed later that the two black jurors held out even against Peter's conviction over the tennis disruption. They were joined by others in refusing to convict on the much more serious and imprisonable rugby and cricket tour counts. On those the judge directed that 'verdicts of not guilty be recorded'. He ticked Peter off, fined him £200 and he was free to go.

After all the efforts from apartheid South Africa and the huge panoply and expense of a month-long trial in the Central Criminal Court, Peter now had a criminal conviction for peacefully sitting on a tennis court for a couple of minutes. He was elated: the 'Pain for Hain' prosecution had failed in its fundamental objective, to remove him from a leadership role in the anti-apartheid struggle. The verdict was greeted with widespread disappointment in the white South African media. Notwithstanding grim warnings from the prosecutor about the verdict, so far as could be ascertained England's green and pleasant civilisation remained intact.

*

Although Peter was used to being a target for dirty tricks by the apartheid machine, nothing compared with an experience so surreal as to be almost fictional on Friday 24 October 1975, when a bunch of police officers turned up at his front door to arrest him for bank theft.[216]

It turned out to be at a branch of Barclays Bank near his home in Putney, outside which he had demonstrated several years earlier as part of the Anti-Apartheid Movement's campaign to get Barclays to disinvest from South Africa.

Quite unbeknown to Peter, a man roughly his age and roughly his appearance snatched a bundle of five-pound notes totalling £490 from the bank cashier. He ran down the High Street, pursued by several bank staff who were joined by several schoolboys. He then ran up a side street, turned around obligingly, said, 'All right, here you are then', tossed the money back, and conveniently disappeared.

Within an hour, Peter was locked up in a cell for the rest of the day, in a confusing swirl of thoughts as the hours dragged by, nothing happening, no explanations, nobody to speak to. What made it worse was he had not the slightest idea about the theft. How had it happened?

After eleven hours in detention, he was eventually charged despite vehemently protesting his innocence and arrived home at around three on the Saturday morning, shell-shocked. Later that day, the police leaked the news to the media and he found himself facing 'HAIN IN BANK THEFT' headlines.

The unreal sequence of events took another twist on the Monday when his photograph appeared on the front page of the *London Evening Standard* with the caption: 'Peter Hain, due to appear on an identification parade today'. Bank staff later confirmed in court that copies of the newspaper had been in their office and that they had read it before attending the parade. Perhaps this was why the cashier from whom the money had been snatched came down the line and straight back to Peter, placing her hand on his shoulder.

Later that evening, however, came about the only break he got in six miserable months during which the case consumed his life and because of which he had virtually to abandon his Sussex University doctoral thesis. Terry MacLaren, the older of the three schoolboys, saw Peter on the evening television news pictured outside the police station after the identification parade. 'That's not the man. They've got the wrong one,' he told his father, who, fortunately for Peter, contacted his solicitor the next day.

Quite spontaneously, journalists, political acquaintances and others began discussing whether Peter had been set up by the South Africans. This was common currency among almost everybody intrigued by the case, especially as it became clear that he was strongly asserting his innocence as a victim of mistaken identity. But although a South African connection seemed all too plausible, direct evidence was absent. For all he knew he was simply a victim of the vagaries of identification evidence (which at the time was being exposed almost monthly for its notorious unreliability) combined with police malice: during his detention, one of the investigating detectives belligerently told Peter: 'You have caused a lot of trouble with your protests and we are going to make this charge stick on you.'

Various characters approached Peter alleging that a South African agent had committed the theft. Then on 9 March 1976 Prime Minister Harold Wilson astonished the House of Commons when he said, 'I have no doubt at all, there is strong South African participation in recent activities relating to the . . . Liberal Party,' adding there had been 'very strong and heavily financed private masterminding of certain political operations'. This South African participation, he stated, was 'based on massive resources of business money and private agents of various kinds and various qualities'. Later he also referred specifically to the Hain case. This set the media off in pursuit of more details.[217]

In the absence of hard evidence, Peter had to remain content at fighting for his innocence within the rules of a conventional criminal trial, while strongly suspecting that he was really the victim of a much larger South African plot.

*

For two full weeks at the end of March and into April 1976 the Queen v. Peter Hain played to a packed house in the Old Bailey's court eight. One eyewitness gave evidence that the thief was 'South African' in appearance. And the prosecution tried half-heartedly to suggest that, since Peter had been active in the campaign to get Barclays Bank to withdraw from South Africa, Peter might have staged the theft as a political protest. Otherwise South Africa hardly received a mention in the proceedings.

There were no surprises in the prosecution evidence – except that in court it seemed if anything even flimsier. The unreliability – at times in-congruity – of identification evidence featured throughout. As *The Sunday Times* (then edited by the legendary Harold Evans) reported:

> A confusing picture has emerged of the culprit as a sharp-featured, dark-eyed man, sometimes wearing spectacles, sometimes not, aged between 23 and 30 and anything from 5 feet 10 inches to 6 feet 2 inches in height, of medium build, very skinny, quite slim, with a long face, very drawn and white, of normal complexion but needing a shave, a very 'sallow' complexion with a darkish tinge, foreign looking, possibly Spanish, Egyptian or 'Afrikaans', not foreign, with black curly hair worn collar length, not very long fluffy hair reaching just below the ears, shortish wavy brown hair with ginger tints, wearing light-blue jeans and dark trousers as well as a white check shirt, a blue check shirt, a cream shirt with puffed sleeves, a light shirt with dark stripes, a cream waist-coat made of thick velvet wool, white tennis shoes and brown suede 'Hush Puppies'.

The case progressed in a bizarre fashion as even the cashier who had picked Peter out on the identification parade was hesitant, saying she had seen the thief only for a 'split second' and at one point was seemingly unable to pick Peter out in court – even though he was sticking out in the dock like a sore thumb. She also confirmed she had seen Peter periodically on tele-vision well before the theft took place, and in the newspaper just before the identification parade.

Apart from two twelve-year-old schoolboys – whose evidence was em-barrassingly inconsistent – and the cashier, no other witness was able to identify Peter: not even the bank's accountant who had led the half-mile chase behind the thief, who told the court that he knew Peter's face well from television and the newspapers and said he was not the man. The fingerprint analyst confirmed that Peter's prints had not been on any of the notes – though there was a fresh 'unknown' print on the top note.

Fortunately, evidence by Terry MacLaren proved decisive. Peter's soli-citor described him as 'a witness in a million' – he was remarkably composed, fluent and totally convincing in his emphatic insistence the thief was someone else. Peter's QC concluded: 'Members of the jury, the bare bones of the story just don't hang together. This is a classic case of mistaken identity.'

But then came yet another twist to the strange proceedings. The judge, Alan King-Hamilton, was a member of the Marylebone Cricket Club – and Peter its bête noire during the Stop The Seventy Tour campaign. Senior members of the legal profession confirmed later that King-Hamilton had been keen to try the case and that court administrators were equally happy to give it to him. In a quite extraordinary summing up, he suggested without any substantiation that Peter's wife, mother and a friend staying with her, may have been untruthful alibi witnesses; though the prosecution never suggested that. He also introduced a ridiculous new hypothesis – about why the clothes Peter had been wearing were different to the thief's – which he then had to withdraw under joint challenge from defence and prosecution, the latter worried that it compromised their case because no evidence had been presented supporting that hypothesis. Judge King-Hamilton's open hostility shocked even the most experienced lawyers and was the talk of the bar for some time. At best he might have confused the jury and at worst he raised serious doubts in their minds as to Peter's innocence.

Perhaps that helped explain why after five tense hours, during which the jury were called back and advised to reach a majority verdict, they finally pronounced 'not guilty'. Justice done – despite the police, despite the judge – and despite the South African security services behind this 'Putney Plot'.[218]

Although the Putney affair may have appeared an isolated event, a weird one-off, it coincided with an extraordinary period in British politics in 1974–76, during which there was a concerted drive to establish a new right-wing dominance in Britain. This contained a number of different threads which converged into a common purpose and which others subsequently analysed.[219]

By the mid-1970s key sections in the British establishment had become increasingly alarmed at what they believed was a leftward political drift in Britain and had taken steps to reverse this. The escalating crisis in Northern Ireland, the growth of the left in both the trade unions and the Labour Party, successful extra-parliamentary protest and direct action such as STST, trade union and student militancy – all were seen to pose a major threat. Successful miners' strikes horrified conservative forces who viewed these as seditious victories for trade union power over the state and felt the country was staring into an abyss of anarchy.[220]

In 1971 with the crisis escalating in Northern Ireland, the British Army established the Information Policy Unit, officially denying its existence, but which became an instrument of 'disinformation' and 'black propaganda'. Its leading operative was a local army information official, Colin Wallace, who became senior information officer at the army headquarters outside Belfast from May 1968 to February 1975. When he left the service in 1976 after a distinguished career, Wallace provided detailed evidence on 'Psychological Operations' – or psy-ops as they were known in the trade – including establishing front organisations and organising paramilitary projects.

The distinction between 'legitimate' targets, such as the IRA or the Protestant paramilitaries, and 'illegitimate' targets in Britain became increasingly blurred. Wallace confirmed that, over the years, his psy-ops work was steadily widened to cover figures and groups on the left in British politics – and here 'left' was defined in very broad terms, to cover anybody not identifiably on the hard right, including members of the Labour and Liberal Parties, and even 'liberal' Tories such as Prime Minister Edward Heath. By 1973 Wallace and his colleagues were working very closely with the British security services on 'British' rather than 'Irish' intelligence work. The 'Irish crisis' had come to be merged with what they perceived to be a 'British crisis'.

Among the many people Wallace recalled being asked to monitor and sift intelligence on was Peter, who interviewed Wallace at a meeting at his home in Sussex early in 1987. Wallace told him: 'We saw you as an important target in the long term. You were clearly on your way up in politics. Through your anti-apartheid activities and your involvement in radical campaigns, you had offended many people on the right, and it was important to neutralise you.'

Wallace stated that intelligence information fed from MI5 to his office in Northern Ireland was then 'recycled' with the assistance of the CIA to news agencies in America including TransWorldNews, the North Atlantic News Agency and Forum World Features. (Gordon Winter wrote an article in the latter in 1970 on leading anti-apartheid figures, including Brutus and Peter.) When this planted information appeared either in US newspapers or international dispatches from these agencies, Wallace and his colleagues would then pick it up in Belfast as 'hard' information and supply it both to MI5 and to government ministers.

Thus MI5 could use its own recycled information, 'disinformation' or 'black propaganda' – Wallace told Peter that all three types were involved – contained in apparently independent sources to give credibility to its activities against political opponents or provide corroboration for its suspicions. Evidence of a plot involving elements in the British and South African security services to disrupt the Liberal and Labour Parties was confirmed in 1987 by the retired MI5 agent Peter Wright.[221]

Significantly, MI5 was concerned that Labour would take tougher action against South Africa and the illegal Smith regime in Rhodesia – thus 'encouraging Marxist influence in Southern Africa'. Wallace added: 'Most of my work during this period was being used by others for totally unconstitutional ends.' He explained that this created an atmosphere in which he and his colleagues found it steadily more difficult to distinguish between, for example, a suspected IRA bomber and a British anti-apartheid activist. Information on both was being fed across his desk. Both appeared on target lists and in his security files. Both represented a common threat, and both therefore were legitimate targets. Wallace showed Peter a newspaper cutting alongside which he had recorded: 'Hain's family deported from SA for communist activity.'

Fifteen years after the files had been prepared and twelve years after Peter's arrest, Wallace described this technique as 'guilt by tenuous association'. Peter was just one of many to whom it was applied. A flagrantly false entry on MI5 records about his parents' 'communist activity' provided a pretext for Peter's anti-sports apartheid protests to be associated first with Soviet communism and then back full circle to Irish terrorism. As Wallace also confirmed, it was not hard to envisage how, on that basis, action to discredit Peter could be rationalised by members of the security services. Wallace confirmed that, not only did he work closely with MI5 and the CIA but (as Winter had also stated) both these agencies then worked with BOSS.

To summarise: throughout the 1970s there was what may be described as a hard right project to roll back the post-war social democratic political consensus supported by all the major parties – a project which eventually succeeded with the advent of Thatcherism in 1979. This contained perfectly legitimate elements, such as the democratic espousal of new right ideology and the open promotion of Margaret Thatcher for the Tory leadership and subsequently the premiership. But it also contained illegitimate elements. At one end of the spectrum were rightist pressure groups and shadowy military networks. At the other was Peter Wright's MI5 faction.

Over the Barclays Bank theft case, the interests of the British hard right and the South Africans coincided. Wright testified that the MI5 faction was openly sympathetic to white South Africa during the height of the Cold War because it was seen as an ally against 'international communism'.

Wallace corroborated this, adding that information was regularly 'traded' between MI5 and BOSS. Even joint operations were carried out where the agencies shared common objectives, as Winter confirmed.

Consequently, in framing Peter for the theft, BOSS was likely to have had the active or tacit support of members of the rightist MI5 group. This would have given BOSS both the 'cover' and operational back-up necessary. Assistance from MI5 agents would also have opened up channels to ensure he was linked to the crime.

Quoting his former London 'handler' – Winter reported that a BOSS agent had been watching Peter's home in a parked car with a walkie-talkie radio who alerted the real thief to act. Immediately after committing the theft, the man was flown to Paris and then to South Africa to start a new life. Winter added that shortly after the theft BOSS arranged for Scotland Yard to be called to link Peter to the crime. The caller told the Yard to check on Special Branch files where they would find he had campaigned actively against Barclays' involvement in South Africa, including at the very same Putney Branch.

Wallace told Peter he had established through a then serving British Intelligence officer the contents of a record held by the security services in London. According to Wallace, it stated that almost immediately after the bank theft the Metropolitan Police were tipped off by MI5 that Peter was responsible. Wallace said the security service record confirmed BOSS's involvement. The record also showed there was an earlier attempt to set Peter up some weeks before, but this failed to implicate him sufficiently.

However, as with many South African intelligence activities across the world at the height of apartheid, the real crime remained conveniently unsolved and the real bank thief was never identified.

*

Another visible attack on Peter came in the form of an expensive 3,000-word smear-sheet, 'The Hidden Face of the Liberal Party'. It used various reports of Peter's Stop The Seventy Tour campaigns taken viciously out of context. There were lurid photographs of the 1964 station bomb in Johannesburg, implying that the then fourteen-year-old Peter was somehow responsible. Hundreds of thousands of copies were distributed in key parliamentary seats where the Liberals might have been expected to do well in the

October 1974 election.

Contained in the broadsheets (one was also produced on the Labour Party, with a joint print run of about three million) were the by now familiar themes of the hard right: extremism in the Liberals and Labour and allegations of subservience to Moscow. They were published by the Foreign Affairs Publishing Company, which had close links with white South Africa, British Intelligence and the CIA. In view of the huge production costs, the broadsheets must have been financed by the South African intelligence services and indeed fitted an emerging pattern of disinformation, destabilisation and disruption.

*

These dirty trick interventions by the British and South African establishments severely impacted on Peter's day-to-day life in the early 1970s, but he nevertheless continued to be active.

Early in 1972 he was invited to give evidence to the UN Special Committee Against Apartheid in New York, its principal secretary (and later director of the UN Centre Against Apartheid) the redoubtable E. S. Reddy, who did much to further the cause. Other British anti-apartheid leaders including long-serving AAM secretary Abdul Minty were regular witnesses at its sessions, as were New Zealand's Trevor Richards and SANROC leaders. The AAM urged the government to revoke Britain's 'no visa' arrangement with South Africa so that it could ban individual players from entering the country and from 1980, the UN Special Committee worked with SANROC and the AAM to compile an international register of sportsmen and women who breached the boycott, those from Britain together with the United States being by far the biggest offenders: between 1980 and 1987 more than 700 British sportspeople visited South Africa.[222]

Where anti-apartheid activists had succeeded with direct action on cricket, rugby remained a difficult nut to crack. Springbok tours had been blocked in Britain and Australia, but it was very difficult to prevent teams visiting South Africa and, despite opposition, England went ahead with their tour in 1972. By this time the Stop All Racist Tours campaign (SART) of which Peter was chair had been launched, and a group of demonstrators disrupted the England training session in Twickenham. SART also arranged for the team coach to be hemmed in at their hotel in Richmond prior to their departure for Heathrow Airport. Just before the coach was due to leave, the fire brigade was called, which descended on the hotel in force. Additionally, requests were made for several skips to be brought, ostensibly to take away rubble, but in fact to block the team's departure.

However, the tour went ahead, as did one by the British Lions in 1974. Prior to the latter's departure, Peter was one of a dozen activists who broke through security and staged a rooftop occupation of the Rugby Union's offices at Twickenham. Peter also helped organise a demonstration at the Lions' London hotel and occupied its reception area, forcing the hotel management to persuade the captain, Willie John McBride, to meet him. But there was absolutely no meeting of minds, and the Lions proceeded, indifferent to their complicity in sports apartheid. However, the Labour foreign minister, Joan Lestor, a stalwart of the Anti-Apartheid Movement, instructed the British Embassy to withdraw the usual courtesy facilities for a visiting national side from the Lions.

Once there, they played whites-only teams, to return in triumph, unbeaten, their dazzling play with legendary Welsh quarterbacks sweeping all aside. Afterwards much was made of the support they had from black and coloured fans, but the latter had long backed anybody against the hated white Springboks, seen as symbolising apartheid.

Jonathan Steele of the *Guardian* had previously written of the STST campaign on 5 March 1970:

> It is not hard to find South Africans who are delighted by the
> demonstrations against the Springboks. Go into Soweto . . .
> or into any other African township . . . and if you are not accom-
> panied by a white South African, the masks fall. Eagerly they
> want the news confirmed. 'Is it true that they are having to use
> a thousand police to hold back the demonstrators today?' . . .
> Their views on the Springbok tour were straightforward.
> They were against it. And so were their neighbours, and anyone
> else you talked to.

As significant was the realisation amongst South Africa's white rugby fraternity that their now limited scope for international competition had damaged the Springboks' competitiveness.

The Lions returned to face a demonstration at a Heathrow Airport hotel reception. Peter's young sister Sally managed to throw a flour bomb which burst on the shoulder of the former Conservative prime minister, Edward Heath, who was there to greet the team. However, in March 1974, the avowedly Nazi British National Front organised a counter-demonstration in support of the tour against an anti-apartheid protest, one of the their placards emblazoned with 'Repatriate Peter Hain'.

The National Front demonstration and the conspiracy trial, the letter-bomb episode and the Barclays Bank robbery set-up all showed the determination of right-wing forces in Britain, South Africa and other Western countries to roll back progressive advances in a decolonising world. Many anti-apartheid activists suffered similar harassment, if not so dramatic. For example, Kader Asmal and his wife Louise, leaders of the Irish Anti-Apartheid Movement and a SANROC executive member also faced attacks from apartheid agents in the form of false information, and pressure on the Irish intelligence agencies and on their employers.

Inside South Africa, the openly repressive actions of the security agencies that marked the 1960s continued, as shown by the death by letter bomb of Abraham Tiro and assassination of Dr Rick Turner in Durban in the early 1970s. Non-racial sports officials and activists continued to face harassment and persecution. Teachers lost jobs or were transferred to remote areas. Local authorities banned non-racial codes from certain municipal facilities. But these actions did not deter opposition. In fact, they were giving energy to a new wave of resistance that was building in South African sport.

5

SACOS and the revival of the sports struggle inside South Africa

By the late 1960s white rule seemed on the surface to be absolute, apartheid unshakeable. The main opposition groups, such as the African National Congress, Pan Africanist Congress and South African Communist Party, were banned and many of their leaders were jailed or had gone into exile.

The same was true for non-racial sports leaders. Harsh new laws allowed extended periods of detention without trial and apartheid's grand plans were intensified through large-scale forced removals and a school system – known as 'Bantu Education' – which deliberately fostered an unskilled black population. Not only was the white minority running the country with an iron hand, they were also better off than ever before. During the 1960s, the greatest economic boom in the country's history (with a growth rate equalled only by Japan) had bought what one commentator called 'a careless affluence rivalling that of Californians'. Western countries were comfortable with the regime and the American magazine *Fortune* could conclude that 'South Africa is one of those rare and refreshing places where profits are great and problems are small. Capital is not threatened by political instability or nationalization. Labour is cheap, the market booming, the currency hard.'[223]

This confidence was misplaced. The outward signs of unchallengeable, *kragdadige* (heavy-handed) white rule masked vulnerabilities that surfaced from the late 1960s onwards. There were several indications, starting with the growing international opposition to apartheid reflected in the militant anti-apartheid protests in sport, and more significantly in the rapid process of decolonisation taking place in Africa and Asia. A new international architecture arose from the mid-1960s onwards, which created a long-term platform for effective anti-apartheid action, starting with the creation of the Organisation of African Unity and its allied Supreme Council for Sport in Africa, a reshaped post-independence grouping of Commonwealth nations, the growing influence of the Non-Aligned Movement of so-called 'third world' countries, the support of the Soviet Union and its Warsaw Pact allies for anti-colonial liberation struggles, and finally increasing opposition to apartheid at the United Nations.

The cancellation of rugby and cricket tours and Apartheid South Africa's expulsion from the Olympic movement indicated the tightening of international pressure and the real threats of full isolation. The direct-action driven sports boycott from 1970 onward left white South Africa shell-shocked and both its state and sports authorities were forced to ponder on how they could effectively respond without jeopardising the fundamental power structures of apartheid.

Sports-starved whites looked to their government for an initiative. It was forthcoming on 22 April 1971 when the prime minister, John Vorster, unveiled his new 'multinational' sports policy. This allowed the different racial groups in South Africa – classified as whites, Africans, coloureds and Asians – to compete against each other as four separate 'nations' within the country, but only in major international events with foreign participation. 'Multinational' became the buzzword in establishment sport. The significance of this was that it confirmed the essential case for the boycott: that change would only be forced under the pressure of isolation. However, the concession merely expressed the logic of apartheid: that each racial group should develop separately in their own 'nations' – provided of course that the ruling white minority remained in overall control and kept the spoils for themselves. White teams would continue to represent the country abroad. Crucially, Vorster added: 'I want to make it very clear that in South Africa no mixed sport shall be practised at club, provincial, or national levels.'

Thus, in the 'South African Games' in Pretoria two years later, amid a fanfare of publicity aimed at influencing world opinion, black sportspeople were officially allowed to compete against whites for the first time. Photographs of such 'history in the making' were whisked around the world by government propagandists and their sports allies as if to herald a new dawn. But outside these events staged primarily for the cameras and directed at an international audience, the structure of segregated sport from school and club to provincial and national levels continued unabated. The often bizarre, disruptive consequences for sportspeople as a result of apartheid also continued as a result of this 'new' sports policy. Karate Springbok captain Glen Popham won a gold medal at the South African Games but, although his teammates were granted Springbok colours, he was not, because in the meantime he had been hauled before the Race Classification Board and reclassified from white to coloured.

Even in rugby, an image of change was contrived. It mid-1974, when the British Lions toured, almost all their matches were played as usual against white teams (including of course the all-important tests). But two were played against a 'Bantu XV' (Africans) called the Leopards and a 'Coloured XV', the Proteas. The reality behind the facade was revealed by official figures from the minister of sport. These showed that black participation was minimal. In 1975 a total of 6,917 South African sportsmen participated in 'multinational' events. In the language of apartheid, of these 6,393 (92.4 per cent) were whites, 331 (4.8 per cent) 'Bantu' or Africans, 135 (2 per cent) coloureds and 58 (0.8 per cent) Asians. Of the thirty-nine sports in which multinationals were staged inside South Africa, just three (wrestling, golf and tennis) involved people from each of the four racial groups.

By the abnormal standards of apartheid South Africa, the changes introduced were significant – in many respects unthinkable prior to 1970. But they were otherwise entirely superficial. The sports system was given a face-lift, with racial restrictions being relaxed in certain very limited senses and usually during prestige events likely to attract international attention. At club level, however, where fundamental change needed to occur to have any meaning for most sportsmen and women, restrictions were hardly eased at all. The official attitude was that whereas the national level could be controlled and contained, matters could get out of hand in a way that could so easily spill over into the whole of society if sports integration started seriously to occur locally. As an MP said in South Africa's House of Assembly as late as 21 May 1979: 'Integrated clubs and integrated sport constitute far less than 1 per cent of the total sport activities in South Africa.'

Not only was the regime facing growing international pressure from the late 1960s, but it was also being threatened by a resurgence of internal resistance and a changing geopolitical situation which would have a significant impact on both political and sporting developments inside the country in the medium to long term. The banned ANC, with its strong international anti-apartheid connections, showed signs that it was slowly but surely reconstituting itself in exile. In 1968 it launched its first conventional military campaign, clashing with South African and Rhodesian security forces in Wange (Wankie), and the following year it convened the Morogoro Conference in Tanzania, where it adopted a clear programme after dissatisfied cadres called for a re-evaluation of the exiled struggle.

Very importantly, internal protests once again resurfaced after a decade of repression. An emergent Black Consciousness movement came to the fore, particularly after the formation of the South African Students' Organisation (SASO) headed by charismatic medical student Steve Biko. Black Consciousness emphasised the need for black people to liberate themselves psychologically as a prelude to political liberation. Unlike the PAC a decade earlier, SASO readily included in the definition of 'black' people from the Indian and coloured communities, who shared common experiences of discrimination with Africans. However, it decided to 'aggressively reject any involvement with white liberals so as to impress on blacks the need to take the initiative in their own struggle'. The role of white sympathisers was to work for change within their own communities.[224]

As one historian noted, Black Consciousness 'brought to the surface an outpouring of anger and frustration held in check during the preceding decade':

> The message of the movement was simple and compelling. It was
> also flexible and ambiguous enough to accommodate a range of older
> black political attitudes, though . . . not all of them. At the core of the
> message was a call for black reliance and self-assertion . . . A deep sense
> of inferiority, inculcated through the system of Bantu Education and
> reinforced by white arrogance, had to be erased and replaced by pride in
> black values. Fear of whites and of the government had to be replaced by
> a new courage built on group solidarity. All victims of white oppression
> had to draw together, not to indulge in self-pity as victims, but to find
> strength in numbers and to work together to bring about fundamental
> changes. Just how the apartheid system might eventually fall could not
> be foreseen, nor could SASO discuss the subject openly without stepping
> over the line between legal and illegal activity. But no doubts existed
> about the ultimate objective – liberation through revolution – or about
> the urgent need for black South Africans to go on the offensive as a first
> step towards this end.[225]

With its focus on mental emancipation, the Black Consciousness movement also had a strong cultural component. Afro hairstyles and the adoption of African rather than Western names became the vogue. A new generation of writers and poets such as Oswald Mtshali, Mafika Gwala and Mongane

Wally Serote emerged; and Gibson Kente, Mzwandile Maqina and others produced dynamic theatre. On the religious level, black theology became popular, asking the question: 'In terms of our own experience as blacks in South Africa to what extent is Jesus Christ identified with the plight of the black oppressed masses?'[226]

At the same time as the rise of Black Consciousness, economic factors were also conspiring to put apartheid under pressure. Following the world-wide recession that accompanied the Israeli–Arab War and the OPEC oil price hikes in the early 1970s, the South African economy entered a sustained period of crisis and recession, relieved only periodically after that by short upturns made possible by rises in the price of the country's main commodity, gold.[227] The recession brought unemployment and inflation. The government's refusal to recognise the permanence of the ever-increasing urban African population aggravated poor township conditions. Wages were at a poverty level. These conditions, coupled with the lack of avenues for the expression of black views, led to a dramatic growth of militancy and organisation. The repressive calm of the 1960s was broken as workers throughout the country began to organise and make demands, starting with strikes in Durban in 1973. Their actions led to the emergence of a mass-based democratic trade union movement, which by the end of the 1970s had become a significant force in South African politics.[228]

On top of these developments, successful struggles for independence in the neighbouring countries of Mozambique and Angola (and later Zimbabwe) led to the collapse of the colonial rule in those countries. The African revolution had breached the colonial *cordon sanitaire* protecting apartheid South Africa and arrived at the very borders of the white South, infusing the disenfranchised masses with a sense of their own potential. A number of developments in the early 1970s, economic, political and military, thus gave rise to a new militancy within South Africa. Political events moved fast as the black majority emerged from the bleak period of the 1960s and early 1970s in energetic resistance. The role of international campaigners moved increasingly to supporting that internal fight as the torch of resistance to apartheid passed back to those inside the country.

The founding of SACOS, 1973–76

The rise of Black Consciousness, the late 1960s reorganisation of the ANC, the 1973 Durban strikes and the changing international shifts in powers were to have a lasting effect on South African politics, as well as sporting developments inside the country. In 1973, in the same year and in the same city as the strikes, a new national anti-apartheid sports movement – the South African Council on Sport (SACOS) – was established to take further the struggles started by SASA and SANROC before they were bludgeoned into oblivion or exile during the repression of the early 1960s.

The specifically 'non-racial' SACOS was formally launched at a meeting in the Vedic Hall in Carlisle Street, central Durban, on 17 March, with eight national sports bodies as founding members. The delegates represented the SA Soccer Federation, SA Cricket Board of Control, SA Lawn Tennis Union, SA Amateur Swimming Federation, SA Table Tennis Board, SA Amateur Weightlifting and Bodybuilding Federation; SA Amateur Athletics and Cycling Board of Control; and, finally, the SA Senior Schools Sports Association.

The founding organisations of SACOS had been central in the 'inter-race' sport initiatives in the early 1950s (which the government was now two decades later trying to sell as an innovation in its 'multinational' guise). They were also part of the backbone of SASA and SANROC when the move to 'non-racial' sport started taking place in the late 1950s and early 1960s before state repression in the aftermath of Sharpeville destroyed those initiatives inside the country. This continuity was well demonstrated by the presence of veteran administrators such as George Singh, a successful lawyer and confidante and friend of prominent Congress Alliance activists,[229] who had been at the forefront from the outset of inter-race sport and was banned and house arrested together with the likes of Dennis Brutus and John Harris in the 1960s. Also involved was the pioneering non-racial Table Tennis Board, led by Cassim Bassa, which had been accepted as a member of the International Table Tennis Federation as far back as 1956, and which played in the World Table Tennis Championships the next year, instead of the whites-only counterpart body.

The emergence of SACOS was also part of the renaissance in resistance taking place alongside Black Consciousness and the new trade union militancy. Its formation was at least three years in the making, going back to 1970 when the Johannesburg City Council, influenced by one of its councillors, Dave Marais, who was prominent in the whites-only Football Association of South Africa (FASA), banned the well-supported non-racial SA Soccer Federation from using its facilities at the famous Natalspruit ground because it played integrated football. In September of that year, as part of the fight-back against the apartheid sports establishment, the Federation initiated the setting up of a steering committee for a South African Non-Racial Sports Organisations (SASPO), which included all but one of the later SACOS affiliates mentioned above. In the words of non-racial sports historian, Cheryl Roberts, 'taking cognizance of establishment sport's efforts to get predominantly African representative codes to ascribe to subservient affiliation' to the white codes in order for the latter to win IOC approval, 'the non-racial ad hoc committee sought to pre-empt these initiatives by reorganising and structuring sport along non-racial principles.' In 1972 SASPO lobbied the IOC for the expulsion of apartheid sport from all federations, explaining that under this apartheid sports model whites remained in control, 'no mixed play' was allowed and the black bodies were effectively 'stooges and agents of apartheid'.[230] SASPO was reacting to the likes of football administrator George Thabe and Fred Thabede who accompanied the white Olympic officials to the IOC's meeting in Munich to argue for South Africa's readmission to the Olympics that year. In March 1973 the SASPO steering committee mutated into SACOS in Durban and the new non-racial national umbrella sports body immediately began to confront the government and its multinational sports policy head on.

In its first set of resolutions, SACOS said that it

believes that merit selection is possible only if all participants in sporting events are able to compete with each other freely at all levels and calls on all sporting organisations to reject any system or scheme which does not offer equal opportunity, equal facilities, equal training and equal experience at all levels.[231]

Secondly, SACOS

regards the system of multinational sporting events which are being offered as a substitute for non-racial sport as a negation of the principles of non-discrimination in sport and designed to maintain the racial discrimination in South African Sport and calls on all sportsmen to reject any overtures that are being made by racial sporting organisations to organise multinational sports events.

SACOS also demanded a non-discriminatory sports sponsorship system because non-racial sport received almost nothing from the state, local authorities and 'commerce and industry'.

Like the Olympic movement, SACOS in the course of time had five rings on its badge – but these were a chain symbolising oppression rather than the five continents. The new body elected Norman Middleton as president, cricket's Hassan Howa as vice-president, Manikum N. Pather as general secretary and Abdullah Rasool of the weightlifting and bodybuilding Federation as treasurer. The respected George Singh was made the patron. Middleton was also head of the Soccer Federation, which had initiated the moves to form SASPO and SACOS. He was a prominent politician in the Coloured Labour Party, something that would in subsequent years lead to controversy and his ousting as SACOS president as his party participated in the Coloured Persons Representative Council, which was regarded as a stooge body of the government.

It did not take long for the new SACOS to feel the iron fist inside the velvet glove of the new sports policy. Like their predecessors in non-racial sport, both Howa and Pather were subsequently denied passports to prevent them from presenting the case of SACOS and of their codes abroad. Similarly, prevented from travelling to the International Swimming Federation meeting in 1973, Morgan Naidoo, president of the SACOS-affiliated South African Amateur Swimming Federation, was served with a five-year banning order after the white body was expelled by the International Swimming Federation. This prevented him from playing a public role such as being a member of any sports body or even from giving children swimming lessons.

SACOS leaders knew this kind of harassment was what awaited them, but it did not deter them from remaining completely opposed to the government's multinational sham reforms. In mid-1975 *South African Swimmer*, the newspaper of Naidoo's Federation, summed up:

The purpose of multinational sports meetings is stark and clear for it is intended to persuade the unsuspecting outside this country into believing that apartheid does not affect sport. How untrue! We would rather deny ourselves the doubtful 'distinction' of participating in the multinationals and being considered honorary whites for a few days or a week, so long as we suffer, for the rest of the year, the indignity of being contained, confined, controlled and contaminated by the shackles of group areas, separate development, and official state sports policy and the full gambit of racial legislation under which we have suffered since 1652.[232]

For expressing such views, non-racial sports officials and sportsmen faced both intimidation by the security services and actual prosecution.

Together with its principled anti-apartheid approach to sport, SACOS's greatest strength was the close linkage it soon developed with SANROC and the legitimacy and recognition this brought it internationally. The minutes of the second biennial meeting in 1977 list messages of support from no less than thirty organisations and individuals from outside South Africa. They ranged from the UN Special Committee Against Apartheid, to Ivor Montagu, founder president of the International Table Tennis Union, which had admitted the non-racial rather than apartheid body to its ranks in 1956; Fenner Brockway, the British peer famed for his support for anti-colonial movements and one of those who initiated the anti-apartheid movement in Britain around the same time; top officials of international federations; an active New Zealand anti-apartheid community; the Indian Golf Union; and the USSR Olympic Committee. SACOS reserved particular appreciation for SANROC and the Supreme Council for Sport in Africa (SCSA) on behalf of which both Abraham Ordia (president) and Jean-Claude Ganga (general secretary) sent messages.

By 1979 SACOS was an 'Associate Member' of the SCSA and so seriously did it take the sports boycott, that the South African Darts Board of Control, the only non-racial body next to table tennis to enjoy full membership of its international federation, decided in that year to forego 'our right' to participate in the 1979 World Cup. M. F. Johnson, the secretary, explained to his international counterparts:

In taking this decision we took full account of our prime objective of promoting darts and are of the firm opinion that international activity, like our membership of the World Darts Federation, is a natural and necessary extension of this objective . . . [however] the present local situation must take priority [and] our vacant place in the playing arena must be seen as a strong demonstration of our abhorrence for the racial structure existing in South Africa and a total refusal to give any credibility to the 'multinational' sports policy through our participation in the World Cup.

SACOS policy was, thus, initially, to apply for affiliation to international bodies to counter establishment sport efforts, but not to push for on-field playing contacts. One of only four resolutions passed at SACOS's launch in March 1973 read that:

> the efforts of non-racial national sporting organisations to negotiate an acceptance basis with the racial sports organisations which would permit all South Africans to enjoy the benefits of international recognition have been frustrated by lack of co-operation from racial organisations, [therefore SACOS] hereby requests non-racial national organisations to seek membership of the relevant international organisations.

In 1975 SACOS acted in a similar way with regard to its other internationally affiliated code, table tennis. A SATTB team was invited to participate in the World Championship in Calcutta, but the Indian government refused to give it visas. SACOS fully endorsed the barring of its own team, saying 'rather than create for itself future logistical problems', India had 'simply complied' with UN resolution 'fully and squarely'. Non-racial tennis players would suffer, 'but then suffering has been our lot for many decades' and it was worth it to bring about 'the total elimination of all form of racial discrimination in South African sport'. There should be 'no concession on grounds of compassion or sentiment'.[233]

The new internal umbrella sports body kept strictly to this policy for the twenty-odd years of its existence and became an important cog with SANROC, SCSA and the UN in maintaining the international stranglehold on apartheid sport. Year after year, the match programmes and brochures of its affiliates and the well-documented SACOS biennial conference reports were stuffed with messages of support from throughout the world, as well as briefing papers and reports which provided information and ammunition for the fight against apartheid sport. These brochures would even include the full reports from the regime's Department of Sport and Recreation, which provided ready-made lists to alert activists to athletes, companies and countries co-operating with establishment sport.

SACOS, headquartered in Durban, worked particularly closely with

SANROC in London, where the two most important officials were Chris de Broglio and Sam Ramsamy, who both happened to have lived in Durban. De Broglio had represented South Africa at the world weightlifting championships in Hungary in 1958 before throwing in his lot with the non-racial sports struggle and helping to set up SANROC in the 1960s – first in South Africa and then in London after the hanging of John Harris and the imprisonment of Dennis Brutus. He was still SANROC's anchor when SACOS was founded. Not only its long-standing secretary, but also the provider of office space at his successful Portman Court Hotel near Marble Arch.

Ramsamy arrived in London in 1972, a young physical education lecturer from Springfield College of Education in Durban, looking for a teaching job, and knocked on the door of Portman Court. Besides putting him up in the hotel until he found lodgings, the silver-haired de Broglio immediately roped Ramsamy in to help with anti-apartheid and solidarity work, first off sending him to Munich, where the 1972 Olympic Games were about to take place. Ramsamy had coached the SASF's Aces United team to victory in the Mainstay Cup and was involved via swimming in the sports developments in Durban in the period leading up to the formation of SACOS. Fresh from home, he joined a team of volunteers which included several others who had made their way to London from South Africa, including Isaiah Stein, Jasmat Dhiraj, Bobby Naidoo, Stephen Tobias and Wilfred and Dennis Brutus (although the latter did not stay long in Britain). De Broglio proudly described this small band as 'dedicated officials' who 'work around the clock' and who at short notice travelled and lobbied against apartheid. He described the organisation as 'known for its frankness', and one that was 'well ahead of developments that are taking place and has first-hand knowledge in some instances'.[234]

Isaiah Stein was a strong-hearted character who boxed in his youth under the name of 'Boston Tababy' in District Six, Cape Town. Forced out of his home under the Group Areas Act he ended up as an organiser for the Coloured People Congress, partner of the ANC in the Congress Alliance. After being detained, tortured and put under house arrest, he left South Africa on a one-way exit visa in 1968. He was part of the core team in London and the subsequent success of three of his eight sons, Edwin, Brian and Mark, in English professional football helped SANROC garner support for the cause.[235] Brian ended up representing England and Mark played for Chelsea.

Jasmat Dhiraj was a top tennis player who once played against South

Africa's star player, Cliff Drysdale, then ranked number four in the world. Drysdale declared Dhiraj good enough to be picked for South Africa in an upcoming Davis Cup encounter against Spain. Instead of playing in the Davis Cup, and barred from even having a chance, Dhiraj ended up helping get South Africa kicked out of the tournament. Sent by the non-racial South African Lawn Tennis Union to Europe as part of a squad of non-racial players in the early 1970s, he settled in London and testified before the International Tennis Federation, which upheld white-only South Africa's suspension from the Davis Cup.[236]

But it was Ramsamy who was to stand out amongst this small band of exiled sports activists. In 1976, with SANROC's president Dennis Brutus now based in the United States, Ramsamy became chairman and two years later, he was appointed as the first paid, fulltime official of SANROC, taking on the position as executive chairman at a salary lower than that he was earning as a teacher. Ramsamy's name soon became synonymous with SANROC. According to Brutus it was he who had nominated Ramsamy to take over SANROC when he began his US teaching stints which took him to Northwestern and Pittsburgh Universities.[237] Ramsamy travelled with Abraham Ordia and others to the IOC and was on a treadmill of other international sports conferences, building up a deep network of international support. He became the first stop for anyone enquiring about the sports question outside of South Africa, and numerous letters ending with his neat signature, seemingly always drawn with a quality nib, attest to his close support for SACOS.

*

Despite SACOS's aim of non-racialism, where race was merely a social construction and colour did not matter, sport in South Africa was bedevilled by the challenges posed by history. The biggest one facing the new umbrella body would be how to overcome South Africa's historical legacy of racism, segregation and exclusion. South Africans were strictly prevented from living in common living spaces. How then to proceed across these artificial barriers to create communality in sport?

Those who founded SACOS deserve to have their names recorded in history for their vision, courage and intent.[238] The first minutes, however, record that all those present were essentially people forced by law to live in restricted Group Areas set apart for Indian and coloured South Africans. Out of the fifty founding delegates present at the launch conference, the press and observers included, not one obviously African name jumps out, and the single white South African present was the journalist and social activist, Barry Streek, a special guest.

Clearly, the practicalities of developing a vision for integrated, inclusive sport in a highly segregated society was going to pose an immense challenge for SACOS. Although there was no law specifically prohibiting sport across the colour line, a string of broader apartheid laws and regulations continued to make non-racial sport, which aimed to totally disregard race, a precarious if not impossible goal, just as these restrictions affected every other aspect of life in South Africa.

The Native Urban Areas Consolidation Act 1945 controlled black sports facilities and restricted their use by permit. The 1950 Population Registration Act classified every South African by 'race', based on physical appearance as well as general acceptance and 'repute'. For example, as late as 1985, the SACOS biennial brochure reported on the absurd fact that 'with a stroke of the pen 795 South Africans changed in colour last year in terms of the Race Classification Act'.[239] Mind bogglingly, they include whites and 'Blacks' becoming coloured, Indians becoming Malay, and 'Blacks' going further to be 'other Asian'. The Group Areas Act of 1950 in turn segregated the populations of South Africa's towns and cities into separate living areas for these various categories of people – sportsmen and women included. Other laws such as the Reservation of Separate Amenities Act 1953 and the 1928 Liquor Act prevented the integration of ground and club facilities for refreshments, seating, toilets and dancing. African sportsmen and women were also governed by pass laws, which restricted their movements as citizens and prevented them travelling freely to 'away' matches or going on tours.

In October 1973 the sports minister issued Proclamation R228 under the 1950 Act, which enabled multiracial matches to be banned on private grounds as well. The Proclamation was brought in specifically to prevent the Aurora Cricket Club, in Pietermaritzburg, Natal, from playing multi-racial games. The club had been formed early in 1973 by a group of black and white cricketers, breaking new ground in the process. In the event, no prosecution was launched using the new regulation. The government refrained from using its new power to avoid controversy, although members of the Special Branch took names of players and spectators and prepared a report for the attorney general.[240]

Racial or multinational sport within the government framework on the other hand was based on this apartheid spatial planning. 'Groups' would remain in their own regulated boxes, and occasionally come together, before returning to them. For this form of occasional contact, officialdom was prepared to circumvent regulations, and relevant government departments were given discretionary power to issue permits for multinational events.

Apart from SACOS and its affiliates, there were also racially constituted black bodies: that is to say, each main sport might typically have an African body or a coloured one. For example, the ethnic coloured South African Rugby Federation (with its Proteas team) and the South African African Rugby Board (Leopards) ran parallel next to the non-racial South African Rugby Union (SARU) with its open membership. White sports organisations sought co-operations with these separate black organisations to undermine SARU and SACOS and the legitimacy they enjoyed. And while SACOS and non-racial sporting groups began to openly side with the banned liberation movements and supported moves to isolate apartheid sport, these multinational bodies moved closer to collaboration with the authorities.

One area where SACOS was able to gain significant support across artificially imposed boundaries was in the eastern Cape, with its rich century-old rugby and cricket traditions in the African communities (described in chapter 2). This included longstanding co-operation across racial lines in mixed and inter-race sport. SACOS's specific base in the region emerged from a breakaway by rugby players from the racial board in Port Elizabeth in 1971. Ten of the twelve clubs in the first league left and formed the new Kwazakhele Rugby Union (KWARU). Their motto was *Facta non verba* (Deeds not words) and the crest was the sturdy rhinoceros. The Young Turks were led by Mono Badela, a journalist who had been vice-president of the local African board. The initial reasons for leaving were dissatisfaction with the attitudes and perceived corruption and maladministration of the 'old-timers' such as Norris Singaphi, head of the local Bantu Administration Board, and his lieutenants, Curnick Mdyesha and W. L. Dwesi. They assumed political significance when KWARU decided to apply for affiliation to the South African Rugby Union (SARU), and therefore SACOS in 1975.[241]

Other African sporting bodies in the eastern Cape subsequently followed KWARU in defecting from the African rugby and cricket boards to the 'non-racial' counterparts.[242] Feelings between African sportspeople on different sides of the growing divide could be very strong, cricketer Khaya Majola recalled: 'There were times when people chased each other around with knives'.[243]

Those who went over to non-racial sport, soon became locked into conflict with the authorities. The rugby and cricket players were 'kicked out' of the facilities at the Wolfson Stadium and the New Brighton Oval and went to play on the *veld* in Veeplaas, which even today has a look of desolation about it. The Bantu Administration Board ruled that only 'Bantus' (Africans) could play on facilities financed from its Bantu Revenue Account, excluding teams which played across the colour line. The authorities put a spoke in the wheel in various other ways – like preventing journalists on the state-run Radio Xhosa from reporting on non-racial sport.

Nevertheless, KWARU did excellently in the SA Cup rugby competition after crossing over to SARU, reaching the inter-provincial rugby final in only their second season. When the team made the final again in 1975, the match was planned for the Adcock Stadium in Korsten. The authorities informed KWARU that as Africans wishing to play in a coloured area, they needed special permits. KWARU refused to apply. The national SARU started considering venues elsewhere as time was running out. Dan Qeqe remembers, 'We asked them, let us play the final here even if it is on the doldrums'.[244]

One of the remarkable episodes in the history of non-racial sports followed. 'Boet' Dan and a team of volunteers started building a ground from scratch out at Veeplaas, even though there were only two to three weeks to go to the big match. They worked day and night, clearing stones and broken glass, drawing the chalk lines, putting up posts and a rudimentary pavilion. A rope around the field had to serve as the stadium fence. Six thousand people turned up and waited patiently in lines to pay. The organisers could boast that 'no one jumped over the wire'. The game went ahead and the biggest crowd and gate takings yet for a SARU final were recorded. Again in 1976, 20,000 people filled the 'people's' stadium for the SA Cup final between KWARU and Tygerberg. The ground was named the Dan Qeqe Stadium in honour of the indefatigable sports activist. He recalls that this was a 'thrilling period' where people stood together and 'great, entertaining' rugby of the highest quality was played.[245] KWARU was consistently one of the strongest provincial teams and the United Democratic Front leader and later premier of the Western Cape, Ebrahim Rasool, remembers the special aura around this team of Africans when they came to take on Western Province at the Athlone Stadium in Cape Town. 'There was always a buzz and for us it gave meaning to the non-racial struggles.'[246]

The harassment and intimidation meted out against genuinely non-racial sport contrasted markedly with the rewards given to those few black South Africans who did allow themselves to be accommodated by the white bodies. Besides being given opportunities to tour abroad denied to the system's opponents, these 'collaborators' were often given secure jobs as individuals, and offered financial inducements to improve their club and organisational facilities. Such inducements were naturally attractive, given the abysmal level of facilities available to black South Africans and given the fact that the government was spending five times as much money on white sport as it did on black sport – a disparity compounded by the fact that the black population outnumbered the whites by far.

The state also started using black people in its divide-and-rule propaganda and disinformation was employed to disrupt opposition to apartheid sport. One prominent example in the mid-1970s was journalist Leslie Sehume. In a well-oiled public relations drive, he was flown overseas by the state to confront anti-apartheid leaders and to call for support for British Lions and New Zealand rugby tours to South Africa. Sehume had a widely publicised half-hour debate with Peter on BBC television in April 1974. The sports editor of the black Johannesburg newspaper, *The World*, he was presented as the 'true' voice of the black majority. Putting a black spokesperson like him up against both Peter and against New Zealand HART leader, Trevor Richards, was designed to put them on the spot with a message: who did they think they were, these 'foreign whites' trying to dictate to black South Africans? It was a message well received in sectors of the international sports administrative fraternity, who were as keen as white South Africans to have them back.

Sehume received favourable coverage in the right-wing media and was feted by British apologists for sports apartheid, and although cutely acknowledging that anti-apartheid activists had helped 'accelerate change', he was a transparent 'collaborator'. While in London for several weeks, he held forth from a luxurious apartment in the Waldorf Hotel, which was about as far apart from his readers at home as it was possible to get.

In their television debate, Sehume deployed a transparently rehearsed line. Turning to Peter he said: 'If you returned to South Africa now, you would be stoned out of the country – by blacks, not whites.' Powerful stuff which captured the headlines. But unfortunately for him, untrue. Sehume was immediately denounced by his own newspaper, *The World*. Although it had to navigate a careful path because it was then illegal to advocate sanctions and boycotts of any kind, an editorial in the paper took 'the strongest exception to Mr Sehume's remarks'. In an accompanying page-long article it also reported the views of a range of black sports and civic leaders. SACOS president Norman Middleton spoke for most when he said Sehume was being 'used to exploit his own people' and added: 'Peter Hain would be welcomed to South Africa as a hero because he is a fighter for the Blacks.'

As it turned out later, Sehume's sponsor was exposed as a government front in what became known as the 'Information Department scandal', discussed previously. With the active blessing of the prime minister, John Vorster, the Department had moved well beyond the normal bounds of foreign information and propaganda, spending tens of millions of pounds to sponsor front organisations, spread disinformation and secretly financed newspapers at home and abroad. One of these was the Committee for Fairness in Sport (CFS),[247] launched in 1973, the same year that SACOS was formed. Sehume ended up officially on the payroll of the CFS after being sacked by *The World*.

'Normal sport': The Soweto uprisings and government attempts at 'reform'

When SACOS was founded in 1973, the idea of a unity on dignified terms with whites-only bodies inside South Africa was also still very much on the agenda, something that may surprise those who know only of the organisation's later 1980s principled opposition to any such attempts as long as apartheid existed. Only a month after the historic founding conference, on 30 April 1973, SACOS vice-president Hassan Howa led the board of the South African Cricket Board of Control (SACBOC) in its first discussions with the white SACA and African SAACB about co-operation and possible unity. Several such meetings followed, but there was a sticking point from the outset.

SACA and its ally wanted an umbrella federal body, the so-called Cricket Council of South Africa. Each body would stay separate and a Springbok team would then be chosen at a tournament where the standard of all the top players could be measured. Howa refused because this would have amounted to race-based multinationalism. Never at a loss for words, Howa did not shy back from controversy. He rubbed in the fact that until all cricketers in the country were treated equally whites could forget about international competition. He was prepared to change behind bushes to make this happen, but the principle of non-racialism was non-negotiable. The outspoken SACBOC and SACOS leader's condemnation of paternalistic white administrators and apartheid white hypocrisy made him a figure the establishment press loved to hate. Epithets such as 'intransigent', 'hard-line' and 'hot-headed' were routinely used to describe him, but this only reinforced his reputation as the distinctive face of non-racial sport inside the country.[248] His constituency loved his straight-talking and the criticism of him had the effect – like the demonstrations in 1969–70 – of keeping the sports issue on the front pages.

Sam Ramsamy described the ensuing process well, as the white body fumbled its way towards the future. 'Now and then, almost comically,' he said, 'multi-racial sport took place under the noses of the government.'[249] But the establishment cricketers continued to toe the government line and support the system. Three torturous years later, with Howa having been succeeded as SACBOC president by Rashid Varachia, the three cricket bodies, SACA, SAACB and SACBOC, finally agreed in January 1976 to 'hereby adopt the principle that Cricket in South Africa be played on a normal basis under the controlling aegis of one controlling body in South Africa'. Moreover, '"Normal Cricket" shall mean at this stage participation of and competition between all cricketers regardless of race, creed or colour in cricket at club level under one provincial governing body'.[250] It seemed as though unity on the terms of non-racial cricketers was finally a possibility. After the so-called 'normal cricket agreement', a national coordinating structure, the nine-man Motivating Committee, was set up to oversee unity.[251] The provincial boards of the respective bodies were instructed to enter into dialogue to give effect to the resolution and the provinces started making preparations for a single league competition at the beginning of the 1976–77 season.

However, during the off-season, on 16 June, the Soweto uprisings began, fundamentally altering the course of South African history and rendering the normal cricket agreement virtually meaningless. Soweto school students took to the streets to protest against a government directive that Afrikaans be used as a language of instruction in black schools, and were ruthlessly gunned down by police. The protests grabbed world headlines as they turned into a general uprising that spread to many other black townships. As parts of the urban fabric went up in flames, the concession of blacks and whites being able to play cricket together on weekends while apartheid continued unabated in other areas of life seemed a triviality.

Black cricketers started questioning the wisdom of proceeding with the project. The stalling and ambiguous statements of government and the lack of sensitivity and commitment on the part of the white SACA's affiliates were the straws that broke the camel's back. As late as October 1976, with the first round of league matches due to start throughout the country, the minister of sport refused to confirm that mixed cricket at club level would be allowed, although he had given cricket administrators indications that this would be the case. The first few weeks of the season were chaotic, with claims and counterclaims, and on-off-on-off situations throughout the country.

Department of Sport officials stopped a match in Kimberley. The white Transvaal Cricket Union secretary refused to allow the national African player, Edward Habane to play for the white Balfour Park club.[252] SACA president, Billy Woodin, upheld the government line, arguing, 'We and the Minister agreed to club cricket matches between clubs of different races. We never agreed to multi-racial clubs.'[253] Trust was shattered.

Football and cricket star Bravo Jacobs found he was treated as a 'coloured' player, who had to 'sit in the lounge of the clubhouse waiting for the proffered lift [home] while the white owner of the car was quaffing beer with the rest of the teammates in the club bar'. Meanwhile, 'I could not go in there because they were scared of losing their licence.'[254]

While Varachia and other 'moderates' tried to hold the 'normal cricket' line, the desired unity turned out to be elusive and unsustainable given the political situation and conservative white attitudes. Splits within the non-racial SACBOC followed at club, provincial and national level, as most of an irate SACBOC decided to withdraw, although others decided to stay.

In September 1977 Varachia formally took SACBOC and a minority of its players into the new unified South African Cricket Union (SACU). The African Board (SAACB) which had shrunk to a shadow of its former self, also joined SACU and dissolved after forty-five years. However, the majority of SACBOC members refused to join SACU and formed a new non-racial body with the full support of SACOS in November 1977. After being threatened with legal action if they used the old name,[255] the dissidents formed the South African Cricket Board (SACB). 'The Board', insisting it upheld the true legacy on non-racial struggles and principles, soon claimed back the majority of SACBOC members. The split badly affected both bodies: on the one hand, the standard of SACB's cricket declined, as some influential top players left, even if temporarily, and on the other the new 'multiracial' SACU – run in effect by the old whites-only establishment with Varachia as a figurehead – was unable to gain the legitimacy as a representative body that it so craved in order to get back into international cricket.

The split in SACOS's cricket affiliate in 1976–77 was followed in 1978 by the loss of its influential football affiliate and founding member, the SA Soccer Federation, with its long-running Federation Professional League (FPL). As often happens in sport, money lay at the heart of the problem. At the end of 1977, after the white professional National Football League (NFL) collapsed, a victim of its own apartheid policies, which cut it off from the market that sustained it – a black fan base. Some of the white sides, mostly on the coast, then asked the non-racial Federation if they could join its FPL, to which the Federation agreed. But the inland white clubs complicated the matter by asking for and gaining affiliation to the rival African-run South African National Football Association (SANFA) and its professional wing the National Professional Soccer League (NPSL), which had in its ranks township brand names like Orlando Pirates, Moroka Swallows, AmaZulu and the still-young Kaizer Chiefs. These developments set in motion a major reshuffle of the South African football scene.

The outcome was the start of two racially mixed professional football leagues in 1978, both now attracting sponsorship from South African Breweries, a longstanding supporter of whites-only sports, which saw the opportunity to enter the still under-exploited township football market.

In the process the non-racial FPL landed in a triple quandary. Three of its newly affiliated white clubs left for the NPSL halfway through the season because of the better financial prospects the latter offered (as the overheads of playing in the bloated FPL, expanded from eleven to seventeen teams, proved higher than expected). Meanwhile, much to the anger of SACOS, the SASF/FPL and the SANFA/NPSL had started discussions about creating a single professional league from the next 1979 season. The latter's chairperson, George Thabe, was prominent in government's discredited urban community councils and had accompanied white administrators to argue against the sports boycott before the International Olympic Committee. SACOS saw Thabe and his body as an apartheid sweetheart organisation and duly expelled the SASF/FPL in October 1978 for speaking to them. As if the above was not enough, the financial and political uncertainty accompanying this process caused eight of the non-racial FPL's own clubs to jump ship and join the NPSL at the end of that season. The result was that in one year the national professional football terrain was reshaped and united in the most unexpected of ways (while the three separate amateur divisions resulting from apartheid remained intact).[256]

From 1979 onwards, therefore, the African-led NPSL by default became what was described as 'the de facto "Super League" in South Africa' with the flamboyant former SASF vice-president Abdul Bhamjee as one of its most prominent figures. In these complex maneuvourings and changes, SACOS as the flagbearer of non-racialism in sport became marginalised from the football mainstream and lost its best opportunity to find a future mass base for itself.

While these dramatic sporting developments were happening, South Africa was sinking into political darkness. The state – via the police – responded to the Soweto uprising by killing nearly a thousand people during 1976–77. In September 1977 the Black Consciousness movement leader Steve Biko was murdered in detention, causing an international outcry. In October of the same year the government banned eighteen organisations and closed down a leading black newspaper. The opposition forces were once again in disarray because of sustained repression. Thousands of young people fled into exile to continue the struggle and a slow rebuilding of resistance forces started internally.

The 1976 Soweto uprising forever changed the balance of power in South Africa. Minority rule entered a deep-seated structural crisis. Existing institutions could no longer resolve the strains and contradictions within South African society. The uprisings shattered the myth of white invincibility and made it impossible for the white minority to continue to rule in the old way. Forcibly putting down the revolt could not hide the crisis. The government, therefore, began in the late 1970s to seek ways of restructuring and modernising its policies and institutions. The prime minister warned that white South Africans would have to 'adapt or die'. 'Reform' became the new key word.[257]

Apartheid reform involved the governing Afrikaner National Party attempting to broaden its narrow ethnic power base by co-opting English-controlled big business and a black elite into a new multiracial ruling-class alliance. Government sought ways of including the coloured and Indian communities in parliament, recognised independent black trade unions for the first time and promised urban Africans more secure property rights and a new system of local authorities. In this way it hoped to stave off the demands of the mass of black South African for full political rights in an undivided country.

In sport 'reform' translated into the government and establishment much more assertively promoting multiracial or 'normal sport', after the timid introduction of token 'multinational' engagement across the colour line in the early 1970s. As part of the post-Soweto middle-class co-option exercise, black people were now allowed under permit to use what were called 'international' hotels and register at previously whites-only private schools. Between 1977 and 1982 the government made an effort to de-politicise sport, stating openly that it now recognised the autonomy of sport bodies to operate without state interference, and for individuals to make their own choices of where to play. The policy, conceived in increasing desperation to avoid isolation, however, bore no reality to conditions on the ground.

Confusion continued to reign as the right-wing teachers in the conservative Transvaal, for example, stubbornly impeded any attempts to introduce inter-racial sport at school level – and this is where SACOS cleverly made its next move. It adopted a charter on 'normal sport' and said if government was serious about its proclaimed move away from apartheid in sport, integrated sport should happen from school level upwards. This was patently not going to happen, though a few children started making appearances in the new permit-approved private school teams. Government got bogged down deeper in a debate full of ambiguity and confusion, prompting Roberts to observe that while it 'put forward a new legitimacy rationale, certain inherent contradictions found the state continuously on the defensive'.[258]

On the playing field, dozens of black cricketers started playing for formerly white clubs and leagues under SACU and the first black cricketers, led by Omar Henry of Western Province, made their appearance for the first time in the more than eighty years of Currie Cup provincial cricket. Going into the 1980s, Henry and rugby fly-half Errol Tobias became the first black players to play for national Springbok teams in the traditional white games of rugby and cricket. Peter Mathebula became a world boxing champion and his 'white trainers and handlers . . . kept parading him all over, taking him to white municipalities and dinners'.[259] Talented black athletes became regular participants and stars on the track, their achievements trumpeted as signs of major change in the mainstream media. Mixed professional football, involving former white NFL and former SASF clubs playing in the formerly all-black NPSL in a single league, became a new normal, now supported by mainstream sponsors South African Breweries (SAB), which had ignored black and non-racial sport before. The depth of cross-colour sporting contacts increased compared to the patently token first steps in the early 1970s. However, this still took place within a framework determined by apartheid, and numerous incidents that showed that apartheid was still alive, in sport as well, as when the star long-distance runner Matthews Batswadi, one of the first black runners awarded Springbok colours, was assaulted at the 1978 Currie Cup rugby final for using a toilet designated for whites.

Basically, these post-Soweto reforms meant doing away with what was called 'petty apartheid' while keeping in place the fundamentals of white domination and economic prosperity. Although the government was increasingly prepared to turn a blind eye in sport to the flouting of regulations and even the law when it needed to – especially when foreign teams were involved – a full range of racist legislation and regulations remained in force and could be applied at any time deemed appropriate. Resilient racism also meant these changes were not always appreciated. While this greater opening up of sporting opportunities constituted significant progress to white South Africans, and a new discourse of 'change' and 'normality' accompanied it, it meant very little in terms of addressing overall apartheid inequalities and exclusions. This is something that the liberation movements, the 'non-racial' SACOS and SANROC and the international anti-apartheid movement uncompromisingly underlined.

'Double standards': SACOS adopts radical new strategies of non-negotiation and non-collaboration, 1977 onwards

The Soweto uprising and the messy moves towards so-called 'normal sport' in 1976 had a massive impact on SACOS and the non-racial sport movement in two ways. Firstly, destabilised by the dramatic fluidity in sport and politics, the organisation had to struggle to maintain cohesion in its ranks following the breakup of its cricket affiliate (SACBOC) in 1977 and the drama in football ranks the following year. Secondly, it redefined its mission, undergoing a radical change of strategy.

From its traditional departure point of being open to principled sports unity in an incremental way on the basis of non-racialism, which required establishment multinational sport to stop organising on the basis of colour or ethnicity, the non-racial movement now moved to a position of strict non-negotiation and non-collaboration with the establishment and its new-found black multinational sport allies.

The organisation started drawing a line in the sand between it and establishment sport. Anyone who crossed this was banned and declared a stooge or collaborator.

In April 1977 SACOS passed its famous Double Standards Resolution (DSR), which laid out strict sanctions, usually expulsion, for any sportspeople who watched or played multiracial or multinational sport. Individuals and clubs who did so were isolated and declared persona non grata. The DSR stated that no player, administrator or supporter of SACOS or its affiliates could 'participate, nor be associated with, any code of sport which practices, perpetuates or condones, racialism and multinationalism'. This amounted to a ban on sportspeople in any way being linked to white establishment sport or government sanctioned bodies or events.

The punitive action applied even when SACOS players in one code of sport played in or watched events linked to the system in another code. For example, during winter many cricketer 'defectors' found themselves barred from their football and hockey clubs. They felt ostracised as their former teammates and communities shunned them. This became too much for some players. Top provincial batsmen Garth Cuddumbey summed up the dilemma: 'I was very happy with Pioneers during my one-and-a-half seasons with them, but I had to think of my future. I cannot even watch non-racial sport [in the group area suburb I live in] at the moment.'[260] Others, like the aforementioned Bravo Jacobs, came back because the grass was not, as expected, greener on the other side. Mogamad Allie recalls that sometimes neighbours who had previously played for the same club were now on different sides of the sporting fence and stopped speaking to each other for years. This was the universal dilemma unfolding in times of intense societal conflict, when one has to decide on resistance or collaboration and the grey in-between spaces disappear. Bitter personal enmities developed, some of these harboured to this day.

An immediate outcome of the Double Standards policy was that SACOS's founding president Norman Middleton was forced to step down from his position in SACOS after four years at the helm. A member of the ethnic Coloured Persons Representative Council set up by government as the supposed parliament for that apartheid group-ing, he refused to abide by the resolution and was replaced by Hassan Howa later that year.

The charismatic Howa introduced a new slogan, 'No Normal Sport in an Abnormal Society'. It dovetailed neatly with the 'Double Standards Resolution' to popularise the new approach. These twins became instant markers for evolving SACOS policy – and they amounted to a fundamental change of strategic thinking in non-racial sport. Sports change itself was no longer the key issue. Political change was required for sport to become truly non-racial – nothing short of the overthrow of the apartheid system would suffice. It made no sense to be a 'normal' person for sport on a Saturday and go back to being a second-class citizen for the other six days. Only when political and socio-economic equality existed could the non-racial sports dream be realised.

A key requirement in the Double Standards policy was that no non-racial sportspeople should apply for permits to use racially segregated government facilities, either for sport or social and personal reasons. In the years to come, several sporting dramas resulted from this principled position. The apartheid government had for a long time used its system of passes and permits to control the movement and labour of black bodies, in sport as well. For example, when members of the mixed New Brighton-based United CC, who lived in the nearby coloured group area, wished to join their teammates, they were required by law to have permits as non-Africans to enter an African township. Non-racial sportspeople refused to comply with this, leading to various of them being charged over time.[261]

In 1979 SACOS extended the DSR to include the off-field prohibitions of members sending their children to private white schools or from using so-called 'international' hotels, which had been given permits to serve black guests. Some SACOS members who decided to send their children to these private schools to get a better education decided to give up playing rather than subscribe to the ban. SACOS explained that in both cases the apartheid government set unacceptable conditions with these permits. For example, there was a ceiling for the numbers of black children who could attend the open schools, and those going there would additionally be mustered into playing multinational sport with their new schoolmates. Also, while black people could be accommodated at the hotels, mixed dancing and the use of the swimming baths was not allowed – an insult.

The same applied to government facilities, such as civic centres and halls. One top cricketer was banned after some of his provincial fellow players reported him for having his wedding celebrations in Port Elizabeth's council-owned Feather Market Hall, where 'non-whites' were required to apply for a permit to use it. He was due to play in a provincial game next day, but was removed from the team, upon which four of his clubmates pulled out in solidarity, setting the scene for impassioned disagreements on the local sports front.

Cheryl Roberts viewed these interventions as attempts by SACOS to intervene in the area of middle-class life and 'disciplining the Black petit bourgeoisie', while on the other hand also aiming to sabotage government's efforts to co-opt a black middle class into the system through the relaxation of what was called 'petty apartheid': that is small concessions, which did not imperil the grand plan of apartheid. As SACOS correctly argued, after 1976 the state and business 'decided to adopt the strategy of creating a black middle-class which they thought would act as a buffer between the state and the black masses during times of uprising.'[262] The Urban Foundation, set up by the Anglo American corporation and its big business allies for exactly this purpose, was one of those groupings SACOS explicitly prohibited its affiliates from co-operating with. This resulted in its tennis affiliate, the Tennis Association of South Africa, refusing to have dealings with the Soweto-based black Tennis Foundation because of the support it received from the Urban Foundation, despite the opportunity this provided to forge closer links with African sportspeople.

In response to the class-based 'reform' initiatives of the system, SACOS increasingly looked beyond exclusions on the basis of colour to emphasise class and it began to prioritised sport as a vehicle for promoting working-class as much as non-racial interests.

The extension of the DSR beyond the sports field in 1979 also specifically targeted segregated state institutions such as the 'dummy' coloured, Indian and African local councils meant to represent disenfranchised black South Africans in their segregated living areas. People serving on these councils could not be members of SACOS and its affiliates. This helped to delegitimise apartheid's ethnic institutions. One outcome though was that it complicated access by non-racial sport to municipal facilities in racially segregated neighbourhoods. SACOS's next secretary Colin Clarke noted that where clubs refused to apply to these ethnically based management committees, facilities were often diverted to multinational sport and in certain case SACOS clubs were forced to disband.[263] Sometimes SACOS affiliates refused even to play on municipal facilities if they were also used by multinational bodies. But the organisation later changed the policy, allowing sportspeople, especially in small towns, to apply for playing facilities 'under protest' as they might otherwise not been able to play at all.

So committed was the post-1976 SACOS to non-collaboration that in Kimberley the non-racial athletics association disbanded rather than apply for a permit to use the De Beers Stadium. It found 'it could no longer function', so SACOS's SA Amateur Athletics Board 'lost a strong affiliate'.[264]

SACOS also decided to boycott the black ethnic-based universities or 'bush colleges' created under apartheid. This was a controversial decision as many black students had no option but to study there and by excluding them SACOS deprived itself of both prime facilities, especially in the rural areas, as well as a ready-made constituency. Those students who were not dedicated enough to find off-campus clubs were lost to the organisation. This resolution regarding universities was rescinded in the mid-1980s for this reason and some of the educational institutions became focal points for non-racial sport.

As a result of the splits in the non-racial sports movement from 1976 onwards, SACOS and its affiliates had to engage in serious repair work in certain areas of the country where relatively large defections occurred. At its October 1977 meeting, SACOS gave 'caretaker status' to the SA Non-Racial Cricket Committee, which was busy consolidating into a new organ-isation the large amount of disgruntled SACBOC players who did not follow the Varachia wing of the organisation into the new multiracial white-dominated SACU. This led to the formation of the new South African Cricket Board in November 1977. As well as serving as SACOS president, Hassan Howa also became president of SACB and that season it started its new competitions with the Howa Bowl as the premier trophy.[265] Many of the SACBOC elite players were initially enticed by the bigger playing oppor-tunities in SACU, but most came back to 'the Board', as it was called. Attention had to be given, too, to strengthening grassroots organisation in provinces such as Transvaal, which were badly affected by the splits.

SACOS set up several other new affiliates, like the SA Cycling Board to replace the old SA Cycling Association, which had gone rogue, and in football the SASF and its FPL professional wing were admitted back into the SACOS fold at a meeting in Cape Town on 1 September 1979, after sympa-thetic inputs by Howa and the veteran George Singh. But not before these football officials ate humble pie and were grilled by the delegates. Both organisations admitted 'we have made mistakes'. They apologised 'for the harm they have caused to the aspirations of oppressed and disenfranchised sportspersons of South Africa', and were reinstated after promising to abide by the constitution and all rules and resolutions, 'and especially the resolution on Double Standards'. SACOS was unambiguous: 'no further concessions of any nature would be considered'. The footballers were on a final warning. But it was clear, really, both sides needed each other. SACOS depended on the Federation's 65,000 members for much of its strength – and the remarkable part of it was that two years after Double Standards the politically maligned Norman Middleton was still the SASF president on its readmission to SACOS.[266]

All unity talks with the establishment came to an end and SACOS slowly recovered from the blows of the late 1970s. It emerged both tested and on a new, more radical trajectory. In the gloomy times following the death of Steve Biko and yet another round of bannings of organisations and individuals, SACOS remained a symbol of resistance that was in fact strengthening. It was given observer status by the forty-six-nation Supreme Council for Sport in Africa at Rabat, Morocco in 1977 and was thereafter invited to attend SCSA annual conferences.[267] This gave it a political importance far exceeding its strength in numbers and small budgets. Together with its close ally SANROC operating from exile, SACOS effectively had veto rights over the entire establishment sports structure of apartheid South Africa with all its capacity, sponsorship and state support. Employing the threatening double-speak so typical of the apartheid government, the minister of sport warned SACOS in 1979 that they would be 'passing final judgement on themselves' if they 'carry on prejudicing South African sport'.[268] But, in the new decade of the 1980s the influence the organisation exerted would grow even stronger.

*

Nearly fifty years after the founding of SACOS (and nearly thirty years after its demise), debates still rage in an imperfect present-day South Africa, with its deep and persistent inequalities in sport and society, about the merits and demerits of those radical non-collaboration policies and slogans it adopted in the late 1970s. Were they the way to sporting liberation and equality in South Africa? Or were they political misjudgements despite the purity of the vision? For some, SACOS fought a worthy struggle but the organisation was too rigidly ideological and in the end incapable of achieving its own goals. For SACOS supporters the inequalities and slow pace of post-1994 transformation are the result of the 'sell-out' that took place in the 1980s when non-racial sports movement decisively changed direction and adopted new strategies.

The debate goes on and on and it has become cardboard and mechanistic, a to-ing and fro-ing of fixed old either-or ideological and political positions. For greater understanding of the historical complexity involved, it is necessary to look afresh at the details of each phase of the unfolding sports and political struggle, and the contradictions, constraints and nuances that the different leaders, organisations and streams of thought faced.

One of SACOS's major contradictions came to the fore during this period of recalibration in the late 1970s. Two well-known historians sympathetic to the organisation, Cheryl Roberts and Douglas Booth, have made critical observations about some of the decisions it took then. Roberts, a stalwart sports and gender activist grounded in SACOS struggles, argues that 'the emphasis placed on the double standards and boycott of permit-sanctioned facilities . . . effectively prevented SACOS from establishing and developing into a mass-based non-racial sports organisation'. She says that it proceeded with 'acute aggression and minimal analysis of tactics and strategy' to police its constituency rather than using the opportunities available to it. In the process it gave away ground to the co-optive ruling classes: 'Most of its energies were spent on . . . playing detective to its membership. Those who stepped out of line were suspended or expelled or investigated by commissions of enquiry. Needless to say this involved costly organisational time.'[269]

SACOS 'opted for stringent membership criteria to the liberation struggle instead of organisation building', and Roberts points out that this change in strategy resulted from an influx of 'activists from the Western Cape in the 1930s and 1940s who proposed boycotts and non-collaboration as strategies without advocating alternatives'. She was talking of groupings such as the New Unity Movement and the influential Teachers' League of South Africa, who were influenced by Fourth International or Trotskyite ideas and were well represented in the school sports movement in the Western Cape. She argued that 'to the detriment of non-racial sport mobilisation this tradition surfaced [and became dominant] within SACOS' at this time.[270]

The biggest weaknesses in SACOS's new, heavily ideologically driven 'ideas' approach was that it ignored two realities. The first was that through no fault of its own SACOS had a narrow, racialised base, being restricted primarily to sportspeople living in apartheid's Indian and coloured group area compartments. This would in the end fatally inhibit its influence in broader national debates and contestations. At the 1979 SACOS biennial conference, which discussed the football issue, there were around eighty delegates. Only one – Don Kali of the Tennis Association of South Africa – was black African. This immediately brought forward the second linked contradiction. While SACOS claimed to represent oppressed sportspeople in South Africa and was beginning to articulate a perspective that the working class should be at the centre of its sports struggle, neither the mass of Africans in South Africa nor the mass of workers (who were mostly African) were directly involved in it. Indeed, under the Double Standards resolution, SACOS defined the teams such as Kaizer Chiefs and Orlando Pirates that the working class in the townships followed as being multinational stooges of apartheid.

Thus, the ultimate flaw in the new, hard-edged principled SACOS approach was that it doomed the overwhelming majority of African sportsmen to the category of collaborators. This at a time when – as the Soweto uprisings showed – African communities were bearing the brunt of apartheid and leading the broad struggle against it.

The way SACOS dealt with the 1978 football dramas perhaps shaped its destiny. By expelling and carpeting the SASF at a time when it was attempting to negotiate a place for non-racial football in a broader South African football scenario, it also cut off its main avenue for future growth.

Roberts points out that with a 'more flexible approach' by SACOS towards the SASF/SANFA 'the two bodies may have merged and a powerful base [could have been] established in the townships' for non-racial sport, a development that might also have facilitated the movement of African football in a more progressive social and political direction.[271] Some township-based sporting associations, such as the SA Softball Federation, did try to reach out to SACOS, but 'found the organisation's principles too difficult to implement'. The result was that SACOS remained with only small pockets of African membership, mainly amongst the strong rugby and cricket codes in the eastern Cape, but also in other pockets of tennis, swimming and football. In general, Roberts claims, by not building this broader base and contesting the spaces in sport more broadly, including sponsorship, the non-racial sports movement gave a 'pass for big capital to score' and re-order sport after Soweto.

Douglas Booth agreed with the essence of Roberts' analysis when he wrote that while the double standards resolution 'was initially a strategy to build internal discipline', it progressively became a tactic of political purification', and SACOS 'willingly sacrificed members and refused to consider alternative strategies'.[272]

At the same time that the non-racial sports movement reached an apex of radicalism in the late 1970s, its base was disconnected from the African masses or what was described in struggle parlance as the motive forces in the liberation struggle. In the years that followed this would become an increasingly relevant contradiction challenging SACOS throughout the 1980s, eventually leading to its demise.

Gleneagles and the United Nations blacklist, 1977–80

As part of its radical new policy positions, SACOS after 1977 strongly reiterated its support for the total isolation of South African sport, including SACOS sportspeople themselves. The tendency to seek affiliation to international bodies, which together with creating non-racial unity characterised its approach before 1977, was also dropped.

Meanwhile, after the Soweto uprising, international opposition to apartheid sport intensified as well. Major milestones in this respect were the adoption of the 1977 Gleneagles Agreement banning sporting contact with South Africa by the Commonwealth countries, followed a few months later, on 14 December 1977, by the acceptance by the United Nations of the International Declaration Against Apartheid in Sport.

The Gleneagles Agreement was unanimously approved by the Commonwealth Heads of Government Conference presided over by the Queen at a meeting at the Gleneagles Hotel in Perthshire, Scotland on 15 June 1977, a day before the first anniversary of the Soweto uprising. Referring to its 1971 Declaration of Commonwealth Principles, the heads of state 'reaffirmed their full support for the international campaign against apartheid and welcomed the efforts of the United Nations to reach universally accepted approaches to the question of sporting contacts within the framework of that campaign'. They also 'accepted it as the urgent duty of each of their Governments vigorously to combat the evil of apartheid by withholding any form of support for, and by taking every practical step to discourage contact or competition by their nationals with sporting organisations, teams or sportsmen from South Africa or from any other country where sports are organised on the basis of race, colour or ethnic origin'.

SANROC and anti-apartheid activists were elated. 'For the first time an international governmental organisation has signed up to our cause', Sam Ramsamy wrote in his diary. And it meant that third parties would also now act against boycott-breakers. The agreement took hard backroom work: 'We are now working behind the scenes, preparing draft statements, finding the words that would satisfy the African nations on the one hand and countries like Britain and New Zealand on the other. As always this is a delicate balancing act', Ramsamy noted.[273] One of the heroes was Canadian prime minister Pierre Trudeau, who 'pressed hard' for a position against apartheid, determined to avoid a boycott of the following year's Commonwealth Games in Edmonton along the lines of the one that had spoilt the 1976 Olympics in Montreal. But it was the Commonwealth secretary general, Sonny Ramphal, who, according to Ramsamy, brilliantly 'orchestrated the whole affair'. To get around the right-wing Robert Muldoon, prime minister of New Zealand, he persuaded Jamaican prime minister Michael Manley (who authored a history of West Indian cricket) to have a quiet chat with him. Manley offered the obdurate Muldoon a drink in the bar – and the rest was history.

Gleneagles was an important step forward for the sports apartheid struggle, though the Commonwealth leaders added: 'They fully acknowledged that it was for each Government to determine in accordance with its law the methods by which it might best discharge these commitments. But they recognised that the effective fulfilment of their commitments was essential to the harmonious development of Commonwealth sport hereafter.'

The South African Olympic Committee called the Commonwealth Code 'the worst thing to have happened to South Africa since our expulsion from the Olympic movement'.

'The agreement was a victory for all Commonwealth countries, since they had all agreed to use their best efforts . . . to break down the system of apartheid in sports,' said British Labour prime minister James Callaghan, adding that each country would work to 'sustain and strengthen' the consensus brokered at the summit.

However, two years later, following the election victory of Margaret Thatcher's Conservative government in 1979, there was a change of stance by Britain. Thatcher was the centre of regular standoffs at Commonwealth meetings, often finding herself isolated in her reluctance to take any practical action against apartheid. In Parliament on 31 July 1981 one of her most ardent cheerleaders, John Carlisle MP, argued of Gleneagles: 'Sadly, the agreement has now become an easy political weapon for anyone wishing to mount a vendetta against South Africa. Indeed, it has given such people a respectability which they do not deserve . . . Great progress has been made in the integration of multiracial sport in South Africa.' A recipient of regular flights and hospitality by white South Africa, Carlisle – dubbed 'the Member for Pretoria' – was one of its chief apologists.

Meanwhile from 1980 SANROC worked with the UN Special Committee to compile an international 'Register of Sports Contacts with South Africa' or 'blacklist', which 'outed' athletes and administrators visiting or participating against South African sports teams, thereby breaking the boycott. Enuga Reddy of the United Nations Centre Against Apartheid brought noted activists such as Sam Ramsamy and Trevor Richards from New Zealand over to the UN headquarters in New York for periods of several months to help him prepare this tightening of sanctions. On the new 'blacklist' were sportspeople and officials who had played against white South African teams or promoted this. Regularly updated, with the help of SANROC, SACOS and international allies, the new blacklist caused some to be refused opportunities to play in other countries, especially in Africa. Many sports stars had to reverse their plans to compete in the country: golfers, tennis players, boxers, athletes and other individual sportsmen and women.

This was important because, although it had become easier to get *teams* – national, provincial or club – to join the boycott, anti-apartheid campaigners were more uneasy about targeting *individuals* with protests out of fear that these would attract sympathy. Just such a case was Zola Budd, the white South African long-distance runner, who competed barefooted. The Thatcher government found a way of morphing her in record time into a UK citizen so she could represent Britain at the 1984 Olympics. (Experiencing protests and constant controversy because she refused to denounce sports apartheid, years later she competed for her native South Africa when it was readmitted to the 1992 Olympic Games.)

The Anti-Apartheid Movement – driven forward by its tireless executive secretary Mike Terry, who played a key role over the decades of struggle – pressed the Thatcher government to revoke Britain's 'no visa' arrangement with South Africa so that it could ban individual players from entering the country. But Tory ministers replied that Gleneagles was 'not in any sense a formal agreement' and took no action. Christabel Gurney has pointed out that 'Together with the USA, Britain was by far the biggest offender:

between 1980 and 1987 more than 700 British sportspeople visited South Africa.'[274] This helps explain why English cricketers were so easily recruited for the boycott-breaking rebel tours that feature strongly in later chapters of this book.

*

Meanwhile, in the period that the Gleneagles Agreement and the UN Blacklist were announced and SACOS was moving towards adopting an uncompromising position of non-collaboration in the aftermath of the Soweto uprising, Peter was involved in a sideshow that had been impossible to imagine just a few years earlier. In 1977 his bitter enemies Danie Craven from rugby and Ali Bacher from cricket, and separately newspaper editor Donald Woods (acting as a discreet intermediary for sports minister, Piet Koornhof) made their way to him in attempts to close the gap between the anti-apartheid sports movement and the white reformist/co-optist elements in government and establishment sport. They each wanted to know if he might be prepared to negotiate an end to the sports boycott in return for the dismantling of apartheid in sport.

Craven came first. Because the number was not publicly listed, Peter's home phone very rarely rang with an unfamiliar call, and the evening in March 1977 was a curiosity. 'Craven, South Africa,' said a guttural voice. 'I would like to talk. Will you meet me?' This from a bitter opponent seven years earlier during the Stop The Seventy Tour campaign. In the early evening the following day, Craven arrived in a taxi and knocked apprehensively at his front door, brusquely declining the offer of tea or coffee, seemingly unsure whether to be aggressive or to return Peter's respectful politeness. Gradually he thawed. Peter suggested that they left 'politics' to one side and talked about changes that would be required in the way sport was played and organised in South Africa to warrant lifting the boycott. For example, fully integrated club and school sport, multimillion-rand programmes to improve black sports facilities and opportunities and changes in a variety of laws that affected sport. Craven took Peter's list of reforms away with him. The two had got on increasingly well as their talks proceeded. Underneath Craven's gruff Afrikaner assertiveness, Peter found a well-mannered gentleman who took a shine to his nine-month old son Sam crawling busily about the small living room-cum-study.

Woods followed next, and five months later, on 9 August 1977, the former South African test cricket captain Ali Bacher, who had been due to lead the cancelled 1970 tour to Britain, beat a path to Peter's door. He aggressively sought to persuade Peter that things were changing for the better and the boycotts should be called off. Peter did not agree, and their exchanges were acrimonious compared with the down-to-earth honesty and warmth of Danie Craven. It made Peter reflect on what his father Walter had told him: Afrikaners, rather than English-speaking whites would ultimately be the ones to win over when a settlement with the dispossessed majority finally occurred.

Peter used the moment of flux in South Africa to take a strategic position, focussing on what change the establishment could push for at the time. The main argument conveyed via the direct-action protests singling out South Africa – that South African sport deserved to be isolated because it was organised on race, not on merit – had been won. Now, for tactical reasons, Peter was specifically talking sport and encouraging them to get real change going.

Alert to the fluid situation in South African sport, Peter held discussions with the Labour minister of sport, Denis Howell, and on 8 February 1977 drafted notes for the government department. He agreed these new tactics with Dennis Brutus and Chris de Broglio from SANROC and managed to win a carefully negotiated policy position after a difficult debate at an annual meeting of the Anti-Apartheid Movement, where people had been sceptical about their approach.

Although agreeing entirely with isolating apartheid as a principle, Peter was convinced there needed to be a complementary political strategy as well for anti-apartheid forces to retain the initiative in sport specifically. He and his comrades had to keep up the momentum – to push out a boat of proposals and see where it sailed. So on 22 June 1977 he drew up a confidential memorandum agreed with Brutus and de Broglio for a 'Proposed South African Sports Summit', with various tough preconditions attached, including a temporary two-year moratorium on all tours while the sports system was reorganised on totally non-racial lines from school and club to national level, with SACOS's endorsement.

For various reasons, neither this proposal, nor a meeting with Koornhof, nor repeated requests via newspapers to return home ever materialised – Peter insisting that any such propositions depended upon the government revoking its 1969 ban on his return and guaranteeing his safety and

221

unrestricted access to non-racial sports leaders. Peter heard years later from Woods, forced into exile for championing Black Consciousness leader Steve Biko, that he had been phoned by Koornhof and asked to meet the head of the South African Bureau for State Security, General Hendrik van den Bergh, who warned that Koornhof was going too far, too fast, and that *he* would like to meet Peter in Paris instead. Peter was not surprised that such an invitation never materialised.

In retrospect, these flirtations were a signal of desperation at their iso-lation and among the last of 1970s-style engagements which saw incremental change as a possibility. South Africa was rapidly heading towards a new decade of increasing state repression and militant mass resistance. Militant tactics and uncompromising language decisively supplanted notions that an unreformable apartheid system could be changed by reforms from within the white power bloc. The goal now was capturing state power. Going for-ward, the calls would be for sport and 'liberation'.

The old boys' club of empire makes a last stand: Near civil war in New Zealand

New Zealand provided the next dramatic chapter in the evolution of inter-national protests against apartheid sport. So fierce were the divisions over the issue by the 1980s that they influenced the outcome of general elections and New Zealand was brought closer to civil war than anyone thought possible.

The campaigns against sports apartheid in the land of the silver fern were more racially charged than in Britain and played out over a much longer period of time, going way back to 1921.[275] Between 1971 and 1986 anti-apartheid activists waged an intense battle that was rarely out of the headlines. In a sense, Prime Minister Robert Muldoon's defence of sports contacts with apartheid South Africa was the last stand of the (white) old boys' club of empire, nostalgic about the 'traditional' way things had been done in the past.

As Robert Archer and Antoine Bouillon show in their impressive book, *The South African Game: Sport and Racism* (1982), of all the white Common-wealth countries, New Zealand (both its government and union) 'played a unique role' in the sports apartheid struggle, mainly because Māori had been so important in New Zealand rugby. They had 'frequently been members of the All Blacks national side, and from the 1920s were the subjects of controversy whenever tours were played with South Africa.'[276] The authors further argued that the reluctance of conservative New Zealand governments – especially under belligerent Prime Minister Robert Muldoon – to sever sporting contacts with South Africa was one of the factors that led African Heads of State to insist all Commonwealth countries sign up to the 'Gleneagles Agreement'.

The Springboks first toured New Zealand in 1921, and there was a match against a Māori XV whom they narrowly defeated, 9–8. But as Māori players began their haka before kick-off, the Springboks turned their backs, Māori winger Jack Blake later remarking that he and the rest of the team were 'seething with anger'. Afterwards a South African journalist touring with the Springboks wrote: 'It was bad enough having to play a team officially designated 'New Zealand natives' but the spectacle of thousands of Europeans frantically cheering on a band of coloured men to defeat members of their own race was too much for the Springboks, who were frankly disgusted.' Māori fullback George Nepia, a star of the 1924 All Blacks tour of the United Kingdom, commented that this statement 'provoked a reaction and bitterness which within the heart of the Maori race have neither been forgotten nor forgiven.'[277] Such strong Māori feelings were compounded by the South African Rugby Board's refusal to allow Māori players to be a part of any New Zealand team touring the country. In 1928, 1949 and 1960, New Zealand rugby teams to South Africa were all-white, each one attracting protests at home.

But the 'winds of change' that the British prime minister, Harold MacMillan, had warned the South African Parliament about on a visit to Cape Town in 1960 were also swirling around New Zealand. Protests against the 1960 all-white All Blacks rugby tour of South Africa saw the largest petition in the country's then history calling for the tour's cancellation. Despite this and the massacre at Sharpeville in March 1960, the all-white tour proceeded, the 'All Blacks' manager, Tom Pearce, declaring 'it is incumbent on every loyal New Zealander to get wholeheartedly behind the team'.

The Citizens Association for Racial Equality (CARE) was formed in 1965 and the campaign to end New Zealand's sporting and other involvements with apartheid South Africa quickly became a principal focus of its activity. Under the leadership of its dogged Auckland secretary, Tom Newnham – increasingly a key anti-apartheid campaign leader – CARE set about raising the profile of the apartheid sports issue.

In 1967 another New Zealand rugby tour of South Africa was scheduled. Again, Māori were to be excluded, which led conservative National Party prime minister, Keith Holyoake to announce in February 1966 that 'in this country we are one people; as such we cannot as a nation be truly represented in any sphere by a group chosen on racial lines'. The rugby authorities got the message and the tour was cancelled.

The role that Māori had played in the first five decades of protest against South African racism in sport was critical. Leading Māori voices against contact with South Africa had included the brilliant All Black fullback George Nepia, the respected Māori doctor and anthropologist, Te Rangi Hīroa (Dr Peter Buck), Māori Arawa leader Te Puea Herangi (aka Princess Te Puea), Eruera Tirikatene MP, and later, his daughter Whetu, also an MP.

South Africa reluctantly accepted that Māori could be included in the touring 1970 New Zealand team, but only on the basis they were given 'honorary white status', and the Halt All Racist Tours movement (HART) was formed in July 1969 to coordinate opposition to the tour. A toxic statement by former South African cabinet minister, Albert Hertzog, railed against the inclusion of Māori – 'Māori will sit at the table with our young men and girls and they will dance with our girls'. This helped mobilise opposition to the tour, but it proceeded nevertheless.

Unlike previous protests where the focus had been on the exclusion of Māori players, HART's campaign against the 1970 tour was outward-looking and internationalist, focusing upon the racist nature of the South African team. HART eschewed extra-legal, direct-action tactics, although some activists, including Tim Shadbolt, the long-time mayor of New Zealand's southernmost city Invercargill, raced across the tarmac at Wellington Airport towards the All Blacks' departing aircraft in a final defiant gesture.

In March 1971, taking the lead from both the failure of the 1970 campaign and the recent success of STST's tactics in Britain, HART announced a policy of 'massive, nationwide, non-violent disruption of racist sport'. The target was the scheduled 1973 Springboks rugby tour of New Zealand, but a number of 'minor' South African sports links were targeted, and tours by a South African women's hockey team and South African golfers were cancelled. In keeping with the international solidarity which was a feature of the campaign against apartheid sport, Peter and other activists, employing trademark STST tactics, occupied the forecourt of a London hotel where the All Blacks were staying, in protest against the planned 1973 Springboks tour.

Peter carried out of Twickenham, October 1969.
The direct-action protests against the Springbok rugby
team in 1969 catapulted the anti-apartheid sport struggle
into the headlines.

Protestors invade Bristol tennis court, July 1969.
Peter in dark glasses.

Cardiff demonstration, 13 December 1969.

Twickenham protest poster, 1970.

Barbed wire surrounding Lords Cricket Ground, 1970.
Cover of *Cricket Monthly*, April 1970.

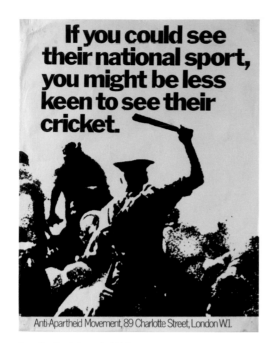

Popular Anti-Apartheid Movement poster, 1970.

Peter speaking at a Stop The Seventy Tour protest, 1970.

Police baton-charge a women's meeting, Cato Manor,
Durban, 1959. Photo by Laurie Bloomfield.

Mike Brearley, future England captain, speaking at the
Stop The Seventy Tour national conference, 7 March
1970, with Peter (far right). Jeff Crawford, West Indian
Standing Conference (left), and Mike Craft, STST, are
sitting next to Brearley.

Christopher Ford, 'Hain stopped
play', *Guardian*, 23 May 1970.

SPRINGBOK SPORTS TOURS — — WHY ALL THE FUSS?

1. **WHAT'S APARTHEID GOT TO DO WITH SPORT?**
   With South African sport, everything! Apartheid decides, on the basis of race, what sport every South African is permitted to play, where he may play it, and with whom he may play it. All sport is rigidly segregated and non-whites are excluded from representative South African sides

2. **BUT WHAT'S APARTHEID GOT TO DO WITH SPORT HERE?**
   Where contacts with South African sport are concerned, a great deal. South African touring teams are 'whites only'. It's no use assuring everybody that "of course we don't agree with apartheid", and then going ahead and playing against apartheid teams. If we genuinely reject racialism in sport, then we ought to show that we do, and the only obvious and effective way of doing so is by refusing to play against racially selected teams

3. **BUT SHOULDN'T WE RATHER "KEEP THE BRIDGES OPEN"?**
   The 'bridges' have no effect upon sports apartheid. During the past 20 years that we have been playing Apartheid teams, racial discrimination in South Africa has got worse, not better. We kept 'the bridges open' when the Nazis excluded Germans of Jewish descent from German teams, and it didn't help them either. Will we never learn that you can't compromise with racialism?

4. **BUT AREN'T DEMONSTRATIONS UNFAIR TO WHITE SOUTH AFRICAN SPORTSMEN, WHO MAY NOT EVEN APPROVE OF APARTHEID?**
   If they don't approve of it, why don't they say so? Each member of the Springbok Rugby team was invited to say that he disagrees with racialism in sport—none has done so

5. **BUT ARE ANY SOUTH AFRICAN NON-WHITES UP TO INTERNATIONAL STANDARD?**
   Surprisingly, in view of the poor facilities and opportunities, many are. Basil D'Oliveira is one; Humphrey Nkosi the ½ miler, Papwa Sewgolum the golfer and Precious McKenzie the weightlifter are others. And there are many more like them. Over 5,000 non-whites play Rugby in the Cape Province alone, and there are over 20,000 non-white cricketers in South Africa

6. **BUT WILL REFUSING TO PLAY WHITE SOUTH AFRICAN TEAMS MAKE ANY DIFFERENCE TO SPORTS APARTHEID?**
   Certainly. Sport is one of the few spheres in which white South Africans are still accepted internationally. It is therefore vital to them to be able to send teams abroad, and important to them that these teams should win. They are sports fanatics. So opposition to their tours troubles them deeply. The only concessions they have ever made have been a result of strong opposition to sports apartheid; they have never reacted to gentle persuasion.
   Above all, real opposition to sports apartheid is a tonic to the morale of the 13 million non-white South Africans

CONVINCED?
Then stop supporting racialist sport; stop going to watch the Springboks; stop making excuses for white South African sportsmen; STOP THE SEVENTY TOUR!
For further information, contact the 'Stop The Seventy Tour' Committee, 21a Gwendolen Avenue, London, S.W.15

Printed by Danny Bros., Bury St. Edmunds.

APARTHEID — — WHY ALL THE FUSS?

1. **BECAUSE APARTHEID IS THE ONLY POLITICAL SYSTEM THAT SETS OUT TO DIVIDE PEOPLE RATHER THAN UNITE THEM**—all South Africans are segregated into groups on racial grounds and integration is a criminal offence

2. **BECAUSE APARTHEID RELEGATES ALL PEOPLE WHO ARE NOT 'WHITE' TO A SUB-HUMAN STATUS**—under Apartheid only whites have the vote and 80% of all South Africans are therefore second class citizens. Only whites are normally permitted to enter South Africa, even on a visit. No African may live as of right anywhere in South Africa—land of his birth

3. **BECAUSE APARTHEID TREATS NON-WHITE SOUTH AFRICANS AS CHATTELS:**
   ★ every African is obliged by law to carry a document called a Pass on his person at all times—failure to have this Pass renders him liable to arrest
   ★ no African may live in any urban area without the specific permission of a white official, which must be entered on his Pass
   ★ no African may visit any area (other than that in which he has permission to live) for longer than 72 hours, without a permit
   ★ no African may work in an urban area without a permit; the permission must be entered in his Pass which he is obliged to have signed each month by his white employer. An unsigned Pass renders him liable to arrest
   ★ no African, apart from a domestic servant, may live anywhere in an urban area other than in a municipal council township
   ★ no African may live in a municipal township without a permit; if his wife is of a different tribe, she requires a permit to live with him, and his children may not live with him after the age of 16 without a permit
   ★ no African domestic servant may have her husband spend the night without a permit
   ★ no African may be on the streets of a town at night after curfew time without a permit from his white employer
   Any of the permissions mentioned above can be withdrawn at any time without reason— 1,500 Africans are arrested in South Africa **every day** for falling foul of these regulations

4. **BECAUSE APARTHEID SEEKS TO KEEP AFRICANS SUBSERVIENT**—there is a chronic shortage of skilled workers in South Africa, but skilled work is reserved for whites and white immigrants are brought in to do jobs which non-white South Africans are eager and able to do

5. **BECAUSE APARTHEID EDUCATES NON-WHITES FOR INFERIORITY**—African education is not only sub-standard in buildings, finance and facilities, but the syllabus is designed to brain-wash Africans into acceptance of second class citizenship

BECAUSE NO OTHER POLITICAL SYSTEM IN THE WORLD SO HUMILIATES HUMAN BEINGS AND DAMNS THEM FOR LIFE FOR AN IRRELEVANT CIRCUMSTANCE BEYOND THEIR CONTROL—SKIN COLOUR

MSS. AAM 1638

Stop The Seventy Tour campaign leaflets written by Walter Hain.

Peter with Australian campaign poster after returning to London, with Rosemary Chester, July 1971.

Meredith (being dragged) and Verity Burgmann arrested at anti-tour protest, Sydney 1971.

PAPWA
GOLF'S LOST
LEGEND
Maxine Case

The achievements of cricketer Basil D'Oliveira dented the myth of racial superiority in South African sport in the 1960s.

Golfer Papwa Sewgolum beat Gary Player and won the Dutch Open despite being excluded from official golf at home.

Lovedale college team, circa 1880s or 1890s.
The mission schools of eastern Cape not only produced the first generations of 'struggle' leaders but, together with the Parsis of Mumbai, also one of the oldest indigenous traditions of cricket in the colonial world.

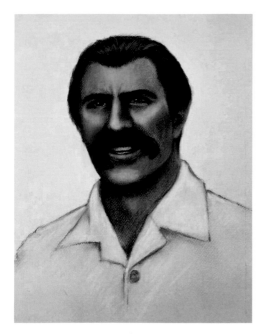

Krom Hendricks was one of the best fast bowlers in the world by 1894, compared by English professionals to 'The Demon' Spofforth of Australia.

Harry Mantenga and Livingstone Mzimba, South African students in the US in their Lincoln University American football colours, early 1900s.

The first football tour from South Africa to England in 1899 was by a team from Bloemfontein, captained by Joseph Twayi, and it played against opponents whose names today make fans drool, including Liverpool, Manchester United, Aston Villa, Tottenham Hotspur and Arsenal.

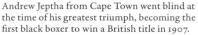

Andrew Jeptha from Cape Town went blind at the time of his greatest triumph, becoming the first black boxer to win a British title in 1907.

Jan Mashiane and Len Taunyane fortuitously took part in the marathon at the Olympic Games in St Louis in 1904.

Aspiring to full citizenship in sport: Members of the national SAARB African rugby team in the 1950s, with their own Springbok badge bordered by an outline of the African continent: Baba Jali (left) and Mbulelo Twaku, with supporters.

The SACBOC brochure for the 1956 Kenya tour, showing how the organisation adopted the same head-only Springbok emblem and aspired to the same opportunities as their segregationist, white, test-playing SACA counterparts.

The 1948 Olympic Games British weightlifting team.
Ron Eland (front left) had to leave his country so he
could participate internationally for Britain in the 1948
Olympics in London.

Another black South African sportsman who had to go
abroad to find greener pastures: Jake Ntuli (Tuli) won
the Empire flyweight boxing title in 1952 after defeating
experienced British and Empire champion, Teddy
Gardner.

Claiming space and breaking taboos: Vicky Valentine-Brown, former Wimbledon tennis quarter finalist, leads the champion Western Province women's team onto the field during SARWCA's inter-provincial tournament in 1954.

Early women's cricket: Nurses playing during the South African War while recuperating British soldiers look on.

Model Victorians. Women students from Lovedale and other schools closely supported local male cricketers and started their own tennis and croquet clubs from the 1880s onwards.

Milase Majola (middle) and members of the ladies section preparing for a local rugby club's Christmas day picnic at St Georges Strand beach in Port Elizabeth in the 1950s.

Dennis Brutus, poet, educator and pioneering non-racial sports activist was first secretary of both SASA and SANROC in a photograph that used to stand on his desk, taken by his long-standing comrade Chris de Broglio.

Weight lifting administrator, G.K. Rangasamy was elected as first SASA president.

A different kind of 'all black tour' during the height of apartheid forced removals.

John Harris with wife Ann returning from representing SANROC at the IOC meeting in Switzerland 1963.

Exiled SANROC campaigner Chris de Broglio set up a small office for the organisation at his Portman Court Hotel in Seymour Street, London W1, which increasingly gave direction to the worldwide anti-apartheid sports struggle from 1966 onwards.

A rare photograph of a football match in the Maximum Security Prison on Robben Island, 1970s.

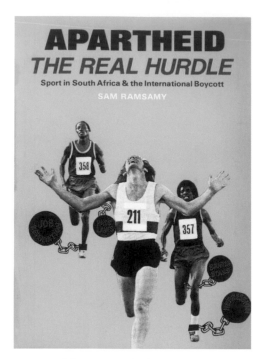

APARTHEID
THE REAL HURDLE
Sport in South Africa & the International Boycott
SAM RAMSAMY

SOCCER!
GREATEST VARIETY!?

INTER-CELL MATCHES TO CLOSE
MFA SOCCER SEASON
DATE: 13TH OCTOBER, 1973   TIME: 2 x 2 HRS
MORNING
BOOMSTRAAT ABAKHULU! V WANDERERS
DIKWANKWETLA   V   MAMBA
AFTERNOON
PULA AYINE!   V   BOMBERS
CABINET XI   V   EXODUS
HAPPY SUMMER REST SOCCERITES!

SANROC and the Anti-Apartheid Movement were highly effective in highlighting the overt and systemic discrimination in South African sport, 1982.

'Inter-cell' football fixture list on Robben Island, 1970s.

'The great challenge [is] . . . to maintain the human and social within you': Club badges and a sport and arts certificate designed by the political prisoners on Robben Island.

238

Robben Island prisoners doing hard labour, 1960s.

An imprisoned society: forced removals in Modderdam in Cape Town in the 1970s. Such removals and laws such as the Group Areas Act were part of the systemic violence that dislocated the lives of millions of black South Africans, impacting hugely on sport and community life.

239

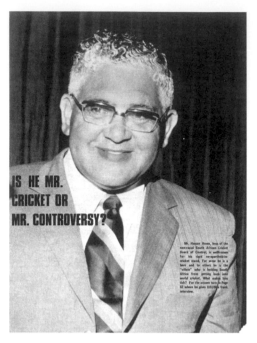

IS HE MR. CRICKET OR MR. CONTROVERSY?

SASF football chief, Norman Middleton (right) was elected first president of SACOS in 1973, but forced to step down in 1977 under its 'Double Standards' policy for participating in the government's Coloured Persons Representative Council. He is pictured here with two other politicians who participated in the government's ethnic bodies, Allan Hendrickse and Chief Mangosuthu Buthelezi.

Hassan Howa, SACOS vice president 1973–77 and president 1977–81, became the feisty voice of non-racial sport in the seventies. Featured here in *Drum* magazine, 8 March 1973.

240

'Facta non verba' (Deeds not words). Mono Badela, Dan Qeqe and the KWARU rugby leaders in the eastern Cape led the move of African sportspeople into non-racial sport under SACOS in the 1970s. Pictured here are Vuyi Domkraag, Mveleli Ncula, Dan Qeqe, Joseph Made, Royi Masoka, Baba Jali, Vuyo Kwinana, Silas Nkanunu and Dennis Siwisa.

M. N. Pather, tireless SACOS secretary for its first decade, speaking with Hassan Howa in the chair. SACOS patron and veteran administrator George Singh and future leaders, Frank van der Horst, Colin Clarke (his successor) and Joe Ebrahim up close and attentive.

(l–r) Morgan Naidoo's first public appearance after being banned for five years. With SACOS colleagues M. N. Pather, Don Kali of the SA Tennis Union, Frank van der Horst, Paul David and Morris Lewis. Naidoo became the third SACOS president in 1981.

241

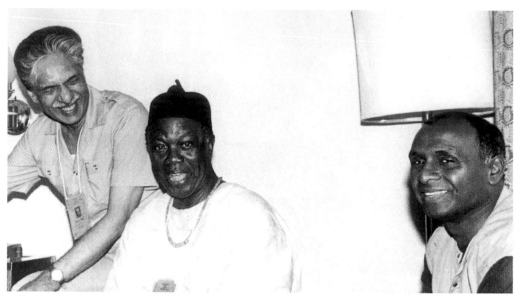

Key figures in isolating apartheid sport in the 1970s and 1980s. (l–r) Enuga Reddy of the UN Special Committee Against Apartheid, Abraham Ordia president of the Supreme Council for Sport in Africa and SANROC's Sam Ramsamy.

CITIZENS ALL BLACK TOUR ASSOCIATION

PROTEST MEETING

WELLINGTON TOWN HALL — WEDNESDAY 12th AUG. at 8 p.m.

NO MAORIS - NO TOUR

To fight racial discrimination in the selection of the 1960 All Black team to tour South Africa. This is an issue vital to every New Zealander. Racial discrimination must be fought right here in New Zealand.

Don't miss this meeting. Those coming in support from Hawke's Bay and North Auckland include:
GEORGE NEPIA and LOUIE PAEWAI
of the famous 1924 "Invincibles"
and VINCE BEVAN and M. N. PAEWAI

ROLLAND O'REGAN, Chairman, C.A.B.T.A.

New Zealand Citizens' All Black Tour Association poster, 1959. Speakers include Māori All Black star George Nepia.

242

'Mobilise May 1st' protest poster against the 1981 tour of New Zealand by the South African Springbok rugby team.

HART leader Trevor Richards at a July 1981 protest.

The HART campaign posters, 'Stop The Bloody Tour', 1981.

A Stop The Seventy Tour poster, 1970.

Peter and sons Sam (4) and Jake (2), at the Mandela
protest, 1980.

Peter acquitted at the Old Bailey in April 1976 after
being falsely accused of robbing a bank, part of a 'Putney
Plot' by British and South African dirty tricks operatives.

André, the only provincial player from the white SACA/SACU to join 'non-racial' cricket under SACOS during the apartheid years, batting at St George's Park, Port Elizabeth, 1982.

André at the mass funeral for the Cradock Four, murdered by the security police, in 1985. It was a defining moment in the struggle against apartheid, and also for him; pictured just to the left of the furthest left gravesite sign, indicating the last resting place of Sparrow Mkonto.

245

Frank van der Horst, SACOS vice president 1977–83 and president 1983–88, at a prize-giving with Colin Clarke (secretary) standing directly behind him. The pair became the new-generation face of SACOS in the 1980s. Announcer Wilfred Daniels standing with microphone looks on.

Frank van der Horst speaking at the Sport and Liberation conference in August 1983, which demonstrated SACOS's turn towards becoming the active 'sports wing of the liberatory movement'.

Oliver Tambo pictured at the ANC's historic 'council of war' at Kabwe, Zambia in 1985. Balancing the armed and underground struggle with international solidarity and legal internal mobilisation, Tambo in 1987 re-emphasised calls for a broad united front against apartheid inside South Africa, including sectoral mobilisation in sport, and for the re-evaluation of the international boycott so that the 'people's camp' internally could be exempted from the isolation imposed on the regime and its allies. This led to the emergence of the National Sports Congress and new strategies in sport.

SACOS held two national sports festivals, in 1982 and 1988. Here, showing its Olympian aspirations, Adeeb Abrahams lights the flame to start the 1988 event.

SANROC's untouchable international standing and
contacts during the the late 1980s and early 1990s
transition from apartheid to sports unity and political
democracy is underlined here. Sam Ramsamy, sitting
next to a gesturing Jean-Claude Ganga of the Supreme
Council of Sport in Africa, and also an IOC member.
Behind them are Lamine Diack (later president of the
IAAF) and South African-born Ismail Bhamjee (later
a FIFA executive member).

Two key figures in the internal sports debates of the late
1980s. (l–r) speaker Jakes Gerwel, called for new sports
strategies, and Joe Ebrahim, next to him, took over from
Frank van der Horst as SACOS president in 1988. With
them is Abe 'Maaantjie' Adams.

Planning the revolution in South African sport: (l–r)
NSC spokespeople, Ben Tengimfene and Ngconde
Balfour, and Trevor Manuel of the UDF/MDM, announce
planned actions against the rebel cricketers, 1989.

Krish Mackerdhuj, president of SACB (foreground), and
next to him Krish Naidoo and Moss Mashishi preparing
for the demonstrations against the Gatting tour with
other NSC activists, 1989.

Peter, travelling undercover, meeting André on his first day back in South Africa in 23 years, Rocklands grounds, Mitchell's Plain, 9 December 1989.

Peter meeting his United CC team mates, Rocklands grounds, Mitchell's Plain, 9 December 1989.

Peter meeting prominent non-racial sports activists in Port Elizabeth: (l–r) Gavin Watson, Khaya Majola, Ronnie Pillay and Cheeky Watson, December 1989.

Days before the arrival of the Gatting rebel team, André shared a platform with SACB president, Krish Mackerdhuj and Mass Democratic Movement leaders, 'Terror' Lekota, Makhenkesi Stofile and Trevor Manuel at a packed meeting in the Cape Town City Hall that set in motion the plans for the national anti-tour campaign, 16 January 1989.

Newspaper headlines of the 'Siege' of Kimberley, January 1990.

Crowd at the Cape Town City Hall to protest against the Gatting tour, January 1991.

TOUR PROTEST . . . Protesters hold up placards outside the De Beers Stadium on Saturday demanding the end of the rebel England cricket tour.

Tour demo ends in township riot

The Kimberley demonstrations sent an unambiguous message to organiser Ali Bacher and Mike Gatting and his team during the first match of the rebel tour, 1990.

The crowd on the Parade in Cape Town hanging on to every word by Mandela on the day of his release, 11 February 1990.

John Nkadimeng, keynote speaker at the launch of the National Olympic and Sports Congress (NOSC), March 1990, with key organiser, Krish Naidoo seated on his far left.

New leadership in South African sport. The executive committee of the NOSC elected at its launch in Langa, Cape Town, March 1990. (r–l) Errol Vawda, Smuts Ngonyama, Errol Heyns, Mthobi Tyamzashe, Rama Reddy, Krish Mackerdhuj, Ebrahim Patel, Mluleki George (president), Cheryl Roberts and Mtwekhaya Nkwinti.

A new era for South African sport. ANC and NSC leaders welcome an IOC delegation to South Africa after the unbannings. (Front l–r) Steve Tshwete, Oliver Tambo, Nelson Mandela, Sam Ramsamy (SANROC) and Mluleki George (president of the NOSC).

Steve Tshwete, the ubiquitous 'Mr Fixit' of South African
sport after the unbannings of organisation in 1990.
At his home base in East London together with fellow
Robben Islander, Walter Sisulu, during a showpiece
SACB match in East London in March 1991. Pictured
with Vido Mgadla (left) and Luxolo Qoboshiyane of
the non-racial Border Cricket Board.

254   Tshwete celebrating a surprise win for South Africa over
Australia in Christchurch, New Zealand, during the
1991/92 cricket World Cup with captain, Kepler Wessels.
He famously shed tears on this occasion, symbolising
the dramatic turnabout underway in South Africa at the
time, before becoming democratic South Africa's first
minister of sport in 1994.

Elana Meyer and Derartu Tulu of Ethiopa doing
a victory lap together at the Barcelona Olympics
in 1992, which foreshadowed post-apartheid unity
with the rest of Africa.

The iconic 'Rainbow Nation' image of Nelson Mandela
wearing a Springbok jersey, handing over the 1995
Rugby World Cup to South African captain, Francois
Pienaar.

Football's turn: Madiba handing the 1996 Africa Cup of
Nations over to Bafana Bafana captain Neil Tovey, 1996.

Minder van dié medisyne nou nodig **bl. 8**

Beeld

netwerk24.com Maandag 22 Augustus 2016 R10,00

Faf gaan nóg beter word, sê Allister **bl. 18**

"
Dit gaan nie oor hoe my teenstanders lyk of klink of wie hulle lief het of hoe gespierd hulle is nie. Dit gaan oor hoe hard ek teen hulle moet werk. En vanaand is ons hier om daaroor te praat. Baie dankie.
— CASTER SEMENYA

SEMENYA

Stryd om beheer van Goudstad vandag op mespunt

Verslagspan

Terwyl die DA en sy nuwe informele bondgenoot in munisipale bestuur, die EFF, gereed maak om vandag finaal die beheer van Johannesburg oor te neem, het die ANC verklaar hy stel ook 'n burgemeesterskandidaat en gaan tot die einde toe veg.

In die jongste ontwikkeling in die opbou na die eerste sitting van die Johannesburgse metroraad vandag het die EFF die ANC daarvan beskuldig dat hy sy raadslede probeer omkoop.

Verder het Geoffrey Makhubo, ANC-tesourier in die Johannesburg-streek, die skuld vir die party se swak verkiesingsuitslae onder meer op die Nkandla-hofuitspraak en e-tol gepak.

Mbuyiseni Ndlozi, EFF-woordvoerder, het in 'n verklaring gesê die EFF veroordeel die pogings van Dan Bovu, uittredende ANC-lid van die burgemeesterskomi-

PRAAT REGUIT NÁ SKITTER-WEDLOOP

Goue Caster troef Rio

Marizanne Kok

oor bespiegeling nie, dit gaan oor die werk wat ons gedoen het.

SA se ander medaljewenners

Caster Semenya, South Africa's golden girl winning her 2016 Olympic gold.

Return of the victorious Springboks after winning the rugby world cup in Japan in 2019.

Although the Labour Party's victory in New Zealand's 1972 general election ushered in a government sympathetic to the anti-apartheid cause, it had campaigned on a policy of not stopping the tour. HART's dynamic leader, Trevor Richards, had no doubt that, like STST, the threat of direct action was crucial. He stepped up plans to disrupt the tour, provoking a frenzied debate about law and order, and a reminder from the New Zealand prime minister, Norman Kirk, that it was *he*, and not Richards, who was 'running the country'. As the pressure increased, the minister of defence was advised that up to 1,000 soldiers would be needed to bolster the police and protect the tour from demonstrations; he said he would 'not commit New Zealand soldiers to bash other New Zealanders at rugby fields or anywhere else'.

It became increasingly clear, as in Britain three years previously, that the Commonwealth Games (scheduled for Christchurch in 1974) were in jeopardy, with black-governed countries refusing to participate if the tour proceeded. Giving an indication of how little rugby thinking had changed since 1960, Tom Pearce (former president of the Rugby Union) declared: 'Where the white man has been, he has brought law and the establishment of his regime for the benefit of mankind. If these things go, we are lost . . . They say if we have a Springboks tour, we won't have a Commonwealth Games – I couldn't give a damn.'

With the pressure mounting and the tour imminent, on 10 April 1973 Prime Minister Kirk announced that the tour would be postponed until the South African team was chosen on the basis of genuine merit. The rugby world was furious, the president of the Wellington Rugby Football Union calling it 'the worst news I have heard since . . . Chamberlain stated that England was at war with Germany.'

It was a decisive breakthrough and a major victory for the international campaign against apartheid sport. But it is a measure of the divisive political intensity swirling around Springbok tours that Kirk knew full well his decision could cost Labour the next election. He was only too aware that opposition from the New Zealand Rugby Union, most rugby fans and many voters would be bitter. Nevertheless, acting bravely and on principle, he believed that stopping the tour was in the best interests of the country, both domestically and internationally. The police had reported to him a few months previously, that 'without drastic Police action, and possibly assistance by the military as well, it is most doubtful that the tour could proceed . . . It is our view that the tour would engender the greatest eruption of violence this country has ever known.' Kirk also believed the tour was inconsistent with how New Zealand should act internationally, and the reputational damage to the country if the tour proceeded.

Backed by Tom Newnham and joining Trevor Richards at the core of HART's leadership for more than a decade were Dave Wickham, Mike Law, Pauline McKay and Don Swan. With Richards the four were labelled – by friends and foe alike – as the 'gang of five'. Although HART became a mass movement with key activists spread around the country, without the gang of five, its progress would have been that much more difficult. As the 1970s progressed, many others played important roles, Auckland schoolteacher John Minto being one of the most prominent.

The period thereafter until the November 1975 election was dubbed by Richards as 'the inter-war years', with steady progress made on a number of anti-apartheid fronts. But Prime Minister Norman Kirk, the strongest supporter of the anti-apartheid cause in Labour's senior ranks, died suddenly in August 1974, and in the election in November the following year, the opposition National Party won a landslide victory on a platform dominated by populist right-wing issues such as welcoming the Springboks to New Zealand.

New Zealand and South African sports officials moved quickly. Within two weeks of the election, six sports had indicated that invitations to South African teams had been issued or were being considered. While these sports were all the subject of protest action, it was the scheduled 1976 All Blacks tour of South Africa that was HART's major target. Richards undertook a seventy-stop speaking tour of the country. At the end of May, shortly before the team's planned departure, 15,000 marched in demonstrations around the country – the biggest anti-tour protest since 1959–60.

But neither the Rugby Union nor the government were listening. As in Britain, HART found it was always harder to stop tours to South Africa than to secure the cancellation of tours to New Zealand. Even the eruption of Soweto on 16 June 1976 – when schoolchildren were ruthlessly gunned down by police – less than a week before the All Blacks were to leave for South Africa, made no difference, though opposition to the tour sky-rocketed. On the eve of the team's departure, a sports minister declared that the team 'left for their South Africa tour with the blessing and goodwill of New Zealanders and the New Zealand Government', a sentiment later repeated by the prime minister.

What followed has been described as New Zealand's greatest foreign policy crisis. With the All Blacks in South Africa and the Montreal Olympics due to open on 17 July, Tanzania announced on 10 July that it was pulling out because of New Zealand's presence, explaining: 'The New Zealand Government is the only Government we know of which openly and enthusiastically encourages links with South Africa'. On 13 July, the Organisation of African Unity called for the International Olympic Committee to ban New Zealand from participation. On 16 July, New Zealand IOC representative, Lance Cross, a long-time supporter of South African participation in international sport, told the IOC that there was 'no significant difference' between the policies of the previous Labour government and the present national administration. He received sustained applause and IOC chief, Lord Killanin, without bothering to call for a vote, declared unanimous support for New Zealand's participation.

This signalled a fight between the old imperial order still governing the IOC and the emerging global order of independently assertive developing world nations, and with SANROC playing a key role in liaison with HART, Nigeria immediately announced its withdrawal from the games. At the Olympic opening ceremony, the extent of the boycott was revealed. Thirty-one countries that had entered for the games withdrew because of New Zealand's presence, and the 1976 Olympics became the smallest Games since Rome 1960. New Zealand had been responsible for the first major boycott of the modern Olympic era, *The Sunday Times* declaring: 'An examination of the facts behind the New Zealand tour leads positively to the conclusion that the IOC should have had no other course but to ban New Zealand from the Olympics.'

Following the cancellation of the 1973 rugby tour, Richards visited Africa periodically, developing close relationships with a number of African governments, particularly Tanzania and Nigeria, with Abraham Ordia, the president of the Supreme Council for Sport in Africa and with the OAU, and was therefore known and trusted in Africa. Regular HART international backgrounders were distributed on developments in the New Zealand campaign against apartheid sport, highlighting the difference between belligerent New Zealand government rhetoric at home and the spin it put on its policies internationally. For this, both HART and the Citizens Association for Racial Equality (CARE) were blamed for the Montreal boycott, and accused by Prime Minister Muldoon – a strident apologist for white South African sports links – of 'telling lies overseas' and of 'acts bordering on treason'.

Nevertheless, the response of the United Nations and the Commonwealth to the Montreal boycott was to take further steps aimed to isolate white South African sport.

The Commonwealth was hopeful that this would spell the end of New Zealand's support for apartheid sport, particularly the scheduled 1981 Springboks rugby tour. But not known at the time was that Prime Minister Muldoon had no intention of taking any notice of the Gleneagles Agreement, and by 1978, HART was spearheading protests against fifteen New Zealand sports bodies involved with South Africa. When Nigeria withdrew from the 1978 Edmonton Commonwealth Games because of New Zealand's noncompliance with the Gleneagles Agreement, the familiar old attacks on anti-apartheid leaders of 'spreading false information overseas' and 'treason' resurfaced, and Richards was once more dubbed a 'traitor'. HART's international work had squeezed the government's ability to exercise its foreign policy options, and it was hurting.

On 1 May 1981, 15,000 marched in Wellington, as many as had marched in the entire country in 1976. Nationwide, between 65,000 and 75,000 had participated in the mobilisation. By mid-May, polls showed opposition to the tour had risen to 51 per cent, with support standing at just 32 per cent, and protesters' anger melted momentarily into hope. But Muldoon calculated that, with the next general election less than six months away, he needed the Springbok tour to shore up his base.

In *Dancing on Our Bones* (1999), Trevor Richards writes:

The passions brought to the surface by the 1981 Springboks tour drove many people on both sides of the divide to take actions that five years earlier, or today, would be totally out of the question. In the 56 days the team was in New Zealand, there were more than 200 demonstrations in 28 centres involving in excess of 150,000 people. Two Springboks matches were cancelled, and over 1,500 people were charged with tour related offences. For the first time in 30 years, New Zealand police baton-charged fellow New Zealanders. To ensure that the test matches could proceed, between a third and a half of the country's police force was required. These were the largest police operations in New Zealand's history. Families, communities and organisations were split. The whole country was deeply and bitterly divided.[278]

Māori activists, as in the early years of protest, were once again to the fore. Tama Poata, who had driven from Wellington to Auckland to attend the meeting that established HART, and who was the person who gave HART its name, was a dominant figure. Syd Jackson was another – his father, the 1937 All Black Everard Jackson, had been asked by the New Zealand Rugby Football Union to make himself unavailable for selection for the 1940 All Blacks tour to South Africa (subsequently cancelled because of the war). Māori filmmaker Merata Mita assiduously filmed the events of 1981. Her film, *Patu* (1983), documents the protests against that year's Springboks tour. Donna Awatere, active in the protests, went on to write the definitive text on Māori sovereignty.

To Oliver Tambo, the ANC's leader in exile, New Zealand's protests were 'the most significant contribution to the anti-apartheid struggle in 1981 from either inside or outside of South Africa.' Fourteen years after the tour, Nelson Mandela told New Zealand governor-general Dame Catherine Tizard that when on Robben Island he heard the news of the cancellation of the Hamilton game, 'it felt like the sun coming out'.

The rugby tour had immediate consequences for New Zealand. In 1982 its attempt to gain a seat on the Security Council failed, with African delegates actively lobbying against. Earlier in the year, the Commonwealth Games Federation introduced a code of conduct, which was incorporated into the Federation's constitution. Under it, power was given to it to stop a country taking part in future Commonwealth Games for 'gross non-fulfilment . . . of the objectives of the Gleneagles Agreement'. Another tour like 1976 or 1981, and New Zealand would automatically be out. In 1976, African boycotters were condemned for disrupting the Olympics. Now the Federation's constitution labelled the act of playing with apartheid disruptive. Muldoon's National Party had scraped home in the 1981 general election, but in 1984 Labour won a landslide victory, and the ban on South African sports teams visiting New Zealand was immediately re-imposed. The new government told the Rugby Union that the scheduled 1985 All Blacks tour of South Africa was not in New Zealand's national interest, and the government did not want the tour to proceed. But whereas the Rugby Union had responded positively to a National Party prime minister in 1966 and had called off a scheduled tour, eighteen years later rugby was past listening or caring. The tour would proceed. Two lawyers responded by bringing an injunction against the Rugby Union to stop the tour. South African non-racial sports administrator and underground ANC activist, Rev

Arnold Makhenkesi Stofile, flew to New Zealand to testify in support. Shortly before the team was due to leave New Zealand for South Africa, the High Court granted the injunction. The tour was off. A rebel rugby team visited South Africa the following year, tacitly supported by the governing body, but there was to be no more official contact until the unbanning of the ANC and the release of Mandela from prison.

More even than had been the case for Britain in 1970, the New Zealand story was one of a clash of ideology and history, which escalated beyond the international sporting level to an inter-governmental level. On the one hand, sports officials, fans and right-wing politicians reflected reactionary and racist attitudes from colonial times; on the other, radical progressive opinion beat to the tune of the emerging new global order; sport was caught uncomfortably between the two. New Zealand society was split down the middle, dividing families and friends, and the issue became central to the country's politics.

Secret Kruger Rands and the start of rebel tours as apartheid sport tries to buy itself out of isolation

After a frustrating decade of isolation, the establishment cricket union, SACU, led by Rashid Varachia, Joe Pamensky and Ali Bacher, started seeking new ways out of the cold. As the New Zealand tour strife indicated, the door was closing tightly on apartheid sports teams going abroad. The limited internal changes since 1976 and the poor quality of private invitation teams visiting South Africa from abroad, sponsored by conservative friends like millionaire English sports promoter Derrick Robins, were not providing the answers. So, at a time when the isolation of apartheid sport was deepening and the newly launched World Cup and Kerry Packer's World Series cricket were rejuvenating the game internationally, the South African sports establishment and its few black allies decided to use the cheque book to buy their way back into international cricket and legitimacy.

The result was seven so-called rebel cricket tours between 1982 and 1990. SACU offered attractive amounts of money to international and fringe players from England, Sri Lanka, Australia and the West Indies to buck policy and come to play so-called 'tests' in South Africa. The visits of the West Indians in particular created much excitement,

After the change of government in 1984 and the ensuing successful court injunction against the New Zealand Rugby Union touring South Africa in 1985, SA rugby went rogue too, hosting rebel tours by the New Zealand Cavaliers invitation team, supported unofficially by their rugby hierarchy which had labelled international sanctions 'extraordinary, arrogant and intolerable'.

The new generation of business-minded cricket leaders running SACU proceeded confidently with rebel tours during a decade marked by high levels of repression as the white minority government tried to cling on to power in the face of increasing resistance, having failed to co-opt black middle-class allies through 'reforms' such as the Tricameral Parliament. Violence, the suspension of (in many cases already dubious) rule of law measures and heavy state repression became a feature of the 1980s. Non-racial sports administrators, affected by 'restrictions on freedoms of press, speech and assembly', regarded the rebel tours as obscenities in this context.

The establishment efforts fitted in with the total onslaught strategy and the new National Security Management System (NSMS) put in place by the South African government in the 1980s. The state propaganda narrative emphasised that South Africa faced a full-scale assault by the forces of 'international communism' and its allies, including the black liberation movements and even the Western media. Therefore, all sectors of the population – including business, the press, and other institutions – had to be harnessed in support of this total strategy. This meant clamping down on opposition and 'winning hearts and minds' (WHAM). 'If you are not with us,' the reasoning of the government's total onslaught went, 'you are against us.' To ensure continuing tight control of the 'change' process, the national security system was restructured. A new State Security Council (SSC), heavily influenced by the military who were close to the new head of state, P. W. Botha, became a kind of 'second cabinet' or 'shadow government' set up to monitor the performance of the NSMS. Its full repressive capacity would become evident in the 1980s as South Africa entered the age of full-blown states of emergency, mass detentions, troops occupying black townships, cross-border military raids in neighbouring countries and extra judicial assassinations of anti-apartheid activists.

Commentators noted that the government was now not so much the party of Afrikaner nationalism, as the party of unrestricted free enterprise and militarism.[279] Once again, sport was be intertwined inextricably with what was happening in this broader context, and one of the strategies used by apartheid sport was for SACU to plead innocence and to try to buy itself out of isolation through the rebel tours with the help of government and the business establishment, with which Bacher, Pamensky and others were heavily connected in Johannesburg.

Meanwhile the growing cost of playing and administering non-racial sport by the late 1970s and early 1980s was demonstrated by the experiences of Dan Qeqe and the eastern Cape rugby players in KWARU who had moved across to join SACOS, as well as the case of the Watson brothers who sensationally deserted Danie Craven's rugby board to play in the townships with KWARU in 1977. Cheeky Watson, a Junior Springbok on the verge of selection for South Africa, Valence, flank for Eastern Province, and six other white players turned out in a match between KWARU and Grahamstown-based South Eastern Districts Rugby Union (SEDRU) at Dan Qeqe Stadium. The minister of sport said that they would be arrested if they went ahead and they were threatened with suspension by Danie Craven. One of the brothers was taken to security police headquarters and told: 'Go back and tell your brothers that . . . they're not such fucking heroes that they can get away with anything. If you betray your kind, you'll get what's coming to you.'[280] The players decided to go ahead, avoiding roadblocks at the main entrances to the townships and 'a mass of armoured vehicles' at the stadium. Ten thousand people were present and 'pandemonium broke out as they approached'. Cheeky Watson scored two tries as KWARU beat SEDRU 23–14 and the brothers became instant icons of the non-racial sports struggle.[281]

The rugby match also forever changed the lives of the Watsons. Branded as 'white kaffirs', the brothers were shunned, harassed and victimised by the white community and the police. Several attempts were made on their lives and the family home was burned down. They, in turn, deepened their commitment, eventually joining the underground struggle of the banned African National Congress. Cheeky was quoted as saying: 'The pressures on us have been tremendous. We all realise we have given up our careers as white players and even the chance of Springbok colours. But we are now serving a far greater cause.'[282]

Non-racial sportspeople who were not African faced arrest and charges for entering a township without permits. This made the mixed membership of the New Brighton-based United Cricket Club all the more significant: with post-democracy Springbok coach Allister Coetzee and South African Football Association president Danny Jordaan, who hosted the 2010 FIFA World Cup, and other coloured team members. They were sometimes angry when Eastern Province Cricket Association (EPCA) clubs refused to come into the township or expected to be met at the entrance and escorted in. 'Eventually, we told them to find their own way to our grounds, just like in any other club,' Maxwell Jordaan recalled. Then there were the security police, who were particularly vicious in Port Elizabeth as later testimony to the Truth and Reconciliation Commission and the murders of Steve Biko, Matthew Goniwe, Simphiwe Mthimkhulu and others showed. Sportspeople were targeted as well. KWARU founder Mono Badela had to leave town for his own safety, and in 1977 Dan Qeqe was arrested after 'defending' school children held by the police in the aftermath of the youth uprisings of 1976. 'I was there at Algoa police station and Colonel Goosen, head of the local security Police, said to me, *Kom*,' Dan remembers. 'No one came close to you if you were followed by the Special Branch of the time. It was only your family. Those chaps were vicious. They didn't even care for a king's son. They were the kings of the country.' In 1978, shortly after Biko's death, newspapers reported that prominent cricket and football official Yusuf Lorgat had resigned from his positions after security police had twice visited his house.

The situation was deteriorating, and sportspeople were coming much more directly into the firing line. From now on it would not be unusual for the non-racial SACOS and its affiliates to be banned from calling meetings and for its officials to be harassed, detained or imprisoned without trial. Dan and his colleagues in New Brighton were among those on a collision course with the state. In the past, the sports leaders were pillars of middle-class respectability and restraint. For example, Wilson Ximiya, A.Z. Lamani, Sidima Dwesi and Qeqe himself served on the local administration board. But after Soweto these boards, for long derided as 'toy telephones', lost all legitimacy, particularly once the apartheid government promulgated the Black Local Authorities Act to put black local government on a new footing. The local boards were given greater powers than before, but the overall outcome was to tighten control over urban Africans, increase the cost of local administration and confirm the exclusion of Africans from government's 'reform' programme dealing with representation at the national level.[283] Qeqe and his colleagues decided to withdraw from the Administration Boards. They stopped attending meetings and lost their positions. While 'unfortunately some like Dwesi and Mpondo went back', Qeqe now became a member of the Action Committee which rejected the new community council system.[284] He was soon detained by the police for the first time. In 1981 he and Mono Badela were among the four sports leaders banned by the government.[285]

The flipside of apartheid 'reform' was repression. The superficial changes being made to apartheid after Soweto went with a calculated plan for greater repressive control by the state, also in sport. But resistance by non-racial sportspeople was a sign that after a decade and a half of brutal repression and banning of opposition, they were once again openly synchronising their activities with the goals of the banned liberation movements.

Ali Bacher of SACU and other establishment sports bodies employed shallow liberal arguments to contend that their 'mixed' sport and rebel cricket, rugby and football tours were helping to fight apartheid, but this was simply not the case: petty apartheid perhaps, but definitely not grand apartheid. Non-racial sportspeople argued that on the contrary they were helping to perpetuate the apartheid system by giving legitimacy to the claims that real reform was taking place in South Africa when in fact it was only cosmetic change that left the pillars of apartheid such as the Bantustans (the so-called 'homeland areas' for Africans), group areas, Bantu Education and the instrument of racial classification and division, the Population Registration Act intact. They argued that while mixed sport was becoming more commonplace, claims that South African sport was now fully non-racial and had done everything asked of it by the outside world was deceitful. Thousands of sports clubs throughout the country were still racially exclusive, either constitutionally or de facto.

Opponents of the 1980s rebel tours also pointed out that the tours were in fact foreign policy coups in an otherwise bleak period for the government, internally and internationally. The 'astronomical amounts' spent in attracting overseas sports stars to South Africa gave the nationalist government desperately needed political mileage, and clearly reflected the close relationship between government, big business and sport. Indeed, following representations from the SACU leadership, new tax legislation was passed which meant that the apartheid government effectively bankrolled the tours via the Treasury.

Joe Pamensky's biographer explained:

The SACU was running short of money and needed to find some quickly in order to fund the tours. Joe was uniquely placed. He had made important contacts both as President of SACU and through his international financial planning business. He could also easily negotiate his way around South African tax legislation. He and Ali met with the Foreign Minister, Pik Botha, who gave them money for the tour out of the foreign affairs budget. But more was needed and Joe managed to raise this by negotiation with the Minister of Finance, Barend Du Plessis for tax concessions. He managed to secure an amendment to the Income Tax Act, which gave a double tax allowance to sponsors who backed events classified as 'International projects'.[286]

In addition to taking international pressure off the increasingly isolated South African government, rebel tours diverted attention away from the daily suffering of South Africans. The tours were front page news on a regular basis. The 'unrest' and other pressing issues were relegated to the inside pages, even in the more critical and liberal-oriented newspapers. Rugby supremo Danie Craven put it succinctly later in the decade when he said, 'this tour has done wonders for the country. Rugby has changed the front pages of newspapers, we no longer see Mandela's name, he has been moved to page 6 so as to accommodate rugby. And to me this is wonderful. In time to come we should erect a monument to honour the New Zealand players for they have changed the face of South Africa.'

All in all, establishment sport fitted neatly into P. W. Botha's new deal, which had as its catchphrases, 'reform' and 'free enterprise'. This was exemplified by the cricket tours and tycoon Sol Kerzner's Sun City, where big (subsidised) profits were made and millions spent on glittering entertainment and sporting extravaganzas in the midst of surrounding black poverty. To the liberation movement and non-racial sportspeople, the new breed of business-minded, business-linked cricket administrators who took over from the old MCC school-tie type conservatives were the new face of apartheid, perpetuating the system in a new guise.

Non-racial activists warned that:

It is time that white sportsmen and women took a long hard look at themselves. It is no longer enough just to say they are against Apartheid (as they were forced to do by international pressure) and expect to be left alone to get on with the game. Despite the growth of mixed sport over the past decade the white sports establishment is still as much part of an apartheid system as it was in the 1960s when it hid behind Verwoerd's unbending policy to explain its rigidly segregated clubs and competitions.[287]

However, SACU proceeded on its path of justifying and organising rebel tours. Bacher explained that they were necessary 'to keep the game alive'. But far from being about 'fair play', the limited turn to multiracial cricket within the system and the attempt to buy its way back into international competition, apartheid sport was showing itself to be an extension of the broader apartheid system and part of increasingly corrupt covert actions to circumvent sanctions. Pallo Jordan, a top theorist of the ANC in exile, described the kind of reform manoeuvres happening in politics and sport during the first half of the 1980s as 'the new face of the counter-revolution'. He cautioned that it was dangerous to say that no change had taken place. The system was changing and trying to adapt itself to maintain control. This meant that while certain sectors of white society ostensibly promoted change, and some were even prepared to accept one person, one vote, the overall goal of the system's 'reform' initiatives was not democracy but to constrain fundamental transformation and reorganise white control in South Africa in more acceptable ways.

In *Apartheid Guns and Money* (2017),[288] Hennie van Vuuren exposes the shadowy side of the apartheid sanctions-busting efforts against tightening isolation, popularised so effectively by the sports protests and boycotts. His monumental work is a gripping story of conspiracy, assassination, bribery and dishonesty from London to Washington, from Paris to Pretoria, from Moscow to Beijing, from Buenos Aires to Tel Aviv. While the South African government and its allies talked 'reform', there was rampant money laundering through supposedly reputable international banks by the state-owned arms company Armscor, which deployed its networks of international arms dealers and fixers to deliver the arms and pay the money that kept the war going, against both the black majority in South Africa and neighbouring states Angola and Namibia. Van Vuuren methodically and relentlessly ex-poses what he calls 'the arms money machine'. He writes, 'bankers in coun-tries like Belgium and Luxembourg sat back and watched the profits role in, all the while helping Armscor to construct an international system of money laundering ... Swiss commercial banks were among the most significant and long-standing supporters of Pretoria . . . The banking establishment in all the Western world's largest economies wanted a stake in the South African game.'

What Van Vuuren terms apartheid's 'march to militarisation' from the 1960s peaked under President P. W. Botha from 1978. Before that, Prime Minister Vorster's security services had reigned supreme, and used every trick in the book – including bribery of foreign actors, corruption, subterfuge and intrigue in which arms dealers 'made fat commissions'. Between 1974 and 1978, the government's Information Department under Vorster secretly put about £30 million into special projects, including an undercover attempt to buy American newspapers. There was also an undercover attempt to buy the British publishing company Morgan Grampian. Vast sums were spent on wooing Western journalists, broadcasters and compliant politicians, British Conservative MPs and the likes of Leslie Sehume through a front organisation, the Committee for Fairness in Sport.

Eventually this misuse of funds was exposed in the second half of 1978, bringing about the fall of Vorster. With his security empire discredited, President Botha presided over the militarisation of South Africa from government downwards. The centre of decision-making shifted from the Party and the intelligence services to the military-security establishment. The Defence Force budget rocketed and its fighting strength soared.

The militarists took over foreign policy with armed strikes into neighbouring countries by both land and air, killing local civilians, and arming and supporting insurgent bands such as RENAMO in Mozambique and UNITA in Angola. Van Vuuren shows how under the last fifteen years of apartheid a 'war economy' was built with defence expenditure ballooning to well over 20 per cent of the annual state budget, and private companies alongside 'becoming important and highly profitable players in a siege economy' and being drawn into sanctions busting too. Private companies supplied everything from explosives to shoe polish to the military, often in lucrative contracts with cosy relationships to ministers and secret funding to the ruling National Party. There was a clandestine world of government departments with open wallets and private suitors happy to dip in to evade foreign restrictions.

Buying oil on the black market was cripplingly costly, one estimate he quotes put it at over R500 billion in today's value. A covert conduit for oil was the sanctions-busting operation GMR, a key partner to which was Craig Williamson, the so-called South African 'master spy' responsible for infiltration of anti-apartheid groups, murder and mayhem.

The apartheid regime was indeed promiscuous, even doing military work for the Russians and obtaining Chinese arms, both countries bitter enemies in public. However, it found ready allies in Ronald Reagan's America and Margaret Thatcher's Britain and business boomed, both overt and covert: it was, Van Vuuren says, 'duplicity of the first order' from governments supposedly opposed to the doctrine of apartheid.

This led to massive repression inside the country by the end of the 1980s. The most comprehensive and stringent state of emergency yet was imposed, placing the country under martial law. Then the total onslaught really lived up to its name. Organisations were banned, open-air gatherings prohibited and the police and military moved into the townships to detain 30,000 people. The government recruited vigilante bands, paid, armed and turned them loose on radical township activists. Homes were burnt and the offices of anti-apartheid organisations bombed. The security forces looked on, content that their clandestine strategy of arming and organising these vigilantes was proving fruitful. Despite denials at the time, it was confirmed in the 1990s that this strategy was authorised at the highest level of the government.

It is fashionable now to claim we were all against apartheid. After all, only the shameless or deeply prejudiced would have openly allied themselves with the most institutionalised racial tyranny the world has ever known. But the truth is that only a minority did something about it. The majority expressed their distaste but got on with business as usual: in sport, in diplomacy – or as Van Vuuren's book exposes so devastatingly – by supplying arms, trade and finance to underpin white minority oppression. The rebel sports tours in the 1980s, secretly arranged with the connivance of government and business, were part of this bigger picture.

Although the anti-apartheid struggle was ultimately victorious, by then sanctions-busting all the way from oil and arms embargoes to other strategic goods, right down to sports tours, had become the norm, leading to what van Vuuren described as 'systemic corruption and economic crime that was common in the late apartheid period and that stubbornly persists today . . . the struggle against [former President Zuma-inspired] corruption in South Africa is undermined by a basic lack of appreciation of the nature of that corruption and the criminal networks that facilitate it – namely, that they are continuities of a profoundly corrupt system that predates the first democratic elections of [1994].'

6

Preparing to govern:
Struggle, disjuncture and new strategies
for sport in South Africa

A journey to Cradock

At the end of 1983 André returned to South Africa after several years of studying in Britain, where he became a cricket 'blue' at Cambridge, with the opportunity to play first-class cricket, including a half-century on debut against Leicestershire and a man-of-the-match 72 at Edgbaston against a Warwickshire attack that included well-known internationals Bob Willis, Gladstone Small and Dilip Doshi.

At home he immediately went in search of the struggle, despite the entreaties of his father to beware that 'communists' used well-intentioned people like him for their own nefarious purposes. He had decided that as a white South African he could no longer say he was against apartheid and sit on the fence; he wanted to be part of the fight against it.

But where to start in this country of two worlds? André was reporting for work at the University of South Africa in Pretoria, the capital, memorably called *snor* (moustache) city in an Afrikaans protest song after all the military personnel and government bureaucrats who worked there. He approached a few well-known public commentators and was not satisfied with the middle-of-the-road advice they gave. Then, the *City Press* newspaper for township readers announced that the newly formed UDF, started a few months earlier to campaign against the government's sham reforms for a new racially based tricameral parliament, would be launching a million-signature protest campaign at the Catholic Church in the nearby dormitory township of Soshanguve. Its minister, Father Smangaliso Mkhatshwa, had been in detention for several months. Completely oblivious as to what to expect, and going alone in case of 'trouble', André nosed his way into the township, parked his car at a 'safe' distance, a hundred metres from the church lest there were any police actions and, not without apprehension, approached the venue. He was going in cold.

Through the doors and into another world entirely. Rousing struggle songs about bazookas and P. W. Botha's imminent demise, scarcely twenty kilometres from the seat of power at the Union Buildings. Toyi-toyi, the war dance imported from the guerrilla training camps in Angola, the dirge *Senzeni na?* (What have we done?) and *Bamb'isandla sam Oliver Tambo* (Hold my hand Oliver Tambo). Moving hymns, oratory, energy, smiles of welcome and solidarity, a feeling of safety, even though the mere act of organising this meeting and being present invited surveillance and danger. Though one of only a handful of different-shaded faces there, André soon knew he had found a home.

Also very moving for André was the dinner he had with Liz Floyd and Yvette Breytenbach, partner and friend respectively of trade unionist Neil Aggett, who had died in detention the year before after a terrible seventy days of sleep deprivation and interrogation. Workers downed tools to re-member their fallen comrade – and 15,000 came to his funeral. Archbishop Desmond Tutu said it was 'the kind of salute and tribute that the black townships provide only for really special people'.[289] When his body was 'discovered' hanging in his cell in the notorious John Vorster Square (but, it is suspected, after his interrogators had placed him in that position sub-sequent to his death) the colourful wrap-around *kikhoi* of African woven cloth Yvette had given him as a present was around his neck. Neil Aggett was the first white detainee out of fifty-one to have died in detention up to that stage and for André, just a few months younger than him, just entering the struggle, it was no routine drive home that night as he mulled over the meaning of the meal he had just shared.

Next step was to join non-racial cricket. The reference point was Aggie Mangera in Lenasia, the township on the outskirts of Johannesburg, near Soweto, designated for 'Indian' people who had been forced out of the city centre after the passing of the notorious Group Areas Act. Mangera was president of the Transvaal Cricket Board, brother in law to Abdul Minty (secretary of the Anti-Apartheid Movement in London) and sometime courier for smuggling in messages or money for local activists from Sam Ramsamy. They had met at the first International Conference on Sanctions Against Apartheid Sport in London the previous June. André had simply arrived at the event at the Belgravia Hotel next to Victoria Station and been allowed in, and it had made a big impression on him. Mangera welcomed his queries about joining the SACOS-affiliated non-racial South African Cricket Board. In his letter of application, André emphasised that 'Since my schooldays I have been committed to sports and political change in South

Africa.' But that had meant taking an oppositional stance within the white South African bubble of which he'd been part. Now it was time for a paradigm shift, which would amount to the destabilisation of the self that Nobel Prize-winning novelist Nadine Gordimer's biographer described as a necessary part of her journey 'from whiteness and into humanity'. This would necessitate metamorphosis which 'places the self in chaos', rather than an empathy, where 'a stable self extends itself in sympathy, magnanimously, towards the ... other'.[290]

André has noted in retrospect that 'the decision to get involved was probably the most important I had ever made.' It changed his life fairly dramatically. Doors swung shut loudly behind one, family felt betrayed and the figurative strange men in overcoats started watching you. The decision amounted to a paradigm shift from a life and ideas informed by a white colonial (and, ultimately, European derived) paradigm to a framework which drew on African perspectives and historéical experiences, identified with the oppressed, and demanded a certain humility. However, 'One felt totally alive living through that period and being able to participate in modest ways.'[291]

Peter noted that was not an easy move to make. He was often denounced by whites for 'betraying' his origins and praised by enlightened people all over for his own role; but he was campaigning from the relative safety of Britain and, crucially, surrounded by a family steeped in the struggle. André came from inside the system – becoming a 'subversive' in a security state – painfully at odds with his family and peers, undertaking a very personal journey without connections yet to support networks that like-minded people, for example, at the English-speaking universities perhaps had.

After meeting top non-racial cricketers and also the antagonists Rashid Varachia and Hassan Howa as a student in the mid-1970s, a door had opened for André. While still at university he wrote and self-published *Cricket in Isolation* (1977), dealing with the politics of the game in South Africa, and followed this with *Vukani Bantu!* (Rise up you people!) on early black political mobilisation in South Africa. This research on the nineteenth-century mission-educated intellectuals and activists who had mobilised extensively to start the first black newspapers and protest organisations was a revelation to him, and also news to the historical profession. He was bowled over by their path-breaking experiences and the ideas they had articulated a hundred years before. They had, to boot, adopted cricket as their game. Having also seen something of the world out there during his studies abroad, André could no longer bear the propaganda on state television and the newspapers, the stultifying pettiness and meanness of the justifications for 'separate development', the blindness, the inhumanity of it all. For him it was time to match beliefs with action. So he jumped from a high fence, explaining to the non-racial cricket hierarchy that 'My experiences made me increasingly aware of the social, political and economic realities of South African life and eventually led me to challenge and become disillusioned with the narrow framework within which I was operating... and I now wish to join the [SACOS-affiliated] SACB so that I can participate actively in the struggle for democracy in South Africa – both on and off the sports field.'[292]

The *Cape Times* reported, 'Odendaal defects to SACB', which got a young advocate-to-be, John Campbell going. He lambasted the newspaper for using the term, as well as for its 'cursory' reporting of non-racial sport, while the white SACU in contrast received 'acreage of space' and 'fawning' coverage which allowed their administrators 'to reiterate ad nauseam why they think they are the victims of an international conspiracy'. '"Defection" is a word with unpleasant and sinister connotations, often related to the notion of betrayal', he said, pointing out that Chambers 20th Century Dictionary (New Edition) defines it as 'desertion; a failure; a falling away from duty; revolt'. The headline, while 'unfortunately no surprise', raised unfair connotations 'about a sincere decision of conscience', he concluded. Campbell's parting shot was a slap across the face for Bob Woolmer, the England rebel cricketer who settled in South Africa and had in his recent autobiography come up with 'the usual trite anaesthetic about SACU having done all they can and Hassan Howa being "obsessed" with showing overseas visitors the terrible state of pitches on which they play, and the appalling rooms they change in – by their own choice.'

The *Cape Times* writer, Franklyn Heydenrych, later to become editor of the *South African Cricket Annual*, wrote that Woolmer's reasoning is 'lucid' and that he 'has the facts at his fingertips'. Campbell replied. 'So lucid is Woolmer, and so conversant with the facts, that he never once mentions the Group Areas Act, the pass laws, discriminatory government spending on public sporting facilities, the bantu education system and so on. This is the concrete reality of sport on the other side of South Africa's statutory colour bar.'

For André, this was an encouraging polemic to mark the start of his new journey. But he would forever be the guy who had crossed the fence in cricket and become 'ANC', seen as an almost mystical embrace of danger and unthinkable taboo in the world he had come from. It was after all a time when 'total onslaught' and *rooi gevaar* (red danger) were at their height. And within months he received his first visit from the security police. He found that for the next two decades virtually every conversation with people from his past would, after the obligatory greetings, start with questions like, 'So what is the ANC . . . ?' It was like having a brandmark on your forehead.

Being the only provincial cricketer from white cricket ranks to join 'the other side' during the apartheid years has remained meaningful for him, but he was not entirely alone: a small group of other like-minded sportspeople made a similar journey, also in other sports. The most famous 'defectors' being, of course, the legendary rugby-playing Watson brothers and the racially mixed Aurora Cricket Club in Pietermaritzburg which trooped en masse across to the non-racial SACB in the 1970s.[293] Most of these dissidents were students at the self-styled 'liberal' universities in Cape Town, Grahams-town, Durban, Pietermaritzburg and Johannesburg. André points out that the stands they made need to be acknowledged and that some, like Chris Nicholson (SA Schools and SA Universities) and Raymond Rogers (SA Schools), were more talented cricketers than him. The brilliant social documentary photographer from Afripix, Paul Weinberg, who became a struggle friend and mentor, and Richard Compton, son of the English post-war batting cavalier, Denis Compton, were others who played provincial cricket in the non-racial fold.

Joining the struggle was a profound moment that changed André's life forever. He recalls courageous people, laughter, warmth, generosity, learning, respect, purpose; not sacrifice but liberation, entering a whole other world full of immeasurably rich experiences. What he called a lifelong PhD course in humanity, mentored by dignified South Africans of every variety. The Queensland CC in Lenasia, which he joined on Aggie Mangera's recommendation, embraced André as family. Ali Osmany was the life and soul of the club. A Black Consciousness supporter close to Dr Abu Baker Asvat, and later director of the foundation named after the assassinated struggle icon, Osmany and his new teammates treated him like a brother, spoiling him so that when he hit the 'Golden Highway' on the long drive back to Pretoria before the days of speed limits there was always a parcel on the back seat, *barakat*, something left over from what one was blessed to share with others. The playing conditions were not great. Certainly not Newlands, St George's Park, Edgbaston, Lords, Hove, Fenners or The Parks where he had been fortunate to play on only a short while before, but the meaning was the same. Then a piece of sheer magic. One day, padding up with his car boot as changing room, someone came up quietly and said, 'Kathy sends his regards.' A frown. This guy does not make sense, André thought. Ahmed Kathrada, the stranger clarified, always known as 'Kathy'. A message from Robben Island for André. Twenty years after escaping the death sentence with fellow Rivonia trialists such as Nelson Mandela, Walter Sisulu and Govan Mbeki, Kathrada was still in touch with what was happening on his home turf. His and André's lives would become closely intertwined in the future.

This message reinforced what the move to non-racial sport was all about for André. The new cricket season starting that October coincided with a momentous moment in South African history. Massive protests broke out in the Vaal townships. After the overwhelmingly successful boycott of the tricameral elections two months before, President Botha's plan to gain political legitimacy for reforms by shuffling around deck chairs on the Titanic while keeping the basics of apartheid intact was stillborn. Apartheid had reached a political dead end. Instead of pacifying opposition, the new tricameral parliament and related black local councils inflamed it. On the day that Botha was inaugurated in his new capacity as president (upgraded from the prime ministers of the past), people took to the streets determined to make apartheid ungovernable. The uprisings caught flame and spread quickly to different parts of the country. Government buildings that symbolised apartheid control were torched, and local collaborators were targeted, chased from their homes and often killed. The state then dropped all pretence of accommodation and tolerance. On 23 October 1984, 7,000 soldiers and policemen cordoned off the Sebokeng township – not far from Lenasia where André played – and carried out a door-to-door 'anti-crime' operation in the middle of the night. A resident testified: 'At about midnight I saw there were soldiers all over the street . . . At about four o'clock they knocked on the door as if they wanted to kick it in . . . Before they left they took a sticker and stuck it on a cupboard. It said, "Trust me, I am your friend."'[294]

By the end of the year some 32,000 troops had been deployed in ninety-six townships for the purpose of 'preventing or suppressing internal disorder'. Casualties rocketed as the siege of the townships spread. The number of deaths for 1985 alone was just under 800. On the twenty-fifth anniversary of the Sharpeville massacre on 21 March, twenty people were shot dead by the police in an unprovoked attack at Langa near Uitenhage. The was the first of a number of mass killings – followed by powerful mass funerals, often in sports stadiums – that became a feature of South African life during the next few years.

The state was rapidly closing existing avenues of legal protest and organisation and trying to cripple and criminalise the UDF. Mysterious assassination and abduction squads began to appear. By early June the UDF listed at least twenty-seven people missing and twelve victims of political assassination. Anti-apartheid activists were forced to go into hiding or flee the townships. These acts of terror were aimed precisely at areas where resistance was strongest.

In July 1985 André started a new job at the University of the Western Cape in Cape Town. Commonly referred to as 'Bush', because it once was the site of a 'squatter camp' and started as an ethnic institution for coloured people only, UWC became one of the hotbeds of campus militancy in the country. Under new rector Jakes Gerwel (later first director general in the office of President Mandela), UWC styled itself the 'an intellectual home for the democratic left', making a formal commitment to aligning itself critically with the democratic forces and the 'third world communities' that its students came from. André's world – like so many others – became one of full-time activism: campus protests, riot police tear gas charges, people's education experiments, community activism and other challenges to autocracy that would sometimes cross the bounds of an oppressive legality. *Hek toe!* (To the gate!) became the rallying cry of a campus in ferment.

Within days of his arrival at UWC, the state sent out a chilling reminder of its new approach of naked extra-legal terror. Matthew Goniwe, a dynamic young leader who had risen to national prominence, and three of his comrades were murdered in the eastern Cape. Their charred and horribly mutilated bodies were found several days after they were declared missing en route to Cradock after a meeting in Port Elizabeth. They were murdered soon after the State Security Council sanctioned their 'permanent removal' from Cradock.

Thirty thousand people from throughout South Africa streamed to the dusty little Karoo town for the funeral of the 'Cradock Four', which came to symbolise the whole spirit of mass resistance in the country. UWC staff raised a R 100,000 reward for information leading to the arrest of the killers and André was on one of the busses that left from Cape Town for the funeral. Cradock was only ninety kilometres from where he had grown up in Queenstown and, this time, instead of turning left at the T-junction outside Lingelihle township to take the road to Port Elizabeth, or right for the one to Cape Town, he was going into it. At that moment this dusty little settlement was the eye of a national storm. Security forces in their yellow-painted, oddly named 'Casspir' armoured vehicles and their ubiquitous surveillance equipment, kept menacing watch from a nearby vantage point. The newspaper headlines next day trumpeted the fact that for the first time, flags of the banned ANC and South African Communist Party were openly unveiled in public. The people were unbanning the liberation movement themselves.

Steve Tshwete, who had been so prominent in organising sport in Robben Island Maximum Security Prison as general secretary of the Robben Island Recreation Committee in the 1960s and 1970s, and Rev. Makhenkesi Arnold Stofile were among the speakers who made powerful calls to arms from the podium that day. After being released from prison, Tshwete had helped set up the UDF and by 1985 he was being hunted again by the security police. As they entered by the front gate of his house in Peelton, soon after the funeral he slipped over the back wall and into exile in Zambia, where he soon became a leader in the armed wing of the ANC, *Umkhonto we Sizwe*, and a key player in the 1980s debates about the direction South African sport should take.

Rev. Stofile, a former rugby captain of Fort Hare, the nursery for many liberation leaders, was prominent in both the UDF and as a regional under-ground leader of the ANC in the eastern Cape. Some in SACOS identified him as its future president. He had just come back from testifying on behalf of the UDF at the court case in New Zealand which successfully stopped the planned All Blacks rugby tour to South Africa. He was arrested soon after-wards and jailed in the Ciskei Bantustan for 'harbouring 'terrorists'. The funeral, and the actions of these two leaders, demonstrated the growing convergence between the armed struggle of the ANC in exile and the mass mobilisation of the internal democratic movement. Also the link between sport and resistance. As the funeral progressed and the dry wind bit, André, fresh from playing for Transvaal, bumped into fellow players, Khaya Majola from the legendary Eastern Province sporting family, and Border all-rounder Greg Fredericks. Greg had hosted him and his teammates before a recent provincial fixture, when they slept on the floor in schoolrooms in the Buffalo Flats township near East London before their game. Sport and life intertwined in the most profound way. And as André watched the coffins being lowered into the grave he joined the crowd singing *Senzeni na?*, clenched fist raised, with a complete sense of oneness and belonging: it was for him a moment of life-defining clarity, close to where he was born.

Afterwards at the washing of hands ceremony at the home of one of the departed, a comrade of André's, a lefty who believed bathing was an unnecessary bourgeois invention and was therefore sometimes a little odorous, asked way ahead of his time for vegetarian food. The women of the house laughed good-naturedly. 'A man who does not eat meat!' High on the wall of the room they sat in was a small black-and-white portrait framed in discreet green and gold braiding. It was Rev. James Calata, secretary general in the 1930s and 1940s, from Cradock, who with Dr A. B. Xuma had helped rescue the ANC from oblivion and put it on the road to becoming a mass movement. His grandson, Fort Calata, was one of the freedom fighters they had just buried.

The people in Cradock were in the presence of history in more than one sense on that July day in 1985. And they were sending out a message that no oppressive force could defeat a struggle as ingrained as this.

As the buses rolled out of the dusty township that night, President Botha appeared on television to announce a state of emergency. The regime was now officially resorting to martial law. The UDF marshals announced through loud hailers that the mass movement was going to embark on a consumer boycott in response: 'Your bus will not be stopping at any shops on the way home and we call on you to be disciplined'.

The emergency regulations gave the South African Defence Force (SADF) and police unrestrained powers, as well as virtual indemnity from prosecution. No one could bring criminal or civil proceedings against any member of the SADF, the police or government if the minister of law and order believed they had acted in good faith. More than 10,000 people were detained during the first six months of emergency rule. Emergency rule was accompanied by reports of a new phenomenon: from Pietersburg in the north to Cape Town in the south, bands of right-wing 'black vigilantes' with links to the state's community councillors, Bantustan authorities and the security apparatus, started waging war on anti-apartheid activists. Assault, arson, slashed or over inflated car tyres, dead cats nailed to doors, bricks crashing through windows, bombed and burgled offices, and the ever-present threat of death . . . these were the grim realities that anti-apartheid activists and organisations now had to face.[295]

But successive states of emergency failed to provide the solution envisaged by the apartheid state. Although seriously disrupted, militant resistance persisted within the country and international action against apartheid reached new heights.

As South Africa descended into a state of virtual civil war, being an enthusiastic member of a UDF Area Committee and SACOS, and now also UWC, placed André inside the cauldron.

'Sports wing of the liberatory movement': SACOS's growth and new strategies in the 1980s

Meanwhile, SACOS itself was pulsing, growing stronger along with the rising wave of resistance. Though alternatively ridiculed or ignored in the mainstream media, looked upon with distaste by white-establishment sports bodies and harassed regularly by government, it grew in stature as the undisputed representative organisation for non-racial sport inside South Africa. SACOS's status was underlined by its close working relationship with its 'overseas representative' SANROC, operating from its Portman Court hotel offices in 28 Seymour Street in London W1, its associate membership of the Supreme Council for Sport in Africa, and the recognition and the support that came with these two connections from the entire international anti-apartheid sports network, including the United Nations Special Committee Against Apartheid.

In April 1980 a SACOS delegation flew to New York to attend the session of the Special Committee, rubbing in the fact that it enjoyed the legitimacy that establishment South African sport craved. The organisation's biennial meeting reports continued to carry numerous messages of support from outside South Africa and its growing international status was reflected by the fact that the SCSA president, Abraham Ordia and its secretary Jean-Claude Ganga were made SACOS patrons in 1981, alongside the ageless George Singh, still there after helping set up the SA Soccer Federation thirty years earlier. When Singh passed away soon afterwards, SANROC's Sam Ramsamy was brought in as third patron to formalise the triple alliance that effectively held the future of South African sport in its hands.

While South Africa's white-dominated sports establishment tried to buy itself international allies and opportunities in the 1980s, all the time staying tucked in behind the coat tails of government, SACOS and its affiliates sought to adapt to the changing circumstances of that decade, especially the emergence of a new wave of internal resistance from 1983 onwards.

To celebrate its tenth anniversary, SACOS organised a national Festival in Athlone in Cape Town in October 1982. Twenty-one affiliates participated in this 'people's festival of sport', rugby being the only exception. In each of the codes a SACOS team, the 'best representative national team', was selected to take on the second-stringers in the form of a president's team, and in several cases the latter won. SACOS was unable to attract any significant sponsorship for the event costing an estimated R 70,000, but 'realising the plight' a local travel agency and some local businessmen rallied in support. The festival kicked off with a march past of the participating teams under lights, all dressed in matching black tracksuits, and a gymnastics display by hundreds of local children forming the SACOS letters.

The president, Morgan Naidoo, described the festival as a high point in the decade of SACOS's existence: 'Whilst individual non-racial sports codes have persevered in promoting the game against a climate of adversity, pre-occupation with more fundamental issues governing sports in the country has virtually sapped us of any initiative towards staging sports activities under a singly coordinated effort. Today . . . we cannot help but be proud that at long last a significant milestone has been achieved.'[296]

Apart from the lack of sponsorship, the organisers had to deal with attempts by the system to sabotage the event. Mysterious pamphlets were distributed giving incorrect times and venues for events. 'We do not know who was responsible for this despicable act,' SACOS said, 'but the intent is very clear.' And a few days before the event, 'officials discovered the dumping of over forty loads of sand' in the stadium where the main events were due to take place. A bemused festival coordinator, Frank van der Horst, was pictured inspecting the mounds, dotted neatly across the entire infield, clearly making it impossible to use under those conditions. Municipal officials, feigning innocence, said they were 'under the impression that only the tracks were hired and not the grounds'. Going with this disruption was the 'huge propaganda machinery at work' as the hostile apartheid establishment, including the minister of sport and the heads of the official Olympic and rugby bodies attacked the 'enemies from within'.[297]

Executive member Allan Zinn argued that it was 'essential' for SACOS to have this kind of 'mass activity every year'. To make it more affordable and workable, he suggested a decentralised model where winter and summer sports, as well as indoor games such as table tennis, weightlifting, body-building, chess, snooker, darts and squash, would hold three separate events in different regions every year.[298]

But no such programmes materialised, and it was not until 1988 that SACOS was able to organise another such umbrella sports Festival. Other than the introduction of an annual sportsperson of the year competition from 1984 onwards, it left the organisation of sport to its affiliates.

A feature of SACOS's first ten years was the consistency of its leadership. Between 1973 and 1981 there was a single patron, George Singh; only two presidents, Norman Middleton and Hassan Howa; two vice-presidents, Howa and Frank van der Horst, a civil engineer and trade unionist from Cape Town; one person in the key role of secretary, Manikum N. Pather; and two treasurers, Abdullah Rasool and Pather (holding dual positions for one term). From 1979 a secretary for literature (later publications secretary) was added to the top positions, probably to keep up with the high flow of information needed for international anti-apartheid campaigns and to counter the propaganda of government and establishment sport. Naidoo was given this task. A small group of four additional members, generally made up of presidents of national sporting codes, supported the top leadership.

In 1981 Howa resigned as president after delegates passed a motion of no confidence in him 'because of his individualistic approach'. Other reasons such as his suspected support for negotiations with establishment sport and ill health were also advanced. Howa's stepping down roughly coincided with the deaths of stalwarts like Singh, Pather and several former heads of national associations, such as Cassim Bassa, Monnathebe Senokoanyane, Shun David and Abdullah Abass, in the early 1980s. The change of guard heralded in a new era of leadership for SACOS. The power swung both more to Cape Town from Durban, the headquarters in the 1970s, and to a younger generation of administrators with radical left political leanings. SACOS completed its journey from the adoption of militant non-collaboration after the Soweto uprisings, to become emphatically in its own words the 'sports wing of the liberatory movement'. As both repression and resistance increased in the 1980s, revolutionary perspectives supplanted a more old-world style of jacket-and-tie sports administration, schooled in the 1950s struggles.

Durban's Naidoo succeeded Howa for a brief period as president (1981–83) before Frank van der Horst (1983–88, vice-president since 1977) and Joe Ebrahim (1988–95) took the lead, with Colin Clarke the reliable secretary from that time into the 1990s. The latter three – a civil engineer, an advocate and pharmacist respectively – became the face of the organisation in the 1980s.

Besides veterans such as Reggie Feldman, Harry Hendricks and Raymond Uren, some fine administrators came to the fore as leaders under SACOS in that decade, among them Dr Errol Vawda, elected treasurer in 1981, Krish Mackerdhuj, who took over as national cricket head from Howa, Mervyn Johnson, Don Kali, James Letuka, Allan Zinn, Abe Fortuin, Ebrahim Patel, Clive Vawda, Abe Adams, Silas Nkanunu, Makhenkesi Stofile, Rama Reddy and others.

These people came from a variety of political backgrounds, which existed in a cooperative tension in the sports movement. People had well developed political positions but did not necessarily 'report back' politically as sports administrators. Thus, for example, Naidoo, mentored by Singh and others, entered sport with a Natal and Transvaal Indian Congress 'Charterist' background, but over many years worked closely with people from other tendencies and was later 'traumatised' when political splits occurred in SACOS. Krish Mackerdhuj, perhaps encouraged by his educational experiences at Fort Hare, was similarly Congress-aligned. Fellow Durbanite, Errol Vawda, was not 'NIC or TIC' but came from a 'non-collaborationist' Marxist-inspired Unity Movement perspective and became a strong supporter of the independent trade union movement in the 1980s. The Unity Movement was well represented in SACOS's leadership. The likes of Raymond Uren, Reg Feldsman, Harry Hendricks, Abe Fortuin and younger leaders such as Allan Zinn and Avis Smith rose through the ranks. But here too, there were different perspectives and styles. For example, Frank van der Horst in Cape Town belonged to a Unity Movement faction loyal to I. B. Tabata, which split from the dominant grouping under Ben Kies to form the African People's Democratic Union of Southern Africa (APDUSA). Van der Horst, also active as a trade unionist, worked closely with the highly regarded Cape Action League and National Forum theorist, Neville Alexander, in the 1980s. His successor, Joe Ebrahim, emerged from the South Peninsula Education Forum (SPEF) discussion groups and civic association activities in Cape Town and was closer to the Unity Movement mainstream. He also had a softer political approach. Working for a while in the same law firm as the later ANC justice minister Dullah Omar, and briefing Ben Kies as their silk, they worked regularly with a range of human rights lawyers to support political trialists of different persuasions.

The hard-working new general secretary, Colin Clarke, came from a

1970s Black Consciousness background. His code tennis had formed an alliance with similar-thinking Johannesburg-based African tennis players to form the Tennis Association of South Africa (TASA) in 1979, and it was via this channel that the Black Consciousness-supporting Don Kali graduated to the SACOS executive. In the eastern Cape African townships, on the other hand, the loyalties were more traditional: SACOS-affiliated rugby leaders Arnold Stofile and Mluleki George were detained and imprisoned for ANC activities, and the strong KWARU rugby affiliate from Port Elizabeth was led by the likes of the legendary Dan Qeqe and Silas Nkanunu (ANC) and treasurer Dennis Siwisa (PAC). As political temperatures rose in the dramatic 1980s, these non-sectarian approaches and SACOS's definition of non-alignment would come under pressure.

Reflecting the deeply patriarchal nature of South African sport historically, no women were elected onto the SACOS executive in the 1970s and only one, Avis Smith, in the 1980s. She was elected as 'internal secretary' in 1985, in the new portfolio created to provide support to the general secretary two years earlier, her appointment underlining the nurturing and support role that women were traditionally expected to fulfil in sport. Smith was a high school history teacher, who was forced under the Group Areas Act to move from the Port Elizabeth sea front area to the marginal West End, where she brought up two children as a single mother, and went on to become general secretary of AVASA, the Amateur Volleyball Association of South Africa, an affiliate of SACOS. Her appointment seemed to be in response to mounting criticism against sexism from within the organisation.

In this respect SACOS was little different from sport organisations generally: men dominated, held the top positions and made 'history', though women were there from the beginning. As late as 1987, in the codes not exclusively for women, 'A national school sports association with only three women's representatives out of 33 is typical',[299] one internal report explained. But given that SACOS was an organisation closely linked to broader struggles against injustice, it was not surprising that some of the earliest internal criticism against sexism in sport emerged within its ranks. In 1984 the supporters club of the FPL Bluebells professional team wrote to the SACOS general secretary criticising the 'cattle parade' in the form of a beauty contest organised during the FPL's cup final activities. In 1985 the prize-giving ceremony at the TASA national tennis championships started immediately after the men's final while the one for women was still under way. Women's champion Charmaine Carollissen lashed out against her treatment while later receiving her trophy. Critiques of sexism in SACOS started appearing and in 1987 SACOS itself published a document on 'Sexism in sport and society' following its seventh biennial conference held in Johannesburg that October.

In 1988 table tennis star Cheryl Roberts, who won the 1985 SACOS Sportsperson of the Year Award (incidentally, covering both men and women), took the debate further when she published a version of her master's thesis from York University on the history of SACOS. The examples mentioned above are taken from this work, and Roberts deserves recognition for subsequently going on to become one of the leading gender activists in South African sport, writing and self-publishing numerous pieces in the three decades since then, including her monthly *South African Sports Women*.[300]

SACOS started its 1987 discussion paper on sexism by explaining that this was 'a vital area for debate and practical implementation' and encouraging its affiliates to hold 'ongoing workshops' at grassroots and national levels 'to change attitudes, practises and values on this key issue'. It concluded: 'Social liberation from racial discrimination, national oppression and class exploitation will not be complete without anti-sexism in sport and society.'[301]

South African sport was late in catching up with a resurgent feminism after the 1960s, but as a result of the 1980s struggles the notion of black women being triply oppressed – on the basis of colour, class and gender – had gained increasing currency within the non-racial sports movement. Seeing itself as part of the liberation movement, it was appropriate that SACOS and successor organisations would from now on have the issue of gender equity permanently on the agenda, as a specific discourse and goal if not yet even close to that reality.

Howa's departure in 1981 was a sign of the turn to revolutionary ideas in SACOS. Naidoo leap-frogged over vice-president van der Horst to become president, but the latter defeated Naidoo by a 'small majority' in the 1983 contest for the top position. Colin Clarke explained that after Howa stepped down, 'The executive was extended with the view of establishing a collective leadership.' But 'in the first years this was not very successful'. The tensions inherent in the notions of individual versus collective leadership did not go away under van der Horst. The new president soon found himself at odds with his executive and at a meeting in 1984 he felt 'compelled to ask for a vote of confidence' in himself. Delegates pointed out this would amount to asking them to choose between president or executive. In the end, peace was restored, and the motion was withdrawn.

Van der Horst had very clear ideas about where he wanted to take SACOS. He said that SACOS faced a new situation, just as it had in 1976. Then it had introduced the Double Standards Resolution to draw clear lines between those opposing the system and those collaborating with it, and to 'cleanse our sports bodies from traitors and defectors who were corrupted by racist sport'. Now it again needed to adapt and make the necessary changes. The challenge for the 1980s was firstly to change the way SACOS was working. Secondly, it had to be more directly involved in mass struggles 'being led by the working class who must be free from ruling class and conservative black middle-class influence'. He said, 'A leaf had to be taken out of the manner in which the democratic working-class input operated in the Trade Unions ... Decisions can no longer be made on behalf of affiliates in a bureaucratic manner but they had to be involved in the decision-making process.' The SACOS leadership had to re-evaluate its role because it no longer 'merely represent[ed] an Executive or an organisation conducting its affairs in a purely administrative manner.' It would now also have to 'give guidance' to make sure 'the organisation was on the right path in the struggle'. Instead of relying on international actions, SACOS also had to be more in the forefront in directly challenging rebel tours and the government's new constitutional plans on the home front. And, he warned, 'We will be entering a period of increased repression where a certain amount of courage was required.'[302]

In line with these ideas, SACOS decided at a meeting in Lenasia in 1983 to join the nationwide campaigns against the introduction of the regime's new tricameral parliament. Van der Horst travelled the country, with little help from his executive, he complained later, speaking and attending various protest events against the 'new deal fraud'. This was followed up by a major Sport and Liberation conference organised by SACOS itself in Hanover Park in Cape Town from 20 to 21 August 1983.

Close on 2,000 invitations were sent out to national, provincial and club affiliates, as well as 'trade unions, schools, civic organisations, and youth movements'. Over a thousand delegates attended and 200 organisations sent messages of support. The purpose of the conference was described as follows: 'to confirm the commitment of sportspersons to the liberatory struggle and to involve the rank and file sportspersons in active struggle in association with other organisations and to put the oppressed and exploited working class in the vanguard of the liberatory struggle.'[303]

A wide range of papers were presented on the relationship between sport and the unfolding political situation, including separate papers on sport and the nation, the worker, the student and the constitutional proposals. There was also one on 'The role of the non-racial sports person in the liberatory struggle.' These were subsequently published in detail in a special edition of the *SACOS Bulletin*.[304]

SACOS reaffirmed its bedrock policies regarding multinational sport, the sports boycott, Double Standards, and the 'new deal fraud', declaring also that 'the struggle for non-racial sport is part and parcel of the liberation struggle and [we] call on all the non-racial sportspersons and organisations to promote and support in all possible ways this struggle on a principled basis.' There was therefore now a complete identification of the sports movement with the broad liberation struggle. But in the massive upsurge of resistance in South Africa in the early to mid-1980s, some fundamental differences started emerging between SACOS and the leading organisations in the struggle, and these differences revealed themselves on the very weekend of its Sport and Liberation conference, organised on 20 August 1983, the same day as the historic launch of the United Democratic Front barely ten miles away in Mitchells Plain outside Cape Town, where a crowd of 12,000 people filled the civic centre to the rafters. It turned out to be the genesis of one of the game-changing struggle organisations in South Africa in the 1980s. Among those in attendance were 2,000 delegates from 320 organisations claiming to represent over one million people. To thundering applause the UDF leader and president of the World Alliance of Reformed Churches, Allan Boesak, made the call that would be taken up throughout the country: 'We want all our rights. We want them here. And we want them now. Now is the time!'

It was illegal to identify openly with the ANC or propagate armed struggle, but the UDF stressed that it shared the broad aims espoused by the ANC when that body was still legal. Using creative methods and campaigns, it opened up a new front in the struggle, dramatically changing the dynamics of internal politics, drawing support from all segments of society and crossing race drawn boundaries in a way not yet seen in South Africa. The UDF emphasised that it was complementing, not superseding the struggle of the respected exile movement. ANC veterans were made patrons of the UDF, and among the ten was also the recently deposed SACOS president Hassan Howa. Appropriating songs, slogans, and symbols from the 1950s, many of the UDF's affiliates also subscribed to the ANC Freedom Charter as a guiding document.

This informal ANC-UDF alliance was given a massive boost in 1985 with the formation of the giant trade union federation, COSATU, the largest in South African history with over one million members. COSATU significantly decided to move beyond what was described as a 'workerist' approach focussing exclusively on factory floor issues, to one of involvement with the community and political struggles sweeping the land outside the workplace under the unofficial ANC/UDF banners. This gave tremendous muscle to the struggle and by 1987 COSATU had also adopted the Freedom Charter as its basic programme. Its first sentence proclaimed, 'South Africa belongs to all who live in it, black and white.' The exiled ANC movement's alliance with two newly launched and rapidly growing popular mass movements operating on the ground within South Africa constituted a tri-partite alliance and led to a functional grid of resistance operating throughout the country, and in different spheres of society. The activities emanating from this newly constructed base of struggle was to change the course of the nation's history.

The UDF launch also created something of a dilemma for SACOS. Although the organisation pursued a policy of non-alignment in regard to liberation movement politics, the sympathies of its leadership tended to be more in the direction of organisations grouped together in the National Forum (NF), a rival of the UDF. Also formed to oppose the government's new deal, the NF was a smaller alliance of Black Consciousness and socialist parties including the New Unity Movement, Azanian People's Organisation (AZAPO), Pan Africanist Congress (PAC), African People's Democratic Union of Southern Africa (APDUSA) and the BC-oriented National Council of Trade Unions (NACTU). It came to constitute an important political fringe within the broader 1980s liberation struggle.

From 1983 it became either one or the other of these above-mentioned coalitions in internal struggle politics. The pronouncements of the SACOS president van der Horst, the speakers at the Sport and Liberation conference and its policy enunciations showed SACOS's close ideological affinity to the National Forum groups. Among the views that separated SACOS and the National Forum from the UDF/ANC were their opposition to the involvement of white 'liberals', sometimes an umbrella term for anti-apartheid oriented whites, and the linked rejection of the Freedom Charter with its claim that South Africa belonged to all who lived in it, black and white. SACOS also developed a particular analysis of 'racial capitalism' and a general emphasis on anti-capitalist over anti-apartheid or nationalist aims. Its 'workerist', trade union focus under the van der Horst leadership also resulted in different understandings of how a broad front against apartheid should be constituted, showing a clear bias against the multi-class, multi-ethnic mobilisation of the UDF and the ANC. BC-rooted references to 'Azania' in SACOS debates and publications also underlined the different emphases in analysis and strategy between SACOS/National Forum and the so-called 'Charterists'.

The leaderships of SACOS and the UDF met for the first time in October 1984, a year after their clashing conferences, by which time it had become obvious that the latter was rapidly developing into the country's leading internal resistance force, working closely with the ANC in exile. The entire SACOS executive and the presidents of several national federations were present. Besides the common ground established, the UDF made three important points. Firstly, it was committed 'to make government structures unworkable and 'would give consideration to assistance [from/to SACOS] at regional level'. Second, while the UDF opposed the government's community councils in African areas, its approach to those serving on them 'in certain instances' was to 'win them over to progressive organisations and not to isolate them'. It also stressed that 'Many UDF people in Soweto supported the National Professional Soccer League [which SACOS saw as a stooge body] and it would be folly of the UDF to isolate them.' Thirdly, the SACOS minutes recorded that 'fundamental policy differences like the role of liberals and NUSAS [the National Union of South African Students] in particular were not resolved at the meeting'. The UDF defended its relationships with anti-apartheid white South Africans and, indeed, Andrew Boraine, president of NUSAS, had been elected onto the UDF's first national executive. In return, SACOS made the point that its autonomy had to be respected 'and no political tendency within the struggle could expect SACOS to establish formal links to it'. Indicating the perhaps contested nature of the discussions, the two organisations agreed that 'the right to constructive criticism was fundamental' and they would stay in contact via their secretariats.[305]

Expressed here were some of the important fault lines between the main struggle organisations and the main sports body inside the country. Notwithstanding, the agreement to continue working together, the gap between SACOS and the UDF/ANC gradually widened. This led slowly but surely to contending approaches and internal challenges to the dominant direction within SACOS – and eventually to the rise of a new National Sports Congress

(NSC), which during a key phase of the liberation struggle in the second half of the 1980s would adopt significantly revised strategies for organising non-racial sport.

Revolution within a revolution:
Oliver Tambo and the ANC look to the future

In his traditional 8 January statement, on the seventy-fourth birthday of the ANC, the soft-spoken ANC president Oliver Tambo send out a hard-line message into the country. Broadcast and distributed clandestinely inside South Africa, the message was to 'intensify and transform the struggle into a real people's war'. Nineteen eighty-six was designated the 'Year of *Umkhonto we Sizwe*, the People's Army' and the call to those in the struggle was 'Every patriot a combatant'. Yet, even as a buoyed ANC and its broad front internal allies in the UDF and the newly formed COSATU exhorted the masses in the most militant terms to intensify the struggle against an unreformable system, Tambo embarked on that very day at his headquarters in Lusaka on discreet diplomatic and political initiatives which amounted to a revolution within a revolution.[306]

At the very height of the insurrection – not as a sign of weakness but of confident strength – he appointed a constitution committee to start drawing up constitutional guidelines for a future South Africa democracy on 8 January 1986. One of the members of this committee worked closely as an executive member of SANROC with Sam Ramsamy; this was law professor, Kader Asmal, head of the Irish anti-apartheid committee who was based at Trinity College Dublin.

Uniquely for a liberation movement, Tambo and the ANC leadership started planning purposefully albeit very discreetly for the eventuality of negotiations and a future constitutional dispensation. Tambo – also in discreet communications with the imprisoned Mandela – understood that every war ends with the antagonists sitting around a table. Now, judging that the balance of power was beginning to turn decisively in favour of the long-suffering disenfranchised majority, he decided that it was time to open up this new, interlinked terrain of struggle.

Tambo gave the instruction that the guidelines to be drawn up by the Constitution Committee had to ensure three things. National sovereignty – that is, the transfer of power to the dispossessed so that they could decide on their own futures – as well as a multi-party dispensation and system based on the protection of the *individual* rights of every South African. This latter point was strongly made as the ANC was determined to prevent at all costs a future model based on *group* rights, which the regime and its allies at home and abroad favoured as a way of protecting and reproducing entrenched apartheid privileges, sometimes disguised as 'minority rights' or de facto white privileges. (Tambo was laying here the foundations for South Africa's much-lauded Bill of Rights.)

Secondly, the ANC president started preparing his own party to speak to the enemy, A platform had to be created for this to happen. Any South Africans who communicated with the illegal ANC or were caught reading or quoting any of its banned literature, faced severe penalties from a repressive surveillance state. One worker was sentenced to four years in jail for having 'Mandela' scratched on his coffee mug. So instead arrangements began to be made for democratically minded South Africans to start travelling beyond the borders to have discussions. Between 1985 and 1989 the ANC held close on 200 meetings with a wide range of delegations from inside the country in Lusaka, Harare, Dakar and other venues. These contacts grew incrementally from nineteen known meetings in 1985, to twenty-seven in 1986 through to thirty-nine in 1989. Well over a thousand South Africans participated in this new process of engagement in a period of just over four years.[307] The narrative of the ANC as a dangerous and devious enemy which could not be trusted started crumbling. And as the crisis facing the regime deepened and the legitimacy of the ANC grew, the distinctions between 'outside' and 'inside' resistance groups and politics started dissolving quickly, particularly from 1987 onwards. This allowed the ANC, the UDF and COSATU also to better coordinate the underground and legal above-ground struggles more effectively. From being caricatured and demonised in decades of Cold War 'total onslaught' propaganda as a dangerous 'terrorist' stooge of the Soviet Union, unthinkable to even talk to, the ANC now became the host whose party you could not miss. Sport would become part of the unusual procession of 'safaris' to consult with the Zambian-based ANC.

The increasing number of contacts with home were also part of the ANC and its allies' plan to create the broadest possible front against apartheid so that when South Africa reached the stage of transition the groundwork for a future national unity had been laid. Using successful UDF campaigns as examples, Tambo said this should include whites, as well as progressive elements in the Bantustan structures. As part of this wider, deeper mobilisation, the ANC started pushing hard for greater sectoral mobilisation, encouraging people involved in education, the churches, the factory floor and the legal, medical and other professions to organise against apartheid in their own specific areas of life. Building on the consolidation of community and political groups into the UDF in 1983 and of workers into a new super federation, COSATU, in 1985, a host of new sector-specific organisations emerged over the next two years. These included the National Education Crisis Committee (NECC), the United Women's Congress (UWCO), the Congress of Traditional Leaders of South Africa (CONTRALESA), the South African Youth Congress (SAYCO) and the National Association of Democratic Lawyers (NADEL). It was not a coincidence that some of these organisations were formed after the 'safaris' by internal people to Lusaka and Harare. The new formations joined existing sympathetic sectoral groups such as the important faith-based South African Council of Churches (a leader of which was Archbishop Desmond Tutu) and the Call of Islam (and later Jews for Justice) in making sure that the mass democratic movement was able to operate on a deeper level within South African culture and society. In tandem, calls came for SACOS and its affiliates in sport to follow suit and widen its base so that they could unite a broader cross-section of sportspeople in pursuit of the push forward towards a transfer of power.[308]

The final component of the new political and diplomatic strategy followed by the ANC and its allies was to start reassessing and honing boycott and sanctions strategies which had become carved in stone, also within SACOS. They called for rethinking them in a way that could strengthen those identifying with the 'peoples camp' inside South Africa while at the same time further isolating the regime and its allies. From 1986 Tambo started suggesting that instead of a total boycott and isolation of South Africa, why not target apartheid specifically and recognise and encourage those who aligned with the mass democratic movement. He first clearly enunciated this position at the Canon Collins Memorial Lecture in St Paul's Cathedral in London in 1987: 'Indeed, the moment is upon us when we shall deal with the structures our people have created and are creating through struggle and sacrifice as the representatives of the masses. Not only should these not be boycotted, but more, they should be supported, encouraged and treated as the democratic counterparts within South Africa of similar institutions and organisations internationally. This means that the ANC, the broad democratic movement in all its forms within South

Africa and the international solidarity movement must act together.'[309]

These unfolding ideas and strategies, as the ANC started preparing itself for the transfer of power, were in direct conflict with some of the key principles underlying SACOS's operations. The leading forces in the liberation movement and the sports movement were beginning to go in different directions. Serious family squabbles lay ahead for non-racial sport.

The emergence of the National Sports Congress, 1987–89

Not long after the meeting between SACOS and the UDF in October 1984, the UDF set up a sports desk in 1985. Emboldened by Makhenkesi Stofile's successful visit to New Zealand in that year, where his lobbying and court testimony in co-operation with the wider anti-apartheid movement, helped to torpedo the planned 1985 All Blacks rugby tour to South Africa, the UDF started becoming more involved in sports-related campaigns. At first these were organic actions, not aimed at challenging or dividing SACOS, but by 1987 the idea of linking sport to the broad-front strategies of the advancing struggle started taking concrete shape.

On 2 April a paper prepared by a collective of sportspeople in Durban critical of SACOS was approved at a meeting of the Natal Council of Sport (NACOS), a provincial version of the national SACOS where the different affiliates met. The drafters argued that while the country was faced with a societal crisis that needed addressing, SACOS 'is itself in a state of crisis', adding: 'Up to the present, SACOS has no coherent response or programme of action, and certainly no semblance of broad based democratic structures. This means it has remained bound by its rhetoric. It cannot galvanise a broad band of members into any group'.[310] The drafters' argument was that sport should follow the example of the trade union movement in both the way it incorporated the working class and also practised internal democracy.

In the same month, the Johannesburg-based rugby administrator Bill Jardine, who was working virtually fulltime as a volunteer for UDF and its associated groups, travelled to Lusaka where he met with Thabo Mbeki, the newly exiled Steve Tshwete and the ANC's head of culture Barbara Masekela, cosmopolitan sister of the famous trumpeter Hugh Masekela, who had gained several degrees from international educational institutions. It was decided that decisive action should be taken at home. Jardine returned to South Africa with a one-page document that 'set out proposals on how we could mobilise sportspersons across the colour line and provide facilities and programmes to develop them, especially black sportspersons in the goal of creating a disciplined sports movement'.[311]

On 8 April 1987 Jardine approached the struggle lawyer Krish Naidoo to become involved as secretary of a new body to be called the National Sports Congress (NSC). It had been decided, moreover, that the president of the new body should be Mluleki George, a rugby administrator and former Robben Islander who headed the ANC's underground structures in the Border region. Jardine followed up by approaching the Natal-based head of the South African Cricket Board, Krish Mackerdhuj (a former Fort Hare student), and NACOS executive member Harry Naidu to help develop policies for the intended NSC. They met in July 1987 and again that September in Durban. There, baseball administrator Errol Heyns from Eastern Province and athletics officials Judy Abrahams and Wilfred Daniels from Cape Town joined the interim committee. Co-opted sometime later were four of the national football leaders and Mackerdhuj's deputy at the national cricket board, advocate Percy Sonn.

By October 1987 the NSC's interim committee had developed a strategy based on the three foundation stones of unity, development and preparation, goals based on broadening the base of sport and preparing for the future both on and off the field. By emphasising unity, the NSC would seek to create the broadest possible front against racial sport in line with broader ANC policy. It was designed to not only mobilise the oppressed as far as possible behind a common vision, but also to reach out to white South Africans to offer them a share in a post-apartheid future, as part of an incipient nation-building process. The emphasis on development was to ensure that black sportspeople disadvantaged over many years were given improved opportunities. This meant providing decent facilities and technical assistance and training, which had not been available to them, including the use of the ANC and SANROC's international allies to send people abroad for coaching and training courses.

The independence of Zimbabwe had shown that non-establishment sport was ill-prepared to take over the reins after independence. Its national hockey team that won the gold medal at the Moscow Olympics six months after independence was simply the ex-white Rhodesian team, and the NSC wanted to avoid this type of situation and ensure sport in the future had a more national character. Sport, too, needed to be as ready as possible when the transition happened.[312] George, Naidoo and Mthobi Tyamzashe travelled to Lusaka in the same month to meet with Mbeki, Tshwete and Masekela; the policy positions were approved and it was agreed that the NSC would act as a pressure group within SACOS 'with the purpose of appealing to SACOS to spread its wings into the townships'.

Meanwhile SANROC's London-headquartered Ramsamy was on board with the strategy to build the NSC as well. In May 1987 in London, he had heard Tambo give his new position on new-style selective boycotts which could empower the progressive groups at home as 'democratic counterparts within South Africa' of the ANC and its international allies. Ramsamy now started making regular trips to Lusaka to meet with Masekela, Tshwete and others to consult and strengthen the new approach.

*

A new alignment of international and democratic forces was underway, well demonstrated at the Culture in Another South Africa (CASA) conference and festival held in Amsterdam in December 1987, a sectoral intervention to put a wide array of writers, musicians, artists, actors, filmmakers, photographers and cultural workers from home in touch with their exiled and international counterparts. Over 300 participated, highlighting the growth of resistance in South Africa and the unity that existed between the ANC, the internal mass struggles and the international anti-apartheid movement.

Amsterdam had been declared the cultural capital of Europe in 1987 and the mayor of Amsterdam, Ed van Thijn, a strong supporter of the anti-apartheid movement decided the way to celebrate would be to join forces with the active Nederlandse Anti-Apartheidsbeweging (AABN) and declare Amsterdam an 'apartheid-free zone' for a week. Tens of talks, exhibitions and performances took place as the South Africans 'took over' the royal theatre and opera, the discos and the restaurants and the city hall and parliament.[313]

The rhythm and the beat took in a wide range of South Africa's top talent from the famous Jazz Pioneers, Basil Coetzee, Jonas Gwangwa, Abdullah Ibrahim, and Dolly Rathebe, to the overtly activist COSATU choir and Amandla Cultural Ensemble of the ANC, to plays by Percy Mtwa, Mbongeni Ngema and Athol Fugard, and writers such as Nobel prizewinner Nadine Gordimer, Lewis Nkosi, Don Mattera, Mandla Langa, Breyten Breytenbach and Njabulo Ndebele. It was truly 'a mix of exiles from all over the world and "insiders" working and living in South Africa'.[314]

Much like the writer and soon-to-be president, Václav Havel was doing in Czechoslovakia where an old Soviet Union satellite system was dying as popular resistance welled up, these artists were seeking to define freedom and envisioning a new birth in ways that had instant political resonance. Amsterdam underlined that they had key roles to play in popularising and legitimising system change. The regime was bankrupt in the popular imagination. Every piece played or enunciated by the resistance artists and musicians present became part of the heartbeat of the revolution.

The possibilities of extending this kind of co-operation in sport were obvious. For sport was something the youth revelled in and could be encouraged in similar ways in the eyes of the ANC and its allied new National Sports Congress. The NSC sports leader Krish Naidoo was at this CASA Festival representing the MDM (an amorphous grouping that replaced the by then banned UDF) in place of Achmat Dangor, who had been prevented from attending by the state; that together with a large ANC delegation which included Barbara Masekela and Thabo Mbeki, with whom both Naidoo and Ramsamy had been consulting on the sports issue, showed the interconnectedness that was starting to dictate a new path in the 'soft' spheres of sport and culture in South Africa.

The top ANC intellectual Pallo Jordan emphasised in his keynote address that the ANC was not trying to impose a 'line' or insisting that artists become political 'pamphleteers' or 'sloganeers'. Rather this was part of a 'continuing dialogue' and they should 'pursue excellence in their respective disciplines – to be excellent artists and to serve the struggle for liberation with excellent art'. The role of artists, he added, quoting Tambo, was for artists to use their craft 'to give voice not only to the grievances, but also to the profoundest aspirations of the oppressed and exploited'.[315]

A decision was taken in Amsterdam about the boycott of apartheid South Africa which would decisively formalise the change in thinking and strategy that was occurring in the ANC and its allies, with a huge resultant impact on culture, academic life and sport in South Africa.

The total boycott had been instituted to isolate the regime. Now, it was decided, the growth of the democratic forces within the country required that 'the cultural boycott as a tactic needs to be applied with a degree of flexibility which takes into consideration the developing situation within the country'. This was in order to 'recognise and strengthen the emerging democratic culture in South Africa'. The CASA resolutions committee consisted of ANC people closely linked to the new terrain of constitutional planning – Jordan, the conference key note speaker, Mbeki and Aziz Pahad – together with sport's Krish Naidoo. The concrete outcome was the setting up of a UDF cultural desk, and the formation of yet another sectoral body, the South African Musicians Alliance (SAMA).[316] This mirrored what had happened within the broad alliance in relation to sport in 1985 and 1987 as well. The struggle, and sport, was heading for a strategic turning point.

*

Sam Ramsamy wrote: 'If the ANC believed it was time to engage on a broader social and political level, then I believed it was important that the sports struggle should follow suit, and ensure the entire sports movement advanced at the same pace.'[317] The first tentative moves were now initiated towards creating a broader internal anti-apartheid sports front drawing in new constituencies with a view to facilitating future national unity – in other words nation-building through sport. Football and rugby – the games of the African majority and the Afrikaner ruling class respectively – were first to get attention and the process started in different ways in each case.

Bill Jardine started to reach out to the South African Soccer Association (SASA), de facto home of African township football though regarded as out of bounds by SACOS. The SASA president was Solomon 'Stix' Morewa, a former Robben Island prisoner and he and his executive were eager to meet with the NSC. After this meeting the NSC met with the SACOS-affiliated South African Soccer Federation (SASF) in April 1988 to take the idea of football unity further. Though ideologically close to the NSC, the Federation's leadership were not enamoured with the idea. One of the reasons being that one of its former leaders, the flamboyant Abdul Bhamjee, had together with Kaizer Motaung helped form the Premier Soccer League (PSL), the professional arm of SASA, drawing various long-standing SASF affiliates away from that body. Bhamjee, a born television-age marketeer, fond of gold chains and with a bold dress sense, was part of the reason why the white sports sponsorship establishment, aware that it had for long ignored the emerging African market, chose to give significant support to the PSL/SAFA. Consequently the non-racial Federation, which had been the pioneer of both professional and 'inter-race' football, as it was called in the 1950s, was in the process of being sidelined, which was a politically uncomfortable fact to deal with. In addition, it charged, Bhamjee had pocketed sponsorship money meant for the Federation during the estrangement between them. Here was proof of the complex historical, racial, financial and cultural issues that the strategy to create unity in sports would encounter – and this was essentially a discus-sion between sections of the oppressed, not yet involving the white body. The next step was for the NSC to organise for the Federation leaders to meet with the ANC in Lusaka later the same year so that these complications could be addressed. The Federation's leadership responded positively and four of its top officials, the president Rama Reddy, Danny Jordaan, Vincent Baatjies and Alex Abercrombie became NSC stalwarts.

The rugby talks were similarly not without drama. In July 1987 Frederik van Zyl Slabbert, former Leader of the Opposition, recently resigned from the white parliament because it had lost relevance, took a large delegation of Afrikaners to Dakar, Senegal to meet with the ANC and pursue the idea of talks. Slabbert invited Tommy Bedford – Springbok rugby vice-captain of the 1969–70 demo tour – to participate. Bedford said he would come on condition Slabbert set up a private meeting for him with the ANC leadership. On the first evening in Senegal, there was a knock on the door. The former top Springbok, a nephew of the writer Laurens van der Post who was a close adviser to Prince Charles and Margaret Thatcher, was called to Thabo Mbeki's hotel room and offered to act as an intermediary in setting up a meeting between the ANC and the white South African Rugby Board. Mbeki immediately saw this as an opportunity that should be followed up on, leading a year later to discussions in October 1988 in Harare, capital of Zimbabwe. Sitting around the table with the ANC, represented by Mbeki and Steve Tshwete, were Craven's SARB delegation (which included the wealthy businessman Louis Luyt, who was to succeed him), and Ebrahim Patel and his non-racial SARU executive, who were sympathetic to the NSC. This started the rugby unity process in the country.[318]

After two days of talks, both sets of rugby leaders expressed a 'common desire' for South African rugby to be 'organised according to non-racial principles' and they 'agreed that rugby should come under one non-racial controlling body'. 'Accepting the good faith and sincerity of the rugby administrators at the meeting', the ANC agreed in turn that if this precondition was met it would 'use its good offices to ensure that non-racial South African rugby' took its place in 'African and world rugby'. To cut out any ambiguity, the point was repeated: 'the accomplishment of the goals stated here is a necessity for South African rugby to take its rightful place in world rugby'.[319] Mbeki was revealing here the more flexible ANC position on the sports and cultural boycott decided on in Amsterdam the previous December, stating that the boycott should be maintained against racist institutions in South Africa, but non-racial organisations had to be treated differently. Craven's fervent desire for tours, particularly with the celebration the following year of the centenary of the white Rugby Board, had led him to do the previously unthinkable and talk with the ANC – still regarded by most whites as the 'terrorist' arch-enemy. His action was an important sign of whites' growing desperation. The fact that Craven was encouraged by the business elements represented by the powerful Louis Luyt also reflected the increasing impatience of business leaders with the apartheid regime. It was also the final vindication of the anti-apartheid movement's sports boycott strategy. Eighteen years after stating at the time of the STST campaign that he would never have a black player in a Springbok side, Craven, as the leading establishment sports figure in South Africa, was breaking his own fundamentalist taboos to talk to the ANC.

In the event, Harare proved to be one of the last throws of the dice from the old sports establishment. Craven was blocked, both within his own Rugby Board and by the government from implementing the agreement with the ANC; true to his position as a member of the conservative wing of the National Party, and only a year before his later reforming role as president in 1989–90, the sports minister, F. W. de Klerk, condemned Craven and Luyt for 'plunging politics knee-deep into rugby' and spelled out to them 'the negative consequences of this kind of action for South Africa in its fight against terrorism'.

After an initial period of silence, President Botha's public condemnation was itself revealing of how powerful the ANC had become. He insisted that the ANC was wrapping itself in a cloak of piousness 'in order to stab you in the back with a dagger'. Sport, Botha chuntered on clinging to an old script, was part of the ANC's terrain of 'subtle subversion' and 'there are still politically blind moles in this country who fail to see this'.

*

The talks in sport initiated by the ANC and its MDM allies via the NSC in 1988, along with an intensification of the armed struggle, international activities to isolate apartheid and internal mobilisation, had direct parallels in the broader political sphere. The talks ranged from encounters with establishment groups of businessmen, academics, Bantustan cabinet members previously hostile to the ANC, white opposition MPs and students, to aligned civil society organisations such as the National Education Crisis Committee. Another was the SA Council of Churches, which very significantly declared in 1988 that it was legitimate for Christians to take up arms against oppressive systems like apartheid, thus endorsing the ANC's armed struggle. The ANC was meanwhile also speaking regularly to allies like COSATU and the UDF to plan the way forward.

In parallel both the jailed Nelson Mandela and Oliver Tambo tried to open up direct lines with the apartheid government. In May 1988 Mandela started 'talks about talks' in prison with a committee of officials appointed by P. W. Botha. In England, secondary informal discussions began between Tambo's diplomatic emissary Mbeki and a group of conservative Afrikaners reporting back to the National Intelligence Agency, after Tambo had opened up a channel via the Britain-based Consolidated Gold Fields mining company, which for a century had been prominently involved in the exploitative South African mining industry.[320]

These direct contacts with the enemy remained secret at first, given sensitivities on both sides. SACOS was not impressed with the initiatives in sport by the ANC, MDM and NSC. The contacts with Stix Morewa's SASA in football breached its Double Standards Resolution of isolating black sportspeople deemed to be co-operating with apartheid, and with the white establishment rugby body – its strict principle of non-collaboration with the ruling classes. A growing disjuncture was developing between SACOS and the dominant political organisations in the struggle and by 1988 the prospects of a public rupture were increasing. 'The ethos of the MDM has not been able to penetrate the non-racial sports movement to the same extent as it has other spheres of social life', noted Professor Jakes Gerwel, the activist rector of the University of the Western Cape.

A former Black Consciousness student activist, Gerwel was now close to the ANC and MDM and emerging as a spokesperson for the NSC. However, Gerwel expressed the feelings of many people loyal to non-racial sport when he warned against the populist rubbishing of SACOS. He said it had in difficult times played a big role in nurturing non-racialism and isolating apartheid and, 'It will be a grave mistake to apportion all the blame for this [growing misalignment] to SACOS or its present leadership or through resorting to allegations about the existence of a cabal controlling it'.

He noted with a sociologist's insight that 'There are more profound reasons for the non-existence of a vibrant non-racial sports movement' in South Africa.[321] Gerwel pointed out that the real problem was that

> while SACOS has been able to penetrate the Indian and Coloured communities, it has not really succeeded in penetrating the African townships both in the urban and rural communities. A non-racial sports movement remains seriously flawed if it does not reflect the democratic composition of our people. In the period when mass struggles have reached such great heights and when the chief content of national liberation is the liberation of the African masses and under their leadership, this weakness of the non-racial sports movement should be the concern of all democrats.[322]

A clear goal of the ANC and MDM since the formation of the UDF in 1983 was to attract more enlightened sections of the white community into the struggle so that, in the language of the struggle, cracks could be created in the ruling block and the broad front that constituted the 'people's camp' consisting of many different persuasions and ideas could be strengthened. As Gerwel put it: 'The success and prestige of the MDM have to be paralleled by the sports wing. We need to clarify and pursue vigorously a policy that attracts increasing numbers of white sportspersons in the non-racial fold. In this way we will deepen the democratic gains made by the democratic movement as a whole.'[323]

From both trade union and MDM political perspectives, there were also calls for SACOS to become more participatory and reform the way it operated and was structured so that grassroots sportspeople could be more involved. It was seen as tightly controlled by ideologically driven officials policing sport with ideas that would make growth difficult, at a time when black sportspeople needed to be more organically involved and given more opportunities and access to facilities and training in preparation for the future. Writers like Hein Willemse and Ashwin Desai, both deeply involved in the radical movements of the 1980s, explain how 'the politics of refusal . . . spawned its own contradictions' in SACOS during these times. Desai recalls that:

> Like religious zealots, what the line was between sell-out and revolutionary grew more stringent. Just when we thought it reached

301

its acme a South African Council of Sport (SACOS) leader told us that it was when we stopped playing sport altogether that the highest point of the struggle would be attained. But was not sport a way of organising, learning and dare we say it enjoying life under the repressive gaze of apartheid? For me and many of the Black and a few of the white students at Rhodes University it was all that. Every weekend we left the sanctuary of Rhodes to play soccer in the local townships, learn at eye level street politics and party in the shebeens.[324]

Hein Willemse makes similar observations in Cape Town:

a spirited debate raged on campus on whether the new UWC tartan track and sport stadium should be used. Hardliners within the SACOS fraternity insisted that UWC was an ethnic institution, that attending it amounted to collaboration with the apartheid government and that no sport events should be held at the stadium. The argument left me . . . perplexed . . . What was the alternative? Had the non-collaborationist ethic of the 1950s and 1960s not kept up with the dynamics of the politics of the 1980s? Was the impending boycott of the sports stadium the result of a difference between two anti-apartheid forces, i.e., the Fourth International-inspired left and the United Democratic Front/ Congress movement, or was it something else?[325]

Internal critiques by Durban-based SACOS leaders like Dr Errol Vawda and the affiliated provincial Natal Council on Sport in early 1987, as well as the annual M. N. Pather Memorial Lectures, where trade unionists Gwede Mantashe and Alec Irwin, and much harassed Catholic priest and MDM leader Father Smangaliso Mkhatshwa gave sports-related inputs between 1987 and 1989, were pointers to the persistence of these perspectives. The implications were clear for those advocating new directions for SACOS. In the same way that the MDM 'has to contest and penetrate all the key social spaces in our society – education, religion, the factory, sports and so forth', one commentator said, SACOS as the sports wing need to be more dynamic in engaging with the whole sporting constituency in South Africa. There was a clear parting of the ways on the ideas and strategy happening in non-racial sport, and this was grounded in the deeper realities of life and politics in the country. The bitter, personalised accusations of betrayal, 'sell out' or individuals acting purely for personal gain that would follow masked the deeper reasons for the cracks that were appearing in SACOS.

*

The divorce happened slowly over two years in 1988 and 1989; it was not easy for either partner, and in retrospect it was traumatic for the sportspeople under their wings. SACOS's Sam Ramsamy recalled that he was at the Olympic Games in Seoul in September 1988 when Essop Pahad, a close confidant of Thabo Mbeki, phoned him about the plan to meet Danie Craven in Harare. Ramsamy had no problems with the meeting with the proviso that 'we must be sensitive and ensure that the non-racial sports movement in South Africa feels involved and is always kept fully informed of the process'.[326] By this he meant increasingly the NSC because strains between him and SACOS were already showing by then. For example, Ramsamy had initially not invited SACOS to the major third International Conference Against Apartheid Sport in Harare from 5 to 7 November 1987. After a last-minute scramble, a SACOS delegation did manage to attend and its report back noted that there were also 'a number of other [unnamed] invitees from South Africa', most likely meaning sportspeople from the emerging SANROC/NSC alignment.

SANROC organised the widely attended conference together with the Supreme Council for Sport in Africa, the Association of National Olympic Committees of Africa and the Union of African Sports Confederations in co-operation with the Zimbabwe government and national Olympic committee. President Robert Mugabe, then also head of the Non-Aligned Movement, opened the proceedings and Joseph Garba, chairman of the UN Special Committee Against Apartheid, gave the keynote address.

Besides tightening the screws on apartheid sport and recognising the violent repression happening in a country under a state of emergency rule, the ensuing Declaration of Harare Against Apartheid Sport unambiguously confirmed Ramsamy and SANROC's leadership role on the South African sports issue (and through him that of the ANC). The conference called on the international community to give SANROC meaningful backing and, in apparent reference to the NSC policy position of preparing athletes and administrators from the oppressed communities for the future, it emphasised, 'Governments, sports bodies and other organisations should provide

SANROC, which has made an outstanding contribution to the international campaign over the past 25 years, with resources adequate to meet its expanding responsibilities.' Moreover, 'The UN Special Committee Against Apartheid, the Supreme Council for Sport in Africa and other bodies should further strengthen their co-operation with SANROC for more effective co-ordination of the international campaign.'[327]

Following various press reports indicating that something was brewing in non-racial sport, the interim NSC leadership officially informed SACOS of its existence on 6 April 1988. SACOS noted in its documentation that 'immediate steps were taken to arrange a meeting with the organisation'. Ebrahim Patel, the SARU rugby president, who worked closely with Bill Jardine on their home turf in Johannesburg, was asked to set up a meeting. This took place on 7 May 1988, the day on which the NSC team witnessed a palace revolt in SACOS, according to Krish Naidoo. Frank van der Horst was attacked by his colleagues in a stormy meeting, leading to his resignation as SACOS president two months later in July 1988 when he was succeeded by lawyer and later judge, Yusuf 'Joe' Ebrahim.

The first NSC and SACOS meeting ended with a calm, non-controversial statement: the two parties discussed the sports situation in the country and declared that 'Newspaper speculation on the formation of a rival organisation and a split within SACOS are unfounded.' They said the status of SACOS was 'recognised and confirmed, and they would report back to their constituencies and then 'ongoing discussions will be necessary'.[328] In reality the backroom climate was much tenser. Naidoo explained, that when the NSC team sat down with the ten SACOS representatives that May evening, no less than half of them – the presidents of football, rugby, cricket, table tennis and squash – were sitting on the other side of the table but secretly supported the NSC. In its reports of the time, SACOS in turn explained how it made unsuccessful attempts to organise a follow-up meeting in July because the NSC people did not come back to them on this. It was becoming a painful separation. When the two sides did eventually sit around the table again in November 1988 in East London, Naidoo noted that 'it was an unpleasant meeting'.

By this time mutual suspicions were high. SACOS maintained the NSC 'persistently stated that it regarded SACOS as the authentic non-racial sports organisation in the country' and that its role would be 'to organise non-racial sport in those areas where SACOS affiliates for a number of reasons were unable to do so'. However, other SACOS sources reported that the 'NSC has decided unilaterally to go it alone and have nothing further to do with SACOS'. The next SACOS meeting in Port Elizabeth in February 1989 brought matters to a head. As debate raged about the NSC's proposal that affiliates be allowed dual membership, the delegates were asked to show their loyalties physically: delegates had to move to the left (for the proposal) or the right of the hall for those against. The ayes had it but the SACOS leadership would not accept the situation and before the end of the year SACOS declared the NSC a rival body.[329]

Peter and André, who was active in an aligned UDF Area Committee and had met some of the banned ANC leaders at the 1987 Dakar Conference in Senegal, were supportive of these ANC-led initiatives, which stressed the need for intensified struggle as well as a strategy for sport to move forward alongside the unfolding political process. Peter thought the ANC was extremely sophisticated – sometimes in ways not appreciated by activists schooled in the harsh and necessary arts of 'no compromise' – and that its demonstration of flexibility at the Harare rugby talks had strengthened the anti-apartheid movements, not least because it revealed to the world that all the blockages were from white South Africa. From now onward, sport became a means of offering sportspeople on both sides of the divide a glimpse of a new post-apartheid South Africa.

But there was a new decisive act in this sporting drama to follow – a rebel cricket tour organised with incredibly clumsy and provocative timing right in the middle of key developments that saw the release of Nelson Mandela from prison and his seamless transition from prisoner to president of a new democratic South Africa.

7

Sport and nation-building: The final push for national liberation and democracy, 1989–96

From Harare to home: The rebel sports tours and preparations for the decisive push against the apartheid regime, 1989

In mid-1989 news leaked out that yet another covertly organised rebel cricket tour was being planned under England cricket captain Mike Gatting. But unknown to the apartheid sporting establishment promoting it, a perfect storm was brewing. A wide range of political, community and sports organisations started making plans to make life uncomfortable for the visitors and when they arrived, thousands of protesters went out onto the street, miring the tour in unprecedented controversy. Sport was about to be drawn directly into the final decisive campaigns for the release of Nelson Mandela and the unbanning of organisations.

In a jackboot state, it had simply been too dangerous to attempt anything on a similar scale before. The police, security apparatus and, not least of all, testosterone-powered whites-only apartheid-supporting crowds were ready to swing into action against any moves such as this in state-of-emergency South Africa. André was present at the match between the British Lions and Southern Universities in 1974 when a small group of anti-apartheid protesters suddenly ran onto the field at Newlands. The immediate response – even before officials could act – was for dozens of spectators to pursue them onto the pitch ready to impose rough, summary justice. André wondered for years what had happened to those poor souls. But the story had a happy ending. Decades later, the well-known labour lawyer Paul Benjamin wrote about how he and a few University of Cape Town students had invaded the pitch on that day. It was in the time before strictly fenced-off fields and mercifully the pursuing hordes were so many that they started tussling with each other, enabling the statement-makers to sneak away unseen and unmolested.

This time it would be different. By mid-1989 South Africa was hurtling towards a final denouement between the liberation movement and the apartheid state. A spiderweb of fast-paced interconnected developments stretching across continents was unravelling at breakneck speed. At his modest offices in the Alpha building off Chachacha Road and Cairo Road in Lusaka, Oliver Tambo, the kingpin in the ANC around which the democratic forces in South Africa were increasingly coalescing, faced a complex set of challenges. If not handled properly they could imperil the very future of his movement and the outcome of the liberation struggle.

*

Communicating via a recently developed secret encrypted communications network in May 1989, Oliver Tambo informed his underground head, Mac Maharaj, who was deep undercover at home as part of Operation Vulindlela (open the road) that 'The race for who will control developments in our country has started in earnest, & we should be in the lead.'

Namibia was moving towards independence under international supervision, involving a host of outside countries: South Africa, Angola and Cuba, as well the United Nations and the observing superpowers – the United States and Soviet Union – together with Britain. The focus shifted to South Africa as the geopolitical issue to resolve. Caught offside by the growing popularity of the ANC, the international face of the counter-revolution, Margaret Thatcher, rushed to get involved, seeking to influence events in a way that would reign in the liberation movement's agenda as much as possible. Strategically far-sighted as always, Tambo moved therefore to assemble a solid international coalition of forces to ensure that the Constitutional Guidelines for a Democratic South Africa, adopted by the ANC in 1988, formed the basis of any future settlement. To this end, he started drafting with urgency with his closest aides and brother presidents in the frontline states what would later become known as the Harare Declaration.

Talk of negotiations speeded up dramatically after 5 July 1989 when the now frail despot, P. W. Botha, finally acceded to the long-standing demands from the imprisoned Nelson Mandela for a meeting where they could establish common ground for a future meeting between government and the ANC's National Executive Committee.

To make sure that the liberation forces were not caught offside, Tambo had to juggle these major geopolitical realignments and the unfolding internal changes, while at the same time attending to his regular job as commander-in-chief. This entailed overseeing the interrelated armed actions of *Umkhonto we Sizwe* and the underground operations and mass mobilisation within South Africa in ways which increased the pressure on a regime seeking a way out of the corner it had been backed into politically. The fact that a new president, F. W. de Klerk, would be installed to replace the retiring Botha in September following a general election only added to the pressure on Tambo and his organisation. The former maths teacher and aspirant priest turned reluctant revolutionary, who had succeeded in keeping the ANC together through nearly three harrowing decades of exile, was facing his greatest test yet.

The ANC and its allies in the Mass Democratic Movement (the renamed alliance between COSATU and the now banned UDF) decided in June 1989 in Lusaka that the MDM should launch a defiance campaign inside the country to challenge the ongoing state of emergency and to demand the release of Mandela and substantive negotiations which could lead to the transfer of power. Though hobbled by the emergency, the MDM was riding the crest of the wave of popular support and it duly proceeded as planned on 2 August with its hunger strikes, deliberately 'illegal' mass marches, invasions of segregated beaches, demands for treatment at whites-only hospitals, campaigns against whites-only schools, the demand for the release of Nelson Mandela, stay-aways to protest against the white elections and generally making known that the people's organisations were 'unrestricting' themselves from the apartheid police state's shackles. Images of Archbishop Tutu, his wife Leah Tutu, and other leaders being arrested during one of the protest marches in Cape Town raised international attention and put the government on the back foot.[330]

Just one day before the start of the defiance campaign, news leaked that a rebel cricket tour was being planned by Ali Bacher and SACU. The first report of the tour came during the fourth and final test in the Ashes series between England and Australia in Manchester, which ended on 1 August 1989. Sport was already becoming firmly part of the strategy to isolate the regime and simultaneously build unity with a view to preparing South Africans for a common future. The planned tour immediately raised temperatures and fed into the endgame activities of defiance campaign planning. Bacher, it was reported, had signed up no less than nine of the players who had been involved in the Ashes series, including Mike Gatting, one of the England captains. The players were promised £50,000 each for three seasons, a huge figure for the time.

There was an uproar in England and the rebels faced negative press. As one journalist put it, 'the studied ignorance of the tourists remained unfath-omable'.[331] It was terrible timing for Bacher and his fellow organisers, exactly the wrong thing to do at exactly the right time for the forces of change, who were flexing their muscles at a turning point in South Africa's journey.

As part of the defiance campaign, the MDM protested against two matches by a World XV versus the Springboks – approved by the International Rugby Board and supported by the mainstay sponsor of apartheid sport, South African Breweries – to celebrate the centenary of the white SARB. But it was the Gatting tour that would be the real test.

Ramsamy, tipped off by a journalist friend, contacted the ANC in Lusaka to inform them of the developments and after the necessary deliberations the fledgling NSC and SANROC were drawn directly into the planning for the broad ANC and MDM offensive. Ramsamy and leaders of the NSC were asked to fly to Lusaka at short notice to decide on the steps ahead. He could stay for only a few hours as he had obligations in London the next morning, but he left feeling the importance of what was being planned made the flying visit very worthwhile. The group met at the house of Thabo Mbeki in Lusaka. Present were Mbeki, Ramsamy, the ANC's Head of Culture Barbara Masekela, and the key NSC officials, Mluleki George, Mthobi Tyamzashe and Krish Naidoo. There, given the strains within SACOS, the decision was taken to go it alone and formally launch the NSC as a new organisation and also that the NSC and SANROC working in tandem with the MDM should stop the impending rebel cricket tour if it went ahead. Going with these actions, it was agreed, the focus should increasingly fall on uniting South African sports bodies in order to win over sections of the ruling block and put the regime on the offensive ahead of political negoti-ations that now seemed inevitable.

Mbeki had been at Tambo's side ever since the latter had decided at the height of the insurrection in 1985 to prepare for the moment when the antagonists would one day sit around a table together. He had been a key figure in many of the safari meetings with internal groups – totalling around 150 by this stage – and was involved as Tambo's envoy in secret talks in England which led in September 1989 to the first formal contacts between the ANC and the regime's National Intelligence Agency to prepare the logistics for the release of Mandela. Mbeki was thus a key person in the ANC's inner circles and was becoming directly involved in the sports debate at a crucial moment in the country's political history. This in turn elevated the importance of the Gatting tour and its outcome. It provided the exiled liberation movement and the internal forces with an ideal opportunity to demonstrate to the regime and the white establishment in South Africa that their days of dictating events was over.

SACU duly confirmed that a team captained by Mike Gatting would be visiting South Africa during the summer of 1989–90. It seemed like business as usual for the white sporting establishment. Up to then, white cricketers had operated without restraint in running the show inside the country. Smug about their cricket 'cultures' and their positions of privilege within the apartheid system, they were ill-educated about the realities of apartheid faced by most South Africans. SACU had recently celebrated the centenary of the former whites-only cricket association SACA (which had nominally been absorbed by SACU) by inviting a large contingent of overseas administrators, ex-players and media to the country on an all-expenses-paid holiday for the celebrations. Parading as a misunderstood and wronged liberal, Bacher had also made a major speech at a Wisden dinner in London that April, hinting at a tour. Bacher was intent on showing the white establishment's muscle. While in England, he started approaching top English players for the tour.

But much bigger events were imminent. On 15 October 1989 Mandela's fellow Rivonia trialists were released from prison and received home in huge welcoming rallies. Meanwhile defiance campaign marches saw tens of thousands of people take to the streets, starting in Cape Town with Archbishop Tutu and Reverend Allan Boesak in front, and going on to Johannesburg (20,000), Uitenhage (80,000) East London (40,000), Durban (20,000), Port Elizabeth (50,000) and even small towns like Oudtshoorn (8,000), according to figures provided by Anthea Jeffery of the SA Institute of Race Relations. After the release of the Rivonia leadership, Bacher met the same week with cabinet minister Gerrit Viljoen, responsible for the constitutional development portfolio and came back emboldened.[332] Despite the liberal image he was projecting to the cricket world, he was playing a straight down the line ruling-class game. His position: 'It's totally unfair to expect cricketers to come out and say they are against the government. I can assure you I wouldn't have signed a statement deploring apartheid or the South African Government if asked by [Peter] Hain or anyone else.'[333]

The anti-tour campaign now got going in earnest. Krish Naidoo, who was at that time helping to facilitate secret unity talk between South Africa's four football bodies, contacted Bacher to start discussions about calling off the tour. The NSC also started pressing SACU sponsors to withdraw support if it continued with the plans. At an NSC-organised sports conference at Witwatersrand University at the end of October, the MDM committed itself to supporting the NSC actions against the tour. It was decided that two MDM leaders, Murphy Morobe and the trade unionist and poet Mi Hlatshwayo, together with SACB president Krish Mackerdhuj and Ngconde Balfour of the NSC should go to London to lobby for it to be called off.[334] Balfour had just been released from nine months of detention, where he had been kept in solitary confinement and had a gun pushed into his mouth under torture. Refused entry to Lords, they eventually met with Gatting and John Emburey, who refused to back down. André, on sabbatical in Britain at the time, was asked by Ramsamy to speak out against the tour on television, and he attended the delegation's press conference in London in support. On returning home, André was invited by Ramsamy to join a delegation of non-racial sports leaders for a meeting in Harare with Ethiopian-born Fekrou Kidane of the International Conference Against Apartheid Sport which signalled another step forward in the realignments on the sports front, and was soon active on the interim committee of the NSC in the Western Cape as education and training officer or 'the commissar', as his comrades teased.

On 8 November the NSC delegation which had been to Lusaka, plus Harry Naidu, Ngconde Balfour and Bill Jardine, met formally with SACU requesting the tour be cancelled. The NSC said that if SACU called off the tour the ANC would work towards creating unity and an eventual return to international cricket for South Africa. But no guarantees about the timing could be given. The key issue was that 'the NSC was expecting SACU to come to a decision and could not ease it for them by offering guarantees of future tours'. Naidoo explained: 'We are asking them to be part of a process of change. And in being part of a process you have to show good faith. They must decide whether they want to be part of the decaying apartheid system or part of a new South Africa. If SACU choose the latter road, the NSC may have to give them a clearer idea of what they will meet as they travel along it.'[335]

Despite scratching for funds, the NSC had hired a conference room at an upmarket hotel to impress the SACU cricket executive consisting of ten suited middle-aged white men and their one solitary 'coloured' colleague. However, next day a complacent SACU quickly decided to go ahead with the tour. Flip Potgieter, a prominent Eastern Province SACU administrator, coming back from one of the many meetings now taking place in Lusaka, had stopped over in Johannesburg beforehand to warn Ali Bacher of the new direction developments were taking, but Bacher was dismissive about the threats to the tour, or the need to speak to the ANC, as his counterparts in rugby and football were doing. Professing to be 'liberal', he and his colleagues were still solidly rooted in the white ideas world of apartheid South Africa. Indeed, the tour itinerary had been leaked in a newspaper report the day before the meeting, and it noted that SACU 'would not even consider cancelling the tour'.[336]

From 9 to 11 December 1989 the internal anti-apartheid forces staged a large Conference for a Democratic Future, in Johannesburg. Some 4,600 delegates from 2,000 organisations attended. Six months in planning since the June meeting between the ANC and MDM in Lusaka, the purpose was to unite the widest possible range of internal South African groupings behind the ANC's key constitutional proposals and pre-conditions for negotiations, as outlined in the Constitutional Principles for a Democratic South Africa and the Harare Declaration. Reports noted that 'The principal objective of the conference was achieved to demonstrate that the exiled ANC and the MDM speak on the central question of negotiations, with one voice.'[337] The keynote speaker was the recently released Rivonia prisoner and mentor to Mandela, Walter Sisulu, who said the democratic forces had a prime opportunity to take the initiative given 'the government's loss of control over the process'. Though dominated by the MDM, for the first time representatives from rival tendencies such as the Black Consciousness movement also attended. The Conference (or CDF as it was known) endorsed the Harare Declaration, already adopted by the Frontline States in Lusaka, the OAU in Harare, the Commonwealth in Kuala Lumpur and the Non-Aligned movement in Budapest, and it now took wings to the UN General Assembly which unanimously approved it in the form of the UN Declaration on Apartheid. The UN gave the de Klerk government six months to fulfil the demands in the document and the secretary general was instructed to report back after that to ensure it was complying.[338]

Crucially, the Conference for a Democratic Future also came out in full support of a call to SACU to 'cancel its rebel tour forthwith' and said SACU 'by its action is perpetuating apartheid'. Alongside the set of resolutions meant for the United Nations were five others on the need to stop the tour, which the CDF declared 'retards the creation of a truly mass-based sports movement in South Africa'. Member organisations and sports and community groups in the democratic movement were being asked to take to the streets again, this time with the future of sport as the focus.

Thus, in the last month before the advent of the 1990s, two momentous sets of events had been set in motion alongside each other. In New York, the United Nations ratified in a modified form the Harare Declaration and, on the ground in South Africa, the sports movement prepared itself to launch the first large-scale direct action protests in sport in South Africa. This would be launched from a strong platform provided a large range of supportive community and political organisations. In Cape Town, André and his NSC colleagues, working in a not altogether stress-free relationship with SACOS comrades, were heavily involved in anti-tour work. That December he was amongst the fifty-three local activists detained briefly for disrupting a match in progress at the Avendale fields in Athlone, where England international Bob Woolmer was coach. All over the country similar mobilisations started taking place.

The Harare Declaration and the sports protests were the final chess moves in a strategy developed over five years by Tambo to isolate the regime and force it to release Mandela and enter into substantive negotiations. The liberation movement was in the process of effectively checkmating the regime politically. It had the solid support of the international community and the governing National Party was now tied into a pre-decided framework of talks about talks.

This was to be a South African summer of momentous, happening at the same time as the festivals of protest in Europe which heralded the collapse of the Berlin Wall and the Soviet system controlling Central and Eastern Europe.

The oppressed were saying, 'no more'.

Sport and history had converged yet again in South Africa.

A secret assignment

André, due to represent the National Sports Congress as one of its Western Cape delegates at the Conference for a Democratic Future, was excited about the opportunity, especially as it had been billed by supporters as a modern-day version of the Congress of the People where the Freedom Charter had been adopted in 1955.

But then the phone rang. It was SANROC's Sam Ramsamy on the line from London. He had a request, or rather an instruction. 'I want you to look after someone coming to Cape Town soon.' André tried to explain that he was on his way to Johannesburg, but Ramsamy said, 'This is important.' In those days of tapped telephones and working with information on a need-to-know basis, it was enough to let André understand that – whence it was coming from – this was a serious request which he could not ignore. He withdrew grudgingly from the delegation to Johannesburg, wondering what on earth Ramsamy's call was all about.

Come 9 December and it turned out the person he had to look after was Peter Hain. It was Peter's first day back in South Africa in twenty-three years – their first ever meeting, in extraordinary circumstances.

Peter had for some time been planning to be part of the anti-Gatting tour subterfuges. Worried that the rebel Gatting cricket tour could trigger the start of major breaches of the boycott and attracted by the opportunity to expose in a television documentary the still deeply entrenched racism in the sports system, he agreed to go to South Africa undercover for nine days to film for ITV. It was an extremely risky trip for him to make at that stage, but he decided to take the chance.

Having been banned from returning to South Africa in October 1969, vilified by white media and politicians, then in June 1972 targeted courtesy of the security services by letter bomb, for Peter to contemplate secretly visiting the country to make a television documentary on the eve of the Gatting 'rebel' cricket tour might seem foolhardy. As seasoned journalist David Beresford pointed out, he was 'detested' by white South Africans for his role in initiating the damaging sports boycotts. His parents pointed to new evidence that officially sponsored death squads were responsible for the murder of over fifty anti-apartheid activists. His wife was equally opposed to the notion. But Linda McDougall, a renowned TV producer, persuaded him that the hazardous mission could be accomplished for Granada Television's *World in Action*, well versed in shooting films covertly whether in Eastern Europe or within South Africa, as Linda had done several times. She came up with an ingenious solution to Peter's conundrum. He was to change his name by deed poll and *World in Action* would negotiate a new passport.

With his parents and wife sworn to secrecy, Peter briefed his sons Sam, aged thirteen, and Jake, aged eleven, the night before he left with a warning that he might be captured if they breathed a word (they didn't). Booked for the first time in his life in business class, wearing a suit and clutching a copy of the *Financial Times*, Peter Western Hain boarded a British Airways flight from Heathrow to Cape Town on 8 December 1989 with a new name. The overnight flight went without hiccup, and he was excited to see out of the window as the plane circled down Table Mountain with its legendary 'table-cloth' cloud draped over. Anxiously blinking into the Cape brightness and feeling hot in his suit, he walked across the tarmac and tried to appear relaxed as his passport was examined. The white official looked up disinterestedly and muttered, 'Purpose of visit?' 'Business,' Peter replied, and he was waved through into the unknown.

After a tense delay waiting for a missing suitcase, he found McDougall outside, by now also frantic with worry. Thus began his flying visit, travelling with a film crew illicitly around the country, feeling he was always on borrowed time. Interviewees had been told only that there was a visiting British TV presenter, certainly not that it was Peter.

First off was meeting André for the first time in Mitchell's Plain, the large group area for coloured people on the Cape Flats. He was getting ready to bat for United, the non-racial cricket team he had chosen to join on moving from Pretoria to Cape Town. Their meeting was to be the beginning of a long friendship.

For André, it was an electric moment and made even more so by the whiff of danger that surrounded Peter's arrival. Astonished by the identity of this mystery visitor, he introduced him as a friend from England to team-mates at the windy Rocklands ground close by the sea and he passed the first test – they did not recognise the now respectable-looking, short-haired figure behind the dark glasses.

Expecting that both he and Peter might be arrested, André had drawn up list of people for his then partner, Liz Offen, to phone in case that happened. On top were Percy Sonn and Alex Abercrombie, part of the engaged circle of 'struggle lawyers' in Cape Town, who were both involved with the NSC. Among the journalists were the brilliant cricket and features writer of the *Guardian* in London, Matthew Engel, with whom André had corresponded and developed great respect for. But all went smoothly. André remembers: We spent Peter's first night back in South Africa after twenty-three years at my home in Woodstock under the mountain chatting away until the early hours of the morning. It was a magic moment on a perfect Cape summer's evening. It seemed right that we spent most of it around a braai fire that seemed mesmerizingly bright that night. An enormous day for both of us, fuelled by close feelings of solidarity, and the champagne provided by *World in Action*. It was the beginning of a special relationship with Peter, his parents and family – and, ultimately, also the genesis of this book.

Peter experienced a whirlwind of mixed emotions on his first visit back to South Africa. Eerie and dangerous – the most frightening part was when he spotted their car was being tailed by the Port Elizabeth security police in New Brighton township, a flashback to his childhood a quarter of a century before when surveillance by Pretoria's security police was the norm. The crew hastily dumped all the camera equipment in a dry-cleaners considered secure by local resistance leader Mkhuseli Jack.

In Oudtshoorn, a backwater in the Karoo desert, security police patrolled busily in cars outside as Peter interviewed Reggie Oliphant, who had lost his job as a teacher in 1981 because of his campaigns for non-racial sport. A fierce opponent of the Gatting rebel tour, he greeted with incredulity the very notion of mixed sport in a town like Oudtshoorn where sports facilities for blacks and coloureds were almost non-existent by comparison with lavish provision for whites. Oudtshoorn's black pupils, deprived not just of sport but of school places, were prevented by the government from filling an empty white high school, a training college and a technical college – all unused because of over-provision for whites and which together could have offered nearly a thousand places to needy black children.

Carefully staged coaching sessions for black youngsters in a handful of well-known townships like Soweto could not conceal the reality that sports apartheid was alive and well in Oudtshoorn, with its 80,000 strong population rigidly segregated.

As Oliphant explained all this to Peter, a security policeman who was bugging the office phoned up, issuing threats over the 'shit' being told to 'these foreign journalists'. (Since Peter's name was expressly not mentioned they were unaware of his presence inside.) Only four months previously, Peter was assured, the police would have burst in and rounded everyone up, having previously shot at and wounded one of Reggie's activist comrades. Yet here was Reggie telling Peter the facts of sports apartheid, refusing to be intimidated by threats to his family and on his own life. The certainties of the iron fist regime were crumbling.

Across the country, it was officially estimated at the time that well over 90 per cent of sport was still segregated. In Gugulethu, one of the squalid townships on the Cape Flats to the south-east of the city, teachers spoke to Peter about the absence of sports facilities in their government-controlled schools. As they talked on the township's only football field, covered by an uneven stretch of fine grey gravel littered with glass, they could not give their names for fear of dismissal. And this was the reality the Gatting cricket mercenaries were blessing with their tour.

In Port Elizabeth, Ronnie Pillay and Khaya Majola, top black cricketers with the non-racial South African Cricket Board, told Peter despairingly how cricket was dying among their people because of abysmal facilities. Official statistics showed that for every thousand rand the government spent on sport, just one rand went to the black population. Of every hundred cricket fields only fifteen were available for black people to play on – and most of these of very poor quality.

Although some mixed sport existed in 1989–90, it was overwhelmingly in the larger cities, Johannesburg and Cape Town. In small towns in the middle of the country, such as Oudtshoorn, there was virtually no mixing at all on the sports field. A survey of sports facilities in the Natal town of Pietermaritzburg found that whereas 11,567 white school pupils shared thirty-two cricket fields and sixty-five cricket nets, 13,608 coloured and Indian pupils shared just one field and five nets, and there were no sports facilities in black schools. In the black townships of Umlazi and Lamontville outside Durban, 330,000 Africans shared six football fields and two swimming pools. In Durban itself, 212,000 whites had 146 football fields and fifteen public swimming pools. For the country as a whole, despite being under one-tenth of the total population, whites possessed 73 per cent of all athletic tracks, 93 per cent of all golf courses, 83 per cent of all hockey fields, 85 per cent of all cricket fields, 93 per cent of all squash courts, 80 per cent of all badminton courts, 98 per cent of all bowling greens, 84 per cent of all swimming pools and 83 per cent of rugby fields.

More than this, the deliberate squashing of non-racial sports bodies outside the white-dominated racial structures continued. Non-racial sports officials still had restriction orders imposed on them. When Peter interviewed him, the president of the Western Cape National Sports Congress, Ngconde Balfour – subsequently minister of sport in the new ANC government – had only recently emerged from nine months' detention, mostly spent in solitary confinement.

Meanwhile white companies refused to offer sponsorship except to government-approved bodies like Ali Bacher's South African Cricket Union, which had invited the Gatting rebel tourists. The idea that cricket could be separated from politics remained risible, especially since the government was bankrolling the rebel tour by granting 90 per cent tax rebates to companies providing the several millions of pounds needed in sponsorship. Significantly, however, the sponsors, once keen to proclaim their support, were now keeping very quiet for fear of a black consumer boycott and trade union reprisals – another indication of the changing balance of power.

For Peter it was both exciting and extraordinary to see the ANC's distinctive green, gold and black colours worn so openly and with pride. ANC graffiti decorated black townships to an extent unimaginable when he was last in the country in 1966.

In an audacious move, Peter even interviewed white rugby supremo Danie Craven at his beautiful wood-panelled rugby headquarters in Stellenbosch. He reacted in amazement as Peter walked in on camera. 'Aren't you scared?' he asked. Peter's team had counted on Craven having an old-fashioned sense of honour in upholding a promise he had made to Linda McDougall beforehand not to mention the interview until they had returned safely to London. To his credit he stuck to this, and the meeting made a dramatic moment in the film. Other interviewees, like Oliphant, forewarned only that a 'British journalist' wanted to talk to them, stared at Peter as if seeing a ghost – and the burly Khaya Majola even burst into tears.

Thankfully for Peter, the trip proved highly successful and he returned to his family safely undetected. However, after taking off from Johannesburg airport, then notorious for its steely security, the stress of the venture got to Peter because, unusually, and despite a very smooth flight, he was sick on the plane. Despite a few curious questions on his return about having a tan in the middle of a British winter, the whole venture was kept secret over Christmas until two weeks later when the film – entitled *Return of the Rebel* – had been edited and was ready for transmission.

News was simultaneously broken in the British and South African morning papers in early January 1990, with Cape Town residents startled on the drive into work to see banner headlines on posters alongside the road stating 'HAIN WAS HERE'. Later there were angry questions in the South African Parliament about how Peter had got in.

As an exercise in lifting the protest profile around the Gatting rebel tour, it could hardly have been more successful. There was widespread media attention in Britain and the film got good ratings. More important, Peter's predictions that the tour would be disrupted by angry demonstrators helped create a frenzy of interest within South Africa as there were stories in all the papers, making the link between the STST protests and the opposition likely to be faced by the rebel cricketers. Peter ensured videos of his film were smuggled into the country and they were widely distributed by NSC activists.

Peter remained convinced that the sports boycott was as necessary as it had ever been. He gained the impression during his visit that white authority seemed rather punch drunk, unsure about the new ground rules. Thus, the press were banned from carrying Nelson Mandela's picture, but the ANC's colours were worn or displayed openly. Some protests were being permitted, provided they received prior police permission and conformed to tight restrictions. Others were still repressed. At the same time morale among white police had collapsed due to government legitimisation of protest and defiance. The exposure of officially sponsored 'death squads' also destabilised the security forces.

The striking thing for Peter about going back at this moment was the extent to which the government was being forced to change, not out of desire, but of necessity. The pressure from an increasingly defiant black majority was growing, their trade unions powerful and their consumer power threatening white business. And the limited sanctions over loans and investment had an impact: the economy was in bad shape and whites complained constantly about depressed living standards and economic expectations.

Time did seem to be running out for whites-only rule, Peter wrote on his return. There seemed a realisation that they no longer had sufficient bullets. But he also sensed that whites were losing their political will to govern in the old way, ruthlessly maintaining their privileges by force and where appropriate outright terror. Following President Mikhail Gorbachev's reforms and the collapse of the Soviet bloc, there was a sniff of the same demise in South Africa of an old order which in 1989 in East Berlin allowed people to pour buoyantly into security police buildings which they had passed by in fear only days before. The armed might of South Africa's police state was still intact, and the white political power was still immense. But, Peter assessed, there comes a psychological moment when that doesn't count any more, just as in Romania, at the same time as his visit, the old Stalinist dictator Nicolae Ceausescu was extraordinarily swept from power.

'Goduka (go home) Gatting!':
Direct action in sport comes to South Africa

Twenty years after Peter and his colleagues tried to invade the opening match of the 1969–70 Springbok rugby tour at Twickenham, the first such concerted direct-action mass protests in sport also finally happened in South Africa.

By early January 1990 the anti-Gatting tour committees in every area where matches were scheduled were going about their preparations with unprecedented militancy in sport. Following the resolutions of the Conference for a Democratic Future the previous month, in every region the Mass Democratic Movement and affiliated community structures at the heart of the growing 1980s resistance, and often covertly linked to the ANC, were working closely with the NSC. More than one hundred organisations became involved: for example, in Bloemfontein, the UDF, COSATU, Bloemfontein Women's Congress, the Mangaung and various other youth and student congresses, the civic association, the local Advice Office and teachers union, as well as various taxi associations, Tomay Printers and the owners of the local Nova Pax Hall to help with transport, publicity materials and a meeting place.[339] Krish Naidoo and Johannesburg-based NSC officials such as Bill Jardine and Moss Mashishi, who became an active anti-tour media spokesperson, were at the heart of the national coordination.

On 7 January 1990 the South African Sunday newspapers almost without exception ran pages full of the clandestine Hain visit and film. 'SA whites still don't play ball', was the message in the *Sunday Tribune*, counterposing pieces by Peter and Ali Bacher. If the rebel tour had not been the main news until then, it was now.

André was one of the speakers at a big anti-tour rally on 16 January 1990 that filled to overflowing the Cape Town City Hall. He shared the stage with Rev. Makhenkesi Arnold Stofile, Terror Lekota, local UDF leader Trevor Manuel and SACB president Krish Mackerdhuj. Besides successfully lobbying in New Zealand for the cancellation of the 1985 All Blacks tour to South Africa, Stofile had after that been detained and jailed for three years for 'harbouring terrorists'. Lekota had spent ten years on Robben Island and emerged as one of the charismatic UDF national leaders during the late 1980s upsurge of resistance.

For four hours the city hall was alive with toyi-toying (African struggle dancing), as the leaders André was with said the tour had to be stopped.

He was wearing an 'ANC Lives' T-shirt, meant to show that the still-illegal organisation had unbanned itself. He conveyed the message: 'Ali Bacher always says he is against apartheid, but he always ends up on the side of the system.' And the timbers shook with applause, when he put in three languages the unequivocal message of the anti-tour protestors to the tourists. 'Go Home Gatting!' Then, in Afrikaans, the guttural, *Gaan huis toe, Gatting!* Followed by the short, sharp, *Goduka Gatting!* in isiXhosa.[340]

Newlands was originally due to host the first so-called 'test', but as it turned out SACU decided to change the tour fixtures in order to avoid hotspots where demonstrations were expected, particularly the eastern Cape and western Cape. The direct-action protests in Cape Town extended to the damaging of practice nets in Stellenbosch and the pitch at Newlands, an unlit firebomb being thrown through the window of one establishment administrator's home, oil being dumped into the pool of another, and the ANC-armed wing, *Umkhonto we Sizwe*, planting bombs at the Avendale clubhouse (where the fifty-three anti-tour protesters had been detained the month before), and later also at an entrance gate at the Newlands cricket ground. These explosions could have emanated from a meeting where André, Percy Sonn and a few others were present.

The regional NSC chairperson, Ben Tengimfene or 'Ta Ben' as he was fondly called, was a respected school principal, who had served time on Robben Island. All four of his children had gone into exile and he had not heard from them for years. He had decided to travel to Lusaka to see if MK leader Chris Hani could give him clarity about their whereabouts and wellbeing. 'Tell him we need some fireworks at Newlands', someone remarked to sounds of approval and nervous laughter. A few days before the tourists arrived, the *Cape Times* carried a headline, 'Hani: ANC bombed Avendale club house'. As spokesman for Umkhonto we Sizwe at a press conference in Lusaka, Hani said the action was 'in defiance of the rebel tour'. He said the building had been extensively damaged, but 'no lives were lost' in the blast. The *Cape Times* reported that it blew out several windows and damaged the entrance and ceiling of the clubhouse.[341]

Subsequently a bomb went off during the middle of the night at a ticket box at Newlands. Nearly thirty years later a new book, *Voices from the Underground* (2019), revealed that the latter explosion had been the work of a unit of the Ashley Kriel detachment of MK, named after a young local guerrilla who had been shot in the back by the security police a few months earlier while handcuffed and under arrest. On the same night, the unit planted similar devices at the magistrates' court in Paarl and the Parow Civic Centre where the semi-fascist Afrikaner Weerstandsbeweging (AWB) of Eugene Terre'Blanche was due to meet.[342]

Similar intense preparations and activity was happening in the other main centres in South Africa. *Die Burger* newspaper had responded to reports of Peter's visit by describing him in 'total onslaught' terms 'as a 'reactionary leftist' and 'arch boycotter', who together with his 'spiritual kin' were out spoil the government's well-intentioned reform plans with 'classic revolutionary' actions. Peter could not be given all the blame though, the newspaper added, because there were certain internal radical groups already mobilising, as certain recent disruptive actions aimed at cricket in the Cape had shown.

André wrote a 'No!' opinion piece against the tour in a newly launched progressive Afrikaans newspaper, *Vrye Weekblad*, his position counterposed to that of star batsman, Jimmy Cook, whose view was, 'Yes, definitely!' André gave an account of Peter's secret mission and the impressions their brief time together had left him with. Far from being the sewer rat of white folk lore, André said he was well informed, 'unpretentious and charismatic and possessed of an inner warmth'.

After a very long absence, André noted, Peter found the cities more racially mixed than he expected and the 'big shiny cars' of the black middle classes were a surprise to him, but 'all in all it was the same South Africa that he had years before learned to know', and he was shocked by visits to the Brown's Farm informal settlement camp with dedicated activist Val Rose-Christie of the Black Sash, a women-led social movement offering support to the most vulnerable people under apartheid. The visit made everything very 'real' for him again. André said white South Africans should take note of the NSC because it would soon be playing a central role in South African sport. Besides incorporating black South Africans in the townships in ways SACOS had not managed to do, it was intent on creating a broad front which could act as a basis for a united post-apartheid sporting dispensation.[343]

The response of white cricketers varied from hard-nosed support for the tour, to a naive 'we just want to play cricket' and the usual wishy-washy sophistry about 'fair play'. In a 'Crosstalk' piece with André in the *South* newspaper (also reported on in the *London Evening Standard*), similar to the debate with Jimmy Cook above, former England cricketer and rebel tours apologist Bob Woolmer said he experienced segregated post offices when he first came to South Africa, but 'much of that has changed now and therefore I cannot understand now why the group of demonstrators [at Avendale] took the action which they did. They appeared to have such hardened attitudes.'[344]

In his autobiography, *White Lightning* (1999), South African fast bowler Allan Donald said, 'To a naive kid like me, who just wanted to bowl as fast as possible, political considerations were irrelevant.' The young Gerhardus Liebenberg mirrored this feeling, 'I just want to play cricket. I love sport. As you can see on the wall [covered with awards he had received] I'm a sportsman, so that is all I live for.'[345] The batting genius, Peter Kirsten, André's old flat-mate at Stellenbosch, who he had challenged not to play against the tourists, said, 'I'll admit I'm confused on the issue. If this was a normal country one would just get on with it and play. But Dr Ali Bacher and the guys have had meetings with the NSC and still decided to go ahead. If I pull out I will be ostracised completely. But what do you do? They [the NSC] want to use me to gain credibility while I have nothing to gain from it. It's a bit difficult to divorce yourself from what you've been doing since a kid.'[346]

White public opinion was in line with *Die Burger*'s hard-line stance, and these attitudes were sometimes articulated in unusual ways. Like letter-writer C. Bentley's admonition: 'To Krish Naidoo and his followers . . . if you turn your attention to God and channel your energies there, you would achieve much more than protesting against an innocent game of cricket.'[347]

The disgust of those opposing the tour was well known by now. SANROC's Sam Ramsamy, long a thorn in the side of apartheid sport, warned that the rebel tour would be an act 'of racism, immoral and intended to serve the predominantly white constituency at a very high financial and political premium to the country'. The Pan-Africanist Movement said, 'We wish to remind [them] that we regard their actions as grossly insensitive to a war-torn situation.' This tour 'brings to the fore that we are living in two different worlds in this country', added Trevor Manuel of the MDM. Hard-hitting Frank van der Horst of SACOS had long ago described those taking part in such tours as having 'sold their souls to the violent devil of apartheid'. Along the same lines Ebrahim Patel, president of the South African Rugby Union, although referring to a recent rebel rugby tour, summed up the general feeling of the non-racial sports movement when he said, 'It is sickening to note that the arrangements for the tour were concluded by means of intrigue, secrecy and deception and with callous disregard for the feelings and political realities of the oppressed people of South Africa.'[348]

Johannesburg-based Abdul Bhamjee of the National Soccer League simply offered the thought that 'If Pele, Garfield Sobers and Muhammad Ali had been South Africans where would they be now?' And John Murphy, later to become a judge also soberly noted, 'As a lawyer it troubles me to learn that the sum of money to be spent on the rebel tour approximates the total annual budget of the Legal Aid Board. Eighty-five percent of people charged in our criminal courts are without the benefits of legal representation. One can only despair at the provocative arrogance of Ali Bacher and his cronies.'

The battle lines were drawn. SACU remained gung-ho and its president, Geoff Dakin, not known for his genteel behaviour, spoke in Churchillian terms about how the cricket body was ready to take on the demonstrators. He said, 'sophisticated plans were in place to neutralise the protests'. He rejected suggestions that the SACU's team take a commercial name to lower temperatures, saying there was no chance that they would be called anything else but the Springboks. He said those who wanted to watch the cricket could rest assured that precautions would be in place. When pressed for what these were, he declared, 'When the Allies planned for the longest day in the attack of Europe they did not phone the Germans to give their tactics away.' Cartoonists had a ball. Dakin, cigar in mouth, was depicted standing in the middle of field surrounded by barbed wire, marching soldiers, gun emplacements and a dozen air-filled Zeppelins overhead saying, 'We will fight them on the pitches. We will never surrender.'[349]

In early January 1990 Gatting himself said that 'Peter Hain is entitled to his views but we have to be guided by Ali Bacher . . . We are going out to play cricket and we accept that as a result we will all be banned from international cricket.' He was harassed by protestors at the team hotel and the departure of the rebels on 18 January was delayed for several hours at London airport after an anti-apartheid activist had telephoned a hoax bomb warning.

At Johannesburg airport, dogs, tear gas and batons were used to attack peaceful demonstrators led by Winnie Mandela awaiting their arrival and exposed to the world's media the brutality still at the heart of apartheid. Mrs Mandela was present at the special request of Ramsamy; she didn't hesitate after he phoned her from London saying, 'Comrade Sam, I will be there.'[350] The police action also showed how worried the authorities were about the growing movement which threatened to disrupt the rebel tour.

The white communities inside South Africa and opinion leaders in Britain had seriously underestimated the level of organisation and the strength of feeling and bitterness the tour had provoked among the majority of South Africans. Not only was there understandable resistance to a move which sought to smuggle white South Africa back into international competition, there was also a burning resentment that the rebel tourists were getting millions of pounds in fees which could have gone towards upgrading the abysmal level of black sports facilities.

They had a victory almost right away. The newspaper and television headlines announced 'blood flows as tour starts' and the first three matches were rescheduled away from urban strongholds of political militancy to more isolated centres. Carefully staged photo-calls for Gatting's team to coach black youngsters in a handful of well-known townships like Soweto had to be abandoned. The furore following the ugly scenes at Johannesburg airport simply compounded the grotesque miscalculation made in staging the tour in the first place.[351]

The first match, scheduled for 25 January 1990, was moved without publicity to Kimberley. When this became known, the MDM, NSC and SACOS jumped into action. Newspaper headlines reported, 'Forces gather for siege of Kimberley', bringing to mind the famous wartime siege of the town eight decades before during the South African War.[352] Despite having just forty-eight hours to prepare, the anti-tour forces were soon in action. Bill Jardine delivered a memorandum of protest to Gatting at the team hotel, community activists mobilised local people and despite the police turning around buses from out of town at roadblocks, some 4,000 people marched to the gates of the stadium when the sanctions busters finally took to the field. The preceding mass rally in the Civic Centre in Square Hill Park was so full that 'they literally had to carry the main speaker, Terror Lekota (fresh from the Cape Town rally a few days before) to the stage. Everything was full, the aisles, windowsills and the stage', recalled Eugene Jacobs, later a fellow provincial CEO colleague of André's. 'He conveyed the message that we would be targeting the airport, the hotels and the field. We were deployed to the stadium.' The situation was balanced on a knife-edge. The organisers were marching without having asked for permission and Naidoo and Bacher were involved in a face-to-face stand-off, which the latter tried to defuse by phoning the minister of law and order to ask for the march, already in progress, to be permitted.[353]

The five-kilometre walk to the stadium started symbolically at the Kemo Hotel, whose long-time owner, the deceased president of the non-racial rugby South African Rugby Union (SARU), Abdullah Abass, had always made available for sport and community meetings. 'We often had meetings there and never paid hire because of his commitment to non-racialism,' Jacobs explained. A pleasing feature was seeing both SACOS and NSC posters side by side in the crowd. The marchers eventually got to the stadium: 'We ended up at a side gate. We weren't allowed to get the main gate because they thought we were going to invade the field and stop the game . . . What I can remember there was a very big police presence at the gate. The more the guys tugged at the gate, the more cops would cock their guns.'[354]

When the marchers dispersed later in the day and ran through the streets for the four kilometres back to the township, a policeman's house was burned down. Eugene went to the assistance of the white motorist whose car was stoned. Her face is a picture of concern in the newspaper photo. He recalls, 'I went to her and said I am sorry that she was caught up in this, and she was trying to get out the car and I said, don't worry, you aren't being threatened. This was to show that our struggle was non-racial, not against whites.'

That day of direct action was later described as meaning for sport what the Soweto uprising of 16 June 1976 did for politics. It was a defining moment. No longer would sportspeople permit apartheid sport to go on as normal. When Gatting and the team walked into the Tom Cat restaurant in the town on 26 January, the black staff walked out and the ill-fated captain, pictured in an apron, helped the restaurant owner prepare the meal. Similar fiery acts of opposition followed for matches two and three in Bloemfontein and Pietermaritzburg.

On the day of the Bloemfontein match, the *Cape Argus* front-page headline shouted, 'Mayhem as police break-up anti-tour meeting'; pictured were people who had fled the Pax Nova Hall in Mangaung township returning to look for their shoes, 'left behind in panic when police fired teargas into the hall'.[355] On being shown the scar where one of the protestors had been shot with pepper bullets during the 2,000-strong anti-tour rally, Gatting said: 'He was not hurt here – pointing at the group of protesters outside Springbok Park – what happens in the township is not related to the cricket.' But Richard Streeton, writing in the London *Times* said, that cricket was now irrelevant after ten days of 'an ill-timed and hapless tour'.[356]

In Pietermaritzburg, up to 10,000 marchers gathered in the Market Square for the three-kilometre walk to the razor-wire-surrounded stadium where the rebels were playing. Trade unionist Pat Bhengu chaired the local anti-tour committee, with Cassius Lubisi (later an important official in the president's office as chancellor of the national orders), Yusuf Bhamjee (carrying the memo for Mike Gatting in a plastic bag) and Mike Hickson from Aurora CC prominent as the procession moved forward. The pro-testors walked behind a slow-moving car in which the march leader and ailing struggle veteran, Archie Gumede, took his position. After four hours in the blazing sun, Bacher, Gatting and John Emburey emerged to accept the memorandum, asked to speak and were denied the opportunity by the protestors. It was not their platform.

From place to place came stories of energetic planning, organisation and action. The odour the rebels were emitting was forcing traditional SACU allies to distance themselves. The mayor of Cape Town, Gordon Oliver, who had walked in front during one of the Defiance Campaign marches, indicated the city would not give the rebels a civic reception. All such events were then cancelled on the flimsy pretence that the tourists would be 'too busy'. MDM allied trade unions responded positively to requests from the protest coordinators to make life uncomfortable for the team at the hotels they stayed in. Southern Suns, a traditional SACU supplier, agreed not to take action against staff who chose not to serve the tourists. At some places noisy placard demonstrations took place. In Bloemfontein, a picture of a young white boy unloading baggage for the team appeared in the news-papers. As security scares increased, the peace around the team disappeared.

Scarcely a week into the tour, Connie Molusi reported in *City Press* that 'The protest action . . . has been the largest in the history of sport in this country.'[357] 'Government worried protests could derail reform', the news-paper headlines declared on 29 January 1990. Unnamed 'ministers' were quoted as saying, if the protests continued and 'sparked action reminiscent of 1985', then government's 'plans to ease the state of emergency might have to be postponed'. And, 'Some even believed the proposed release of Mr Nelson Mandela and the unbanning of the ANC might have to be postponed.' The general consensus in government circles was that 'the rebel tour has not come at a time that is helpful to national reconciliation in South Africa.'[358]

Four days later, on 2 February 1990, President de Klerk opened the first session of the new Parliament and did indeed announce the arrival of a 'new South Africa', stunning the country by unbanning of the ANC and other outlawed organisations, and giving momentous notice of the impending release of Nelson Mandela and other political prisoners. He declared his readiness to enter into negotiations with them to work out a new consti-tution.

327

The apartheid regime had finally realised that it was impossible to preserve apartheid without the total collapse of the country. Under pressure from the liberation movements, it agreed to unban the liberation forces and enter into negotiations, these seismic political developments making continuation of the tour untenable. After three warm-up games and a mismatched first test which was easily won by the SACU national team, still calling themselves Springboks, a decision was taken to end the tour early. The second test was cancelled and the tour was cut from eight to four matches. It was the end of the rebel tours. SACU realised it was moving into a dead end. It acknowledged that 'In the present political climate, tours are counterproductive to the medium to long term aims of the SACU and to the wider interest of South Africa as a whole.' Bacher and his tour organisers were humiliated and the cricket rebels went home prematurely, their disappointment tempered by payoffs averaging over £100,000 each.

Sport and its close connections to the release of Mandela and the unbanning of organisations, February 1990

The people poured onto the streets. The news was spreading. 'Mandela is going to be released today.'

André was due to play a cricket match that Sunday, 11 February 1990. It was at Green Point Common – described as 'the flat ground by the sea at the Lion's tail' in the first reports on cricket in South Africa after the arrival of the British 184 years earlier. But both teams agreed this was a day like no other. They would abscond and abandon the match when it was confirmed that the legend was on his way to Cape Town's gathering place on the Grand Parade in front of the city hall from his final place of imprisonment, Victor Verster, an hour away in the Cape Winelands.

In thirty years of playing, for André this was definitely a first. He made his way to the venue still in his cricket kit. As it happened, they could have played on for a while, because the crowd that looked and felt a hundred thousand strong were kept waiting for five, six hours in the hot sun . . . and still no Mandela. In his entourage there were fears for his security.

He was being driven by 'Comrade Rose' – the UDF leader Mzunani Roseberry Sonto – in a second-hand Toyota lent to the comrades by the Western Cape Traders Association without whom the UDF would not have been able to afford all the creative T-shirts and posters that they produced over the years. As the motorcade neared Cape Town's Parade and the extent of the crowd dawned on them, his minders, including COSATU's Cyril Ramaphosa (from 2018 president of South Africa), spoke to event coordinator Willie Hofmeyr, not long out of hunger strike of several weeks during the defiance campaign, and they decided to retreat to nearby Rondebosch. Willie was André's housemate that year and André's university colleague, Saleem Mowzer, was driving Rivonia trialist Wilton Mkwayi in the car behind Mandela's. At the tête-à-tête that followed, someone asked Saleem, 'Don't you live near here?' And thus the procession made its way to his father's house undetected. His sister, Nizaad, responded to the knock on the door to see with surprise it was Madiba. And that is how it happened that the world's most famous person on that day had his first cup of tea as a free man at 44 Hayward Road in modest Rondebosch East.

Now what to do? In those days before mobile phones, the comrades got onto the landline. One of the options was to call off Mandela's appearance altogether. Madiba borrowed spectacles to do some reading, probably his speech. In the rush he had apparently left his behind somewhere.

Meanwhile, back at the Parade the people remained happy, good-natured. Friends in their struggle T-shirts greeted each other and waited with delicious expectation for history to happen. Squashed together, balancing precariously on statues, scaffolding, dustbins, lampposts, finding whatever vantage points could be gained, even on the roof of American senator Jesse Jackson's abandoned limousine, they waited. Only as dusk approached did they become restless. Allan Boesak the orator trying to keep the party spirit alive said, don't worry comrades, he is coming. But they were tired, wanting only Madiba now.

Mandela's entourage asked, was it safe for him to come to the Grand Parade? The whole world is here, was the answer they got from Hofmeyr and the likes of Archbishop Tutu and Dullah Omar.

Suddenly – there he was on the balcony. Fists raised in excitement with the ANC's emblematic chant: *Amaaandla!* Total bedlam. The trusted Walter Sisulu at his side. For André and everyone else, an awareness that they were present when something great was happening.

Then the words that the world had been waiting for: 'I greet you not as a prophet but as a humble servant of you, the people.' This time borrowing Winnie's specs to read his speech. 'Your tireless and heroic sacrifices have made it possible for me to be here today.' And recommitting himself to serve the people after twenty-seven years of incarceration, even if it meant dying for the cause of freedom, he said, 'I therefore place the remaining years of my life in your hands.' As he came to the end, he repeated the words he'd uttered facing a possible death sentence at the Rivonia trial decades before:

> During my lifetime I have dedicated myself to this struggle of the African people. I have fought against white domination, and I have fought against black domination. I have cherished the ideal of a democratic and free society in which all persons live together in harmony and with equal opportunities. It is an ideal which I hope to live for and achieve. But if needs be, it is an ideal for which I am prepared to die.

South Africa would never be the same again.

In London, Peter had watched on television with his family, hugging each other, tears in their eyes, his parents weeping with joy as the world's most famous political prisoner, kept out of sight for over a quarter of a century, stepped to freedom through the gates in the fence around Victor Verster Prison. It was one of those defining moments in history, which hundreds of millions watching across the world would always remember. With his wife Winnie by his side, Mandela walked towards the massed ranks of TV cameras and spectators. Except for his obvious humility, he looked regal, a giant among his people. The government had several months before carefully pre-released the first photograph of him in a generation, revealing not the burly bearded freedom fighter in the prime of his life, for decades his image the world over, but a slim, dignified elderly statesman with a smile of destiny hovering somewhere between the benign and the all-knowing.

*

The South African summer of '89 irrevocably changed the country and sport was in the centre of the interrelated entanglements that lead to Nelson Mandela's release, the beginning of negotiations and eventually the unexpected arrival of democracy in 1994. Unbeknown to the thousands waiting on Cape Town's Grand Parade that historic day, 'talks about talks' between the ANC and the government and its proxies had been going on for some time behind the scenes, and one of these meetings was in fact happening that very weekend.

Building on the new strategies started in 1985 (discussed in chapter 6) and, at roughly the same time that they raised the related need for new approaches in sport and a new sporting body in the form of the NSC, ANC leaders had begun to engage envoys of the apartheid regime in a purposeful manner for the first time from 1988 onwards. Differing in regularity and intensity, these secret 'talks about talks' became regularised during that year and continued into 1989, though it was only in the second half of 1989 (at the same time as ANC/MDM/NSC decided to actively oppose the Gatting rebel tour) that they became focussed and started delivering practical political outcomes. The platform was created by the close to 200 known 'safari' contacts between the ANC and a whole range of internal and international stakeholders between 1985 and 1989. The first, more concentrated set of discussions involved the jailed Mandela meeting forty-eight times with a state-appointed committee of prison and national security officials in the twenty-one months between May 1988 to his release from prison in February 1990. Mandela's main purpose had been to set up a meeting between the government and the leadership in Lusaka. The second set of interactions – seven in all between November 1987 and February 1990 – took place in England between a small ANC group led by Tambo's emissary, Thabo Mbeki, and some establishment Afrikaner intellectuals, at least one of whom was an agent reporting back to the National Intelligence Service (NIS), whose head Neil Barnard was also part of the state committee talking to Mandela in prison. Less frequent and more tentative and indirect at first than those Mandela was involved in, the main purpose of these latter Consgold talks was to open up channels to the government and to get Mandela released.

Thabo Mbeki had in September 1989 been in direct contact with the NIS about the logistics for Mandela's release. Now, on the weekend that this would happen, he was in England speaking to the Afrikaner academics and some business leaders. The beleaguered Gatting tour was still in progress and, as they started their weekend of discussions in January 1990 over dinner, one of the Afrikaner businessmen asked Mbeki if he couldn't help 'get the protests and unrest surrounding the rebel cricket tour ... under control.' He lived near the Newlands cricket grounds. His children went to school in the area, and 'things were becoming unsafe', he said. Those talking behind the scenes feared that the activity on the streets could complicate the moves to build a closer relationship between the government and the ANC with a view to starting talks between them, and after some discussion it was

331

decided that Mbeki and Aziz Pahad would phone Sam Ramsamy and that the businesspeople would phone a close colleague of Ali Bacher with whom they had work ties.[359]

The calls home to South Africa continued until after midnight that Friday and then went back and forth for the next seventy-two hours before a decision was reached. Krish Naidoo came back home from being tear-gassed at the Wanderers Stadium that Saturday to get the message direct from Mbeki. The upshot was that he, Bill Jardine of the NSC and Bacher met on the Sunday 'after watching Madiba's release from prison on television'. They agreed to 'make their best endeavours to find a way of resolving the impasse'. The NSC leadership, in conjunction with SANROC's Ramsamy in London, agreed to call off the protests in return for a curtailed tour and no such repeats in future. They had difficulty persuading their comrades in the big cricket centres to allow the last few one-day matches to proceed. The NSC in Cape Town flatly refused to agree that the rebels play at Newlands and SACB president Krish Mackerdhuj was of the same mind in Durban. Not even an appeal by Ramsamy could change his mind.[360] The coastal areas, including Port Elizabeth and East London, where non-racial sort was most firmly rooted, remained no-go areas for the rebel tourists.

Such a prospect had been inconceivable seven years before when the first English rebel cricket tour took place when protest organisers could have faced bullets, beatings and detentions from the once omnipotent, but now faltering apartheid state.

The anti-apartheid sports campaign had come full circle. Where direct-action protests had set the seal on tours abroad twenty years before, they had once again showed themselves to be effective in propelling a sports tour into prominence and putting an end to a serious breach of the sports boycott. But this time, momentous political change was also in the air. Sport was showing itself to be an important ingredient in the unfolding societal dramas.

At the same time, while the diplomatic manoeuvres to end the tour were going on behind the scenes and unknown to the Consgold participants – still reflecting on their sumptuous dinners and socialising around log fires at Mells Park in Somerset, deep in the English countryside – an ops team of the Ashley Kriel detachment of Umkhonto we Sizwe, made up of Sidney Hendricks and Melvin Bruintjies, planted the bomb that went off at the turnstiles at Newlands on that Sunday night of Mandela's release. A Gatting 'test' match against South Africa was due to be played five days later, according to the original schedule issued in November, and this was the unit's way of celebrating the stopping of that match. Its commander Shirley Gunn recalled, 'In our underground house in Northpine, we watched Nelson Mandela's release from Victor Verster Prison on TV. What a joyous moment!' Mandela confirmed in his speech that, 'The armed struggle is not abandoned' yet. So, to demonstrate that we were combat-ready and poised to follow through on the orders of our freed commander-in-chief, we pulled off three simultaneous operations that evening.'[361] This is how Newlands, a hall in a nearby suburb where the semi-fascist AWB were due to meet and the Paarl magistrates court were hit that night. This confluence of a microcosm of events on 11 February showed the immensity of the task that lay ahead for South Africa if it was to transform into a free country and united nation as per the strategic planning of the ANC leadership.

Oliver Tambo and his closest confidants had deliberately opened up new terrains of struggle with the aim of pushing back the regime and tying it into substantive negotiations through which the ANC could engineer a universal franchise, the transfer of power and an unlikely settlement of what had long been seen as one of the world's most intractable political conflicts. This meant carefully combining secret overtures and 'talks about talks' with armed struggle, political mass mobilisation, underground activity and the coordination of international anti-apartheid actions to push the regime into a corner. And, during the Gatting tour, at a turning-point, these struggles and strategies intersected directly with those in sport.

Rainbow dreams: Attempting to build national unity as sport and political negotiations processes run alongside each other, 1990–96

When Nelson Mandela walked to freedom on 11 February 1990, he declared his readiness to enter into negotiations and to work out a new constitution which would guarantee all South Africans equal rights. Thus, when Krish Naidoo claims that the protest of 26 January 1990 in Kimberley was 'the first punch which spelt [sic] the knockout blow of the Gatting tour and the beginnings of negotiations for a new South Africa,'[362] it is not far off the mark. Sam Ramsamy has said of that last rebel tour, 'I look back on these dramatic events now, and believe they may well have been the single moment when victory was secured in our long, difficult struggle against apartheid in sport.'[363]

The apartheid regime realised that it was impossible to preserve apartheid without the total collapse of the country. Under pressure from the liberation movements and the international community, including by now its allies like Margaret Thatcher, it agreed to unban the ANC, PAC and other groups, release Mandela and enter into negotiations with them. But the intention of the last apartheid president was still to control the change process and forestall a democratic dispensation that would lead inevitably to majority rule, or what he termed a 'winner take all' outcome. However, as one commentator noted, the genie was out of the bottle. The white minority were no longer in charge of determining the future.

The elusive dream of freedom and democracy was in sight. Now it was time for the long-disenfranchised people of South Africa to finish the last stretch to the winning post in what had been the most painful and uphill of history's marathons.

After February 1990, a parallel process of negotiations began in sport and in the broader political domain. Both processes would be complex and fraught with dangers and contradictions of different kinds, but both would eventually lead to unity – that is, to single non-racial organisations in every sport for the first time, and more importantly a new constitution for a South Africa that could be called one country for the first time after three centuries of subjugation.

The process of sports unity was pursued in a similar way as the late 1980s struggles by the NSC and SANROC working alongside the ANC, with the ever-present Steve Tshwete, freshly returned from exile, playing an increasingly important role. By 1992, all the major sports codes were both united and participating in international sport, with cricket and the Olympic movement in the forefront.

But first the NSC had to formally establish itself. In the three years since the idea of a mass-based sports front using the muscle of the struggle had been discussed in Lusaka in early 1987, the NSC had become a powerful new force, but it was still an interim sports body. It was finally launched officially four months after the Gatting tour, in early June 1990, in Langa near Cape Town. Now called the National Olympic and Sports Congress of South Africa (NOSC), it added the word Olympic to its title, after consultation with its allies abroad, in anticipation of leading post-apartheid South African sport into the international area.

The launch event was opened by John Nkadimeng, a senior member of the ANC. His colleague, Tshwete, on the way to becoming the key sports

334

figure in the country, delivered the main address, and was to the point about the priorities that lay ahead: 'The most urgent duty of sportspersons is to destroy apartheid and simultaneously lay the foundations for a mass-based movement within sport in preparation for a united, democratic and non-racial South Africa.' For this to happen it was necessary for sports organisations 'to identify themselves with progressive movements' in the way that the NSC was doing.

The NOSC with its message of unity in sport now held 'centre-stage' in the sports arena, Tshwete said. 'The changing political climate in this country had forced white sport to follow the road of unity. Therefore, although the first priority would be to consolidate black sport amongst the disenfranchised black population, 'we at the same time must also work to encourage whites ... to accept non-racial principles in sport.'

Tshwete also called on sponsors who had in the past supported the apartheid establishment in sport to become part of the process of building a non-racial future. Once the NOSC had established a broad mass-based sports movement the next step would be to build international relationships, and this would happen to the exclusion of racist sports, he added. Aware of its growing international stature, the more forward-looking establishment bodies were now lining up to speak to the NOSC.

The South African Road Running Association (SARRA) was present and its president, Mick Wynne, was congratulated for his stand against foreign competitors in the recent Comrades Marathon. The new NOSC was also giving special attention to boxing. Delegates warmly applauded Solly Selibi of the National Boxing Crisis Committee, which has been set up to democratise the professional boxing set up in South Africa. While 98 per cent of boxers in the country were black, control was vested in a small coterie of unaccountable officials appointed by the government under the outdated Boxing Act, Selibi said. The NOSC and the Crisis Committee had the support of the influential World Boxing Council (WBC), which had adhered strictly to the international sports boycott. The NOSC also decided that school sports should be one of its priorities.

Tshwete said that the NOSC should no longer allow itself to be distracted by the political debate with SACOS. This body had shown itself to be incapable of moving with the times. Instead the NOSC should forge ahead with its plans to create a broader unity in South African sport. The choice of the venue in Cape Town in the township adjacent to SACOS's biggest strongholds, was deliberate. At the conference two of SACOS's biggest affiliates,

335

the SA Soccer Federation and the SA Cricket Board, announced that they were joining the NOSC. Their presidents, together with Ebrahim Patel, president of the influential SA Rugby Union, which was expected to soon follow suit, were elected on to the new executive. The NOSC's rapid rise, together with the recognition it had received from the ANC and international bodies, was to prove a fatal blow for SACOS, which had been the main standard bearer for non-racial sport for the previous two-decades. It slowly started to disintegrate.

The full executive of the NOSC was Mluleki George (president); Rev. Makhenkesi Stofile, Krish Mackerdhuj and Ebrahim Patel (vice-presidents); Mthobi Tyamzashe (general secretary); Errol Heyns (administrative secretary); Cheryl Roberts (publications secretary); and Errol Vawda, Rama Reddy and Mntwekhaya Nkwinti (additional members). Krish Naidoo, who had guided the NSC into the limelight as secretary, was unavailable for election as he intended to pursue his postgraduate studies abroad. Murphy Morobe of the United Democratic Front officially closed proceedings, underlining the strong support base the new organisation could draw on.

A host of international sports and political organisations began recognising the NSC as the authentic voice of South African sport, including the Supreme Council for Sport in Africa, the United Nations Special Committee Against Apartheid, the World Boxing Council, the International Campaign Against Apartheid Sport (ICAAS), SANROC and the Association of National Olympic Committees of Africa (ANOCA).

Emerging out of the MDM and ANC strategies of mass struggle, the NSC's rise had amounted to a step-by-step march with history as it unfolded. Its growth mirrored the three key phases of the struggle from the mid-1980s to 1990. Firstly, the organisation came into being as part of the ANC and MDM's strategies to deepen mass action and sectoral mobilisation with the aim of building a united front against apartheid. Secondly, the NSC shot to prominence in the MDM-led protests against the rebel Gatting tour, which almost by accident became part of Oliver Tambo's final push to force the regime to the negotiating table on liberation struggle terms via the Harare Declaration and the Conference for a Democratic Future in late 1989. Then, the new Sports Congress and the protests became closely bound up with one of the most decisive moments in the history of modern South Africa – the release of Nelson Mandela from prison.

Now sports unity became the overwhelming priority. With it came rapid admission to international federations and competitions, which was sooner than expected (or desired) by many of the non-racial sports activists, who first wished to see concrete change happening internally, but driven by the ANC in its attempt to build national consensus around a four-year-long advance to democracy in South Africa led by the liberation movement.

SANROC and the NOSC became the vehicles for the new phase of negotiations in sport. When the new NOSC and its affiliates entered talks with the establishment bodies they insisted on the importance of the process whereby non-racial unity could be built – on the terms of the majority in South Africa. The goal was first 'unity' on specific conditions, followed by 'development' and only then would 'participation' in international competition happen, SANROC and the NOSC argued. This process the establishment bodies were required to bind themselves to first was:

- Recognising the NOSC's definition of non-racialism and the MDM's vision of a united, non-racial and democratic South Africa.
- Supporting the international sports moratorium until such time as an acceptable political solution was reached.
- Acknowledging the historical injustices and inequalities in South African sport, and the need to address these through the redistribution of resources etc.
- Participating in a programme to upgrade facilities and skills in the townships and the rural areas in consultation with community-based structures and the non-racial codes.
- Campaigning to deracialise school sports and to create single junior bodies in the various codes that could affiliate to the NOSC.

The Olympic movement and cricket were the first to get their unity processes underway. Sam Ramsamy, working closely with his long-time ally, Jean-Claude Ganga of the Association of National Olympic Committees of Africa, led the Olympic process, and Tshwete acted as facilitator in the case of cricket.

At a meeting of the IOC Apartheid and Olympism Commission in 1990, Ganga and ANOCA were requested by IOC head Juan Antonio Samaranch to report on the best way to deal with the unfolding developments in South Africa. Ganga asked Ramsamy to go to South Africa as a one-person commission and report back.

Arriving in South Africa for the first time in nearly two decades on 11

337

August 1990, Ramsamy had a whirlwind twenty-six meetings in eight days. Not surprisingly, he concluded along the lines of the same process he had helped shape; 'With few exceptions, the political and sporting leadership on both sides subscribed to the NOSC mantra of unity, then development, then participation.' He reported back at the fourth International Conference Against Apartheid Sport in Stockholm soon afterwards and there Samaranch, Ganga and himself decided that unity talks between the five current macro-sports bodies in South Africa – SANOC (South African Olympic Committee), COSAS (Congress of South African Students), SACOS, the NOSC and SANROC – should be convened under the auspices of ANOCA in Harare. This meant SANROC and its long-time allies in the underground and inter-national anti-apartheid movement were in control of the process.

The Harare meeting happened from 3 to 4 November 1990 and it was decided to form the Coordinating Committee for Sport in South Africa (CCSSA). Ramsamy was elected chairperson at the CCSSA's first meeting in Johannesburg in January 1992 and from there on developments unfolded swiftly. At a follow-up meeting between CCSSA and ANOCA in Botswana on 9 March 1991, the Interim National Olympic Committee of South Africa (INOCSA) was set up with Ramsamy as chairperson. The quick establishment of INOCSA was partly a plan to pre-empt moves which Ramsamy and Ganga suspected were being hatched between the establishment administrators and elements within the IOC to take control of the process. At a ceremony in Lausanne Switzerland on 9 July 1991, INOCSA became the National Olympic Committee of South Africa (NOCSA) and was recognised officially by the IOC. Ramsamy, the pint-sized roving diplomat for the anti-apartheid sports movement, acting as both referee and captain, had delivered unity and the control of sport in South Africa to the liberation forces at a key moment in the still hard-fought political contestations happening in the run-up to democracy.[364]

Ramsamy commented: 'Sport began to play an important trail-blazing role within the wider political and social transformation, and it was our responsibility as sports leaders to accelerate our talks and keep moving forward.' In the process, he was 'bolstered by the constant support and encouragement, both in private and in public' of Mandela, Tshwete, Thabo Mbeki and Barbara Masekela, who was now one of a group of powerful women running the newly released Mandela's office. As the ANC's head of culture, she had been involved from the mid-1980s, but stayed behind the scenes.[365]

In cricket, SACU sought to recover from its humiliation during the rebel tour by negotiating with its counterpart SACB led by Krish Mackerdhuj via the offices of the NSC and 'Mr Fixit' Steve Tshwete. The two teams agreed on 4 August 1990 to enter into discussions. The first meeting followed on 8 September in Durban. At a follow up meeting in Port Elizabeth on 16 December SACU and SACB issued a joint declaration stating inter alia their intention to form 'one non-racial democratic controlling body under a single constitution' and to 'contribute through cricket to a just society in South Africa'. The two bodies set up a national steering committee to drive the unification process. It decided 'to administer and share, with immediate effect, the resources within the development field'.

After the next joint meeting in January 1991, SACB announced that Khaya Majola had been appointed to start work with Ali Bacher on a national development project as from 1 February 1991. This was one year to the day after the unbannings of political organisations like the ANC. The national steering committee instructed the provinces to prepare the foundations for unity by May 1991 so that a new organisation could be established by the following month. The result was the launch of the new United Cricket Board of South Africa on 29 June 1991. Twelve days later on 10 July 1991 South Africa became a member of the International Cricket Council with Tshwete and Ramsamy, fresh from the induction of NOCSA to the Olympic movement in Lausanne the day before, present.

A sport which at one stage during apartheid had seven different controlling bodies, now only had one. One hundred and eighty-five years after the first recorded matches in South Africa, all cricketers in the country began playing together under one umbrella for the first time. For SACB unity held out the promise of finance, facilities and equal opportunities for people who had long been denied the most basic chances. For SACU the most significant thing was that it helped remove the restrictions and stigmas of the past and bring opportunities for a new normal which included international competition. What was striking about the new period of cricketing glasnost and perestroika is that the process had been so amicable and bloodless. According to a SACB source, to start with 'you could see the tension in them' but the progress thereafter was smooth. Mediating the unity agreement was a triumph for the ANC – it showed South Africans: here is the organisation that can bring people together and create normality in a divided society. Another victory for the ANC on the political front with sport in the vanguard.

By 1991 no less than twenty codes were talking unity. Even SACOS – which had strongly opposed the new ANC, SANROC and NOSC-led initiatives – quietly joined the unity bandwagon – and a number of its affiliates started participating, realising that unless they did so they would be doomed to irrelevance. In some cases dubious, opportunistically created dummy bodies, such as the South African Hockey Congress (SAHCON) in hockey and the South African Amateur Athletics Congress (SAAACON) in athletics, were set up to ensure the conditions for membership set by ANOCA were met, that is the participation of a non-racial body. This and some other short cuts taken undermined the long-term effectiveness of unity in certain cases. For example, SACOS had a very healthy athletics organisation built around a popular inter-schools athletics programme in the Western Cape and these administrators were sadly left behind.

The UN General Assembly endorsed the unfolding scenario in South Africa in December 1991. It resolved to support 'academic, scientific and cultural links with democratic anti-apartheid organisations' and contacts with non-racial sports bodies.

As Christabel Gurney, a senior figure in the British Anti-Apartheid Movement noted, 'The international solidarity movement was entering new and uncharted waters. South Africa's non-racial sports bodies were looking for international support to make up for generations of deprivation, and were negotiating their way back into world competition'. She added, 'The AAM publicised the UN resolution, but tried to hold the line by pledging that it would still boycott 'institutions which continue to promote apartheid in the sports, cultural and academic fields'[366]. However, the doors were being opened and the successful policing role the international anti-apartheid movement had played since the late 1960s came to an end as South Africa and its sport rapidly moved into a new era.

*

In the unity talks between 1990 and 1992, SANROC, the NOSC and the ANC deliberately linked sports unity and the attendant negotiations to the broader process of talks that started slowly to get off the ground after Mandela's release and the first meeting between ANC and government delegations from 2 to 4 May 1990 at the Groote Schuur estate, home of South Africa's head of state. Though the discussions in sport happened as a sideline to politics, it was clear that similar goals drove both processes and no quick-fix sports agreement could be reached independently of the political process. An NSC publication summed up the broader purpose of the sports unity process and the highly sophisticated strategy and understanding of its leaders:

> Since February a new situation and new tactics have emerged, but the basic strategy and aims remain – to strengthen the forces of democracy, while at the same time undermining the regime and the right wing, so that when the constituent assembly is put in place the masses will use their votes to return the Nelson Mandelas and Trevor Manuels to parliament.
>
> The task of creating the broadest possible front against apartheid remains extremely important with a negotiated settlement (and elections?) on the agenda. Hence Mandela even meets with [tricameral parliament collaborator, Allen] Hendrickse, Bantustan leaders and others, to the obvious discomfort of a membership schooled in the white-hot struggles of the 1980s. He does this not because he believes these people have suddenly become forces for change, but in order to cut their moorings to the National Party and to isolate de Klerk as much as possible from any potential allies.
>
> We in sport are faced with a similar situation. If we use the weapon of sport with its huge popular appeal as strategically, as effectively and as politically as possible, we can play an important part in helping tilt the wider balance of forces in favour of the oppressed. White South Africans are fanatical about their sport and, having tried every trick in the book, they are now seriously looking at the NOSC as the way forward, for opportunistic reasons. We hold the political initiative and if we succeed in bringing about unity on our terms we will have helped take forward the broader struggle for a united, non-racial, democratic South Africa based on the will of the majority.[367]

The interweaving of the sport and broader struggles in the run-up to democracy and after was to be highlighted by several dramatic events going forward.

In the months after Mandela walked out of prison, released prisoners and exiles were welcomed back at massive and ecstatic ANC rallies. Having been banned for three decades, the ANC set up its headquarters at Shell

House in Johannesburg and, together with the SACP and PAC, started re-establishing itself legally within the country, the UDF disbanding in deference to its return. Mandela was soon leading negotiations that after four turbulent years were to see him become the country's first democratically elected president. Following the historic first meeting, the ANC and the minority government signed the Groote Schuur Minute in which they committed themselves to opening up official channels of communication between themselves and working towards a climate conducive to future negotiations. In a second round of talks three months later, the bitter old enemies signed the Pretoria Minute on 6 August 1990 and agreed 'the way is now open to proceed towards negotiations on a new constitution'.[368]

Two days before that, the two national cricket bodies had announced their intention to start unity talks under Tshwete. The ANC then decided to unilaterally suspend the armed struggle – 'In the interest of moving as speedily as possible towards a negotiated peaceful political settlement' – and the regime approved indemnity and the release of even more political prisoners. Six months later, on 12 February 1991, the long-standing adversaries took a third formal step towards negotiations and a new constitution when they signed the D. F. Malan Accord at what is today's Cape Town International Airport.[369] This was soon after cricket had put together its joint task force on development and announced its intention to be unified by June of the same year.

Twelve days after cricket unity, on 29 June 1991, Steve Tshwete and the cricket leaders were at Lords Cricket Ground in London to witness South Africa's admittance to the International Cricket Council – on the very pitch that, twenty-one years earlier, had been ringed with barbed wire to thwart demonstrators. Mandela had written a special letter to the Caribbean governments and their cricket boards asking them to support South Africa's admission, as the West Indies were wary of lifting the boycott. Sam Ramsamy was also in London after being asked to lobby the ambassadors of the Caribbean nations. With South Africa readmitted, its first ever tour by a national team to India followed in November 1991. It was also the first time in more than two decades that South Africa officially participated in a cricket venture abroad – except that it was agreed the team could not be called the still hated name 'Springboks', its symbol instead becoming the national flower, the indigenous, hardy protea.

Talks about talks on the political front were followed by the onset of formal negotiations in the next month when the Convention for a Democratic South Africa (CODESA) met for the first time at Johannesburg's Kempton Park in December 1991. There were 228 delegates representing seventeen political organisations – the most representative gathering yet in South Africa.[370] The ANC attempted to create a broad patriotic front to build the widest possible unity, replicating strategies for the negotiations used in exile and in sport.

Progress at the talks table was slow as the liberation movement pushed for a final constitution drawn up by elected representatives of the people, while the representatives of the white minority sought 'guarantees' and a curbing of ANC power. However, the liberation movement slowly but surely pushed back on National Party positions. First the idea of a rigged 'power-sharing' in a new South Africa giving whites an effective veto was discarded, then also the notion of fixed racial group rights, which had been the basis of apartheid and its attempts at self-preservation.

In March 1992 President de Klerk called a whites-only referendum to seek approval for the negotiations. Mandela urged supporters not to disrupt the referendum and called on white ANC supporters to vote in favour. At the time the national cricket team was participating for the first time in the fifth World Cup in Australia and seemingly on their way to victory in the semi-final against England before rain and the system of calculation in operation at that time raised the target to an impossible twenty-two runs off one ball. The turnabout on the sports fields was illustrated by a tearful Tshwete hugging captain Kepler Wessels in Australia. The team reiterated Mandela's call for a yes vote in the white referendum. Media coverage back in South Africa was intense. Live television and saturation press coverage enthralled the white population. And the de Klerk government, in a programme of carefully orchestrated political advertisements and TV broadcasts in its referendum campaign, used pictures from the World Cup to urge a yes vote as the only means of keeping and extending such international sports participation.

Where sport had been used as a stick to force change, now it was a carrot to encourage further change, and de Klerk won with a two-thirds majority on an 85 per cent turnout. Ramsamy commented on the ANC's 'enthusiasm for international sport as a vehicle for morale-building transformation'.

Football's 'Bafana-Bafana' (the boys) followed cricket into international sport when they played Cameroon in Durban on 9 July 1992 in Durban, winning 1–0 thanks to a penalty by Doctor Khumalo, who went on to become a household name South Africa. This after the new South African

Football Association (SAFA) was formed on 8 December 1991.

Rugby launched the new South African Rugby Football Union (SARFU) on 19 January 1992, and that August followed the route into international competition as well, playing the All Blacks in Johannesburg and the Wallabies in Cape Town. Though very active in the NOSC, which made unity and this rugby tour possible, André supported Australia. The reason: radio reports of the chauvinistic waving of the apartheid flag and the singing of the apartheid anthem, 'Die Stem' (The Voice) at the stadium. Agreeing with those who felt the process was being rushed too much, in favour of culling the springbok as the national sporting emblem, and wearing an ANC T-shirt to show his loyalties in this cauldron of old South Africa passions, André was intimidatingly followed by two khaki-dressed AWB supporters who discussed in not very delicate language how they would like to *moer* (thrash) him. To André's relief, the Wallabies ran out easy 29–6 winners, sparked by the genius of David Campese, but this cameo showed the at times confusing complexity of the process underway in sport.

Mandela and Tshwete were also working closely with Ramsamy in help-ing to steer South Africa back into the Olympic Games due to be held through July and August 1992 in Barcelona, Spain. Mandela flew with Ramsamy to meet Olympic chief Juan Antonio Samaranch, a former fascist politician in Franco's Spain, to pave the way for a mixed contingent to march out under a neutral flag and using the Olympic anthem – Beethoven's 'Ode to Joy' – as its own. De Klerk and National Party spokespeople called this a 'slap in the face for all South Africans' and threatened to withhold financial support. A right-wing leader reported Ramsamy to the police for 'treating the national flag with contempt' and the Afrikaans press had a field day against him.

Far worse was the crisis caused by the Boipatong massacre of June 1992 in which forty-six people were slaughtered by sinister 'third force' elements supported by the state. The ANC withdrew from the negotiations demanding an end to 'the regime's campaign of terror'. To drive home the seriousness of the matter, the ANC concluded that South Africa should also withdraw from the Olympic Games. An outraged Archbishop Desmond Tutu also called for the reinstatement of the sports boycott. With only a month to go to the Games, Ramsamy was summoned to the office of ANC chief negotiator, Cyril Ramaphosa, but he persuaded the ANC to maintain its initial position; after all, he argued, the ANC had made participation possible and going to Barcelona would send a strong message about a transforming South Africa.

When the mixed South African delegation entered the stadium, walking behind the marathon runner and flag-bearer Jan Tau, Madiba was there as the honoured guest.[371] The ghost of John Harris must have been looking on.

Jonty Rhodes's iconic dive to break the wickets and run out Pakistans's Inzamam-ul-Haq at the 1992 World Cup; 800-metre silver medallist Elana Meyer's lap of honour with Derartu Tulu of Ethiopia at the Barcelona Olympics; and the consistent presence of the gravelly voiced Mr Fixit, Steve Tshwete, all pointed to a future in which the ANC planned for sport to be a complementary part of the road to political freedom.

Three months out from Boipatong, with the national situation worsening following another massacre of ANC supporters at Bisho and a large general strike, the government and the ANC came back to the negotiating table. A 'Record of Understanding' to proceed was signed in September 1992 and serious negotiations commenced again in March 1993.

The most fraught moment of the whole negotiation process came in April 1993 when the struggle icon, Chris Hani, was assassinated. With the country teetering on the brink of open conflict, Mandela was allowed access to the state-controlled SABC to speak directly to the nation to maintain calm, de facto recognition that he and his party controlled South Africa's destiny. The situation cooled, but instability and uncertainty remained high. White right-wing elements of the AWB drove an armoured vehicle into the negotiations hall and threatened a coup. It was touch and go as to whether the whole transformative process would be derailed.

After many clashes and compromises, and with minds focused in the critical period after Hani's death, in July 1993 agreement was finally reached on an election date, and in November 1993 on a new constitution, which would have to be ratified by a democratically elected constitutional assembly. The outcome was a carefully negotiated compromise. The minority government effectively agreed to relinquish power and the ANC and its partners in turn gave comfort via guarantees for the old civil service, a form of coalition government for five years, significant powers to the provinces and an amnesty for political offenders.[372]

The first democratic elections were held on 27 April 1994. Two weeks later Mandela became president, signalling one of the most remarkable turnabouts in the political history of the twentieth century. Immediately after the momentous inauguration ceremony at the Union Buildings attended by a legion of world leaders, the newly installed President Mandela was whisked off for his first public appearance. It was at Ellis Park Stadium to greet the South African and Zambian football teams at the people's celebration of the events. Zambia had been the chosen because it provided the headquarters for the ANC during its long exile. Mandela walked onto the field to the simple announcement, 'Ladies and gentleman, the president of South Africa, Mr Nelson Mandela.' The announcer was Sam Ramsamy, a member of the inauguration committee and representative of a sports struggle that had helped change a country. Ellis Park erupted in deafening adulation.

After three centuries of colonialism and apartheid, the disenfranchised mass of South Africans had at last reclaimed their national sovereignty and ushered in full-scale political democracy. 'Freedom' arrived amidst unprecedented scenes of national joy and celebration.

A feature of the negotiating process, initiated by Mandela from his cell and Oliver Tambo from exile in the 1980s, was the way in which the ANC outmanoeuvred opponents determined to block true democracy, as well as the constructive relations it managed to build with key opposite negotiators and groups At the time of the unbannings, de Klerk and his allies at home and abroad believed that they could control the process and outmanoeuvre the liberation movements, including through security and 'third-force' violence to kill or destabilise ANC grassroots activists. But in a short four years, three centuries of white rule were formally annulled. Mass mobilisation kept the pressure on the regime to the end, and the ANC's Harare Declaration and Constitutional Guidelines for a Democratic South Africa, drawn up in the 1980s, remained the essential template for change. Instead of a new version of Botha or de Klerk, South Africa got democracy, Mandela and one of the most enlightened constitutions in the world, which entrenched via its Bill of Rights and a constitutional court, the rule of law and the rights of every citizen. Against all expectations, and the run of history, South Africans had found resolution to a historic conflict that had, seemed unsolvable, fixed in granite, like Palestine, Ireland and elsewhere.

SACOS stalwart Basil Brown summed up what happened in sport during the tumultuous and surprisingly quick transition to a vote for all and the formal transfer of power in South Africa in 1994: 'As negotiations proceeded and agreement was being reached on the terms of the "settlement", one of the key concessions that the ANC and its allies needed to make was to guarantee that the sports moratorium would be lifted and that South Africa would be re-admitted to the IOC and other international sports federations.

This to allay the worry of whites that they were not getting much in exchange for agreeing to hand over political power to the black majority.'[373]

The positive side of the unfolding process was that South African sportspeople formally united for the first time in more than a century of organised sport, and that the international bodies endorsed a 'new South Africa' committed to different values and a different vision from the old. International contacts, increased income and sponsorship, television coverage, new facilities and development programme at grassroots level were actively being pursued in order to ground the emerging new visions for sport. Opportunities never before available to the great majority of South African sportsmen and women opened up – like Josiah Thugwane coming from obscurity to win Olympic gold in the marathon at Atlanta in 1996 – and the country soon hosted its first world cups in rugby, cricket and football, which were marketed and seen as examples of what long-awaited democracy had brought the new 'Rainbow Nation'.

However, there were also negative sides to these quick-moving developments in sport and politics in the first half of the 1990s. Firstly, the rapid demise of SACOS, an organisation which had bravely flown the banner for non-racial sport since 1973. It soon became a shell of its former self, and by 1995 had been 'reduced to an executive of six members and no national codes of sport', before quietly expiring.[374] As writer Hein Willemse observes, groups linked to the National Forum, such as the New Unity Movement and APDUSA – influenced by Fourth International left ideas, anti-race theory and non-collaboration – and the Black Consciousness-linked AZAPO, found particularly strong expression in sport via SACOS and its 'no normal sport in an abnormal society' slogan, but the rise and rise of the ANC and its internal allies from the mid-1980s onwards brought this ideological dominance in sport to a somewhat abrupt end. Secondly, of deeper social significance was the fact that in the liberation movement's haste to ensure a transition to peace and political democracy using sport as a 'unity' carrot, the inequalities and power and commercial relations in sport remained essentially unexplored and untouched. This was a process that could not be done overnight – even if five years was counted as one day. The launch pad for the future had been created and the goal of a wholly 'transformed' sports' dispensation was clearly articulated, but the real struggle over its final form was in a sense only just beginning.

In one of its final major statements, SACOS argued before the United Nations Special Committee Against Apartheid Sports (UNCAAS) that:

'The entire unity process has been bedevilled by bad faith, behind the scenes machinations, and jockeying for positions. There is not a single example of unity being established in good faith and on a principled basis nor has the previous gains made by non-racial sport been entrenched. Imbalances are not being addressed and in certain areas development programmes are non-existent.'

SACOS was 'sacrificed for political expediency', Brown claimed, implying the whole process of unity was a 'sell out'. However, this strongly expressed view was a minority one. In the 1994 general elections, with an exceptional 86.92 per cent voter turn-out, the political organisations which shared SACOS's general ideological perspectives garnered a minute percentage of the vote, the PAC (1.25 per cent) and the Workers' List Party (0.25 per cent) doing best against the 62.39 per cent of the ANC.

There were undoubtedly shortcomings in the unity process, conducted under immense pressure, with sport being used as a strategic bargaining tool in the final stages of struggle, as South Africa hurtled towards a conclusion whose outcome was unclear. Until the last moments of May 1994, the question was whether a relatively peaceful transfer to democracy would actually happen. However, the sell-out claims against those (like Tshwete) who through mass struggle and great personal risk and cost brought apartheid sport to its knees and forced the change that happened in sport border on the ridiculous. André and Peter agree with the more restrained position among SACOS loyalists that non-racial sport 'gave up too much too soon'.[375]

Could SACOS, with its screaming absence in African communities and ideological puritanism and goal of a socialist and classless society before there could even be talk of sport being normalised, ever have succeeded in implementing a transformed, effective, mass-based, national grassroots sports system in post-democratic South Africa? How would they have done this? These questions are purely hypothetical because by 1995 it had collapsed under its own internal contradictions.

The hard reality is that SACOS faded out despite its heroic goals and struggles.

On the other hand, following the stitched-together sport solution, would the ANC/NSC be able to deliver the radical social transformation that both they and SACOS sought? Again, the hard reality is that South African sport today is far behind the vision for grassroots transformation and redress in 1990. Are the contradictions now not on the other side? The burden of history, the inability of post-apartheid ANC governments to re-order

348

fundamentally apartheid socio-economic relations and spatial planning, the changed context of globalisation and the massive commercialisation of sport in the past few decades, going with a dominant neo-liberal international order, have meant that the majority of South Africans remain systemically marginalised in economic and sporting terms. This situation has been exacerbated by the poor delivery of services, looting and loss of the moral authority of the governing ANC in the era of 'state capture', with its corruption, cronyism and undermining of institutions.

Restrained by deep-seated external factors, both SACOS and the NCS – in different eras and contexts – were unable to implement what they wished for, though they both took South African sport forward in significant ways.

Critics claim in retrospect that the political negotiations and sports unity process followed in the 1990s led to neo-liberalism becoming the dominant feature of post-democracy South African sport and society, and this explains its current economic and social crisis.[376] This has given momentum to both such class-analytical critiques and a growing 'race'-informed, youth-driven Black Consciousness platform that calls for the completion of a stalled decolonisation project, rejecting the whole notion of 'non-racialism' and inclusive political transformation which guided the sports struggle. This analysis sees 1994 as a failed 'compromise' and the ANC and Mandela as part of a neo-colonial project. It also scoffs at the idea from the much-quoted opening sentence of the Freedom Charter that South Africa belongs to all who live in it, black and white.

However, these latter-day criticisms, feeding off the unfilled promises of democracy, are still vigorously contested. Those who say the deal that gave us this republic was a sellout, 'defile those – living and dead – who [struggled for and] negotiated our passage to democracy', argues *City Press* editor Mondli Makhanya.

But the high levels of inequality in South Africa a quarter of a century after democracy cannot be glossed over and give these critiques growing validity. For André and Peter, the struggles for liberation and the accompanying non-racial sports struggles, despite ever-present contradictions, were in their totality efforts with heroic dimensions to them, nourished historically by a deep reservoir of humanity, vision, courage and self-sacrifice. And they took place in a context where liberation leaders had to avoid debilitating civil war and probable economic collapse, which could have permanently damaged the country and rendered 'victory' meaningless. Hence this book's concern to help record and acknowledge the contribution

of all the sports struggle groups from SASA and SANROC to SACOS and the
NSC. And, concomitant with this, against the background of deep systemic
restraints of a global neoliberal economic order entrenching social injustice
and inequality, the struggle for human and sporting equality and dignity
needs to continue unabated, even amidst ever-present contradictions on all
sides of the argument

*

A year into his Presidency, on 24 June 1995 Mandela awoke at his customary
early hour and confessed to being tense – more, he claimed, than awaiting
his swearing in as president.[377] The reason? That afternoon was the Rugby
World Cup final between the Springboks and the New Zealanders not too
far from his home in Johannesburg. In a masterstroke of message-marketing,
he turned up to greet the teams in a Springbok cap and jersey, in a calculated
act of national unity, cheering them on to a famous rugby victory.[378]

The crowd, in what was one of rugby apartheid's citadels, Johannesburg's
Ellis Park Stadium – 99 per cent white, mostly Afrikaner, many still seeing
his organisation as the devil in disguise – rose to cheer him, chanting,
'Nelson! Nelson! Nelson!' Even just a year into his government, sport was
still as potent a force for change as it had always been in the rise and fall of
apartheid. Mandela, a sports fan himself, knew all along that victory could
help promote a feeling of unity between white and black South Africans:
they loved sport, and he was right; the 'feel-good' effect was spectacular.

Another dose of 'Mandela magic' came a year later in 1996 when he
celebrated in a similar way with South Africa's football captain, Neil Tovey,
lifting the Africa Cup of Nations trophy for the very first and still only time.
The national team, known as 'Bafana Bafana', was coached by Clive Barker
who, months before the tournament, had been called to the phone at his
Durban home by his eight-year-old niece. 'It's a man called Nelson and he
says he wants to talk to you, Uncle Clive.' The president began regularly
engaging with the team privately to inspire them. But publicly he was
engaged in his key strategy of nation-building through football about which
the township masses were fanatical. 'He brought an extra pressure because
he made sure you got the sort of message: "You know what happened with
the rugby,"' Barker told writer Ian Hawkey. 'But he was great with the
players, always asking after their families, very hands-on when he mingled

with them. Sometimes he would bring his grandchildren to the hotel. It was a real influence on us.'[379]

Opening the African Cup hosted by South Africa, Mandela spoke of 'Africa rising', and the national team was ecstatically cheered as it progressed with thrills and spills to the pulsating packed final in Johannesburg's Soccer City, beating Tunisia by 2–0, the goals coming electrifyingly late into the second half.

*

Sports apartheid had provided probably the starkest instance of the in- exorable connection between politics and sport. It encompassed a story of absolute racist segregation growing out of British colonialism and insti- tutionalised by apartheid, ultimately overthrown by courageous domestic resistance combined with decades of international protest.

That story progressed through the 'stick' of global isolation and non- racial sports struggles inside the country under apartheid, to the 'carrot' of global readmission if it was abolished and South African sport became for- mally organised, as it always should have been, on the idea of inclusivity, opportunity and merit, not race and exclusion.

Now here was Madiba – the global icon of the age – celebrating togetherness, carrying the hopes of a new country that it could break with the past and create a new future where all had the same rights and all children were given a fair chance.

8 Making sense of sport and globalisation today

From beer money to £100 million footballer contracts: Neo-liberalism and modern sport

When their father was prevented by the apartheid government from working in South Africa, Peter and his younger brother Tom knew they would be exiled to London. Their only consolation was the prospect of seeing top British football teams play.

In Pretoria, late 1965, the two teenagers studied a map of London, a strange and faraway city, about to be their new home. A political friend had made available a flat in his large house for the Hain family to rent, and the stadium of a nearby club stood out. Stamford Bridge, home to Chelsea, whom they'd listened to on the BBC World Service on Saturday afternoons. So, aged fifteen, Peter became a keen (some might say fanatical) Chelsea fan, which he remains, along with the whole Hain family, to this day.

But the stadium Peter and Tom went to excitedly on the first possible Saturday in London in April 1966 was very different to that on the same spot today, and so is the club, symbolising the neoliberal globalisation of the sport.

For a big match like Manchester United in the late 1960s, they had to arrive at least two hours early, queue for an hour inching forward on a packed pavement from Fulham Broadway underground station to reach a turnstile, then search for a spot to stand an hour before kick-off, which meant being on their feet for around four hours by the time the match ended. The pitch was muddy and corrugated in winter, surrounded by a dog-racing track. On a rainy day, spectators got drenched. Men who'd had a few too many beers beforehand sometimes unzipped and had a pee in front of everyone on the terraces.

Today, Stamford Bridge is a mostly covered all-seater with a well-drained, smooth green pitch. Access is pretty quick. There are plenty of toilets, as well as hospitality lounges for thousands willing and able to pay a premium for a meal with drinks.

Back in the 1960s and right through the 1980s, Chelsea's finances were precarious. The club was in turn relegated and promoted. Stamford Bridge was sold to property developers during the late 1970s when the club faced bankruptcy, and was nearly demolished and turned into houses and super-markets, until the developers themselves went bankrupt and the ground was bought back in 1992.

Suddenly in June 2003 its fortunes changed dramatically when it was bought by Russian billionaire Roman Abramovich – his opulence garnered in the lawless Wild West of privatisation and wheeler-dealing after the fall of the Soviet Union and Western-driven 'shock therapy' to an ailing statist economy. He invested massively in top players, managers, stadium upgrades, a state-of-the-art training facility and a youth academy. Chelsea was cata-pulted from a quixotic, middling performer to a serial champion, joining the global elite of Real Madrid, Barcelona, Manchester United and recently Manchester City.

The old First Division became the Premier League, the richest, most popular in the world, powered by multibillion satellite television revenues.

Chelsea's top players earned up to £200,000 per week, Manchester Uni-ted's Alexis Sánchez £390,000 weekly. In 2019, Chelsea star Eden Hazard was sold to Real Madrid for a fee reportedly climbing to £150 million.

Other global billionaires soon followed Abramovich. Qatar's Sheikh Mansour invested massively more in Manchester City to propel it from relative obscurity into the elite, above even Chelsea.

*

The gap between the Premier League and Britain's lowest football divisions became gargantuan. In 2019, when Manchester United signed England international defender Harry Maguire for £80 million, just one pound was all a businessman needed to snap up nearby Bury FC in League One. One estimate put Maguire's worth at more than *all* the League One ('third division') together with *half* the Championship ('second division') clubs – getting on for forty of them, some top-flight famous football names of past generations like Blackpool and Stoke. That might well have been Chelsea's fate without Abramovich.

Football quintessentially (but most globally branded sports too from cycling to rugby) have followed the neoliberalism of recent decades – an

353

ideology favouring market forces wherever possible and tolerating regulation only where absolutely necessary: in practice a free-for-all, with growing and grotesque inequality between the top 1 per cent and the rest.

From 1945 to the mid-1970s Britain and most Western European nations grew quickly by pre-war standards, due in part to Keynesian economic policies, with extensive public investment and everyone sharing in the greater material prosperity to some degree, and real incomes growing as national wealth grew and poverty reduced. There were three decades of expanding welfare services, economic stability and relatively fast growth, greater equality and fewer class differences.

But around 1980, with Margaret Thatcher in power in the United Kingdom and Ronald Reagan in the United States, began a systematic drive for a right-wing neoliberal alternative. In the following four decades, even the concept of society was called into question, and the role of the state acting on behalf of society to promote the common good was belittled. Public services were derided and privatised, and social infrastructure starved of funds. Top rates of income tax paid by the few were halved as taxes on spending paid by the many were doubled. Financial institutions were deregulated, 'free' markets lionised, and a 'greed is good' mentality applauded. Seeds were sown in the 1980s and 1990s that bore fateful fruit with the 2008 financial crisis, bringing the entire global economic system to the very brink of complete collapse: the apotheosis of neoliberalism.[380]

Commenting upon the 2019 FA Cup Final when Manchester City thrashed a very good Watford side 6–0, *Guardian* columnist Jonathan Wilson said this proved that 'football is broken' because without Watford being bought 'by a sheikh, oligarch or nation state looking to enhance its global reputation, there is no prospect of them being able to challenge over any sort of sustained period'. Pointing out that a similar situation applied in Spain and France, he added: 'Greed has won, big finance has won. Whatever small role elite clubs still play in the local communities from which they grew is dwarfed now by their position as global brands. It is desperately sad to say it but if the future is more mismatches like Saturday's, or the sort of coronation procession that so many leagues have now become, maybe the least bad solution is just to let them go, let them have their super league.'

Another *Guardian* columnist, Barney Ronay, pointed out in February 2019 that UEFA Champions League knock-out finalists, Paris Saint-Germain were owned by Qatar, which also sponsored Champions League Bayern Munich and Roma. 'Real Madrid are sponsored by the Emirates airline of the UAE. Another of the emirates, Abu Dhabi, owns Manchester City. Manchester City are taking on Schalke, who are sponsored by Gazprom, which is owned by Russia, which is in effect at war in Syria with Qatar, which is being blockaded by Dubai, which is a financial services partner of Manchester United, whose next opponents [in the knock-out stages] will be Paris Saint-Germain, who are owned by Qatar. Which is pretty much where we came in.'

Ronay added that the newest member of the UEFA Executive Committee was Nasser al-Khelaifi, also chair of BeIN Media Group, which paid UEFA for its Champions League TV rights. UEFA in turn was 'investigating claims of financial fair play breaches by PSG where he is – do keep up – the club chairman. Another circle of life, another wheel within football's wheels. It should be pointed out this isn't just a Gulf state thing. UEFA is also sponsored by Adidas, which owns a stake in Bayern Munich . . . This is nothing new in itself. Sport has been bought, sold, fluffed, preened, primped and generally co-opted by those in power ever since it first appeared as a public spectacle.'

Ronay concluded by deploying a phrase first coined by Amnesty International in December 2018 on the ownership of Manchester City: 'sportswashing'. He argued that this 'describes the way sport is used to launder a reputation, to gloss a human rights record, to wash a little blood away. The phrase itself involves a value judgment. It stems from a belief in moral absolutes, the idea we can say with certainty a particular ideology or regime should not be "normalised" by close association with sport.'

After Saudi Arabia bid to take over Premier League Newcastle United in 2020 the beIN sports channel, sponsored by the Qatari government (itself in a cold war with Riyadh), wrote to every other Premier League Club objecting. As Jonathan Liew caustically observed: 'This, in a way, was always the danger of opening up the Premier League so accommodatingly to the toxic influences of global geopolitics . . . And so, welcome to the new orthodoxies of English football. Saudi Arabia is good. Amnesty International is bad. New signings are more important than murder, broadcast rights are more important than women's rights, and a sense of basic humanity is ultimately expendable if you can scrape into next season's Europa League.'[381]

In May 2019 Arsenal's Henrikh Mkhitaryan did not join his teammates in Baku, Azerbaijan, for the Europa League final against Chelsea because – as an Armenian – he believed his safety could not be guaranteed in the city, as Azerbaijan refused entry to Armenian nationals over the disputed territory of Nagorno-Karabakh. Echoing the sophistry of sports apartheid apologists, the Azerbaijani ambassador to the United Kingdom accused Mkhitaryan of 'playing politics'. Perhaps the real 'politics' came from awarding Baku not only the Europa League final but Azerbaijan as host for four matches during the Euro 2020 nations cup. An award, commented the *Guardian*'s Paul MacInnes, that was 'seen by some to be not unrelated to the potential revenues to be made from the oil-rich country'. He added: 'In the modern age, however, football has gone on to acquire a sociopolitical status far greater than that which it had in the past. In today's world, particularly at the elite level, it is almost more difficult to find a match that has no political subtext. Wolves versus Bournemouth? It's the Chinese Belt and Road Initiative against Russian expatriate cash. Liverpool versus Newcastle? The international synergistic conglomerate versus the bargain basement retailer. Manchester City versus Manchester United? Less a city divided than two polarised principles on the accumulation of debt.'

*

The inequality in British football is a microcosm of that in society. Over a quarter of clubs in the English Football League, the three divisions below the Premier League, faced bankruptcy or winding-up petitions by 2020 – and that was before the coronavirus left the game flat on its back. Although financial mismanagement was a common factor, right across the industrial north-west, small-town clubs like Bury and Bolton Wanderers that once formed the bedrock of English football have been sinking, reflecting the economic decline or collapse of a region that was once the industrial bedrock of England.

As sports journalist Jonathan Liew wrote:

> this is a tale whose origins go deeper than the game itself. And in a way, the decline of north-west football fits neatly with the decay of small-town industrial Britain, the extinguishing not just of vital services by a decade of government cuts, but of something less tangible: community, dignity, hope. Both Bury and Bolton have long since been swallowed up by Manchester's sprawl, their local councils subjected to vicious austerity cuts, their affairs ignored by a largely metropolitan, London-based media. For decades, football acted as a bulwark against all this: knitting these small towns together, restoring some of their former esteem . . .

[But] where do the Burys and the Boltons of the world fit into the
future of football, a sport being stretched and riven by the forces of
globalisation and rampant capitalism, by the increasing concentration
of money and power in the hands of a gilded elite? [382]

Bury's expulsion from the Football League on 27 August 2019 came just
days before Europe's elite Champions and Europa Leagues announced the
distribution of the 2019–20 season's £2 billion revenue and rumours of a
megamove for Brazilian star Neymar from Paris Saint-German to Barcelona
for £135 million; though as it happens that was not consummated at the
time.

Bury's near neighbour, a club with an even more illustrious pedigree,
Bolton Wanderers, only narrowly escaped liquidation. After 145 years as a
founder member of the Football League and having spent seventy-three
years in the top division, Bolton's plight underlined the chasm between top
and bottom clubs. It prompted Nigel Clough, manager of fellow League
One side Burton Albion, to speak out. Premier League clubs had a responsibility to use their financial clout to help bail out stricken lower league teams
such as Bolton and Bury, Clough told the *Guardian* on 30 July 2019. He said
the plight of Bolton and Bury 'saddens everyone in football' and called on
elite clubs to step in and help.

It's very difficult but I think there's enough money in football at the
moment to look after everybody. I would look up for it. When there's
billion-pound TV deals and everything, I think the Football League
[lower league clubs] should have just a little bit more. I think it's been
the lifeblood for many years in providing players for the Premier League
and even the international team – you've got the likes of Kyle Walker
and Harry Maguire. I think there's an overall responsibility to try and
look after those clubs . . . I don't think there are too many sane people
looking to buy football clubs. What do they say? The quickest way to
go from being a billionaire to a millionaire is buy a football club.

Although the Premier League does distribute 'parachute payments' to
relegated clubs, to cushion the blow, and 'solidarity payments' linked to the
value of their former share of broadcasting rights, Clough's plea again highlighted the massive inequality in the game, in turn reflecting the wider and
growing inequalities within a neoliberal world.

Commenting on this, the *Guardian*'s Barney Ronay wrote on 29 August 2019:

> The top-tier game has become . . . an orbiting super-industry, immune to parochial concerns but the plight of Bury is not something to be glossed or shrugged over, chalked up as another casualty of the market . . . As for parliament, well, successive governments have overseen the creation of our current state of archcapitalism, where the only real sin is interfering with the flow of the free market, and where a football club is simply a business like any other . . . The broader question is how many other clubs are teetering close to a similar state of collapse, futures in hock to the greed and ineptitude of their owners; and to a sport that is willing to treat its own cultural wealth so carelessly.

*

If there were an equivalent in South Africa for Chelsea's transition to sporting globalisation and neoliberalism, it was cricket's 9/11 moment – the ICC World Twenty20 that took place in South Africa in September 2007. At the time André was Chief Executive Officer of the historic Newlands cricket ground under the mountain in Cape Town, which was one of the hosting stadiums. On 11 September 2001 a surreal kamikaze attack reduced the Twin Towers in New York to rubble, changing the world as we knew it. But fast-forward to 11 September 2007, and, amidst ubiquitous media analyses of Osama bin Laden's first video in three years and the broad impacts of 9/11, the first ICC World Twenty20 tournament kicked off in South Africa.

Many commentators saw T20 (as it was dubbed) as little more than a gimmick, taking place almost as an afterthought to the Cricket World Cup in the Caribbean earlier in the year. It was in every sense a last-minute arrangement. The exclusion of Jacques Kallis from the South Africa squad dominated pre-tournament coverage. His mate, Mark Boucher, weighed in with dismissive comments about administrators and the format itself. It is not real cricket, most people said, and they argued that T20 (with only thirty-three international games played to that point) should remain restricted. The Rugby World Cup further distracted local media attention.

However, a minority sensed that cricket was possibly entering a new era,

André amongst them. He commented in pre-tournament interviews and articles that by tournament's end 'Twenty20 will be established, with its own life and statistics.' He predicted also that cricket was living through a period of birth, like the late nineteenth century (for test cricket) and the 1970s (for one-day internationals), which would reshape its future.[383]

Readings on the chaotic and 'completed unpremeditated' beginnings of test cricket in 1877 and opposition to the launch of one-day cricket in the 1960s on the basis of 'it's probably destructive effects on technique',[384] gave him a sense that perhaps this kind of scepticism is predictable in the face of fundamental change, and this made it easier to visualise T20 as a revolution ready to take off.

On 11 September 2007 South Africa took to the field against the West Indies (who would have been barred under apartheid) at the Wanderers in Johannesburg, and a massive Bob Beamon-type performance of 117 in fifty-seven balls by Chris Gayle set the tournament alight. An emphatic fight-back by South Africa, led by the mercurial Herschelle Gibbs, showed that T20, too, could trigger the fiercely competitive patriotism that so often underlies classic sporting encounters. People sat up: this is magnificent cricket, magnificent entertainment.

A fortnight later India played Pakistan in the final. Not good news for South Africa, but it set up the new product perfectly in global terms. Seven plane-loads of Indians arrived that morning, including Bollywood heart-throb, Shah Rukh Khan. The crowd buzzed every time he was shown on the big screen or when he waved from the balcony. Bollywood met T20 in Johannesburg amidst a cacophony of sound, fireworks and action.

India won by five runs with two balls to spare in a game that Pakistan should have sewn up. The tournament kept its grip on the crowd and, more importantly, the global television audience, to the very end. The flag-waving winners circled a field bedecked in Indian flags. People were smiling, hugging and patting backs in the long room as Cricket South Africa and ICC big brass watched the final ceremony and said their umpteenth good-byes. We had seen something new being born in cricket.

The next day Stewart Hess waxed lyrical in *The Star*: 'Let the doubters and critics now shut up. Twenty20 cricket is here to stay following one of the most thrilling matches in the sport's history between its two most popularly supported sides . . . a most magnificent encounter that forever cements Twenty20 cricket'. This was the universal reaction. The ICC was happy too. The organisation's post-tournament review underlined the superb South African organisation. It noted also that 400,000 people went through the gates and that three billion people in 105 countries watched on television, including over 750,000 for the final. And don't forget the bottom line: the ICC members had raked in over $45 million in revenue.

India, who had never played a T20 international before and had to be persuaded to enter, went home as the victors to a massive welcome and outpouring of enthusiasm. The tournament's success and a challenge to the Board of Control for Cricket in India (BCCI) by India's largest listed media group, Zee Telefilms, now took T20 to a new level.

Peeved at losing out on official television rights, Zee's owner, Subhash Chandra, announced the launch of his own private rebel T20 Indian Cricket League (ICL). He set aside R170 million and it was announced that the top international limited-overs players would be offered R16 million each for a few weeks' work. The BCCI now speeded up plans for its own domestic T20 Indian Premier League (IPL). In recent times, India had started realising the economic potential of the huge cricket market in a country of 1.2 billion people. The result was that it increasingly became the fulcrum for world cricket in a post-modern, post-colonial world. As Guha and Bose, top historians of Indian cricket point out, when Indian cricket's megastar Sachin Tendulkar batted against Pakistan's 'Rawalpindi Express', Shoaib Akhtar, the viewing figures virtually equalled the population of Western Europe. A mega step forward in this regard was when Nike reputedly paid the BCCI over $600 million for rights to the playing shirt, putting the Indian team on par in value with Serie A football teams in Italy. Hands were rubbed for the new product of T20.

The announcement about the new IPL was made in October 2007 and thereafter a remarkable sequence of events unfolded from December 2007 when tenders went out for media rights and new franchises, to be privately owned and based on city teams. First, on 14 January 2008 a $1.026 billion deal with Sony/WSG for the IPL media rights for ten years, then two weeks later eight new IPL franchises were sold for $723.6 million. They were Bangalore, Chennai, Delhi, Hyderabad, Jaipur, Kolkata, Mohali and Mumbai. Some of India's richest people and biggest celebrities, including Mukesh Ambani, Vijay Mallya, Shah Rukh Khan and Preity Zinta, become owners, bringing glamour to the new product.

Soon the Indian commercial property developer DLF became the IPL title sponsor for $50 million, with another $125 million following from leading corporates including Kingfisher Airlines, Honda and Pepsi. That was topped by sensational 'player auctions' in Mumbai and over fifty international stars were signed up by the IPL for a staggering figure of around $30 million, and cricketers entered a whole new world of financial opportunity. One South African superstar earned R1 million *a week* for playing in an Indian domestic cricket competition, fully one-tenth of the annual budget of a local South African franchise, and around three times the annual salaries of the top non-nationally contracted South African domestic players.

On 18 April 2008 the IPL kicked off, with fifty-nine matches spread over forty-four days, all televised live during peak global viewing hours. The brainchild of the new IPL commissioner Lalit Modi and developed by a team from the International Marketing Group under Englishman Andrew Wildblood, it was an instant, spectacular success. In a few months, a new cricket product worth well over R12 billion had been created. Modi rapidly acquired the title 'Mr Cricket' in the new era of cricket globalisation. Indian stadiums for domestic cricket were filled in an unprecedented way, Indian newspapers routinely carried five pages of coverage, with the Indian nation glued to its television sets, surpassing the viewership figures of the most popular film channels. So much so that the Bollywood summer release season was delayed until the tournament ended as cricket brought India to a standstill.

Then followed a frantic rush behind the scenes as other countries tried to cash in on the new product. During South Africa's Lords test in July 2018, British Sunday newspapers revealed multibillion-pound proposals to start an English Premier League built on city franchises, which most English counties were against because they feared losing out.

In September 2008 the England and Wales Cricket Board picked its team for a series of one-off matches with the West Indies sponsored by the billionaire Caribbean cricket lover Allen Stanford (self-styled 'Sir Allen', later jailed for numerous offences including fraud, and given a 110-year sentence at the United States Penitentiary at Coleman, Florida). The projected winner-takes-all prize money was $20 million dollars annually for five years.

In the same month it was reported that for the first time ever England, with annual revenue of over £79 million, had been overtaken as the biggest national income earner by India, who had jumped ahead on the back of the IPL takings. Compare those figures with Cricket South Africa's four-year income stream of $70 million at the time and there is a sense of the revolution that was unfolding.

At the time André asked what the impact of this revolution in cricket would be, and tried to provide something of an answer. He predicted that the game as it had been known was going to change radically. An immediate positive was the emergence of India as a twenty-first-century global economic power, together with its neighbour China, which meant that cricket was well placed to remain financially competitive in relation to other sports, many of which had narrow traditional British colonial bases. T20 was becoming one of the outstanding innovations product-wise in global sport in that decade.

But one-day cricket and even test cricket were under threat, as the absconding of virtually the whole Bangladesh team to the rebel ICL in September 2008 showed. At a conference on cricket and globalisation at Leeds Metropolitan University in the same month, cricket historian Rob Steen predicted that T20 would take cricket into an era of ten-day events, like golf and tennis tournaments, with grave implications for formats and tours.

The power of elite players would in all likelihood grow dramatically as opportunities and the pickings in a free market rose. Looking at the West Indies, the noted commentator Sir Hilary Backles commented that the post-colonial marriage between nationalism and cricket, which had underpinned the success of the great West Indian teams (and, indeed, national identities) in the Caribbean in the 1960s to 1980s, ended in the 1990s when Brian Lara arrived on the scene in an early period of globalisation as the ultimate saleable individual commodity with a 'me first' approach. Money and individual interest now started counting for more than loyalty to a bigger cause. South Africa would probably follow the same trend, André predicted.

Since non-racial unity was forged in 1991, the identity of South African cricket had been constructed primarily around a national project of meaningful social change – development, transformation and redress – but market forces began significantly undermining those crucial priorities and the opportunities they generated. The agenda of elite players, the business establishment and television would increasingly shape the direction forward, probably leading eventually to the same kind of divorce between new democracy nationalism and cricket that happened in the Caribbean, André argued.

Infighting between the transformation-minded Cricket South Africa president Norman Arendse and CEO Gerald Majola, who was driving the business-first corporatist agenda and relations with India, led to the former's resignation in the aftermath of the Indian and T20 revolution. Some saw it as a sign that the control of South African cricket was essentially passing to business, where old white establishment forces in new cricket corporate reincarnations became influential. No possible alternative cricket models based on anti-globalisation arguments were even being thought of. And the dependence on corporates was exacerbated by the collapse of physical education in official school curricula and the paltry investment by government in much-needed community sporting facilities since the end of apartheid.

For two decades from the late 1980s, SACOS and the NSC and their struggles for equality and non-racialism set the agenda in South African sport. André now noted that this influence had perhaps passed by permanently. He added: 'Whichever way you look at it, there is no question that 2008 to 2009 was the year in which cricket orbited into the era of hard globalisation. We in South Africa will be massively influenced, even though we still have very little sense about the long-term impacts, for example on grassroots amateur cricket.'[385]

And the successful 2019 ICC World Cup showed that many of his predictions then were busy happening. As in football's English Premier League, the gap between the big three – India, England and Australia – and the rest began growing. South Africa, left out of that threesome oligopoly, dropped into the second tier. Its best player, AB de Villiers chose the T20 circuit over country. A drain of talent began happening in rugby and cricket with busy agents moving their 'assets' abroad, as one of them noted. By 2020 there were some 1,000 South Africans from these two codes playing in Britain and France, readily open to being paid in stronger euro and pound sterling currencies. After the 2019 World Cup, Cricket South Africa also restructured its team management along professional football lines – one director of cricket henceforth to be in charge of the entire playing operation. The careful control of the change management process since unity and democracy by a representative board conscious of its obligations to change in line with new democracy imperatives began to fall away, taking power away from where it had existed since unity in 1991.

What does this all mean for the transformation vital to redress the harsh racial exclusions of 200 years of colonialism and apartheid in South African sport? Stepping down as CEO at Newlands in 2015, André warned his colleagues about a headlong rush into corporatisation in South African cricket:

A parting word of caution though about the new buzzword of 'cricket is business'. Cricket is more than business. It is also about creating meaning and promoting youth and community development and social cohesion. Like a school, mosque, church or university, the game has a social dimension which cannot be commodified or monetised from A–Z. It is part of a social economy whose value is inestimable, particularly at the grassroots club, youth and provincial levels, and in our often-fractured communities. Cricket's leadership has a huge responsibility which will demand of them considerable maturity and multi-dimensional skills to run the game well, while also balancing social and financial imperatives in a way that is broad and visionary, rather than simply mimicking corporatist cultures and leadership styles which often are narrow, top-down and overly reifying of the bottom-line. If this delicate balance (and transformative impulse) is not understood and managed, the ones who will mainly benefit in the long run will be those at the top end of the pyramid – already well paid star players, cricket bureaucrats and string-pullers in business – at the expense of the base. Cricket would have been bought and we would have let down the game and a country in transition if this happens.[386]

*

Under globalisation in this modern neoliberal era, sport has become more of a commodity, increasingly commercialised with widening inequality showcased by the Olympics and World Cup finals. Hundreds of millions view on television their favourite billionaire football clubs and multi-millionaire footballers who inhabit a different planet from the weekend players and fans. That said, sport retains its own magic for all people, black or white, rich or poor, religious or atheist, fit or infirm, political or otherwise. The tongue-in-cheek parable of legendary Liverpool Football Club manager and socialist Bill Shankly applies to all sport: 'People say football is a matter of life and death. They simply don't understand . . . it's far more important than that.'

Racism and football in a post-truth world

A regular attendee at Chelsea home matches in the late 1960s through the 1970s, Peter became acutely aware of racist attitudes amongst some Chelsea and away-team fans. And by the mid-1970s this was becoming a serious threat.

The main fascist, racist group in that era was the National Front, which had pushed the Liberals into fourth place in parliamentary by-elections and in the 1977 Greater London Council elections polling fully 10 per cent. Just as significant, it was attracting some following amongst disaffected working-class youngsters unable to get a job; there was a fashion for Nazi insignia and regalia amongst 'skinheads', working-class youth who menacingly shaved their heads and wore heavy Dr Martens boots. Wherever the National Front was active, there was also a disturbing inevitability about rises in local instances of racist violence and intimidation.

The National Front were also active at football matches, distributing their racist leaflets, including at Chelsea where a hardcore group congregated at the legendary 'shed end' and spread their propaganda and chanted racist slogans. Peter helped form the Anti-Nazi League launched in 1977, becoming its national spokesperson. The National Front leaders did not hide their Nazi ideas and the ANL encouraged supporters to form groups of their own peers – such as 'Teachers Against the Nazis', 'Students Against the Nazis', 'Miners Against the Nazis', even 'Vegetarians Against the Nazis' and 'Skateboarders Against the Nazis'. Each had their own badges and leaflets, each taking their own initiatives and involving their own people, including amongst football clubs where fans organised their own groups like 'Chelsea Against the Nazis'.

Within a year of its launch the Anti-Nazi League had mobilised hundreds of thousands across the country. Wherever the National Front tried to demonstrate or leaflet – such as at Chelsea's Stamford Bridge – they were opposed by the ANL, and also denied platforms to spread their hate. This confrontation strategy was highly controversial – some critics argued it amounted to a denial of free speech – but Peter and other ANL activists insisted it was essential to stop the National Front swaggering through black or Jewish communities with intimidation and violence the result. 'Free speech' did not mean the freedom to preach hatred against minority groups, so denying *their* freedom.

Such was the power mobilised by the ANL that within a few years the

365

National Front was out of business. One of its leaders, Martin Webster, publicly admitted that the ANL was the cause.

That may have helped remove the main organised agency for racism within Britain's football matches, but it did not eliminate the problem that reflected much deeper racist attitudes within British society, going back to the colonial era and slavery, underlining once again the societal link between politics and sport.

An English professional footballer, Paul Canoville, become the first black player to be signed by Chelsea in 1981. Peter and members of his family were thrilled to see him play, his attacking style helping them win the Second Division title in 1983–84. By then, Peter was regularly taking his two young sons Sam and Jake to home matches, sitting them on either side, his arms around them, on top of a crush barrier in the Shed End where he was often recognised and warmly received.

Canoville later became a Chelsea cult hero, paving the way for subsequent home-grown black British players to represent the club throughout the 1980s and 1990s, including Eddie Newton and Frank Sinclair. But he had arrived in professional football when racism was endemic in the British game, and like other black players at the time (including England internationals John Barnes, Viv Anderson, Cyrille Regis) suffered horrendous abuse from not only opposing fans but also from sections of Chelsea's supporters.[387] When he made his debut, it was against a backdrop of racist chants and slurs from his own fans: 'We don't want the n-----! Sit down n-----! Oi, you golliwog, go home!' Another was 'Sit down you black c---!', 'You f------ w-- – f--- off!'[388] Facing tough and even at times dangerous obstacles to his progress, Canoville was a pioneer, to be followed by later generations of foreign black international stars at the club, including Ruud Gullit, Marcel Desailly, Michael Essien, Jimmy Floyd Hasselbaink, Didier Drogba and N'Golo Kanté. By 2019 a host of black English youth internationals players had broken into the first team from its youth academy including Callum Hudson-Odoi, Reece James and Tammy Abraham, all becoming England internationals like Raheem Sterling and also suffering torrential social media abuse.

Cheered on by the vast majority of Chelsea fans, the club, along with the rest of the Premier League, had by then adopted and put into practice vigorous anti-racist policies, expelling any fan found guilty of racism. Canoville became a club ambassador on match days and in the community, occasionally playing for Chelsea Legends. Despite the horrendous treatment he received in the early 1980s from sections of Chelsea supporters (and indeed from some club officials), he remained a Chelsea supporter. Immensely popular with fans, and received standing ovations when introduced to the crowd at matches and events, Peter, his sons and grandchildren meeting him periodically at matches.

But just as the adoption of anti-racist stances by European governments could not mask rising levels of racist, anti-Semitic and Islamophobic attacks across the continent, so similar stances by European football authorities did not eradicate racist attitudes, as a country by country survey in the *Observer* on 16 December 2019 confirmed.[389]

Campaign groups like 'Kick It Out' and 'Show Racism the Red Card' continued to press British clubs and football's leadership. Nevertheless, Arsenal's Pierre-Emerick Aubameyang and Manchester City's Raheem Sterling suffered high-profile racist abuse towards the end of 2018, Sterling speaking out forcefully. In November 2018 Kick It Out revealed an 11 per cent rise in reported discriminatory abuse at football matches in 2017 and 2018, compared with the previous season – the sixth year in a row that the number of incidents of reported abuse had risen, over half racist. Cases reported at Football League matches also rose by a third.

But football's continuing problems with racism have never occurred in isolation. Instead they paralleled a toxic convergence across British society of rising attacks on Jewish, black and Muslim citizens. In 2017 and 2018 there were 94,098 hate crime offences recorded by the police in England and Wales, an increase of 17 per cent compared with the previous year, the great bulk 76 per cent race hate crimes. In 2017 anti-Semitic incidents in Britain reached the highest level on record and Islamophobic attacks rose by 30 per cent. It came as no surprise that this followed the ugly increase in xenophobia released by the 2016 Brexit referendum, where 'Leave' leaders and activists had openly exploited racist sentiments, boosting racist and fascist movements. In other words, even admirable leadership at the top of sport cannot always suppress a problem with much deeper roots in society.

In January 2020 the UK government revealed that over 150 football-related racist incidents had been reported to the police in the previous season – a jump of more than half on the season before and more than double three seasons before. As a spokesperson for Kick It Out told the *Guardian* on 30 January:

Racism is both a football and societal issue, and it is clear that we are living in a climate of rising hatred and tribalism across the world. In this country, the situation is no different and the language of division has become normalised within our political debate – and our politicians must take the lead in countering that. In that context, it is no surprise to see a rise in reported incidents in English football. But it is also important to note that racism in the game has now become a far more mainstream topic – which we believe is encouraging supporters to take action and report abuse they see or hear.

Revealingly, Paul Canoville told *The Independent* on 11 December 2018 of the abuse during his playing days:

I held a lot of tension . . . we're never told to tell our problems outside of the house. 'Your problem stays here. You don't tell anyone nothing.' That's what it was for me. I couldn't talk to anybody. You'd ask me if I was alright and I'd say 'Yeah, I'm smiling.' But I wasn't alright . . . And that's probably why I didn't do anything when I was receiving the racism at Chelsea. I didn't complain. I thought if I complained they're going to think I was a wimp. Or if I did make noise, it'd be like 'Well here's this boy, he can't be accepted, he's making aggro, got to get him out.' That's the reason I kept my mouth shut. I don't know why I went through that for three years and not say a thing.

Over thirty years later – when racism was officially denigrated in a way it had emphatically not been during Canoville's playing days – another black Chelsea player who did speak out was shunned by the English governing body, the Football Association.

Eniola Aluko from Birmingham was one of only eleven women footballers to have played more than a hundred times for England. A prolific scorer for her country and for her club Chelsea, she became the first female pundit on BBC's flagship football programme *Match of the Day*. A qualified lawyer, she graduated from Brunel University London with a first in 2008. Football mad from the age of five, she was the only girl on her Birmingham housing estate who played with the boys, some of whose parents complained she was 'too good' for the then only available boys youth teams. By the time she was fifteen, Aluko joined Birmingham City Ladies, where her coach labelled her the 'Wayne Rooney of women's football'. Stocky with explosive pace, she was soon selected for England's youth team, quickly making her mark with free-scoring skills and later joining Chelsea, becoming an important part of their women's championship and cup-winning sides.

Aluko moved to Juventus in Italy in June 2018, also enjoying a successful time there – winning the league and cup double, and finishing the season as the club's top scorer. But, despite her impressive form, Aluko was not selected for England's 2019 World Cup squad. In January 2020, she was appointed football director for Aston Villa Women.

The story went back to the appointment of a new England women's coaching team in January 2014 under manager Mark Sampson. One coach spoke to her in a fake Caribbean accent. 'I was tempted to speak to him in a Scottish accent, despite knowing he was Welsh,' Aluko recalled. Then she was accused of being 'lazy', an extremely charged word for black footballers. As Aluko told the *Guardian* on 24 August 2019: 'Look, lazy is a generic term. Anybody can be called lazy if you're not tracking back. But if you're black and you're called lazy, it's different. Some words have real context to them, and this dates back to slavery times. In that split second, I'm sure [the coach] didn't think about racial connotations, but that's what racism can be.' In 2004 the former Manchester United manager, Ron Atkinson, was sacked as a TV pundit after remarking quite erroneously that the renowned former French International and Chelsea defender Marcel Desailly 'is what is known in some schools as a fucking lazy thick nigger'.

When in November 2014 Aluko told Sampson that some family members were flying in from Nigeria for an England friendly against Germany, he remarked: 'Well, make sure they don't come over with Ebola.' In October 2015 when her black teammate from Chelsea, Drew Spence, was selected for England, Sampson said: 'Haven't you been arrested before, then? Four times, isn't it?' Spence, the only black player present, had never been arrested. Sampson did not pick her again for England.

Rather like Canoville decades before, Aluko told the *Guardian* that she remained reluctant to call out Sampson's behaviour. 'As black players, you don't always want to be bringing these issues up. You want to just play football. You know that the accusations of "playing the race card" are going to come up. So I would bite my tongue. I'd see the level of ignorance, roll my eyes and get on with it.'

But when in May 2016 she was asked by the Football Association (FA) confidentially to describe her experiences as a black woman in the England team, she said that she felt demoralised under Sampson's management. Despite explicit prior assurances, the exchange obviously did not remain confidential and within two weeks an angry Sampson told her she was being dropped.

Then followed a familiar cycle for whistle-blowers. Despite Aluko putting her grievances into writing in 2016, the FA cleared Sampson and his coaches of any wrongdoing. After Aluko threatened to take the FA to court, it held a second investigation, which again cleared Sampson and his staff, though Aluko received an £80,000 settlement.

It was not until Aluko decided to speak out in an interview in August 2017 with *Guardian* journalist Daniel Taylor that the FA finally began to take her seriously, and soon sacked Sampson, albeit on a pretext. A third FA investigation concluded in October 2017 that Sampson had racially abused Aluko and Spence. Although insisting that Sampson was not racist, the review concluded that 'on two separate occasions, Sampson has made ill-judged attempts at humour, which, as a matter of law, were discriminatory on the grounds of race within the meaning of the Equality Act 2010.' The FA finally apologised to both players, and Aluko gave compelling evidence before the parliamentary Digital, Culture, Media and Sport Committee in October 2017.

In January 2019 Sampson apologised to Aluko and Spence, saying: 'As a whte male, I needed to do more and I've worked hard to educate myself. I spent six weeks with Kick It Out on their educational course for equality and diversity. I need to play a more active role in making a difference. It's something I will do for the rest of my life.'

But neither of the women played for England again. Of Aluko's England women's teammates, only Fran Kirby and Karen Carney (also Chelsea teammates) maintained close friendships, while others failed to stay in touch, let alone support her.[390]

In the European Championship football qualifier against Bulgaria on 17 October 2019, England's black players faced an ugly torrent of racist abuse, monkey chants and *Sieg Heil* Hitler salutes from fans, some of whom were from neo-Nazi groups that had plagued Bulgarian football for decades.

These racists at Vasil Levski stadium in Sofia ignored warnings before the match and the strategically placed anti-racism observers, supplied by Football Against Racism in Europe (FARE), which had been working closely with UEFA to report on any incidents.

Former England under-21 player Marvin Sordell argued that England's team 'should have made a statement and walked off the pitch in Sofia . . . I can't see how . . . staying on the pitch and continuing to get abuse is the players winning.' He criticised UEFA for not having tough enough rules, such as suspending countries and clubs with racist fans from its competitions, though after the match the national team manager, the Bulgarian Football Union president and the entire executive committee resigned.

Bulgarian home supporters had already been found guilty of racist behaviour in matches against the Czech Republic and Kosovo in June 2019; the problem was deep-rooted in society. 'Bulgaria and racism, the two go hand-in-hand. It's our reality, we live it every day. I'm sorry for the England players who were targeted but, in truth, this was pretty minor for us,' a taxi driver described as having a 'dark complexion' told the *Guardian*.

England players had also been racially abused during a Euro 2020 qualifier in Montenegro in March 2019, and Wolverhampton Wanderers' Europa League game away to Slovan Bratislava in October 2019 was played behind closed doors after the Slovak side had been fined €50,000 (£45,000) for the racist behaviour of their supporters and an additional €41,750 for similar transgressions.

Former Chelsea and Manchester United striker and Belgian international Romelu Lukaku in September 2019 scored in his first two games for Internazionale, but also found himself a victim of the worst elements of Italian football culture. After being targeted with monkey chants during their win at Cagliari, he was addressed with an open letter from a group of his own club's fans insisting he ought not to interpret such abuse as racist. The Inter ultras portrayed themselves as the persecuted party. As Nicky Bandini commented in the *Guardian*, 'It is a narrative that ties together with far-right politics: the suggestion that free speech is under attack from an authoritarian establishment.'

That in turn reflects a widespread trend across Europe of far-right groups attracting populist backing, often through frenzied social media, for their claims of 'victimisation', frequently when projecting avowedly racist, Islamophobic or anti-Semitic agendas.

After Chelsea defender Antonio Rüdiger was targeted for racist abuse by Tottenham fans shouting a monkey chant at him on 22 December 2019, Sky Sports commentator and former England player Gary Neville was applauded for saying that the Premier League needed to 'stand up' to the problem. He said that while critics were quick to point out racist incidents occurring abroad, 'we have a racism problem in the Premier League in

England and the Premier League have got to stand up, they hide behind the FA [Football Association] on this issue'.

Importantly, Neville added that racism in football was mirrored in UK politics and criticised both the Conservatives and Labour for not doing enough to stamp out racism in their parties. The Conservative Party had been accused by its former chair, Baroness Warsi, for harbouring hard-right Islamophobia – the leader, Boris Johnson, also having made anti-Muslim comments. Similarly, there was widespread criticism by senior Labour figures and from the Jewish community who accused Jeremy Corbyn, then Labour leader, of tolerating antisemitism.

Human rights and sports issues intertwined

Right across the world, controversies over governmental policy and civil rights continue to bubble up in sport. Under apartheid, there was an umbilical cord between politics and sport. But in many, if not all, other countries the link remains, and commercialism has added to the mix.

The interface between freedom of speech in sport and commercial gain was sharply exhibited during 2019 basketball matches after civil rights protests were suppressed in Hong Kong. Groups of fans expressing solidarity with protesters by wearing masks (like them) and 'Stand with Hong Kong' T-shirts stood in protest at the Brooklyn Nets pre-season finale at Hong Kong's Barclays Center. China's state broadcaster duly blacked out games by teams from the National Basketball Association (NBA), the premier men's professional league in North America, considered to be the best in the world.

Prior to that, the Houston Rockets general manager, Daryl Morey, had tweeted his support for pro-democracy protesters in Hong Kong. But the Rockets stated that his views did not reflect those of the team and the NBA hastily distanced itself from Morey's tweet, regretting it had caused offence. The Chinese government threatened to cut ties with the NBA and some Chinese companies withdrew sponsorship.

Under further pressure, the NBA commissioner Adam Silver said, 'I understand there are consequences from his freedom of speech and we will have to live with those consequences.' In turn Chinese state television announced: 'We're strongly dissatisfied and oppose Adam Silver's claim to support Morey's right to freedom of expression. We believe any remarks that challenge national sovereignty and social stability are not within the scope of freedom of speech.'

The NBA, praised for encouraging its players to voice their views on social and human rights issues, had a relationship with China worth tens of millions of dollars to the league and its players. *Guardian* journalist Marina Hyde wrote on 23 October 2019:

> the tale should also be cautionary for the Premier League and its bigger clubs, which have ever-increasing commercial and even physical presences in China. If athletes or management staff or even banner-toting fans should speak out visibly on this, or other current or future Chinese issues, it feels reasonable to assume some version of the NBA saga could take place . . . All sorts of sports may find their businesses getting sucked into this nasty business because, instead of staying the irrelevance they may prefer, the question is moving centre stage: what price market access?

Former England international footballer Eniola Aluko agreed, arguing in a *Guardian* blog on 19 December 2019: 'Players have beliefs and ideals just like anybody else and so long as they are not discriminatory or offensive they have the right to express them without reprimand. They can use social media to bring attention to certain things that are going on in the game, but they are members of society too and should not be restricted to commenting on football.' She was commenting after Arsenal playmaker Mesut Özil criticised China's discriminatory treatment of its Uighur Muslim citizens.

Özil, a Turkish-origin German and practising Muslim, had described the Uighurs as 'warriors who resist persecution', stating that the Chinese authorities had burned Qur'ans, closed down mosques and killed religious scholars. The Chinese Football Association condemned his comments and Özil was removed from the Chinese versions of FIFA and the Pro Evolution Soccer 2020 video games.

Özil was hardly being controversial. A UN panel and human rights groups had previously condemned the detention of millions of Uighur people in internment camps for compulsory 're-education', with evidence from inmates of torture, rape and abuse.

Clearly embarrassed by Özil's comments, Arsenal publicly stated that they were his personal views and that Arsenal 'is always apolitical as an organisation'. Its match against Manchester City was subject to a Chinese state media blackout with the club warned that this could be maintained if it did not apologise. Former Manchester City star and fellow Muslim Yaya Touré – a vocal campaigner against racism in football – said Özil was 'wrong' and should 'stick to football'.

Guardian journalist Andrew Anthony wrote on 21 December 2019: 'Oddly, Arsenal felt no need to publicly assert their apolitical neutrality when, the day before Özil's message, their vice-captain, Héctor Bellerín, put out a tweet on the morning of the [UK] general election with the hashtag "FuckBoris".' Bellerin had urged a vote for Labour, arguably more overtly 'political' than backing human rights. Anthony continued: 'Özil had spoken out on what is unquestionably the largest, most systematic and flagrant case of religious persecution in the world, and the reaction of his sport was to push him away, as though he were a reckless troublemaker. Cynics might conclude that Özil's isolation is not entirely unrelated to China's growing importance to English football: China recently signed a £540 million broadcast deal with the Premier League, and Chinese investors have put a similar amount into Man City, Southampton and Wolverhampton Wanderers.'

Another *Guardian* journalist, Sean Ingle, wrote on 16 December 2019:

> The decision by CCTV not to show Arsenal's match against Manchester City is another reminder that there is no middle ground here. No way to stick up for human rights and free speech without angering China. You are either for such values or against them. Simon Chadwick, a professor of sports enterprise at Salford University who specialises in China argued: 'The world is in the midst of an ideological battle: western liberalism versus eastern authoritarianism. And sport is one of the front lines. This case reveals a great deal about China's growing power, how it seeks to exercise it, and what it deems to be acceptable and unacceptable. It also reveals how far the balance of power has tipped away from Europe and towards China.'

That geopolitical dimension to sport was also starkly revealed when cricket, tennis and climate change collided.

Bushfires devoured Australia in 2019 to 2020, the hottest, driest year on record, incinerating over 10 million hectares, killing a billion animals, destroying over 2,000 properties and near-eclipsing sunlight. Club and provincial cricket games were abandoned or cancelled, dense dark smoke over the Manuka Oval in Canberra causing one match to be stopped, the ground reportedly toasting bare feet. There were fears that the third test between Australia and New Zealand in Sydney would have to be halted, with temperatures threatening to reach 45 degrees Celsius and air quality near toxic. 'This is a challenge on two metrics: visibility and breathing,' an Australia cricket spokesperson explained.

Barney Ronay caustically observed in the sports pages of the *Guardian* on 3 January 2020:

> in reality sport cares only about growth, profit and consumption. There will be platitudinous noises and pledges. But at the elite level sport is run, funded and used as a reputation-garnish by the world's greatest carbon-gorgers. There will be no rainbow coalition of FIFA-ICC-IOC junketers holding hands to save the planet, not unless the people of the earth can crowdfund a sufficiently tempting 'special payments' fund. As for sport, it is still pretty useful as a way of shining some light. For one thing, here we are talking about climate emergency and destruction of the natural world because the test match might be affected. There are details here you can grasp. That thing you love is in peril. Plus there is something painful and indeed strangely beautiful in the fact cricket is caught up in this, if only because cricket is so vital to the way Australia perceives itself: those dreamy white figures out there in all that pastoral green, a vision of Australia's own youth and strength and righteousness.

The bushfires also disrupted the 2020 Grand Slam tennis match at Melbourne Park swathed in toxic fog, delaying the start by an hour and causing a desperate player, Slovenian Dalila Jakupović, to collapse on her knees, agonised, short of breath and suffering a coughing fit. She was forced to retire midway through her qualifying match and later said she had no previous respiratory issues and had never suffered from asthma. 'I was really scared that I would collapse. I couldn't walk anymore,' she said, criticising officials for allowing the match to go ahead in the first place after other players also struggled to breath and called several medical timeouts.

However, obviously uncomfortable about the way global sport was increasingly finding itself at the epicentre of politics and sport, the International Olympic Committee (IOC) in January 2020 published new guidelines for the Olympic Charter's Rule 50. These prohibited athletes from making political protests, like the anti-racist fists raised by American sprinters Tommie Smith and John Carlos at the 1968 Mexico City Games.

'It is a fundamental principle that sport is neutral and must be separate from political, religious or any other type of interference,' the IOC document stated, 'No kind of demonstration or political, religious or racial propaganda is permitted in any Olympic sites, venues or other areas.' The IOC said prohibited protests included any political messaging, like signs or armbands; gestures, including hand gestures or kneeling; and any refusal to follow protocol at ceremonies.

This came after two US athletes were reprimanded by their own Olympic Committee for anti-racist, anti-President Trump medal podium protests at the Pan American Games in August 2019. IOC president Thomas Bach said politicians and athletes should keep politics out of the Games: 'The mission of the Olympics is to unite and not to divide. We are the only event in the world that gets the entire world together in a peaceful competition. I ask them [politicians and athletes] to respect this mission of the Olympic Games and in order to accomplish this mission we must be politically neutral. Otherwise we would end up in this divisive and boycott situation. I ask them to respect this political neutrality by not using them [the Olympics] as a stage for their political purposes.'

Megan Rapinoe, outspoken captain of the World Cup-winning US football team, was blunt about this IOC initiative: 'So much being done about protests. So little being done about what we are protesting about. We will not be silenced.'

Footballer Eniola Aluko, whose brush with racism and views on free speech have been mentioned above, weighed in, arguing in her *Guardian* blog (19 December 2019):

> From Tommie Smith and John Carlos raising their fists at the 1968 Olympics, to Billie Jean King and the fight for gender equality in tennis and, more recently, Colin Kaepernick's protests about America's treatment of minorities, sportspeople have used their platform to make their voices heard and have an effect on society. They cannot and should not be censored. Sometimes, they are the changemakers we need. There are many issues cultural figures can have way more impact on than politicians and history shows that it is worth players speaking up to support whatever cause they believe in.

In late 2018 Bahraini footballer Hakeem al-Araibi was detained in Thailand for seventy-six days while on honeymoon. Kept in a filthy cell alongside forty-five others, he was not allowed to speak to his newly wed wife. The Bahraini government had placed him on Interpol's Red Notice database – a procedure they and other authoritarian regimes have manipulated to hunt critics. But his detention provoked a global campaign, especially in his adopted country of Australia to which he had fled in 2014 after being jailed and beaten during a crackdown on pro-democracy athletes (he was later sentenced in absentia to ten years in jail for an offence he could not have committed because he was playing in a televised football match at the time).

Al-Araibi's arrest followed his criticism that the Asian Football Confederation president, the FIFA vice-president and Bahraini royal Sheikh Salman al-Khalifa were all complicit in human rights abuses in Bahrain, including of footballers and other sportspeople.

He was finally released after Thai authorities withdrew an extradition case against him, stating that the Bahraini government had decided to end its pursuit of al-Araibi. FIFA and the Australian government had vocally supported the campaign for his release, amongst others. Al-Araibi wrote in the *Guardian* on 27 February 2019:

> Evidently, it is a myth that sports and politics do not mix. Authoritarian states use sports to raise their profile, like the World Cup, or Formula One races. But when athletes and individuals call attention to this practice they are imprisoned and forcibly silenced. For example, activist Najah Yusuf was harshly interrogated, threatened, physically abused and sexually assaulted for speaking against the Bahrain Grand Prix two years ago. Formula One has never called for her release. Another strong voice, jiujitsu champion Mohamed Mirza, a Bahraini from my hometown, is currently serving an unlawful ten years' imprisonment handed down to him by the military court. He was subjected to brutal torture and continues to languish in the notorious Jau prison. Some people consider my release as a great victory. While I'm happy to be home [in Australia], I cannot help but think that my personal fight is not over. Even now, Bahrain has vowed to 'pursue all necessary legal actions' to drag me back to the place I fled. My brother remains imprisoned there, and I don't believe that I am safe from the Bahraini government.

Television analyst Craig Foster, a former Australian football captain, who had strongly campaigned for al-Araibi's release, wrote in the *Guardian* on 12 February 2019:

> this was a huge challenge for global sport, particularly football. We think that this campaign showed what sport can be, and our job as former players or athletes is to ensure that all sport becomes the vanguard for human rights. Stepping forward to uphold the human rights of everyone within the game should be a natural part of its value system. As players, we believe in protecting a fellow colleague very deeply and will take every step to do so, now it is time for those in positions of governance to be held to the same standards.

In Berlin at the time of the Nazi Olympics in 1936, the topography of terror encompassed gypsies, Jews, homosexuals, people with physical disabilities and mental problems, liberals, progressives, socialists and trade unionists targeted randomly by the SS and the police with an overriding loyalty to the Führer. The Nazi creed was that homosexuals were 'sexual degenerates', destroying the purity of the Aryan race, just as Jews were.

The rampant homophobia of that time was widespread across the world, and continued also in Britain, ameliorated only in 1967 when homosexuality was decriminalised. Homophobia across all sports was widely institutionalised and remains rampant, with players still being targeted by clubs and national officials in sport globally.

In the 1980s and 1990s Chelsea and England star Graeme Le Saux faced homophobic crowd rants and prejudice from opposing players even though he was not gay: this prejudice was apparently directed at him because – usually for a top footballer – he read the *Guardian* newspaper and expressed progressive views. He also played in fundraising matches for the ANC and at her eightieth birthday party in South Africa House in 2007 presented Peter's mother Adelaine with one of his Chelsea shirts.

A report by Britain's Parliamentary Culture, Media and Sport Committee in 2017 insisted that sport was not doing enough to tackle homophobic abuse and recommended a zero-tolerance approach by sports authorities, including lengthy bans on offenders. In late August 2019 the Ligue 1 football game between Nice and Marseille was suspended for ten minutes after supporters unfurled banners displaying homophobic messages in the stands and chanted offensive slogans. Earlier that month a Ligue 2 match between

Nancy and Le Mans was briefly stopped amid homophobic chanting and there were also incidents in Brest versus Reims and Monaco versus Nîmes fixtures. But that was simply the tip of an iceberg of prejudice which infected sport just as it infected politics and societies across the world.

Almost nowhere in contemporary times has the intrusion of politics into sport been more stark than in international football matches between the two Koreas. Their World Cup qualifier in Seoul in April 2009 saw the North Korea coach, Kim Jong-hun, entering the post-match press conference flanked by two minders, taking no questions and wearing a trench coat. He accused the hosts of poisoning his players and then stormed out, pushing bewildered South Korea FA officials out of the way.

A few months earlier, the qualifier that had been scheduled to be held in Pyongyang, with the two countries technically still at war, was moved by North Korean Leader Kim Jong-il to Shanghai. That was to avoid South Korea's flag and anthem being presented in the stadium named after North Korea's founder, Kim Il-sung. The game in China was filled with emotion and stiff politeness.

Ten years later, controversy again engulfed their World Cup qualifier when the two teams did meet in Pyongyang on 15 October 2019, playing out a goalless draw in the monster Kim Il-sung Stadium, with no spectators and a media blackout. North Korea's team played like it was 'waging a war', said South Korea's manager, Choi Young-il, when the team returned to Seoul, claiming they were violently swinging their elbows and hands and driving into their opponents knee-first when competing for balls in the air. 'I have never seen something like this in soccer before,' he said. South Korea's captain and Tottenham striker Son Heung-min added, 'It's an accomplishment that we returned from a game like that without injury.'

When not playing or training, South Korea players and staff were holed up in a hotel with no other guests and no outside contact, having been required to leave their mobile phones at the South Korean embassy in Beijing.

*

Saudi Arabia, under its self-styled 'modernising' Crown Prince, Mohammed bin Salman bin Abdulaziz Al Saud (complicit in the grisly 2018 murder of Saudi journalist Jamal Ahmad Khashoggi), had meanwhile launched a big initiative to attract global sports events with lucrative opportunities, such as the heavyweight boxing rematch between Anthony Joshua and Andy Ruiz Jr in December 2019 being a prime-time global TV event. Promoter Eddie Hearn explained: 'The plan is to make Saudi Arabia the home of mega boxing. All due respect to Las Vegas, but this place has the ability to bring any fight they want here.'

Hearn also insisted that criticism of the heavyweight title rematch just outside the Saudi capital, Riyadh, was unfair.

> I was driving up and down the road last night thinking of all the criticism I've been getting. And I passed Gucci, Starbucks, Dunkin' Donuts, Versace and Ralph Lauren. And although it is easy for us to also say Formula E, the tennis Super Cup, and the PGA Tour is here too, I also believe that no one has the right to tell a fighter how and where they can earn their money. Our job is to provide opportunities to the fighters. If I put a proposal in front of Joshua and he said to me he was going to Saudi Arabia, and I advised him against, he would say: 'See ya.'

This despite Amnesty International warning that the Saudi authorities were using the fight to sportswash its image. Amnesty insisted that despite what it described as 'hype over supposed reforms' the country was 'in the midst of a sweeping human-rights crackdown' adding that any regime critics were 'exiled, arrested or threatened', and there is 'no semblance of free speech or the right to protest'.

In response, Hearn stated that the country was modernising for the better. 'The Saudis want to show they are changing. And they want a more positive image worldwide by bringing in events. But isn't that what they should be doing? They have got to change, and they are changing. But the great news is that boxing is going to be responsible for those changes – and that shows you the power of sport. There will be loads of women at the fight on Saturday. The sportswashing thing is something over my head,' he added, in terms redolent of sportspeople playing with apartheid.

Caster, Megan and #MeToo: The new revolution in sport

The last frontier for freedom in twenty-first-century sport is that of gender equality, a strong voice being US women's football captain and World Cup winner Megan Rapinoe. It is unusual, unique perhaps, for a sports star to become a role model for outspoken criticism of homophobia, racism and gender discrimination, despite attracting considerable abuse, harassment and official sanction.

In 2016 Rapinoe expressed solidarity with San Francisco 49ers quarterback Colin Kaepernick's 'knees down' protest against racial injustice, by kneeling during the national anthem for both club and US team football games. In response, the US Soccer Federation passed a bylaw stating that any player who didn't stand for the anthem would face punishment, threatening her place in the national team. She stood firm and was selected anyway, becoming team captain, the US football establishment's unease at her forthrightness apparently supplanted by her enormous ability.

Before the 2019 Women's World Cup, Donald Trump had tweeted criticism of Rapinoe, chastising her for not respecting 'our Country, the White House or our Flag' after she said she did not want to visit the White House whilst he was president. ('I'm not going to the fucking White House', she said.) Rapinoe promptly scored twice in her next game between the United States and France. For good measure, Rapinoe scored again in the World Cup final, which the United States won, and left with an armful of trophies. In media interviews she told Trump: 'Your message is excluding people. You're excluding me, you're excluding people that look like me, you're excluding people of colour'. She also said: 'Being a gay American, I know what it means to look at the flag and not have it protect all of your liberties. It was something small that I could do and something that I plan to keep doing in the future and hopefully spark some meaningful conversation around it.' After coming out in 2012, Rapinoe became a forceful advocate for LGBTQ rights, including working with the Gay, Lesbian and Straight Education Network (GLSEN).

Also vocal about pay equality, she was among five national team players who lent their names to a complaint filed with the US Equal Employment Opportunity Commission alleging wage discrimination and claiming women football internationals were paid up to four times less than their male national team counterparts.

She joined Barcelona legend Lionel Messi in being crowned 2019 players of the year at The Best FIFA Football Awards ceremony. Rapinoe had dazzled on and off the pitch at the 2019 World Cup, finishing with the golden ball, golden boot and World Cup trophy, speaking out against Donald Trump and pressing FIFA to equalise investment in the women's game. Yet receiving the award she quipped, 'I'm a little at a loss for words, that very rarely happens to me,' before thanking her teammates, 'who let me be a little bit wild at times but reel me in when needed.' Characteristically, she then used her FIFA awards platform to say she had been inspired by football bravery the past year. She first cited England player Raheem Sterling's denunciation of racism. Then Napoli's Kalidou Koulibaly, who, subjected to monkey chants by Internazionale fans, had said, 'I am proud of the colour of my skin.' Rapinoe also saluted Iranian computer scientist Sahar Khodayari, who died a week after setting herself on fire in the face of a six-month sentence for defying a ban on women attending football matches; in March 2019 she had tried to enter Tehran's Azadi Stadium (*azadi* meaning freedom) dressed as a man, to watch her favourite football team, Esteghlal.

As a footnote, perhaps Rapinoe's advocacy has had an impact. Six months after Sahar Khodayari's death, and for the first time since the 1979 Islamic revolution, women were permitted to watch Iran play Cambodia in a World Cup qualifier in the same Azadi Stadium. This was on FIFA's insistence or else the match would have been cancelled – and even then women were confined to just 3,500 segregated seats, 4.5 per cent of the capacity. Amnesty International observed that the restrictions and lack of commitment beyond a single event showed that the game was being used as a 'cynical publicity stunt'. The tickets for women reportedly sold out within minutes and photos from inside the stadium showed women football fans excitedly waving Iranian flags and cheering on their team, elated to see Iran win the match 14–0.

'If we really want to have meaningful change, everyone needs to be outraged. That would be the most inspiring thing to me,' Megan Rapinoe had told the FIFA audience. 'We have so much success, we have incredible platforms. I ask everybody here to lend your platform, to lift people up, to use this beautiful game to change the world for everyone.'

After winning the 2019 World Cup, US manager Jill Ellis paid tribute to her Golden Boot and Golden Ball winger. 'Megan was built for this, built for these moments, built to be a spokesperson,' Ellis said. 'She's eloquent. She speaks well and from the heart. I never had any worries about Megan speaking out. The bigger the spotlight, the more she shines.'

Viewing figures for the 2019 Women's football World Cup were huge, reaching over a billion. But although the US women's national team actually generated more income than the men's, their players were paid less. Comparing the $30 million prize pot for the 2019 Women's World Cup with the

$400 million prize pot for the 2018 Men's World Cup, the *Guardian*'s Suzanne Wrack wrote on 22 October 2019, 'it is clear that we are putting separate values on the two competitions. Somewhere it has been decided that the women's tournament is worth 7.5 per cent of the men's.' Pointing out that the Women's World Cup viewing figures were 31 per cent of the men's, she asked, 'why do we not use that figure to determine the women's share?' As Rapinoe insisted, the women's game 'has proved World Cup after World Cup, year after year that we are worthy of investment and the quality on field is there and we need the business step to be in line with the steps we are making in performing on the field.'

Upon being nominated for the *Guardian*'s Footballer of the Year, Rapinoe told Wrack (30 December 2019):

> Everybody has a personal responsibility to do what they can to make the world a better place in the most impactful way that they can. This is it, this is the moment and I'm so aware and understand that. I'm not just winning all these awards because I had a great year. It's the culmination of it all. And with that comes so many other people: it comes with the team and what we've been able to do and the way we are organised and the way we fight together on and off the field; it comes from Colin Kaepernick, from MeToo; it comes from all of these other movements.

Rapinoe told Wrack that she had no regrets over rebuffing President Trump. Responding to the criticism that she could 'just stick to the football' to quieten things, Rapinoe said, 'I just don't compartmentalise that way.' She could not understand how footballers steered clear of having a say on politics and society: 'You live in the world, in the city, you pay the taxes, you are affected by it all, so to think you can just be away from it is stupid.'

Also unrepentant about speaking out against racism, Rapinoe said: 'Being white is part of the reason why it's culminating with me. The system is alive and well, so I think it's important to just say that. It's not my fault I'm benefiting but I am, so it's my responsibility to acknowledge that and to try to dismantle that system. I think it's really important to say those words, say "white privilege", acknowledge the fact it's happening.'

*

If Rapinoe and the US football team are an example of American women fighting systemic discrimination and opening up new vistas in sport, Mokgadi Caster Semenya is the most famous South African athlete who has reached great heights and crossed new thresholds.

A world and double Olympic 800-metre champion, Semenya won around thirty consecutive top flight races between September 2015 and May 2019, and became a global icon – at great personal cost – forcing the tradition-bound sports world to confront gender questions of 'What is the definition of a genuine women'.[391] Indeed, the dramatic publicity she generated 'changed how the sport interprets science and human biology'.[392]

Her case triggered gender ructions throughout athletics and sport in general. From poverty-stricken girl to world-beating woman, the complex and sensitive issues she faced surfaced to the top of raging controversies over transgender athletes, as well as the historic discrimination against sportswomen, who still suffer in terms of status, opportunities and rewards.

Semenya found herself unfairly enveloped in the trans-gender cauldron, when she had been diagnosed by some as having 'intersex' characteristics: that is, according to the UN Office of the High Commissioner for Human Rights, individuals who 'do not fit the typical definitions for male or female bodies'.

Prominent British Paralympic multi-gold medallist, Tanni Grey-Thompson – a brilliant athlete competing in her wheelchair and in retirement a champion for disability access and equal opportunities for women – comments: 'As ever, there is more politics in sport than in politics. In testing for performance-enhancing drugs, testosterone is one of many substances where there are levels which are accepted as naturally occurring in male and female athletes. The debate then often gets conflated and rolled into the debate of transwomen in sport which, while different, also discusses what is an appropriate level of testosterone in the system. Where the two worlds cross over is the debate about what level "male" advantage gives, with the media often mixing the two up.'

In an article in *The Times* on 3 September 2019, British transgender rugby player Debbie Hayton argued passionately that the slogan 'Trans women are women' was 'vacuous rhetoric that has led us away from truth and into a land of make-believe . . . By carrot and stick – appealing to their good nature while denouncing dissenters as bigots – women have come under pressure to accept trans women like me not as allies but as actual women. Objections based on biology are dismissed as unkind in a world

where feelings take precedence over facts.' She added: 'However, incon-
venient truth is still truth and in sport, biology matters when segregating
the sexes. Whatever female hormones transwomen might take, we are still
on average taller, faster and stronger than women. We keep our larger hearts
and male muscles, and we do not lose bone density.'

She insisted that in rugby, the inclusion of transwomen is not only unfair, it's unsafe: 'Research backs up my own experience: we transwomen
maintain a competitive advantage over women when we transition, despite
hormone treatment . . . The answer to this problem is staring us in the face.
We transwomen should compete against, and alongside, men in open competition. We can campaign for separate facilities to protect our dignity –
and distinct record-keeping that recognises our success – but let's leave
female sport to female people. We owe it to our daughters.'

A speech by Dr Emma Hilton, a specialist in biological medicine at the
University of Manchester, set out the main questions on the male/female
athletic comparison in a lecture on 10 July 2019: 'That males as a class are
stronger than females as a class is not controversial . . . Males can run faster,
jump longer, throw further and lift heavier than females. So early does the
gap emerge, the current female 100-metre Olympic champion, Elaine
Thompson, is slower than the fourteen-year-old schoolboy record holder.'

Dr Hilton cited a long list of physical differences producing greater male
athletic prowess: 'The majority of these differences are likely driven by
testosterone-fuelled puberty – it is one hell of a drug. It has delivered us
athletes like Usain Bolt and Michael Phelps. As the original anabolic steroid,
used widely in the 1980s in state-led doping programmes, it has almost
certainly delivered us a fair few elite females too.'

Semenya grew up playing football a world away from such complexities
and controversies, in the village of Masehlong in the rural Limpopo province, where even today people are smelled out for being 'witches' who bring
misfortune to the community; she played with boys, training daily and,
often running between villages, developed a pace and an unerring instinct
to win.

She was talented enough that by the time she left school she was offered
a place at the new University of the North West, which, ironically, incorporated the formerly whites-only Potchefstroom University for Christian
Higher Education, where the last white apartheid president had studied.
At the age of eighteen, she became the African junior champion in both the
800 and 1500 metres, and later that year, in August 2009, caught the atten-

tion of the athletics world by winning gold at the World Athletics Championships in Berlin.

With her skill and determination, she made the unlikely journey to the top, only to be hit by a tsunami of bureaucracy, convention and international attention that turned her life upside down.

She was forced to undergo what were called 'gender verification tests' by both the national body in South Africa and the International Athletics Federation (IAAF). These tests, critics argued, were not only an invasion of her personal rights, privacy and dignity but also 'a misnomer as gender is a social construct and what was essentially being tested was her biological sex' – something that in itself could not be exactly defined scientifically.[393] The process she was compelled to submit to and results were leaked – sensationally – to the media, which hyped and distorted the story. She was a 'woman and a man', the New York Daily News headline declared.[394] The Sydney Daily Telegraph reported sensationally that the IAAF was 'expected to advise her to have surgery to fix the potential deadly condition'.[395]

The truth was, the IAAF found, Semenya was a woman with a combination of XY chromosomes, and not the XX chromosome combination found amongst most of her competitors, meaning she had significantly higher levels of naturally produced testosterone in her body than the majority of women athletes. This naturally occurring genetic combination gave her 'intersex' characteristics described by the IAAF as 'hyperandrogenism'. Experts have pointed out that 'thousands of women' have similar characteristics,[396] the South African Medical Journal explaining, 'If it were not for the regulations most women athletes with intersex traits might not even be aware of them.'[397]

While the IAAF claimed that thresholds for men and women could be measured accurately in a scientific way, other experts including the World Medical Association disputed that and additionally found such testing unethical. A study of testosterone levels among women and men athletes, for example, found that 13.7 per cent per cent of top women athletes exceeded the 'upper limit of the normal reference range for women', some far above it, while amongst men 16.5 per cent fell 'below the normal male reference range', some far below it.[398]

After her 2009 win, Semenya was declared ineligible to run for eleven months by the athletics authorities. They lifted this ban in July 2010, after she reportedly agreed to subject herself to hormone replacement therapy, a drug treatment to artificially reduce her natural levels of testosterone.

Seemingly as a follow-up, the IAAF in 2011 introduced new 'Hyperandrogen-ism Regulations', setting a maximum level of testosterone. Semenya led the South African team into the stadium as the flagbearer at the 2012 Olympics in London, but her times were noticeably slower and she came second (her medal was subsequently upgraded to gold as the winner had been a doping cheat).

In 2014 the Indian women athlete Dutee Chand legally challenged the IAAF regulations after refusing medical intervention to change a condition that was natural. She won her case and the Court of Arbitration for Sport (CAS) ordered the IAAF to suspend the regulations. It was after this that Semenya enjoyed her run of Olympic and World Championship golds and remained unbeaten for over three years. Her Olympic gold medal in Rio de Janeiro in 2016, won under immense pressure, when she surprised her opponents by going to the front from the start, was one of the performances of the games.

However, in March 2018 the IAAF made it known that it intended changing its regulations once again with regard to what it called 'Athletes with Differences in Sex Development' (DSD). These were formally adopted in April 2019 and came into force that November. Semenya and Athletics South Africa asked the Court of Arbitration to once again resolve the matter. The three-person CAS panel sat in February 2019 and upheld the IAAF regulations with a split decision, despite concluding that they were 'prima facie discriminatory' in nature.[399]

Semenya's lawyers argued that she and other DSD athletes had been born female, had grown up as girls and become women, participating in female sport since childhood. Yet the IAAF's new rules had erected a barrier just when they reached the top of their sport which was palpably unfair. It was tantamount to saying that 'a DSD person is the same as a male athlete' and this was 'a leap beyond the evidence'. American professor Jaime Schultz has written that though Semenya might have benefitted from higher testosterone levels, her times in fact 'don't come anywhere near the times of elite male runners'. And it has been shown that some athletes with heightened tes-tosterone (like Dutee Chand and the earlier example of Maria José Martínez-Patiño) were not particularly competitive in women's events either.

During her travails of more than a decade since 2009, South Africans united behind Semenya saying she was the victim of patriarchy, sexism, racism, human rights violations, poor science and Western arrogance; a talented African women held back because she did not fit outdated binary norms about gender. They declared she was 'our girl' – promoted in newspaper front-page headlines after Rio 2016 to 'our golden girl'. She herself declared, 'God made me the way I am and I accept myself. I am who I am and I'm proud of myself.'[400] In a sense, this was a liberated South African turning the colonial gaze back on Europe itself.

In the popular South African newspaper *City Press*, Mike Siluma criticised the IAAF for 'publicly dissecting athletes like laboratory specimens' and for releasing Semenya's 'intimate anatomical details': 'the actions of the IAAF bring back memories about how science has historically colluded with colonialists and racists to prove the sub-humanity of black people'.[401] He and others specifically linked the case to the experiences of Saartjie Baartman, the 'African Venus', who was transported to Europe to be displayed naked in public, and whose remains were kept in a museum in Paris in the interest of 'science' until they were finally repatriated and buried in South Africa in 2002.[402] The *South African Medical Journal* was amongst those who saw Eurocentric cultural bias at play. It said that Semenya has 'a physique that differs from the traditional European archetype of femininity, but it is considered normal in the global South' and concluded that in this case – acting against a non-doper and prescribing drug treatment – the IAAF 'should be considered the cheat'.[403] The *Guardian* (1 May 2019) reported an expert argument at the court hearing: 'There are some really important questions of science, some of which have answers, many of them that don't. And you had adversarial parties – they want the science they want.' As the debate about Semenya unfolded, it brought to the fore the wide range of prejudices women still experienced in sport, especially those patently not conforming to its patriarchal history, traditions and notions of femininity.

Some gender activists saw the tests on Semenya as part of a historical continuum of discrimination against women in sport. After the Second World War, participating countries at the Olympics had to submit certificates to confirm the athletes were female. They were also 'visually scored' on whether they were women or not according to the oddly named Ferriman-Gallwey hirsutism scoring system and for a short while, the IOC introduced 'a visual inspection of the genitalia of female Olympians by a panel of physicians'.[404]

Madeleine Pape competed for Australia in the 800 metres against Semenya in the 2009 World Athletics Championships; in an article in the *Guardian* (1 May 2019) she argued that the IAAF and CAS were wrong for excluding Semenya and other women athletes for with naturally high levels of testosterone. Having initially opposed Semenya competing against athletes like her, she 'encountered the vast literature written by advocates of women's sport who oppose the exclusion of women athletes with naturally high testosterone for both scientific and ethical reasons: scientifically, because biological sex and athletic ability are both far too complex for scientists to reduce to measures of testosterone, and ethically, because these regulatory efforts have always been characterised by considerable harm to the women athletes singled out for testing.'

Semenya's supporters made the case that her genetic advantages were no different from those of other exceptional athletes – such as the Finnish cross-country skier Eero Mäntyranta, who was born with a genetic mutation that increased his haemoglobin level to about 50 per cent. Or Usain Bolt with his fast-twitch fibres. Or Michael Phelps with a body uniquely shaped for swimming. Silvia Camporesi, a lecturer at King's College, London, argued that Semenya would never have become an international guinea pig 'if she had had not run so damn fast', adding: 'The fact remains that female athletes who do not conform to the norms imposed by society . . . are challenged under the guise of biological or genetic abnormalities that bestow an unfair advantage.'[405] Camporesi continued: 'Olympic athletes are way out at the tail ends of the Gaussian curve of normal species functioning because all kinds of generic and biological variations that, together with character traits such as mental toughness, make them what they are: elite athletes'.

Human rights and constitutional lawyer Pierre de Vos has argued that in a patriarchal world, gender stereotypes are made to seem 'normal' or 'natural' and that the patriarchal culture is deeply invested in 'promoting and policing these stereotypes'. The language used by the IAAF when it said women could only compete if their testosterone levels were 'below the male range' was an example of this 'highly problematic and stereotypical view of who can be a women and who are not allowed to be thought of as women', he said.[406]

Support came also from international tennis icon, Billie Jean King, the UN Human Rights Committee, which supported South Africa's contention that Semenya's treatment was in breach of international human rights conventions,[407] and the World Medical Association (WMA), which advised 'physicians around the world not to implement the new eligibility regulations'. The WMA said these were scientifically flawed, 'contrary to a number of key WMA ethical statements' and should be withdrawn.[408] The *South African Medical Journal* weighed in on a similar level, saying that by 'scrutinising their perceived femininity' the IAAF had for decades been legitimising 'suspicion, speculation and widespread surveillance of female athletes' with the resultant erosion of their 'rights to human dignity, privacy, health, freedom to make health-related choices, employment and livelihood.[409]

The debate around the Semenya's case has been fuelled by the growing assertiveness of twenty-first-century women's rights movements as represented, for example, by the global #MeToo movement and the rise of the Rhodes Must Fall student protests in South Africa, which set in train calls to decolonise educational institutions and their curricula and highlighted gender discrimination as a thread running through the unacceptably high socio-economic inequality and cultural exclusions in the country.

Though the days are long since passed since W. G. Grace said women who played cricket were 'neither ladies nor cricketers', and the founder of the modern Olympics, Pierre de Coubertin, expressed his belief that it was 'against the laws of nature for women to do athletics', prejudices against women in sport remain rampant today.

The three-person CAS panel noted that the Semenya issue involved 'a complex collision of scientific, ethical and legal conundrums' and also 'incompatible, competing rights'. While the panel noted that it 'is the right of every athlete to compete in sport, to have the legal sex and gender identity respected, and to be free of any discrimination' and moreover recognised that the IAAF's regulations were 'prime facie discriminatory', it voted in favour of the IAAF policy to protect certain 'protected classes' of women from others, and accepted the scientific basis on which the IAAF reached its decisions. Thus sporting 'rights' and traditional binary distinctions and views on gender were given precedence of over individual human rights in athletics. The *Guardian*'s Andy Bull, noting that the Court of Arbitration effectively decided that the IAAF is 'justified in discriminating against that minority because it protects the interests of the larger group', concluded that 'rather than resolving the debate, [the decision] has really only just started it'.

IAAF president Sebastian Coe responded: 'It may be in thirty years, forty years' time society takes a different view and we have other classifications, I don't know. But at this point my responsibility was to protect two classifications and that's what we feel we've done . . . I see this as the right decision.'[410]

Semenya's cause became another front in a culture war changing the discourse of sport. She accused the IAAF of using her as a guinea pig and warned she would 'not allow the IAAF to use me and my body again'.[411] She has declared: 'I just want to run naturally, the way I was born. It is not fair that I am told I must change. It is not fair that that people question who I am. I am Mokgadi Semenya Semenya. I am a woman and I am fast.'[412] After her latest banning by the IAAF (upheld by a Swiss federal tribunal in September 2020), she sent out a tweet with the word 'resist' accompanied by a photograph of her with a clenched fist salute in her athletics gear.

In an off-field challenge to old-fashioned gender bias, in 2017 Caster married her fellow athlete Violet Raseboya in a white wedding which was widely reported in South Africa.

Whether activists by inclination or due to the vagaries of history, Semenya and Rapinoe have found themselves engulfed in controversy as pioneers helping to open up twenty-first-century spaces for women in sport and society.

Dream delayed: From 1994 to the 2010 FIFA World Cup and the present

By the time South Africa hosted the FIFA World Cup final at Soccer City stadium in Johannesburg in July 2010, the dreams of 1994 were rapidly fading. Nelson Mandela attended, his deteriorating health abundantly evident as he arrived wrapped in a thick coat and Russian-style fur hat to brave the winter cold, caringly and unavoidably supported by his wife Graça Machel. Nevertheless, his iconic charisma still radiated. Beaming and waving, nearly 85,000 spectators gave him a thunderous standing ovation, with roars, applause and deafening blasts on their vuvuzelas, the raucous trumpet-like horns which had been the hallmark of the matches during the finals. Mandela graced the biggest sporting event in Africa's history – one that would not have been secured in the first placed without his active advocacy. He had 'passed a late fitness test to make the final' somebody tweeted.

As Richard Calland, Lawson Naidoo and Andrew Whaley wrote of the 2010 World Cup staged across South Africa, the first on the continent: 'Oh what fun! Sport is a great escape. That is why we love it. The drama, the intensity and the scale of it – especially football. It is so simple, and yet so profound . . . Like 1994 and Mandela and the "rainbow nation" stuff, the 2010 World Cup will be etched in the collective memory of all South Africans. It reached surprisingly deep.'[413]

They added:

> Every four years the World Cup commands the attention of literally
> billions of people . . . This is the ultimate paradox: the simplest game in
> the world has the most complex political economy; to hold the four-
> yearly festival of football requires an immense organisational capacity;
> yet millions play it in backyards and street alleys and rough-hewn fields.
> Poverty is no bar to playing the game; but the World Cup itself is a
> pageant of elite wealth as well as vivid spectacle. But this is the power of
> football . . . It is the biggest global audience for the globe's biggest sport.

All the international Afropessimist predictions of visitors being robbed, or raped or mugged or killed, of transport chaos and power cuts were completely confounded. The *Financial Times* gave its verdict: hundreds of thousands of visitors to South Africa 'enjoyed a safe and efficiently run tournament'. It proved one of the best ever.

However, there were also the usual downsides to these mega events. The high expense of the grand facilities was challenged, tender irregularities and collusion pushed up prices, bribery and even murder were reported on but not proved, and the inevitable legacy of debt followed, for example, in the Cape Town stadium, which had yet to prove itself financially sustainable a decade later. And, as others pointed out, mega carnivals like this always end up silencing social activists and the poor trying to bring social issues and problems to the attention of those in power.[414]

Madiba's deteriorating health in 2010 and his passing in 2013 in many respects heralded the passing of the dream. In that decade, South Africa descended into an abyss of 'state capture' where a sick liberation movement with a proud history turned into a kleptocratic government practising corruption with smug self-justification. It has been estimated that as much as a trillion rand of state funds were looted or wasted by a self-serving leadership elite and its private sector allies. With the theft and short-sighted arrogance of power, came increasing non-delivery and disregard for the constitution, a betrayal of the visions of the struggle. Then came the stealthy coronavirus in 2020, delivering a double whammy and plunging South Africa's fragile economy into 'junk status', just as it massively affected the global economy.

The South Africa of the 2020s is very different from the one in 1994, and also that of 2010. Those upbeat moments seem far away, the contemporary sometimes a sad parody of the dreams and visions of the past.

Democracy and the free society brought many magnificent benefits, but the country remained deeply fractured and gripped by systemic crisis. Though a sizeable black middle class developed, the great apartheid divides between rich and poor remained a chasm, with unemployment hovering around 40 per cent, and youth unemployment as high as 65 per cent in some areas. Despite a doubling in numbers of black pupils, poor school standards betrayed their potential. Services everywhere fell into parlous decline, a point driven home at the time of writing by the virtual collapse of the national energy generator, Eskom, and the emergence of a new term in the national lexicon – 'outages', regular, unannounced, extended disruptions in the electricity supply bringing national despair and costing the country billions.

Electricity, education, sewerage, water, transport, police, municipal government – a bold auditor general, the former NSC anti-Gatting tour activist, Kimi Makwetu, reported for several years running that only a small percentage of municipalities – not even twenty out of some 270 – were able to provide a clean audit and are therefore properly functional. In his 2020 report, he explained how the Metsimaholo municipality in Free State spent R21.7 million on a sports centre for the local community, but auditors found only a fence. The municipality wrote the amount off as fruitless expenditure and no-one was held accountable for the fraud and non-delivery.[415] In Graaff Reinet in the Eastern Cape, R20 million out of R25 million provided by the government for drought relief went missing and 'cannot be traced'. And while sewage oozes into township streets and water supplies, unauthorised government expenditure ran into hundreds of billions annually, figures that ceased registering on a benumbed citizenry – their trauma exacerbated by the fact that after a quarter of a century in power, the government was by its own admission permeated with corruption from top to bottom, and that state looting and state capture were indeed a reality, Peter in November 2019 giving evidence to an official commission to investigate the crippling problem. Cronyism replaced competence at all levels, disabling the public sector. Crucial state intuitions like the National Prosecuting Authority, Intelligence Services and the Revenue Service were captured and their missions prostituted to turn a blind eye to state-sanctioned criminality.

The once powerful struggle message of unity, hope and accountability invited cynicism and a discourse of division.

The bottom line is that democracy has not distributed its benefits widely enough to meet the needs of the marginalised majority. It is widely accepted across society that the mass of African people in whose name the struggle was waged are excluded from the mainstream economy, and if this situation persists, endemic instability lies ahead for South Africa.

For this reason, too, sport has failed to transform in deep-rooted ways. Inequality in South Africa is systemic and the government and private sector have failed to create a sustainable platform for ensuring socio-economic stability, including well-functioning sports facilities and sports opportunities in the areas where most South Africans live, in the townships. Schools should be the starting point, but these remain inadequately re-sourced and far from being able to provide the levels of coaching and organised sport required. These underlying economic factors – compounded by the poor service delivery and corruption mentioned above, are made worse by attitudinal factor. Old style white privilege and attitudes remain resiliently intact (and fundamentally racist) in many sports, resulting in very slow progress in producing a critical mass of well-supported, top-perfoming young black athletes.

As we have demonstrated in this book, sport mirrors society in many ways. Writing at the time of the celebration of ten years of democracy, André noted that as in broader South African life there had been 'dramatic highs – and dizzying falls, and for every two steps forward in sport, there had been one step back.' This does not seem far off the mark today either – except at times it appears the other way, two staps back and one step forwards.

South Africans have excelled at the Olympics, from Elana Meyer at Barcelona 1992 and Josiah Thugwane at Atlanta 1996, through to the magical Rio 2016 double gold of Caster Semenya and Wayde van Niekerk, and the achievements of Penny Heyns, Chad le Clos and Cameron van der Burgh in the pool. Sibusiso Vilane became the first African to summit Everest and a line of boxers followed the people's champion, Baby Jake Matlala, with his gigantic heart and silky skills, smiling down from the billboards at the time of democracy. The Premier Soccer League is among the ten or so richest leagues in the world and South Africa world cups were spectacular, most notably FIFA 2010. Cricket reached number one in world under rock-jawed Graeme Smith and the Springboks won the Rugby World Cup three times, including the sheer joy of Yokohama 2019.

Three obvious gains on the general level are that sport has been de-racialised (though access to opportunity is still largely shaped by colour). Access and opportunity have increased dramatically. For example, when André was administering at Newlands, the number of children playing cricket in Cape Town had doubled from 11,000 in the early 1990s to 25,000. And in keeping with the equity imperatives of the new democracy, the participation of women in sport has also grown considerably. The women's national football team, Banyana Banyana, under coach Desiree Ellis, captain Janine van Wyk and with star player Thembi Kgatlana, dazzled to reach the 2019 Africa Cup of Nations final. And the first professional women rugby, football and cricket players, as well as sports CEOs and television and radio commentators, have emerged. Girls and women are asserting themselves everywhere in sport.

Fluffy sports unity and notions of sports development moved towards deeper transformation and redress, as glass ceilings were broken around 2000, and today few dispute that the nearly 90 per cent African component of the population demographic of young people constitutes the future sports market and constituency for sport in the country – incidentally, beginning to realise the seemingly impossible inclusive dreams expressed in SACOS and NSC debates about non-racial sport and the goal of a grounded national unity in the 1970s and 1980s.

But the persistence of old anti-transformation attitudes; endless arguments over (necessary for redress) quotas, administrative squabbles and the absence of sport at many schools topped off by inadequate delivery of facilities and resources by government in poor areas remain obstacles.

Pitch Battles deals mainly with the historically grounded struggles against apartheid in sport to create an inclusive, non-racial sporting dispensation, in the quarter of a century or so between those first direct-action demonstrations in 1969–70 and the arrival of democracy in the mid-1990s. The analysis of the following quarter of a century deserves another book. But, summing up: only gradually – and for many, painfully slowly – has sport transformed, become more equal and provided more opportunities. Yet the situation is infinitely better today than it was then. And the struggle for dignity and human rights in sport remains an ongoing necessity, though the context now is a struggling young democracy just turned 26 not an autocratic system of racial tyranny.

Thus, two constant obstacles remain – on the one hand, unacceptable living (and sport) conditions for many sportspeople, and on the other, the persistence of prejudice in play in the form of old mindsets emanating from seventeenth- and eighteenth-century slavery, nineteenth-century British colonialism and twentieth-century apartheid racism. This book hopefully helps explain how they came about and how they can be understood, resisted and changed.

The liberation and sports struggles and the post-1994 democratic government bequeathed South Africa a series of crucial, powerful counter-vailing forces to elitism, inequality and corruption – vital positives not found in many other countries: a robust political opposition; a vibrant civil society; independent media; assertive judiciary not afraid to take on the government; a solid framework of law, financial regulation and corporate governance; and large numbers of public servants who still work hard, resist corruption and political manipulation, and strive for excellence.

Just as sport is shaped by politics, so sport cannot on its own overcome societal inequalities and divisions of class, race, gender, sexuality or religion – especially as in South Africa with deep systemic inequalities and a racist heritage that runs long and deep. But it can and should be organised around the principles of equality for all and against discrimination of any kind. Its leaders and its stars should be expected to stand up for human rights and identify with the challenges of society, including those resilient socio-economic ones that so affect the most vulnerable citizens.

And as brilliant American sports historian Mike Marqusee has reminded us, the idea of the level playing field always operates within societies and contexts which are 'anything but level' and 'access to the level playing field has always been unequal': 'But there is a sting in the tail. On sport's level playing field, it is possible to challenge and overturn the dominant hierarchies of nation, race and class . . . The level playing field can either be a prison or a platform for liberation.'[416]

The 'Mandela miracle', which sport helped to nurture, engendered myths about the transition from brutal apartheid to rainbow democracy, encouraging a tendency to frame the South African story too simplistically. Although the exceptional struggles and visions of that generation with its deep notions of African humanism need to be striven after, its dreams cannot be realised overnight. Advancing social justice whilst delivering economic success in a world of increasing inequality, gripped by the growth-stifling economics of neoliberalism is a formidable challenge.

South Africa's bitter-sweet, up-and-down journey with its many contra-dictions since political freedom in 1994 continued at the IRB rugby World Cup in Japan in late 2019.

'Our Siya'

> *There will be a black Springbok over my dead body.*
>   Dr Danie Craven, 1969

Fifty years after the whites-only Springboks were battered by British anti-apartheid protesters, a multiracial Springbok team under a black captain battered the favourites England to be crowned Rugby World Cup 2019 champions.

Ecstatic scenes back in South Africa prompted captain Siya Kolisi to pronounce: 'I have never seen South Africa like this. We were playing for the people back home. We can achieve anything if we work together as one.'

It is, for us, a fittingly emotional end-point for *Pitch Battles*. Those who ran onto pitches to harass and disrupt the Springboks half a century earlier would never have dared to dream that dream. Equally, those who sacrificed much for the anti-racist sports struggle back home could only marvel at the achievement of what was – arguably for the first time – a world-beating Springbok team that could claim to represent the whole country, even if there was still much to be done to achieve genuine equality of opportunity in rugby, as in all sports. The apartheid ban on black athletes representing their country may have been removed a quarter of a century before, but the struggle against sporting injustice and equality remained unfinished.

Kolisi's journey was an extraordinary one, from abject community poverty to world rugby pinnacle, reported globally as a symbol of transformation. Aged sixteen and living in Port Elizabeth's impoverished black township of Zwide, he watched the Springboks triumph in the 2007 final in a local *shebeen* (bar); it is not recorded if he had eaten that day. As a boy he went to sleep hungry on a pile of cushions on his grandmother's living room floor, never knowing when his next meal was coming. His mother, Phakama, was sixteen herself when he was born, and died when he was fifteen, so Kolisi and his siblings were raised by his grandmother, Nolulamile, who struggled to feed them. Only as a young man did Kolisi get to know his absentee father – yet embraced him at the final, having ensured his father was there on a first ever trip outside South Africa.

Kolisi's local rugby club in Zwide was the African Bombers and, fortuitously spotted for his talent, he was plucked from poverty and went on a scholarship to the prestigious Grey High School, the launch pad for his Springbok career. Still he struggled. Almost all his schoolmates were affluent and privileged whites, and language was yet another hurdle. 'I struggled with my academic work and I was scared to speak as a result,' Kolisi said.

Imagine I didn't go to an English school like Greys, I wouldn't have eaten properly. I wouldn't have grown properly and I wouldn't have had the preparation the other boys did. I had to compete against boys who had been eating six meals a day, each and every single day of their lives. It's tough. So if you force someone into the Springbok team, and maybe if they're not good enough and they have one bad game, you probably will never see them again. I wouldn't want to be picked (for a team) because of my skin colour because that surely wouldn't be good for the team, and the guys around you would also know. It's tough for us as players because when you put a certain amount or number on it (transformation), are you actually there because you're good enough or . . . even if you are good enough you (a black player) can doubt yourself.

To his great credit, Kolisi has not pulled up the ladder of opportunity behind him like some sports stars from humble origins.

I just think about where I've come from and about the people that look up to me. For me to be able to help people inspired by me, I have to play every week. That is my duty. And I'm not only trying to inspire black kids, but people from all races. When I'm on the field and I look into the crowd, I see people of all races and social classes. We as players represent the whole country. I tell my teammates that you should never play just to represent one group. You can't play to be the best black player or to be the best white player to appeal to a community; you have to play to be the best for every South African. We represent something much bigger than we can imagine.

Married to a white woman, in post-match interviews afterwards he carried his two children proudly together with her; commentators also noted that he had adopted his two half-siblings. He epitomised the enormous progress, albeit very patchy and nowhere near finished, that South Africa had made since Mandela walked out of prison a year before Kolisi was born.

Under a headline 'South Africa's triumphant side simply had more to play for than England', the *Observer* journalist Andy Bull concluded:

If there has been a theme of the World Cup, a lesson for us all, it is this: the game sometimes runs on strange and powerful currents. It is not necessarily the sharpest, smartest, fittest, fastest or strongest team that wins, but the one who wants it most. The difference, this time, is they were led by a kid from the townships. Kolisi said he did not dream about winning the World Cup when he was young, because he was too busy dreaming about where his next meal was coming from, a captain leading a team who had more to play for than the likes of you, and I, and England, could possibly fathom.

That win in Yokohama, Japan, on 2 November 2019 by 32–12, included two 'black' winger tries from dazzling thrusting Makazole Mapimpi and jinking scorching Cheslin Kolbe, together with eight kicks and 22 points from inspired 'white' fly-half Handré Pollard.

Makazole Mapimpi caught high balls and lunged past hapless England defenders, scoring the thrilling first try. The only surviving member of his family, he used to walk ten kilometres to school every day whilst trying to play rugby on dishevelled dusty township fields in Mdantsane outside East London.

Tendai Mtawarira, affectionately known as the 'Beast', led the South African scrum to pulverise the England forwards. Fifteen years before, aged nineteen, he arrived at the Sharks Club training ground, his only possessions in a small kit-bag and wearing threadbare rugby boots, having walked there in Durban's humid heat. He trained for two years before acquiring a bike. His predominantly white teammates – all hailing from elite rugby schools and comfortable backgrounds – were in awe.

South Africa's formidable hooker, Mbongeni Mbonambi, was from a similar background and, with their Afrikaner lock Lood de Jager, had to leave injured in the heat of the opening twenty minutes.

Small blonde scrum-half Faf de Klerk harried and darted making a thorough nuisance of himself, squaring up and grinning provocatively at huge England forwards towering over him. Formidable number 8 Duane Vermeulen was ferocious in contact, winning the gain line battle almost single-handedly, and dominating the breakdowns, deservedly named man-of-the-match. Willie le Roux towered under the high ball and made raking kicks.

England lost the collision battle, bullied and broken in contact. South Africa – despite the apartheid legacy of inequality and destitution that thwarted sporting opportunity – showed much greater resilience, the best of the country epitomised by the magisterial yet humble Kolisi.

The epic 1995 Rugby World Cup victory over New Zealand achieved legendary status because Nelson Mandela donned the Springbok cap and jersey in front of the 99 per cent white crowd: in one of his trademark acts of 'nation healing', he handed the trophy to the white captain Francois Pienaar. But there was just one black player in that team; by 2019 black players constituted half, selected on merit and, like Kolisi, overcoming huge personal obstacles.

As he was presented with the World Cup trophy, Kolisi was wearing the same number 6 jersey as both Pienaar and Mandela wore on the podium nearly a quarter of a century before.

His was predominantly a team of 'white' Afrikaner hulks from farms used to eating well, combined with 'black' hulks from deprived townships where food was rare, their unity flagged virally on social media by a kiss from gigantic 'white' lock Eben Etzebeth on the head of his injured 'black' teammate Trevor Nyakane. The team sang the national anthem with common purpose, white players raucously in the Xhosa and Zulu verses of the freedom struggle song *Nkosi Sikelel' iAfrika*, black players with gusto the Afrikaans and English verses.

Another vital difference from a quarter of a century earlier was the popular reaction. Back then the 'Mandela Magic' moment touched only a comparative few outside the white community.

But in the normally crime-ridden square of Newtown Junction, right at Johannesburg's centre, the crowd swelled as the game went on. Black and white, young and old, men and women, all gathered in front of the big screen. Beforehand, the Springboks had been written off. But with victory seeming possible, shoppers and gym-users flooded in, nearby fast-food queues disappearing.

Black spectators in bars and cafes and squares began singing *Shosholoza*, a regular at sporting events in the new South Africa, its haunting lyrics once the provenance of black gold miners swinging their pickaxes deep underground during the apartheid regime.

But in the decades since 1990, when Mandela so regally lit up his country and beyond, South Africa has remained one of the most unequal societies in the world. Ten years of mismanagement and institutionalised corruption under one of his successors, President Jacob Zuma, crippled the economy and decimated services: there is mass unemployment among the black population, drought, water shortages and regular power cuts in part triggered by looting of the state electricity provider Eskom. The day before the final, the country's international credit rating was downgraded to negative, the murder rate stood at nearly sixty daily and rapes at nearly 120 daily, and crime remained rampant.

Yet somehow rugby, once the game of apartheid, acted as a unifier. The Springbok coach, Rassie Erasmus, explained how the team prepared as the underdogs:

> We started talking about pressure. In South Africa pressure is not having a job. Pressure is one of your close relatives murdered. It is easy to talk about going through hard times and struggling to get opportunities, but it is tough when there are days when you didn't have food or couldn't go to school or didn't have shoes to wear. Because South Africa has a lot of problems, we started talking about how rugby shouldn't be something that puts pressure on you. It should be something that creates hope. But you can't create hope just by talking about it, hope is not something you say in a beautiful tweet. Hope is when you play well. Hope is when people watch the game on a Saturday, and they have a BBQ, and they feel good about themselves, and no matter your political differences, or your belief differences, for those eighty minutes, you all agree. It is not our responsibility as players to create that hope, it is our privilege.

Kolisi added: 'Since I have been alive, I have never seen South Africa like this. With all the challenges we have, the coach said to us that we are not playing for ourselves any more, we are playing for the people back home, and that is what we wanted to do today.' Showing he hadn't forgotten his roots, Kolisi spoke with an eloquence and empathy lacking among many of today's global sports stars: 'We appreciate all the support – people in the taverns, in the shebeens, farms, homeless people and people in the rural areas. Thank you so much. We love you South Africa and we can achieve anything if we work together as one.'

As the national anthem started playing over the big screen at the only stadium in Kolisi's home township of Zwide, the crowd, including whites who had never before ventured there, rose to their feet chanting their captain's name. For eighty minutes they didn't sit down, singing and toyi-toying. As he lifted up the trophy, the noise became deafening, children on shoulders, Springbok flags in the air, with the crowd crying 'our Siya, that is our Siya, we are here for him'. When Kolisi mentioned the homeless, joyous shouts erupted from Ladles of Love, a volunteer-run soup kitchen in Cape Town convened specially for the screening of the game.

With his unique ability to capture the moment, Archbishop Desmond Tutu spoke frankly about governance failures since the dark days of apartheid, but added: 'We are a special country, and an extraordinary people. On days such as this we understand that when we pull together the sky is the limit. When we believe in ourselves, we can achieve our dreams.'

Two days before the match, journalist Craig Ray painted a broader canvas in the *Daily Maverick*:

Tommie Smith and John Carlos raising their gloved right fists at the medal ceremony after the 200m final at the 1968 Olympic Games in Mexico City is one of those sporting moments that was about far more than sport. Smith and Carlos were raising awareness for Black Consciousness. Nelson Mandela passing the William Webb Ellis Cup to Francois Pienaar at Ellis Park in 1995 was another image that not only isolated a moment in time, but sealed an emotional state of a nation in a frame. It was a picture that captured a mood of hope, of reconciliation and of what was possible in a country ravaged by years of segregation and inequality. Of course, 24 years on, South Africa continues to have many challenges and most of the promises symbolised by that picture of Mandela and Pienaar have gone unfulfilled. But that image is still a beacon of hope, still a small reminder that sport has the power to bring us closer together. It remains a memory to nudge South Africans to forget their differences for a short time and revel in their diversity and their collective love of sport. It's a prompt that sport binds us more than it divides us.

Steven Gruzd of the South African Institute of International Affairs commented: 'Sporting success contributes to a country's "soft power" too, the ability to use culture and non-military means to gain influence on the global stage.'

Veteran South African activist-journalist Dougie Oakes had an uncomfortable, grounded verdict. He saw the now multiracial rugby establishment as culpable in that they have collaborated repeatedly with national and provincial governments throughout the country in pretending that all South Africans have equal opportunities on the country's sports fields. Today more than ever, entry into the game for black players is still a carefully managed and white-controlled process. Players from the townships with aspirations of playing at the highest level have to squeeze their way through a narrow pipeline of elite rugby-playing schools like Kolisi did. To put it bluntly, if they don't get into a Bishops, a SACS, a Paul Roos, a Grey College, or a few other top schools, they will not play top-grade rugby. What have the various arms of government done to improve life in the townships? What has the South African Rugby Union done to develop the game in these townships? The answer is, in capital letters: NOTHING.

Oakes added: 'To speak of transformation is stretching the truth. Rugby in South Africa has NOT been transformed. What has happened is that the small groups of black players who have made it to the highest levels of the game, for which they should be praised for their talent and tenacity, have been ASSIMILATED in what has been described by officials, without a hint of irony, into a "Springbok culture". And this "Springbok culture" is essentially a white Afrikaner, and suspiciously, a pre-1994 culture, give or take a tweak or two.'

President Ramaphosa – elected in February 2018 to reverse the corruption and state sclerosis under his predecessor Jacob Zuma – was present at the 2019 Rugby World Cup final, dressed – as Mandela had been a quarter of a century earlier – in the captain's number 6 Springbok jersey, to celebrate an iconic win, with sport and politics intertwined as ever.

Some asked whether becoming World Champions meant a finale for the Stop The Tour demonstrators of half a century before, some sort of closure for the freedom struggle in sport. No is our emphatic answer. It embodied an amazing new plateau, unimaginable in the bitter apartheid days. But there remains a chasm of unequal opportunity between white and black South Africans, between a minority of youngsters from top schools in manicured suburbs and the majority of young people trapped in under-resourced dormitory townships.

Epilogue

Coronavirus sports lockdown

Perhaps the petrifying Australian bushfires then the rampant floods of 2019 and 2020 should have been a warning to sports fans of biblical pestilence to follow.

A few months after South Africa's momentous World Cup victory in Japan, something much bigger happened to sport.

Where those climate change-induced plagues seriously disrupted Australia's globally-watched cricket and tennis, as if the ecosystem was taking further revenge on its destroyer – humankind – the coronavirus pandemic simply closed sport down globally. No football, no rugby, no cricket, no Formula One, no athletics, no Olympics, no golf, no boxing or squash or snooker or darts. No Wimbledon, no other tennis. What was happening to the world? For all of us billions of sports followers or participants, the weekends emptied, action-replays of old events a poor substitute for addictive live sport on TV or self-participation.

And for professional sportswomen and men, a jolting void. Pay cuts or no pay at all for many, no competition for months on end and none of the proper training together so vital to maintain fitness, sharpness and mental focus for team sports. Self-training of course: but *where*, with gyms closed and parks out of bounds due to social distancing dictums? Two England football internationals and chums, Mason Mount and Declan Rice, were disciplined by their clubs for a kickabout in a London park because it contravened the government social distancing shutdown.

Peter's team Chelsea, off the back of two thrilling wins against Liverpool and Everton, seemed to be returning to form after an indifferent few months of inconsistency and frustration. Which Chelsea would resume after the Premier League's break? His grandsons and granddaughters in Britain also had their football matches and training stopped, frustrating for one because her team had just reached a cup final.

André's daily menu of sport was snatched away. A cricket series against India aborted halfway through. No Premier Soccer League matches. No Super XV rugby. All sport in South Africa was brought to a halt by the 'lockdown'. Uncertainty grew all around. The new South African women's professional football league was put on ice with no guarantee that struggling new clubs would survive. Funding dried up for Paralympic sports stars. Fifty of the country's top sports leaders feared infection following a meeting with the minister of sport, where one of their number tested positive.

Journalist Ernest Makhaya wrote of the South African Football Association's decision to suspend all football activities soon after President Cyril Ramaphosa declared the country in a state of national disaster: 'South Africa is dubbed a footballing country – and one cannot imagine a weekend without competitive matches.'[417]

When the Second World War broke out, Sir Home Gordon wrote in *The Cricketer*: 'England has now begun the grim Test Match against Germany. We do not wish merely to win the Ashes of civilisation. We want to win a lasting peace.'[418] But neither world war entirely shut down cricket, as former England cricket captain turned cricket writer Mike Atherton reminded us in *The Times* on 19 March 2020: 'It seems the virus has done what not even the grimmest of wars could do.'[419]

Ironically, the total shutdown of sport made the dystopian Covid-19 plague more real for most people globally than viewing the first ominous TV coverage from Wuhan of empty streets and shops as over 11 million citizens were abruptly brought to a standstill. Was it the halt to Serie A football matches or the Italian government's ban on travel to or from the virus-riddled Lombardy region (to be followed across the entire nation) that first alerted many to the life-changing nature of the pandemic?

As *Observer* columnist Jonathan Liew wrote on 14 March 2020, a week before Britain closed up shop on government instructions, this was 'the most seismic disruption to the sporting calendar since the second world war, with the possibility that an obliterated spring is simply the prelude to an annihilated summer and a torched autumn . . . as the enormous industrial complex of global sport clanks to a terrifying halt.' All many Premier League football fans could think of then was what would happen to *their* team? Would for example Liverpool fans be denied their desperately craved title, the first in three decades? Would Aston Villa be relegated when they had a game in hand? All the time the bodies piled up, including British doctors and nurses without the requisite personal protection infected by the very Covid-19 patients they were trying to save. Elderly care homes in Spain were discovered abandoned, full of the dead. 'For all the time and money and hope and anger we invest in this business of balls and implements, all of it is ultimately expendable,' said Liew bluntly.

As the world went into lockdown, people retreated not just from their sport but from their families, their friends, their neighbours, their communities, on their own, often in perilous or cramped or isolated circumstances: an ultimate loneliness, their lives and livelihoods stolen, many realising what they had always taken for granted. A post-1945 globalisation generation, the vast majority of whom had never experienced loss like this except in Syria or Yemen or other parts of the world torn apart.

But Liew added that, when sport blinked 'back into life . . . it will feel like a benediction and an irrelevance all at once: a reminder that of all the things that don't matter sport matters most of all.'

In a similar vein, Liverpool manager Jürgen Klopp sent a message to club supporters describing football as 'the most important of the least important things' and urged people to follow expert advice over the coronavirus threat instead of regretting the suspension of the Premier League season.

Coronavirus deaths started mounting in Britain, with health professionals struggling to secure personal protective equipment as cases mushroomed. Refreshingly, another Premier League manager, Brighton & Hove Albion's Graham Potter told *The Times* on 25 March 2020: 'Rather than thinking about football, all football should be thinking about, "How can we help?"' He had further insight:

> With a lot of players, you see it from when they stop playing that there's a big issue around mental health, around how they adapt to life, how they adapt to not having the structure that, okay, at 9 a.m., you go to a training ground, and that's your structure and your life, and that gives you some direction . . . But we are in a time of challenge. Everybody's got challenges. There are big ones everywhere. We've all got to empathise with each other, try to stick together and help each other through . . . In our bubble, we think football is life and death – it isn't.

Yet, as sports journalist Max Rushden pithily explained in the *Guardian* on 19 March 2020:

Sport bonds families, it forges and cements friendships, it dominates
WhatsApp groups. It has its own language, its own set of languages.
It is simultaneously not essential for society but is a society in itself . . .
How quickly it has unravelled . . . The morning routine has changed
dramatically. Mindless transfer gossip, last night's goals and staring at
league tables have all gone. In their place: trying to work out if my wife
has picked up coronavirus from one of her pupils; staring at my arid,
crispy but incredibly clean knuckles; and explaining to my parents that
meeting 'just 10 friends' isn't social isolation . . . Sport is flawed, it is
imperfect. It is governed by money. It facilitates racism, homophobia
and misogyny and fails to deal with them adequately. Marginal gains
blur the lines between records and cheating. At the top there has been
corruption; at grassroots referees are abused and attacked . . . We do
not know what sport will look like when this is over. We have to hope
it looks the same – without forgetting how much it needs to improve.
There is so much talk of money filtering down from the top to the
bottom, from the haves to the have nots. Even if there is the will –
and that's a big if – I'm yet to see anyone explain how it will work.
You don't know what you've got till it's gone . . .

After the organisers finally and very reluctantly accepted that the Tokyo
2020 Olympics had to be postponed by a year, at an extra cost of between
£2 and £4 billion, *Guardian* columnist Barney Ronay wryly observed on 27
March 2020:

Global plague trumps global sport every time and the degree of delay
and fudge was just a function of the political and financial capital
involved, the need to erect sufficient litigation-shields and anti-blame
mechanisms . . . Still, though. This is also a time for unvarnished truths.
Whenever it does end up happening Tokyo 2020 will provide the usual
mix of individual human inspiration and mild economic stimulus.
But it will also – and we can say this now – be stuffed full of bullshit,
revved up on the deeply phoney and self-serving Big Sport model, these
four-yearly events that circle the globe like mobile city states clearing the
fields, raiding the public stores, favouring the local Maharajahs with
their magic dust.

Elaborating, Ronay wrote of

the machine world of modern-day Big Sport, that profiteering global circus that constantly tells you this, sport, belongs to someone else, that it is simply a circus to be consumed at a price . . . But it doesn't have to be like this. In Big Sport, as in so many areas of life, there is an opportunity here for a mass-correction, for a step-change in what we see as acceptable. Strip it back. Flush out the murky corners. Get rid of all the things you never needed anyway. Do we have the guts and the will to make it so?

His theme was echoed by Musa Okwonga in the *Guardian* on 25 March 2020:

Coronavirus provided a moment of self-reflection for sport as bracing as that which the 2008 financial crash provided for the economy. Just as that crisis gave rise to the Occupy movement and its accompanying list of demands for a fairer society, we must ask what demands there might now be for a fairer fandom . . . professional sport must therefore show us – or prove to us anew – that it is more than a distraction; that its senior figures care profoundly about matters beyond the pitch, the stadium and the balance sheet . . . [T]he postponement and cancellation of international and club football and the Olympics, among many other events [were] acts of responsible leadership that eventually placed public health ahead of self-enrichment.

With a mass pause imposed on us all, it is time for sport to rethink its social contract with those who adore it; it is an opportunity to reassure those worshippers who may have become disillusioned that they can one day renew their faith.

Initial assessments show that Covid-19 may well have damaged and re-structured sport as much as, if not more than, any other sector of society. The United Nations reported on a serious financial and health conse-quences globally of the Covid sports shutdown, and detailed the impact upon sportspeople, from loss of professional sponsorship to the clubs they played for going bust.[420] And, while highlighting the social, economic and fiscal benefits of increasing physical activity levels, EMD (the UK national governing body for group exercise) identified a significant and widening gap in physical inactivity between social classes, including amongst children:

the poorer you were, the less opportunity to keep fit during the lockdown.

Observing the lockdown's impact from his front doorstep in Wales, his home for thirty years and where he served as an MP and cabinet minister, Peter noted that grassroots-level sport was hardest hit. The Welsh Rugby Union described the impact of Covid-19 as 'catastrophic'. The Football Association of Wales reported 'massive financial difficulties ahead', and with domestic football in Wales very reliant on match-day and clubhouse income, clubs would have to 'reassess their business models to understand how it works'. A Senedd (Welsh Parliament) Committee reported that sport 'is facing a considerable financial impact which could threaten the ability of sport at all levels to return to a pre-pandemic normal'. It also reported an especially negative impact on women's football, which in Wales had grown by 50 per cent since 2016.[421]

Surely it can't be right that the financial bottom line becomes the all-consuming purpose with fewer and fewer people profiting from more and more money received from more and more sports fans today? Can the 'profiteering global circus' that Barney Ronay wrote about be forced to alter its approaches, or self-correct itself for the greater good? The stakes are high. The Business Research Company and consultancy firm A.T. Kearney in 2019 estimated that the value of the global sports market was between $480 billion and $620 billion per annum.

The top-end figure amounted to getting on for 1 per cent of global Gross Domestic Product, which the World Bank valued at $86 trillion in 2018. In addition to this massive direct investment in sport through television rights, sponsorships, merchandising, gate takings and the like, there is a substantial broader economic yield or 'value add' accruing from the sports industry. According to head of South Africa's pioneering sports marketing company, Megapro, George Rautenbach, sports sponsors typically 'do two spends'. One for purchasing naming or other rights in sport. The other to leverage the relationship with competitions, teams or star players – usually on a rand for rand or dollar for dollar basis – so that the sponsorship translates into greater sales of the sponsors' products. So, for example, South African Breweries spends tens of millions of rand annually on its sponsorships of the South African rugby, football and cricket national teams, and would additionally spend the same amount in marketing to boost its beer and beverage sales. Perhaps coming down to fifty cents in the rand during tough economic times, Rautenbach told André. Apply this example across the board in sport, through to giants like Barcelona, Manchester City, the New

York Yankees, the India cricket team, the Olympic Games and various World Cups, and the tally comes to billions of dollars more being generated indirectly through sport.

Similarly, sport drives spending on infrastructure and event management – mega sporting events in particular – and visiting spectators bring in vast amounts of money for airlines, hotels, restaurants and retail outlets in the tourism and related industries – a fact starkly illustrated by the shocking television images of silent cities, ghost airports and locked stadiums (the cathedrals of our time) during the coronavirus. The Cape Town Cycle Tour is a small example illustrating the wider economic impact of sport. Winding a breath-taking 109 kilometres along the seaside, and circumventing Table Mountain via three peaks, it is the biggest timed cycle race in the world with 35,000 participants (André amongst them), generating an estimated R 500 million for the Cape Town economy in one week.

Furthermore, sport and recreation play a vital role in helping to maintain the health and productivity of society, which leads to tangible benefits for national and global economies. Although its immense social benefits are difficult to quantify fully, a fit population puts less pressure on national health systems, leading to automatic savings. It also ensures greater market returns: stock exchanges, life insurance and private health companies all profit considerably from investments by stable, longer-living, fitter older populations with active, healthy lifestyles.

Consider also the value of the global asset registers of sport in the form of the vast network of public and private spaces, parks, grounds and stadiums in countless towns and cities which constitute the infrastructure for the daily and weekly activities of millions of people in every country. Forbes magazine gives a sense of the financial scale of this global sports grid, socially and privately shaped over generations by countless voices and hands. Topped by the $2.66 billion Los Angeles Memorial Coliseum, home of the Los Angeles Rams and the Chargers, the ten most expensive sports stadiums in the world alone are valued at $13.76 billion. Add the thousands of others throughout the world to this list and try putting a figure to that. Teams are today fabulous assets in financial terms as well. The Dallas Cowboys, valued at $5 billion and with an annual profit of $365 million in 2017, are the richest. With the New York Yankees, Real Madrid, Barcelona and other stellar names following, the top fifty wealthiest clubs in the world are worth just under $140 billion. Most of these, including the entire National Football League (where 'monster' media rights deals bring each team $260 million per year) are American. Just add the hundreds of football clubs in Europe to this figure.

Then there are the assets of individual sports stars. Boxer Floyd Mayweather earned $300 million in 2015. Tiger Woods, in eleven of his more than twenty years in golf, raked in $987 million. Tennis's Williams sisters have crashed through gender barriers to open up opportunities for women as well. In 2017 Serena's net wealth was estimated at $170 million, with Venus not far behind. Cristiano Ronaldo ($93 million), Lionel Messi ($86 million), basketballer LeBron James ($86 million) and Roger Federer ($71 million) are amongst hundreds of sportspeople who have been turned into industrial scale money-machines making previously unheard-of annual incomes.[422]

As Musa Okwonga understood, the coronavirus crisis that began in 2019 shows the extent to which trillion-dollar Big Sport is embedded in twenty-first century globalisation and monopoly capitalism, and how, on the flip-side of the coin, it depends on billions of sports enthusiasts for its survival.

The pandemic has highlighted themes of globalisation, racism, human rights and gender inequality discussed in the previous chapter and, as we hover under the dark cloud of the virus, it is indeed time for sport to rethink its social contract.

#BlackLivesMatter underlines the point

This book ends with the twenty-first-century lynching of George Floyd, filmed as a police officer clamped his knee over Floyd's windpipe. The casual manner in which his plea, 'I can't breathe', was ignored underlined how disregarded black lives still are, despite the slave trade having been abolished two centuries before.

The outrage was immediate and ignited weeks of protests in tens of cities throughout the United States, quickly spreading to Britain and other parts of the world. A multi-generational rainbow coalition appeared as if by magic to challenge a narcissistic, racist Trump-dominated narrative of 'Us' and 'Them'. 'I can't breathe' became a rallying cry, the hashtag #BlackLivesMatter surged. Racism and the systemic way it has been normalised in daily life through five centuries of conquest, colonisation, slavery and economic globalisation was put under the microscope and exposed in a manner seldom seen, resonating with people throughout the world.

411

The Black Lives Matter (BLM) movement has become another milestone in the struggle against racism and the systems that prop it up, following the civil rights movement and Black Power led by Martin Luther King and Malcolm X respectively, the decolonisation process in Africa and Asia, and South Africa's own liberation and non-racial sports struggles.

BLM swept into sport in an unprecedented way. For generations, sportspeople have been in denial about the racism ubiquitous in global sport. Sportsmen and women who had rarely stood openly against injustice or inequality – with notable exceptions – started speaking out.

Breaking the taboos established by a conservative (white) sporting establishment to protest against racism has come at high cost to athletes. After the historic Black Power salute at the 1968 Olympics by US gold and bronze medal winners Tommie Smith and John Carlos, the *Los Angeles Times* condemned them for a 'Nazi salute'. There was also quick retribution for second-placed white Australian, Peter Norman, who stood in solidarity on the podium wearing a human rights badge. Olympic champion Smith was sacked from his job as a car washer and his mother was terrorised by dead rats through her letter box, dying from a heart attack months afterwards. Carlos's wife committed suicide.

Only several decades later were both sprinters rehabilitated and awarded honorary doctorates and a huge statue at San José State University. Norman, the fifth-fastest sprinter in the world, was dropped by Australian officials from the 1972 Olympics and snubbed at the Olympics in his home country in 2000. Ostracised, he died in 2006, aged sixty-four, after alcohol troubles. Only in 2012 did the Australian government issue an official apology, acknowledging that he had bravely advocated racial equality.

Soon after the Olympic 1968 protests, the great Muhammad Ali was stripped of his WBA world heavyweight crown and his boxing licence for refusing to be drafted for the Vietnam War. Famously, he said:

> My conscience won't let me go shoot my brother, or some darker people, or some poor hungry people in the mud for big powerful America. And shoot them for what? They never called me nigger, they never lynched me, they didn't put no dogs on me, they didn't rob me of my nationality, rape and kill my mother and father.[423]

Four decades later, those in control of sport could still enforce their version of 'law and order'. After his 'take a knee' protest in 2016, the American quarterback football player Colin Kaepernick was shunned, blackballed and sacked by the San Francisco 49ers under orders from its parent National Football League (NFL), and encouraged by the US President. The NFL players who took a knee alongside Kaepernick brought this response from Donald Trump. 'Wouldn't you love to see one of these NFL owners, when somebody disrespects our flag, to say, "Get that son of a bitch off the field right now. Out! He's fired. He's fired!"'

Although nearly four decades on from Mexico 1968, all the time the practice of retribution had continued. Black American hammer-thrower Gwen Berry, ranked number three in the world, raised her fist after winning gold at the 2019 Pan American Games in Peru. Her father an Iraq War veteran, Berry grew up in Ferguson, Missouri, where black teenager Michael Brown was shot dead by police in 2014, a racist outrage that impacted hugely upon her. But she fell foul of the Olympic Charter's Rule 50, which prohibits demonstrations and political, religious and racial propaganda. The United States Olympic and Paralympic Committee (USOPC) put her on a year's probation, and her funding was cut from $35,000 to $5,000 by USA Track and Field (USATF) shortly afterwards.

However, after the killing of George Floyd and the surge of BLM, the dam finally burst. An outpouring of solidarity with those opposing racism in sport took place across the board. Whereas in 2016 Colin Kaepernick had been shunned, now many more sportspeople were taking the knee. Building up over decades, a decisive moment arrived, breaking the hundred-year hold of organised sport over the expression of black voices.

The impact of this terrible killing was heightened by the fact that it took place in the middle of the Covid-19 global pandemic, which brought sport to a standstill globally. An unprecedented national clamour about racial discrimination in US sport followed. Quickly sensing the national mood, conservative sport establishments started bending.

Both the NFL and the US Soccer Federation lifted their bans on players taking a knee. NFL chief Roger Goodell appeared on television to say unconvincingly, 'We were wrong not to listen to NFL players earlier by encouraging all to speak and peacefully protest.' He never mentioned Kaepernick, who nevertheless remained unemployed despite being fully able to resume his previous star role. The NFL set aside a fund of $150 million to combat structural racism.

The USATF and USOPC who had thrown the book at Gwen Berry only a year earlier also quickly supported the right to protest, the USOPC athletes' advisory council even calling for Rule 50 to be scrapped.

Sports icons Michael Jordan and LeBron James became figureheads for the growing movement. Jordan donated $100 million to support the 'More than a Vote' campaign, which stretched beyond sport to call on African-Americans, minority groups and young people to register to vote so that they could affect societal change. Sponsors joined in to support change, with Nike benefitting from having supported Colin Kaepernick in bold ad campaigns after he was suspended.

The depth and power of the campaign became obvious when the famous Washington Redskins brand became obsolete because it was regarded as disparaging to Native American sensibilities. Like Danie Craven, who had said in 1969 that over his dead body would a black player wear a Springbok jersey, the owner of the Redskins, Daniel Snyder, declared defiantly in 2015, 'We will never change the name – it's as simple as that. NEVER.' Yet, within weeks of the Floyd killing, the Redskins announced that the name was being retired and that a new one would be announced later.

'After George Floyd, a lot of people were speaking out but I knew a lot of them were insincere,' remarked Berry. 'It's disgusting because a lot of corporations want to be on the right side of history. They want the black dollar so bad they are willing to say anything. Why was nobody saying anything after Mike Brown?'

But CNN sports anchor Christine Brennan was right when she said about the Redskins change of name: 'It's a big deal.'[424] America 'went dark' as major league play-offs in several sports were postponed and at dozens of events sportspeople took the knee against racial discrimination, smashing a psychological barrier of control by the white-led, colonially rooted sport system forever.

*

The impact of Black Lives Matter spread like surface oil on fire across the waters to the old colonial heartland, Britain, and its European neighbours. Protests were held in dozens of European cities and also in Asia. At the same time, sport began to emerge from the coronavirus lockdown in almost dystopian conditions. When top-flight football matches resumed they had to be socially distanced, with each team entering stadiums without handshakes or any spectators present, only medics and substitutes seated prudently apart and wearing masks. In the Premier League, the shouts of coaches and players echoed loudly across empty arenas but were drowned out for viewers on live television broadcasts by artificial crowd noises.

At the start, minutes of silence honoured the many tens of thousands who had died from the coronavirus – Britain having one of the highest death rates per capita globally in mid-2020. Following that silence, 'players took the knee' in solidarity against racism, their shirts carrying BLM logos.

In July 2020, spurred on by BLM, the only black driver ever in Formula One, serial World Champion Lewis Hamilton used the unique platform afforded him by his preeminent position to announce a series of initiatives to increase diversity in motor sport. He told of the racism he had experienced from an early age as a schoolboy in kart racing. He recalled with regret how he had been dissuaded from speaking out when Colin Kaepernick was sacked from the NFL after taking the knee. 'I thought that was a very powerful statement,' said Hamilton. 'Then he lost his job and he was a great athlete. I spoke to him a couple of years ago shortly after that for the US Grand Prix. I had a helmet made in red with his number on but back then I was kind of silenced. I was told to back down and "Don't support it," which I regret. So it is important for me that during this time I did my part.'

In 2020 the British Sporting Equals charity found that only 3 per cent of the members of British national sports governing boards were black.[425] As the English football star Raheem Sterling, himself a victim of racist attacks, said: 'There's something like 500 players in the Premier League and a third of them are black, and we have no representation of us in the hierarchy, no representation of us in the coaching staffs. There's not a lot of faces that we can relate to and have conversations with . . . It's not just taking the knee, it is about giving people the chance they deserve.' Chelsea's former Director of Football, ex-Nigerian football star Michael Emeanalo, also articulated the need for radical change.[426]

Former England and Chelsea women's football star, Aston Villa Women's Sporting Director Eniola Aluko argued for quotas for black Asian and minority ethnic board members when she gave evidence to a UK Parliamentary Committee on 7 July 2020: 'When you rely on self-regulation and people doing it themselves, they tend to just fall back into a comfort zone of what they've always done. We do need a target.'

The same day as her evidence, the England and Wales Cricket Board announced plans to require racial diversity inclusion at boardroom level across the game, with just 4 per cent of those in governance roles within cricket being black, Asian and minority ethnic.

But, as *Guardian* sports journalist Jonathan Liew wrote on 13 June 2020:

> The lack of black football coaches stems in part from a lack of black chief executives and sporting directors and owners. This stems in part from a systematic and racist assumption that black people cannot be trusted with positions of executive or financial power, one that also manifests itself in the lack of black representation in the judiciary, in business, in politics. This, in turn, has its roots in the historical concentration of wealth and power in white hands, often at the expense of enslaved or subjugated black peoples. Try and stitch that to the back of a football shirt.[427]

When test cricket resumed in July 2020, England and West Indies players took the knee during the first resumed test after the lifting of the lockdown. In defining moments in cricket commentary, West Indies fast bowler legend Michael Holding and Ebony Jewel Rainford-Brent, the first black woman to play for England, spoke with emotion about the many hurtful ways in which they had experienced discrimination during their sporting careers.

Off the sportsfields, the complacency bordering on denial about colonialism and its accompanying violence in Britain and the West was vigorously challenged. In Bristol, off the plinth and into the river went the statue of the slave trader, Edward Colston, which had stood there for over a century, marking his largesse to the city gained from forcibly transporting about 80,000 men, women and children from Africa to the Americas. In Belgium, the statue of King Leopold II was removed and the state apologised for the atrocities committed under his rule in the Congo. Similar acknowledgements started coming from other European powers: a turning point, perhaps, in post-colonial thinking about the continent's 500-year conquest – divinely given, it was thought at one stage.

*

South Africa was as surprised as the rest of the world at the popular uprisings in the United States in 2020, even though it had seen the 2015 student protests in support of decolonising South African education on various university campuses.

These highlighted the fact that despite two decades of democracy, systemic racism and exclusions were still rampant in education and every other sector of South African life. Rallying behind the call of #RhodesMustFall, they demanded the taking down of the statue of the arch-imperialist at the University of Cape, amongst whose vices was the formal introduction of the colour-bar into South African sport in 1894 (described in chapter 2). The events in the northern summer of 2020 mirrored in many ways these earlier South African student protests, the impact of which have been particularly powerful because of the large-scale economic marginalisation of most black South Africans and the perceived failure of the democratic government to redress the situation. Rhodes's statue was duly removed and South African students at Oxford University subsequently demanded the same treatment for a Rhodes statue there too.

When Black Lives Matter generated US and British acts of solidarity in July 2020, it had an immediate, dramatic impact in sport in South Africa. Ahead of a special post-lockdown match to mark 102 years since the birth of Nelson Mandela, Lungi Ngidi, voted South Africa's best one-day and T20 cricket player in the previous season, was rolled out for the obligatory press conference. Asked what he thought about BLM, the young fast-bowler commented: 'It is definitely something we would be addressing as a team. And if we're not, it's obviously something that I would bring up. It's something that we need to take seriously, like the rest of the world is doing.'[428]

Ngidi's calm response to a routine question ruffled the feathers of a cohort of former white test players. Tapping into language codes that said more than words, they took issue with him on social media, with Rudi Steyn opening the batting. He was against racism, but if the Proteas stood for BLM 'while ignoring the way white farmers are daily being "slaughtered" like animals, they have lost my vote'. Boeta Dippenaar said that BLM was nothing more than a leftist political movement, started by Marxists whose aim was to break down family life and 'if you want me to stand shoulder to shoulder with you Lungi, then stand shoulder to shoulder with me with regard to farm attacks'. He also suggested Ngidi should do some reading: Milton Friedman and others. Pat Symcox, known as a bullish anti-transformation and change voice, charged in: 'What nonsense is this. He must take his own stand if he wishes. Stop trying to get the Proteas involved in his belief. Besides the fact that right now Cricket South Africa should be closed down. A proper dog and pony show with cricket being dragged through the mud daily. Buy popcorn and watch. Now when Ngidi has his next meal perhaps he would rather consider supporting the farmers of South Africa who are under pressure right now. A cause worth supporting.' These responses drew straight from alt-right perspectives in the US and South Africa. The right-wing lobby group AfriForum had developed close relations with the US alt-right, who took up its narrative that the democratic government was callous to a genocide being levelled against white farmers in South Africa. Commentator Ashwin Desai described the idea that the movement was part of an international left conspiracy sucking in the likes of LeBron James, Lewis Hamilton, the Premier League players who took the knee and the South African cricketers as 'Monty Pythonesque' thinking, noting also that Symcox was consistent with 'his call that his [white] contemporaries should be running South African cricket'. Top all-rounder Brian McMillan then wheeled in to bowl with hardly a thought dismissing the whole issue as 'a load of crap', making one wonder if he could have witnessed the killing of George Floyd.

These comments invited outrage and the debate soon reached tinderbox proportions on social media. Cricketers, led by South Africa's first black captain, Ashwell Prince, were amongst those to respond. He said that the system in cricket and the country was broken and that it was time for honesty and for black players to speak up. He and former teammates started conferring about a collective statement on the matter. Soon thirty-one ex-Proteas and five senior coaches had signed up, supported next day by a powerful statement from Hashim Amla, South Africa's highest scorer in test matches with 311 not out. Top of the list was Makhaya Ntini, first black African player to represent South Africa, who played 100 tests in a stellar career, which saw him take the fourth highest number of wickets for his country.

Ngidi's fellow players commended him for his actions and came out 'strongly in support in support of #BLM'. They noted too the views by Symcox and others and said they needed to be challenged:

> We are not surprised at their comments. Given South Africa's well-known past, black cricketers have borne the brunt of subtle and overt racist behaviour for many years, including from some colleagues. Consequently, there is a need to understand how white privilege feeds into the perpetuation of these old attitudes and assumptions. Our attitude, mistakenly, we now believe, has always been to say: 'These are

teething problems, and that these will be resolved if we are patient'. But after almost three decades of cricket unity, the views expressed from one side of the racial divide are still very much part of our lives, and we now believe: 'Teething problems cannot be allowed to continue for this long.'[429]

Moreover, 'All the signatories to the release stated that they have stories to tell about the racism they have had to endure as they strove to get to the top of their sporting careers. Sadly, these have often been at the hands of teammates.' They asked for Cricket South Africa's support in helping to bring these stories into the open, also for that of their colleagues in women's cricket.

Their statement observed that transformation from apartheid was forever given the blame for problems and poor performances, but when South Africa won the 2019 Rugby World Cup in Japan, 'We cannot recall anyone suggesting that the victory was due to transformation'. This after rugby was said to have been 'dead – killed by transformation' just two years earlier.

Can there be equal treatment, please, the group asked, underlining that they had represented South Africa on merit: 'Far too many white South Africans cannot accept that black cricketers have proved, time without end, that they are good enough to play at the highest level'.

Underlining Robin Petersen's observation that this action was about 'leadership, strategy, non-racialism and love for our country', the players made a point of inviting 'our fellow white cricketers to join in this move to defend human dignity' and said:

We live in a beautiful, diverse country, but where the playing fields are still far from level, and the transformation of cricket and people's lives should be of paramount importance.

We are determined that future generations should not have to experience the pain we have had to endure, and that no South African cricketer should be discriminated against in the future.

Racism is a global problem and, as the great Michael Holding explained, we can no longer just keep on laughing, grimacing and moving on.

Calling on the name of Nelson Mandela in the week of his anniversary, the players stressed finally that lingering racism in cricket 'can be tackled once and for all – for the sake of every child and every cricketer in South Africa' if there were 'honesty and sincerity all-round'.

The cricketers now started talking about their personal experiences. National sports hero Makhaya Ntini explained how he was dropped after his hundredth test match – no farewell series to bid farewell to the fans at each home ground after a decade as usually happened. His career just 'shutted down'. He lost his contract within a month, 'from A+ to nothing'.

But nothing was as powerful as when he spoke about being 'forever lonely' during the time he played for South Africa: seldom would a team-mate knock on his hotel room door to chill or check in on how he was; there would be dinner table chat about where people were going out without an invite to come along; or he would just be left to sit alone. He mentioned it was this feeling of isolation that explained his legendary running between hotel and stadium during international matches – 'the best weapon of my life'; getting air in his lungs and 'running away' from the paradoxical loneliness of the team bus.[430]

Cricket South Africa and its provincial affiliates, as well as the media and civil society, rushed to support the former players and their call for action. When the first cricket match after the lockdown took place on 18 July 2020, a charity event to celebrate Mandela's birth and raise funds for Covid-19 relief, all thirty-six current players and the few officials in an otherwise empty stadium wore BLM armbands and took the knee together.

This breaking of the silence by top players was a catalyst psychologically, shifting South African cricket to the next phase of substantive change. One of those moments where everything changes. The players, acting in solidarity, broke the silence to speak about how the system and old attitudes held black people back. The self-assumed authority and unspoken power that Pat Symcox enjoyed until that moment was gone. A new narrative was replacing the old.

Next day, the newspaper headlines announced that forty-nine of the top black rugby coaches, including six who had played for the Springboks, were backing the cricketers and BLM. They pointed out the facts: '100 per cent exclusion' of black coaches at the strategic national and professional rugby levels, and the same '100 per cent exclusion' for CEOs and high performance managers. Thirty-nine black sportswomen followed next day.[431] They were joined by World Cup-winning captain Siya Kolisi, after his fans questioned his silence. In an Instagram post, he spoke of the language and cultural alienation he felt growing up, and how he was made to 'feel grateful' rather than valued on making the Springbok team in 2013. He said that his silence was now over, even if it meant losing his place in the team.[432]

Thus, the death of a US citizen at the hands of a policeman in Minneapolis reverberated powerfully across the globe to the sports fields of South Africa. There is no gainsaying that top of the agenda in South African sport now is that black lives matter.

*

In June 2020 Danish researchers from *RunRepeat*, looking at media coverage of more than 2,000 statements in eighty matches in the premier British, German, Italian, French and Spanish football leagues, found clear racial biases in the way commentators read the game in European competitions. The study concluded that 'players with lighter skin are regularly and overwhelmingly praised for intelligence, work ethic and quality compared with those with darker skin, who are reduced to physical and athletic attributes.'

RunRepeat ratio-adjusted its numbers to account for the fact there were 1,361 comments about lighter-skinned players and 713 about darker-skinned players and found the former group more widely praised for intelligence (62.6% [of the time]), hard work (60.4%) and quality (62.79%). Commentators are also 6.59 times more likely to talk about the power of a player if he has darker skin and 3.38 times more likely to reference his pace. The study also found that 63.33% of criticism from commentators with regards to the intelligence of a player is aimed at those with darker skin, while the figure for quality is 67.57%.[433]

A Professional Footballers' Association spokesman backed the report and admitted: 'To address the real impact of structural racism, we have to acknowledge and address [this] racial bias.' The study found that by typifying players, for example, Real Madrid's Ferland Mendy, as 'fit and strong' rather than versatile and intelligent played into 'a narrative of black people's primary value laying in their physicality and not their intelligence'. This 'dated back to attitudes [including slavery] that modern society is determined to eradicate'. The chairperson of the anti-racist Kick It Out lobby group, Sanjay Bhandari, said these stereotypical representations were inherently racist and could hold players back from getting positions in coaching, management and at boardroom level, as these kind of negative perceptions preceded them.

In cricket, racial biases were most clearly revealed in the completely flawed notions that in South Africa cricket was a game that Africans had never been interested in. And in the stereotype of West Indian cricketers being spontaneous, cavalier or calypso types, something which grated during the Clive Lloyd era, when attritional fast-bowling strategies – spearheaded initially by the 'four horsemen of the apocalypse', Michael Holding, Andy Roberts, Joel Garner and Colin Croft – caused the old colonial masters to duck, dive and submit during the West Indies' winning streak from the late 1970s to the early 1990s.

Years before the *RunRepeat* report, in 1999, the UCBSA's Transformation Monitoring Committee, chaired by André, commissioned a similar investigation into media attitudes to cricket transformation by Lynette Steenveld from Rhodes University. She found differences in how black and white players were spoken and written about. Fitting in with the European racist tropes, she pointed out how Makhaya Ntini was praised not for his skills but for his physical attributes of running in hour after hour, eager as a racehorse, to bowl. When André distributed this report to the media during a test match at Newlands he was excoriated by *The Star*'s columnist and it was otherwise icily received or simply dismissed by the media. Therefore, seeing the *RunRepeat* report in June 2020 gave him deep satisfaction; some of the journalists who had trashed post-apartheid transformation were positioning themselves as promoters of the change they had disparaged.

After the brouhaha involving Pat Symcox and Boeta Dippenaar, André was amongst the many asked to speak on radio and television about BLM in sport. He welcomed it as a heart-warming example of human solidarity in the age of Donald Trump which also highlighted how entrenched old ways of thinking and power relations remained. Those organising the cricketers' BLM protest asked André for advice and help in drafting their statement. The core group at the forefront of planning were Ashwell Prince, seen as the leader, Robin Petersen, Paul Adams and radio journalist Craig Marais. They had requested the sharp-penned doyen of non-racial sports journalism, Dougie Oakes, to aid them. Adams and Marais suggested roping in André as the players' numbers grew and the core group pondered on the right approach. The players' WhatsApps hummed as they sent in their views. Six former national players committed, then there were more, and soon thirty-one, backed up by senior coaches. Some were afraid of going too far. None wanted to jeopardise South African cricket. Finally, in a wonderful moment at Oakes's home nearby to where 1970s icon Hassan Howa lived, the statement was finalised. The four were wearing masks and trying to socially distance, amidst mounting anticipation. Prince and Petersen, who were isolating elsewhere, but had constantly been in touch, gave the thumbs up and Adams and Marais pressed the buttons to break the story.

*

How does sport serve humanity as whole – most of it impoverished – rather than the one or ten percenters? While the efforts of hundreds of thousands who build the social value of sport in myriad selfless ways through 'sweat equity' go unrewarded financially. The coronavirus crisis has generated a springboard for reshaping the debate, towards a greater balance between sport as an agent of social good and the privatised pursuit of extreme profit, driven by manufactured celebrity that has become integral to top sport.

As with the global picture, much still needs to be done to meet the expectations for change in sport that formed during the transition from apartheid to political freedom and democracy in South Africa. How might sport revive liberatory dreams and promote human dignity and opportunities for young people, at a time when governments all over the world seem overwhelmed in their attempts to address inequalities? The insights from the experiences narrated here can help provide answers.

The courageous SANROC and other anti-apartheid sports activists of the 1960s and early 1970s needed a game-changer to help them disrupt the narrative of a reactionary IOC and Western sports establishment of that era – with direct-action protests flowing from decolonisation and the youth rebellions of those years helping project the anti-apartheid cause from the margins to the mainstream. Where the coronavirus disruption and #BLM developments will settle depends upon how determined the pressure for change remains.

So the struggle goes on – as the writer Ben Okri exhorts us:

> They are only the exhausted who think
> That they have arrived
> At their final destination,
> The end of their road,
> With all of their dreams achieved,
> And with no new dreams to hold.[434]

Abbreviations

AAM	Anti-Apartheid Movement
ANC	African National Congress
ANOCA	Association of National Olympic Committees of Africa
ARM	African Resistance Movement
AWB	Afrikaner Weerstandsbeweging
BOSS	Bureau of State Security
CARDS	Campaign Against Race Discrimination in Sport
CARE	Citizens Association for Racial Equality (New Zealand)
CARIS	Campaign Against Racism in Sport (Australia)
CASA	Culture in Another South Africa
CCIRS	Coordinating Committee for International Relations in Sport
CFS	Committee for Fairness in Sport
CMR	Cape Mounted Rifles
CODESA	Convention for a Democratic South Africa
CONTRALESA	Congress of Traditional Leaders of South Africa
COSATU	Congress of South African Trade Unions
FCC	Fair Cricket Campaign
FIFA	International Football Federation
FRELIMO	Mozambique Liberation Front
HART	Halt All Racist Tours (New Zealand)
ICAAS	International Campaign Against Apartheid Sport
INOCSA	Interim National Olympic Committee of South Africa
IOC	International Olympic Committee
IPL	Indian Premier League
IRA	Irish Republican Army
ITTF	International Table Tennis Federation
KWARU	Kwazakhele Rugby Union
MCC	Marylebone Cricket Club
MI5	British Security Service
MI6	British Secret Intelligence Service
NACOS	Natal Council of Sport
NACTU	National Council of Trade Unions
NADEL	National Association of Democratic Lawyers
NBA	National Basketball Association

424

NECC	National Education Crisis Committee
NOCSA	National Olympic Committee of South Africa
NOSC	National Olympic and Sports Congress
NSC	National Sports Congress
PAC	Pan Africanist Congress
SABCB	South African Bantu Cricket Board
SACA	South African Cricket Association
SACB	South African Cricket Board
SACBOC	South African Cricket Board of Control
SACCB	South African Coloured Cricket Board
SACOS	South African Council on Sport
SACP	South African Communist Party
SACU	South African Cricket Union
SAMA	South African Musicians Alliance
SANROC	South African Non-Racial Olympic Committee
SAOGA	South African Olympic Games Association
SAONGA	South African Olympic Committee
SARB	South African Rugby Board
SARRA	South African Road Running Association
SARWCA	South Africa and Rhodesia Women's Cricket Association
SASA	South African Soccer Association
SASA	South African Sports Association
SASF	South African Swimming Federation
SASPO	South African Non-Racial Sports Organisations
SATTB	South African Table Tennis Board
SAYCO	South African Youth Congress
SSC	State Security Council
STST	Stop The Seventy Tour
TCCB	Test and County Cricket Board
UDF	United Democratic Front
UWCO	United Women's Congress
WPCC	Western Province Cricket Club
YL	Young Liberals

About the authors

Peter Hain has been in politics for over fifty years. Born in 1950 and brought up in South Africa, his parents, Adelaine and Walter, were first jailed then banned for their anti-apartheid activism in Pretoria, and forced into exile in London in March 1966, the South African government having instructed all architectural firms from employing Walter.

He attended a rugby school, Pretoria Boys High, but chose to play football at Berea Park then Arcadia Shepherds. He has been a Chelsea fan since 1965. Upon moving to the UK he started playing club cricket and football. He also follows rugby, cricket and Formula One, the latter an interest spanning South Africa's Kyalami to Britain's Silverstone.

Aged nineteen, Peter became a British anti-apartheid leader, focussed on stopping all-white South African sports tours from 1969 onwards. In December 2015 he was awarded from South Africa the The Order of the Companions of O. R. Tambo for his 'excellent contribution to the freedom struggle'. In 2017–18 he exposed in the UK Parliament money laundering and corruption involving global corporates on behalf of then President Zuma's family and their business associates, the Gupta brothers; in November 2019 he gave evidence to the Commission on State Capture.

In 2018 he chaired the Nelson Mandela London Centenary Exhibition Organising Committee. In 2017 he chaired the Oliver Tambo Centenary UK Committee. He is a vice-president of Action for Southern Africa (ACTSA), successor to the British Anti-Apartheid Movement.

As Member of Parliament for Neath (1991–2015), he served in the Labour governments of Tony Blair and Gordon Brown for twelve years, seven in the cabinet. As secretary of state for Northern Ireland he negotiated an end to the conflict, bringing old enemies together in government in 2007. In November 2015 he was introduced to the House of Lords.

He is the author of twenty-two books, including *Mandela: His Essential Life* (2018), *Ad & Wal: Values, Duty, Sacrifice in Apartheid South Africa* (2014), his memoirs *Outside In* (2012) and *The Rhino Conspiracy* (2020).

Chair of the Donald Woods Foundation, patron of the Canon Collins Trust and a trustee of the Liliesleaf Trust and the Listen Charity, he teaches at Gordon Institute of Business Studies, University of Pretoria and University of Stellenbosch Business School and has been Visiting Professor at Wits Business School, University of the Witwatersrand as well as the University of South Wales.

André Odendaal is a writer, historian and activist who has written and co-authored a dozen books on the history of the liberation struggle and the social history of sport in South Africa. He is honorary professor in History and Heritage Studies at the University of the Western Cape and writer for the Albie Sachs Trust for Constitutionalism and the Rule of Law.

After graduating with a PhD from the University of Cambridge in 1984, André spent thirteen years at the University of the Western Cape, where he founded the Mayibuye Centre for History and Culture in South Africa. He was founding director of the Robben Island Museum (1997–2002), the first official heritage institution in democratic South Africa and a UNESCO World Heritage Site. He subsequently served as the chief executive in charge of the renowned Newlands Cricket Ground in Cape Town and the successful Cape Cobras professional team – one of six in South Africa.

André learnt his rugby and cricket at Queens College, Queenstown where old boy and future England captain Tony Greig was one of his coaches. He played first-class cricket in South Africa under both SACU and SACB and for the University of Cambridge in England. He was the only provincial cricketer designated 'white' to join the non-racial SACOS during the apartheid years, taking a stand against apartheid with a small group of like-minded sportspeople, including the famous case of the Watson brothers in rugby. André was active in various anti-apartheid groups in the 1980s, such as the UDF, NECC and NSC. In the early 1990s, he chaired the ANC's Museums and Monuments Commission. He was also chairperson of United Cricket Board of South Africa's Transformation Monitoring Committee (1998–2002). In 2002 he received the President's Award for Sport for his contribution to non-racial sport.

André is the co-author of *Cricket and Conquest* (2016), which was long-listed for the Alan Paton Award and honoured at the National Institute for Humanities and Social Sciences Book Awards. He also publishes on a small-scale, having started the African Lives Series in 2016. He initiated the project for *Imithetho Yeqakamba,* the first translation of the laws of cricket into an indigenous South African language by Xolisa Tshongolo and a team of language experts, in co-operation with Cricket South Africa, the MCC and the Western Cape Department of Cultural Affairs and Sport (2018).

Note on sources

A formal literature on sport and liberation in South Africa emerged only in the 1960s and 1970s. It was linked to the politics of exile and the internationalisation of the anti-apartheid struggle, emphasising once more the thread tying together political and sport struggles from the start. In the 1960s a stream of revisionist writing by recent exiles began. Some of these intellectuals, including Ruth First and Ronald Segal, were connected to major new African-focused initiatives by publishers such as Penguin and Heineman, which provided space outside of a heavily censored South Africa to keep the ideas of the liberation struggle at the forefront. This was the decade of decolonisation, when a whole new international support network arose as the anti-apartheid struggle became one of the biggest single-issue campaigns in international politics.

A worldwide movement against apartheid emerged, from local church groups and trade unions to national governments and solidarity groupings, as well as transnational forums such as the new Organisation of African Unity (and the allied Supreme Council for Sport in Africa) and the United Nations with its Special Committee Against Apartheid. International scholars and activists linked to the growing international anti-apartheid movement provided the first historical overviews of the anti-apartheid sports struggle. The writings by Chris de Broglio (1970), Peter Hain (1971), Dennis Brutus (1972), Richard Lapchick (PhD 1973, published 1975), Richard Thompson (1975), Tom Newnham (1975), Joan Brickhill (1976), Robert Archer and Antoine Bouillon (1982) and Sam Ramsamy (1982) remain landmarks of this genre. After the formation of SACOS in 1973, the counter-narrative to apartheid sport was both stimulated and reinforced by an internal resurgence of mobilisation, lobbying and writing, for example, the regular SACOS biennial reports and bulletins and a supportive alternative press.

A second generation of activist research and writing in South Africa and internationally, and the emergence of sports history as a discipline in its own right from the late 1970s onwards opened up the field further. André and others accessed an internally generated archive of newspapers and organisational brochures, almanacks and reports on the struggles of marginalised black and women sportspeople in South Africa to start telling the story from the beginning. Today the study of the social and political aspects of South African sports history is becoming a virtual industry.

Peter and André have published over thirty books between them, and in the process accumulated a great debt to colleagues, co-authors, publishers, archivists, librarians, friends and family. Peter's *Don't Play With Apartheid: The Background to the Stop The Seventy Tour Campaign* (1971) was an important source and there are overlaps with his memoir *Outside In* (2012), his parents' story *Ad & Wal: Values, Duty and Sacrifice in Apartheid South Africa* (2014) and *Sing the Beloved Country: The Struggle for the New South Africa* (1995).

André has drawn, sometimes directly, from various of his works, especially *The Story of an African Game* (2003), *The Founders* (2012), *Cricket and Conquest* (2016) and *Divided Country* (2018). He wishes to thank his publishers and, in particular, co-authors and colleagues Christopher Merrett, Jonty Winch and Richard Parry for allowing him to use material and ideas which are in some cases as much theirs as his.

In parts, original sources and endnotes have been redacted, and we ask interested readers to refer to the original works for some of this detail.

Peter and André had support from a number of friends from the anti-apartheid struggle, especially Trevor Richards, who kindly drafted invaluable material on the New Zealand sports campaign, as did Meredith Burgmann on the Australian campaign and Christabel Gurney on the British Anti-Apartheid Movement's crucial role (see also aamarchives.org).

The late Chris de Broglio wrote a long account on SANROC's role in an unpublished paper he sent Peter in 2013, which we have drawn upon and his daughter Michele gave us a private photo together with one of Dennis Brutus.

John Harris's son David Wolfe provided new material on his father's role and David's daughter Katie Clark did important research into Harris's papers on SANROC.

Colin Schindler helped with material he researched in records in the MCC Library, Lords Cricket Ground, for his new book, *Barbed Wire & Cucumber Sandwiches: The Controversial South Africa Tour of 1970* (2020).

We have drawn on a booklet by Geoff Brown and Christian Høgsbjerg, which provides an excellent overview on the British sports apartheid campaign: *Apartheid Is Not a Game: Remembering the Stop The Seventy Tour Campaign* (2020).

For information and the use of photographs, we are indebted to Gerald Majola, the late Dan Qeqe, Allan Zinn, Norman Arendse and the host of former women's cricketers who helped André with his research.

Acknowledgements

André is grateful to many friends and colleagues for their support during his past five years of full-time writing: Albie Sachs, Christopher Merrett, Krish Reddy, Jonty Winch, Richard Parry, Yusuf Garda, Xolela Mangcu, Mwelela Cele, Pamela Maseko, Nomalanga Mkize, Marguerite Poland, Jeremy Whiteman, Charlotte Imani, Ra-ees Saait, John Young, Russell Martin, Mac Maharaj, Pallo Jordan, Xolisa Tshongolo, Lyndon Bouah, Lindeka Rwali, Thabo Tutu, Bennet Bailey, Brent Walters, Ashwin Desai, Michael Weeder, Rashid Omar, Moira Levy, Tyrone August, Neo Lekgotla laga Ramoupi, Noel Solani, Khwezi ka Mpumlwana, Noor Nieftagodien, Geraldine Frieselaar, Olusegun Morakinyo, Tim Wilson, Elizabeth Thomas, Bridget Impey, Maggie Davey, Carmen Herbert, Sibongiseni Mkize, Vusi Kumalo, Janet Hodgson, Theresa Edlmann, Tyrone August, John Weinberg, Andre Mohamed, Anthea Josias, David Wallace, Gordon Metz, Louis, Rafique and Adam Asmal, Tarminder Kaur, Mogamad Allie, Aslam Khota, Francois Cleophas, Philani Nongogo, Archie Henderson, Vernon Joshua, Mthunzi Nxawe, Marion Keim, Hein Gerwel, Greg Houston, Bob Edgar, Christopher Saunders, Colin Bundy, Andrew Bank, Ciraj Rassool, Premesh Lalu, Tyrone Pretorius, Larry Popkas, Nasima Badsha, Patricia Hayes, Paolo Israel, Mariki Victor, Pascall Taruvinga, Brian Willan, Mkhululi Auwa, Elinor Sisulu, Ncwadi Tunyiswa and Landi Cilliers.

He wishes to acknowledge friends and comrades from decades back, in those Queensland CC, United CC, TCC, WPCB, SACOS, NSC, UDF, ANC and UWC days, without whose support he would not have been able to co-write this book.

Pitch Battles is André's fifth book on the history of sport in South Africa since being mandated by Cricket South Africa two decades ago to lead its project of rewriting the history of South African cricket. Max Jordaan has been his point person at CSA in all that time, and André wishes to thank him on his retirement this year, for the support through thick and thin over the years.

Thanks to Oliver Gadsby, Ben Glover, Gurdeep Mattu, Mark Thomson, Dorothy Feaver, Scarlet Furness and the team at Rowman & Littlefield Publishers, who were enthusiastic, supportive and professional from the start. For his active encouragement and backing for the South African edition, thanks to Eugene Ashton and his team at Jonathan Ball Publishers.

André says, 'Without my family – Zohra, Adam, Nadia, Rehana and Mary – the warm humanity and generosity of Tony Tabatznik, and the support of the Bertha Foundation those five years of writing could not have happened. *Ndiyabulela.'*

Peter was privileged to have the active support of his late parents Adelaine and Walter Hain (even into their late eighties) throughout his fifty years of political activism: they remain an inspiration to him as to many others. His sons Sam and Jake and their wonderful wives Paula and Kirsten also sustain him and keep him grounded; and Peter hopes that his grandchildren Harry, Seren, Holly, Tesni, Cassian, Freya and Zachary will learn from and in their own ways carry forward the values underpinning the struggle that *Pitch Battles* commemorates.

Finally, a deep and special thank you to Zohra Ebrahim and Elizabeth Haywood for all the fun, feistiness and reprimands when we are all together, and for their tolerance over the stresses and strains involved in co-writing this book, especially towards the end. Because it became less a task than an all-consuming mission for us both.

Selected bibliography

Alegi, Peter. *Laduma! Soccer, Politics and Society in South Africa, from Its Origins to 2010*. Scottsville: University of KwaZulu-Natal Press, 2010.

Allie, Mogamad. *More Than a Game: History of the Western Province Cricket Board 1959–1991*. Cape Town: Cape Argus/WPCA, 2000.

Aluko, Eniola. *They Don't Teach This*. London: Yellow Jersey Press, 2019.

Anti-Apartheid Movement Archives. Aamarchives.org.

Archer, Robert, and Antoine Bouillon. *The South African Game: Sport and Racism*. London: Zed Press, 1982.

Arlott, John, and Fred Trueman. *Arlott and Trueman on Cricket*, edited by Gilbert Phelps. London: British Broadcasting Corporation, 1977.

August, Tyrone. *Dennis Brutus: The South African Years*. Cape Town: Best Red in association with African Lives, Cape Town, 2020.

Barclay, Theo. 'A Search for Stability: Upper Middle-Class Attitudes to Immigration and Race Relations Between 1968 and 1970, Seen Through Public Reaction to the Stop the Seventy Tour Campaign.' BA Hons diss., University of Oxford, 2010.

Bassano, Brian, and Rick Smith. *The Visit of Mr W. W. Read's 1891–92 English Cricket Team to South Africa*. Ewell: J. W. McKenzie, 2007.

Bell, Roger J. *In Apartheid's Shadow: Australian Race Politics and South Africa, 1945–1975*. Melbourne: Australian Scholarly Publishing, 2019.

Beresford, David. *Truth Is a Strange Fruit: A Personal Journey through the Apartheid War*. Johannesburg: Jacana Media, 2010.

Birley, Derek. *The Willow Wand: Some Cricket Myths Explored*. London: Aurum Press, 2000.

Blake, Robert. *A History of Rhodesia*. London: Eyre Methuen, 1977.

Bolsmann, Chris. 'The Orange Free State football team tour of Europe: "Race", imperial loyalty and sporting contest'. In *Sport Past and Present in South Africa: (Trans)forming the Nation*, edited by S. Cornelissen and A. Grundlingh. London: Routledge, 2012.

Booth, Keith. *George Lohmann: Pioneer Professional*. London: SportsBooks, 2007.

Bose, Mihir. *Sporting Colours: Sport and Politics in South Africa*. London: Robson Books, 1994.

— *A History of Indian Cricket*. London: André Deutsch, 2002.

Bowen, Rowland. *Cricket: A History of Its Growth and Development Throughout the World*. London: Eyre & Spottiswoode, 1970.

Brearley, Mike. *On Cricket*. London; Constable, 2018.

Brickhill, Joan. *Race Against Race: South Africa's "Multi-National" Sport Fraud*. London: International Defence and Aid Fund, 1976.

Bright-Holmes, John, ed. *The Joy of Cricket*. London: Martin Secker & Warburg, 1984.

Brink, André. *A Fork in the Road: A Memoir.* London: Harvill Secker, 2009.

Brown, Geoff and Christian Høgsbjerg. *Apartheid Is Not a Game: Remembering the Stop The Seventy Tour Campaign.* London: Redwords, 2020.

Brutus, Dennis. 'The Sportsman's Choice'. In *Apartheid: A Collection of Writings on South African Racism by South Africans*, edited by A. La Guma. London: Lawrence & Wishart, 1972.

Bundy, Colin. 'On a Sticky Wicket: English Cricket from the Golden Age to the IPL'. Lecture, 'Following On: The History of Cricket, Cricket and History', University of Cape Town Summer School Course (with André Odendaal), 2019.

Burgess, Julian et al. *The Great White Hoax: South Africa's International Propaganda Machine.* London: Africa Bureau, 1977.

Calland, Richard, Lawson Naidoo, and Andrew Whaley. *The Vuvuzela Revolution: Anatomy of South Africa's World Cup.* Johannesburg: Jacana Media, 2010.

Callinicos, Luli. *Oliver Tambo: Beyond the Ngele Mountains.* Cape Town: David Philip, 2015.

Campschreur, Willem, and Joost Divendal. *Culture in Another South Africa.* London: Zed Books, 1989.

Canoville, Paul. *Black and Blue.* London: Headline, 2008.

Carlin, John. *Playing the Enemy: Nelson Mandela and the Game That Made a Nation.* London: Atlantic, 2010.

Carmichael, Shelly, ed. *112 Years of Springbok Rugby: Tests and Heroes, 1891–2003.* Cape Town: South African Rugby Football Union, 2003.

Cleophas, Francois. *Exploring Decolonising Themes in SA Sport History: Issues and Challenges.* Stellenbosch: African Sun Media, 2018.

De Broglio, Chris. *South Africa: Racism in Sport.* London: International Defence and Aid Fund, 1970.

Desai, Ashwin, Vishnu Padayachee, Krish Reddy, and Goolam Vahed. *Blacks in Whites: A Century of Black Cricket in KwaZulu-Natal.* Pietermaritzburg: University of KwaZulu-Natal Press, 2003.

Desai, Ashwin. *Reverse Sweep: A Story of South African Cricket Since Apartheid.* Johannesburg: Jacana Media, 2016.

— *Wentworth: The Beautiful Game and the Making of Place.* Pietermaritzburg: University of KwaZulu-Natal Press, 2019.

Dobson, Paul. *Rugby in South Africa.* Cape Town: South African Rugby Board, 1989.

Dorril, Stephen, and Robin Ramsay. *Smear! Wilson and the Secret State.* London: Fourth Estate, 1991.

Driver, C. J. *The Man with the Suitcase: The Life, Execution and Rehabilitation of John Harris, Liberal Terrorist.* Cape Town: Crane River, 2015.

Duffus, Louis. *Play Abandoned.* Cape Town: Timmins, 1969.

Ebrahim, Hassen. *The Making of the Constitution: The Story of South Africa's Constitutional Assembly.* Cape Town: Churchill Murray, 1997.

Edwards, Harry. *The Revolt of the Black Athlete*. London: Collier-MacMillan, 1969.

Estherhuyse, Willie. *Endgame: Secret Talks and the End of Apartheid*. Cape Town: Tafelberg, 2012.

Friedman, Steven. *Building Tomorrow Today: African Workers in Trade Unions, 1970–1984*. Johannesburg: Ravan Press, 1987.

Frewin, Leslie. *The Boundary Book: Second Innings*. London: Spring Books, 1989.

Froman, Jody. *Papa Joe: 80 Not Out*. UK: Jody Froman, 2011.

Giliomee, Hermann. *The Parting of the Ways: South African Politics 1976–82*. Cape Town: David Philip, 1982.

Goodall, Noel. 'Opposing Apartheid Through Sport: The Role of SACOS in South African Sport, 1982–92'. MA thesis, Wits University, 2016.

Greyvenstein, Chris. *The Fighters: A Pictorial History of SA Boxing Since 1881*. Cape Town: Sigma Motor Corporation, 1981.

Groenink, Evelien. *Incorruptible: The Story of the Murders of Dulcie September, Anton Lubowski and Chris Hani*. Cape Town: Evelien Groenink, 2018.

Grundlingh, Albert, André Odendaal, and Burridge Spies. *Beyond the Tryline: Rugby and South African Society*. Johannesburg: Ravan Press, 1995.

Guha, Ramachandra. *The Picador Book of Cricket*. London: Picador, 2001.

— *A Corner of a Foreign Field: The Indian History of a British Sport*. Haryana, India: Penguin Random House India, 2016.

Gunn, Shirley, and Shanil Haricharan, eds. *Voices from the Underground: Eighteen Life Stories from Umkhonto we Sizwe's Ashley Kriel Detachment*. Cape Town: Penguin Random House, 2019.

Gurney, Christabel. 'In the Heart of the Beast: The British Anti-Apartheid Movement, 1959–1994'. In *The Road to Democracy in South Africa*. Vol. 3, *International Solidarity*. Pretoria: South African Democracy Education Trust/UNISA, 2008.

Hain, Peter. *Don't Play with Apartheid: Background to the Stop the Seventy Tour Campaign*. London: Allen & Unwin, 1971.

— *Mistaken Identity: The Wrong Face of the Law*. London: Quartet Books, 1976.

— *A Putney Plot?* Nottingham: Spokesman, 1987.

— *Outside In*. London: Biteback Publishing, 2012.

— *Ad & Wal: Values, Duty, Sacrifice in Apartheid South Africa*. London: Biteback Publishing, 2014.

— *Back to The Future of Socialism*. Bristol: Policy Press, 2015.

— *Mandela: His Essential Life*. London: Rowman & Littlefield, 2018.

Hammond-Tooke, W. D. *Command or Consensus: The Development of Transkeian Local Government*. Cape Town: Oxford University Press, 1975.

Harris, Stewart. *Political Football: The Springbok Tour of Australia, 1971*. Melbourne: Gold Star Publications, 1972.

Harvey, Robert. *The Fall of Apartheid: The Inside Story from Smuts to Mbeki*. London: Palgrave Macmillan, 2003.

Hauman, Riel. *Century of the Marathon, 1896–1996*. Cape Town: Human & Rousseau, 1996.

Hawkey, Ian, and Luke Alfred. *Vuvuzela Dawn*. London: Pan Macmillan, 2019.

Hilmes, Oliver. *Berlin 1936*. London: Bodley Head, 2018.

Holmes, Judith. *Olympiad 1936: Blaze of Glory for Hitler's Reich*. New York: Ballantine Books, 1971.

Holt, Richard. *Sport and the British: A Modern History*. Oxford: Clarendon Press, 1993.

Huddleston, Trevor. *Naught for Your Comfort*. New York: Doubleday & Company, 1956.

Humphry, Derek. *The Cricket Conspiracy*. London: National Council for Civil Liberties, 1975.

Hutton, Barbara. *Robben Island: Symbol of Resistance*. Cape Town: Mayibuye Books/ Sached Books, 1994.

Huizinga, John. *Homo Ludens: A Study of the Play-Element in Culture*. London: Beacon Press, 1971.

Jeffery, Anthea. *People's War: New Light on the Struggle for South Africa*. Johannesburg: Jonathan Ball Publishers, 2017.

Jeffery, Keith, and Peter Hennessy. *States of Emergency: British Governments and Strikebreaking Since 1919*. London: Routledge & Kegan Paul, 1983

Karis, T. G., and G. M. Gerhart. *From Protest to Challenge: A Documentary History of African Politics in South Africa, 1882–1990*. Vol. 5. Bloomington: Indiana University Press, 1997.

Kathrada, Ahmed. *No Bread for Mandela: Memoirs of Ahmed Kathrada*. New Delhi: National Book Trust, India, 2008.

Keim, Marion, and Lyndon Bouah, 'Sport and Recreation on Robben Island', *The International Journal of the History of Sport* 30, no. 16 (2013).

Korr, Chuck, and Marvin Close. *More Than Just a Game: Football v Apartheid*. London: Collins, 2009.

La Guma, Alex. *Apartheid: A Collection of Writings on South African Racism by South Africans*. London: Lawrence and Wishart, 1972.

Lapchick, Richard. *The Politics of Race and International Sport: The Case of South Africa*. London: Greenwood Press, 1982.

Luckin, M. W. *The History of South African Cricket: Including the Full Scores of All Important Matches Since 1876*. Johannesburg: W. E. Hortor, 1915.

Mandela, Nelson. *Long Walk to Freedom*. London: Little, Brown and Company, 1994.

Mandell, Richard Donald. *The Nazi Olympics*. London: Souvenir Press, 1971.

Mangan. J. A. *Pleasure, Profit, Proselytism: British Culture and Sport at Home and Abroad 1700–1914*. London: Frank Cass, 1988.

Mangan, J. A., and Roberta J. Park. *From Fair Sex to Feminism: Sport and the Socialization of Women in the Industrial and Post-Industrial Eras*. London: Cass, 1987.

Marks, Shula, and Richard Rathbone, eds. *Industrialisation and Social Change in South Africa: African Class Formation, Culture, and Consciousness, 1870–1930*. New York: Longman, 1982.

May, Peter. *The Rebel Tours: Cricket's Crisis of Conscience*. Cheltenham: SportsBooks, 2009.

Melling, Phil, and Tony Collins, eds. *The Glory of Their Times: Crossing the Colour Line in Rugby League*. Skipton: Vertical Editions, 2004.

Merrett, Christopher. '"We Don't Want Crumbs, We Want Bread": Non-Racial Sport, the International Boycott and South African Liberals, 1956–1990', *English Academy Review: South African Journal of English Studies* 27, no. 2 (2010).

Morrell, Robert. *From Boys to Gentlemen: Settler Masculinity in Colonial Natal 1880–1920*. Pretoria: University of South Africa, 2001.

Morris, Jan. *The Spectacle of Empire: Style, Effect and the Pax Britannica*. London: Doubleday, 1982.

Mostert, Noël. *Frontiers: The Epic of South Africa's Creation and the Tragedy of the Xhosa People*. London: Pimlico, 1992.

Moult, Les, and Philip Hartman. *Playing the Game: The Story of Cape Town Cricket Club*. Cape Town: Cape Town CC in association with Western Province Cricket Association, 2012.

Naidoo, Indres. *Island in Chains: Ten Years on Robben Island*. Johannesburg: Penguin Books, 1982.

Naidoo, Krish. *Krish: Struggle Lawyer*. Crown Mines: Krish Naidoo, 2019.

Nasson, Bill. *Springboks at the Somme: The Making of Dellville Wood, 1916*. Johannesburg: Institute for Advanced Social Research, University of the Witwatersrand, 1996.

Nicholson, Chris. *Papwa Sewgolum: From Pariah to Legend*. Johannesburg: Wits University Press, 2005.

Nicholson, Chris, and Mike Hickson. *The Level Playing Field: How the Aurora Cricket Club Stumped Apartheid*. Pietermaritzburg: KwaZulu-Natal Cricket Union/Cricket South Africa, 2015.

Nixon, Ron. *Selling Apartheid: South Africa's Global Propaganda War*. London: Pluto Press, 2016.

Oakes, Dougie. *Reader's Digest Illustrated History of South Africa: The Real Story*. Cape Town: Reader's Digest, 1989.

Oborne, Peter. *Basil D'Oliveira: Cricket and Conspiracy, The Untold Story*. London: Little, Brown, 2004.

Odendaal André. *Cricket in Isolation: The Politics of Race and Cricket in South Africa*. Cape Town: André Odendaal, 1977.

— 'Liberalism and the African National Congress'. Paper presented at conference on 'Liberalism in South Africa', Houw Hoek Inn, 1986.

— 'Resistance, Reform and Repression in South Africa in the 1980s'. In *Beyond the Barricades: Popular Resistance in South Africa in the 1980s*. London: Kliptown Books, 1989.

— 'Robben Island – Bridgehead for Democracy'. Paper presented to Mayibuye Centre Winter School, Celebrating Democracy Festival, University of the Western Cape, 15 July 1994.

— 'Turning History on Its Head: Some Perspectives on Afrikaners and the Game of Cricket'. In *Cricket . . . Developing Winners. A 10th birthday celebration of the United Cricket Board of South Africa's 'Development for all in the game for all'*, edited by Chris Day. Johannesburg: UCBSA, 2002.

— *The Story of an African Game: Black Cricketers and the Unmasking of One of South Africa's Greatest Myths, 1850–2003*. Cape Town: David Philip, 2003.

— 'The Liberation Struggle in South Africa, 1948–1994'. In *Africa Since 1990*, edited by Y. N. Seleti. Johannesburg: New Africa Education, 2004.

— 'The Hundred Years' War: Brown Balls, Bronzed Colonials and the Persistence of Colonial Biases in 21st-Century Rugby Cultures'. Plenary address at 'Afrikaners, Anglos and Springboks, 1906–2006', London, 25 September 2006.

— '"Neither Cricketers nor Ladies": Towards a History of Women's Cricket in South Africa, 1860s–2000s'. In *Sport Past and Present in South Africa: (Trans)forming the Nation*, edited by S. Cornelissen and A. Grundlingh. London: Routledge, 2012.

— *The Founders: The Origins of the ANC and the Struggle for Democracy in South Africa*. Johannesburg: Jacana Media, 2012.

— 'Girls and Boys: Looking Back at Cricket's Strange History'. In *CSA Girls U19 Cricket Week*, brochure. Cape Town: CSA, 2013.

— ed. *'The Gate': Commemorating SA Sport's June 16 Moment and the Non-Racial Struggles that Led to Cricket Unity*. Cape Town: Cricket South Africa, 2014.

— '"Maintain the Human and Social Within You": Reflecting on Robben Island, Sport and Change in South Africa'. Keynote address to the conference on 'Sport and the Struggles for Social Justice', Robben Island Museum and Department of Sports Science, Stellenbosch University, 10 October 2019.

Odendaal, André, Krish Reddy, and Andrew Samson. *The Blue Book: A History of Western Province Cricket, 1890–2011*. Cape Town: Fanele, 2012.

Odendaal, André, Krish Reddy, Christopher Merrett, and Jonty Winch. *Cricket and Conquest: The History of South African Cricket Retold*. Vol. 1, *1795–1914*. Cape Town: Best Red, 2016.

Odendaal, André, Krish Reddy, and Christopher Merrett. *Divided Country: The History of South African Cricket Retold*. Vol. 2, *1914–1960*. Cape Town: Best Red, 2018.

O'Donnell, Penny, and Lynette Simons. *Australians Against Racism: Testimonies from the Anti-Apartheid Movement in Australia*. Annandale, New South Wales: Pluto Press Australia, 1995.

Olifant, Andries, ed. *A Writing Life: Celebrating Nadine Gordimer*. London: Viking, 1998.

Pahad, Aziz. *Insurgent Diplomat: Civil Talks or Civil War?* Johannesburg: Penguin Books, 2014.

Pauw, Jacques. *The President's Keepers: Those Keeping Zuma in Power and out of Prison*. Cape Town: Tafelberg, 2018.

Penrose, Barrie, and Roger Courtiour. *The Pencourt File*. London: Secker & Warburg, 1978.

Player, Gary. *Grand Slam Golf*. London: Cassell, 1966.

Ramsamy, Sam. *Apartheid: The Real Hurdle; Sport in South Africa and the International Boycott*. London: International Defence and Aid Fund for Southern Africa, 1982.

Ramsamy, Sam. *Reflections on a Life in Sport*. Cape Town: Greenhouse Publishing Company, 2004.

Richards, Trevor. *Dancing on Our Bones: New Zealand, South Africa, Rugby and Racism*. Wellington: Bridget Williams Books, 1999.

Roberts, Cheryl. *SACOS 1971–1988: 15 Years of Sports Resistance*. Durban: Self-published, 1988.

— ed. *Sport and Transformation: Contemporary Debates in South African Sport*. Cape Town: Township Publishing Co-operative, 1989.

— *Sport in Chains*. Cape Town: Township Publishing Co-operative, 1994.

— *No Normal Sport in an Abnormal Society: Struggle for Non-Racial Sport in South Africa: from Apartheid to Sports Unity*. Cape Town: Havana Media, 2011.

Sandiford, Keith. *Cricket and the Victorians*. Aldershot: Scolar Press, 1994.

Shepherd, R. H. W. Lovedale. *South Africa: The Story of a Century 1841–1941*. Lovedale: Lovedale Press, 1940.

Schindler, Colin. *Barbed Wire & Cucumber Sandwiches: The Controversial South Africa Tour of 1970*. London: Pitch Publishing, 2020.

South African Council on Sport. [*First*] *Biennial Conference*. Durban: SACOS, 1975.

— *Third Biennial Conference*. Durban: SACOS, 1979.

— *Fourth Biennial Conference*. Durban: SACOS, 1981.

— *SACOS Sport Festival '82*. Cape Town: SACOS, 1982.

— *SACOS Bulletin* 1, no. 6 (September–October 1983).

— *Fifth Biennial Report*. Cape Town: SACOS, 1983.

— *SACOS Sportsperson of the Year Award, 1984*.

— *Sixth Biennial General Meeting*. Durban: SACOS, 1985.

— *Seventh Biennial Conference*. Johannesburg: SACOS, 1987.

— *SACOS Festival '88: A Commemorative Volume*. Cape Town: Buchu Books, 1988.

— *Eighth Biennial Meeting*. Cape Town: SACOS, 1989.

Sparks, Allister. *Tomorrow Is Another Country*. Johannesburg: Jonathan Ball, 2003.

Stoddart, Brian. 'Sport, Cultural Imperialism, and Colonial Response in the British Empire.' *Comparative Studies in Society and History* 30, no. 4 (1988).

Sustar, Lee, and Aisha Karim. *Poetry & Protest: A Dennis Brutus Reader*. Scottsville: University of KwaZulu-Natal Press, 2006.

Tanser, George Henry. *A Scantling of Time: The Story of Salisbury*. Salisbury: Stuart Manning, 1965.

Thomas, Cornelius, ed. *Sport and Liberation in South Africa: Reflections and Suggestions*. Alice: National Heritage and Cultural Studies Centre, University of Fort Hare/Pretoria: Department of Sport and Recreation, 2006.

Thompson, Richard. *Retreat from Apartheid: New Zealand's Sporting Contacts with South Africa*. London: Oxford University Press, 1975.

Trollope, Anthony, and J. H. Davidson. *South Africa*. Cape Town: Balkema, 1973.

Van der Merwe, Floris. *Sporting Soldiers: South African Troops at Play in World War I*. Stellenbosch: FJG Publikasies, 2012.

Van Vuuren, Hennie. *Apartheid Guns and Money*. London: Hurst Publishers, 2018.

Viviers, Gerhard. *Rugby Agter Doringdraad*. Pretoria: J. P. van der Walt en Seun, 1970.

Waite, John. *Perchance to Bowl*. London: Nicholas Kaye, 1961.

Willan, Brian. 'One of the most gentlemanly players that ever donned a jersey': The English Rugby Career of Richard Msimang (1907–1912), *Quarterly Bulletin of the National Library of South Africa* 66, no. 3 (July–September 2012).

Williams, Jack. *Cricket and England: A Cultural and Social History of the Inter-War Years*. London: Frank Cass, 1999.

Williams, Marcus, ed. *Double Century: Cricket in The Times*. Vol. 1, *1785–1934*. London: The Pavilion Library, 1989.

Williamson, Kristin. *Brothers to Us: The Story of a Remarkable Family's Fight Against Apartheid*. 2nd ed. Ringwood: Penguin Books, 1998.

Wilson, Monica, and Leonard Thompson. *The Oxford History of South Africa II*. Oxford: Oxford University Press, 1975.

Winch, Jonty, and Richard Parry. *Too Black to Wear Whites: The remarkable story of Krom Hendricks, a cricket hero who was rejected by Cecil John Rhodes's empire*. Cape Town: Penguin Random House, 2020.

Winter, Gordon. *Inside Boss: South Africa's Secret Police*. London: Allen Lane, 1981.

Woods, Donald. *Asking for Trouble*. London: Victor Gollancz, 1980.

Wright, Peter. *Spycatcher*. Richmond: Heinemann, 1987.

Notes

1 J. Huizinga, *Homo Ludens: A Study of the Play-Element in Culture* (1949; Boston: Beacon Press, 1971).

2 Quoted in D. Birley, *The Willow Wand: Some Cricket Myths Explored* (London: Aurum Press, 2000), 223. André also used these quotes in his writings for Makhenkesi Stofile, which appeared in print under the latter's name in SADET's history of the liberation struggle.

3 See P. Oborne, *Basil D'Oliveira: Cricket and Conspiracy, The Untold Story* (London: Little, Brown, 2004).

4 M. Brearley, *On Cricket* (London: Constable, 2018), 136–45.

5 For Dennis Brutus's recollections of the STST, see L. Sustar and A. Karim, *Poetry & Protest: A Dennis Brutus Reader* (Scottsville: University of KwaZulu-Natal Press, 2006), 135–36.

6 *Eastern Province Herald*, 12 August 1969.

7 For the story of the Stop The Seventy Tour campaign, see P. Hain, *Don't Play with Apartheid* (London: Allen & Unwin, 1971).

8 J. Inverdale, 'Remembering a bitter Springboks tour that paved a way for change', *Daily Telegraph*, 20 September 2006, https://www.telegraph.co.uk/sport/rugbyunion/international/england/2346183/Remembering-bitter-Springboks-tour-that-paved-a-way-for-change.html.

9 Peter was subsequently put on trial for conspiracy in 1972: see D. Humphry, ed., *The Cricket Conspiracy* (London: National Council for Civil Liberties, 1973).

10 C. Gurney, 'In the Heart of the Beast: The British Anti-Apartheid Movement, 1959–1994', in *The Road to Democracy in South Africa*, vol. 3, *International Solidarity* (Pretoria: South African Democracy Education Trust/UNISA, 2008), ch. 5.

11 See T. Barclay, 'A Search for Stability? Upper Middle-Class Attitudes to Immigration and Race Relations Between 1968 and 1970, Seen Through Public Reaction to the Stop the Seventy Tour Campaign' (BA Hons diss., University of Oxford, 2010).

12 Meredith Burgmann, quoted in P. O'Donnell and L. Simons, *Australians Against Racism: Testimonies from the Anti-Apartheid Movement in Australia* (New South Wales: Pluto Press, 1995), 15.

13 The other Wallaby boycotters were Bruce Taafe, Peter Darveniza, Terry Forman and Barry McDonald. (Lloyd McDermott had been the first Aboriginal Wallaby who refused to tour South Africa in 1963.)

14 Other Aboriginal campaigners were Billie Craigie, Lyn Craigie Thompson, Norma Ingram, Tony Koori, Isabelle Coe, Sol Bellear and Bob Bellear.

15 R. Bell, *In Apartheid's Shadow: Australian Race Politics and South Africa, 1945–1975* (Melbourne: Australian Scholarly Publishing, 2019), 278.

16 S. Harris, *Political Football* (Melbourne: Gold Star Publications, 1972).

17 Years later, Meredith Burgmann became a Labour parliamentarian and long-serving president of the New South Wales Upper House.

18 Quoted by C. Bundy, 'On a Sticky Wicket: English Cricket from the Golden Age to the IPL', lecture, 'Following On: The History of Cricket, Cricket and History', University of Cape Town Summer School (with A. Odendaal), 2019.

19 Bundy, 'On a Sticky Wicket'.

20 André Odendaal Collection: Box B33, 9, Scrapbooks South Africa to United Kingdom, 1969–79 (bw), newspaper cutting, 'SABC bans Bok match'.

21 The newspaper sources referred to here

and in unacknowledged references below are from André Odendaal Collection: Box B33, 7–9, Scrapbooks South Africa to United Kingdom, 1969–79 (bw).

22 See G. Viviers, Rugby Agter Doringdraad (Pretoria: J. P. van der Walt en Seun, 1970).

23 A. Odendaal, 'The Hundred Years' War: Brown Balls, Bronzed Colonials and the Persistence of Colonial Biases in 21st-Century Rugby Cultures', plenary address to the conference 'Afrikaners, Anglos and Springboks, 1906–2006', London, 19 September 2006 (organised by the Museum of Rugby, Twickenham, the Centre for the Study of Britain and its Empire, University of Southampton and the International Centre for Sports History, De Montford University).

24 On the Bennion case, see André Odendaal Collection: Box B35, 12, Scrapbooks, General issues (including socio-political) (bw); and Humphry, The Cricket Conspiracy.

25 A. Odendaal, '"The Thing That Is Not Round": The Untold Story of Black Rugby in South Africa', in Beyond the Tryline: Rugby and South African Society (Johannesburg: Ravan Press 1995), 24–25.

26 Quoted in A. Odendaal, 'South Africa's Black Victorians: Sport and Society in South Africa in the Nineteenth Century', in Pleasure, Profit, Proselytism: British Culture and Sport at Home and Abroad, 1700–1914, ed. J. A. Mangan (London: Cass, 1988), 203.

27 This section draws on A. Odendaal, 'Turning History on Its Head: Some Perspectives on Afrikaners and the Game of Cricket', in Cricket . . . Developing Winners, ed. C. Day (Johannesburg: UCBSA, 2002), 29–32.

28 C. Merrett, 'We Don't Want Crumbs, We Want Bread: Non-Racial Sport, 1956–90', English Academy Review: South African Journal of English Studies 27, no. 2.

29 J. Brickhill, Race Against Race: South Africa's "Multinational" Sport Fraud (London: International Defence and Aid Fund, 1976), 8.

30 'An enormous pity, says McGlew', Cape Times, 18 September 1968.

31 'Shock and dismay in South Africa', Cape Times, 18 September 1968.

32 L. Duffus, Play Abandoned (Cape Town: Timmins, 1969), 172–73, 176, quoted by C. Merrett in The History of South African Cricket Retold, vol. 3, 1960–2020 (forthcoming).

33 J. Waite, Perchance to Bowl (London: Nicholas Kaye, 1961), 47.

34 G. Player, Grand Slam Golf (London: Cassell, 1966), 7–10.

35 Player, Grand Slam Golf, 11.

36 The Nelson Mandela Foundation did withdraw its support for Player's annual invitation tournament at one stage, but it continues to be paid annually with never a mention of this incident.

37 See C. Nicholson, Papwa Sewgolum: From Pariah to Legend (Johannesburg: Wits University Press, 2005).

38 R. Nixon, Selling Apartheid: South Africa's Global Propaganda War (London: Pluto Press, 2016), 53.

39 Hain, Don't Play with Apartheid, 104.

40 P. Hain, Outside In (London: Biteback Publishing, 2012), 63.

41 Hain, Don't Play with Apartheid, 163.

42 With thanks to Colin Shindler, who kindly supplied these quotes from his researches in the MCC Library for his own book Barbed Wire & Cucumber Sandwiches: The Controversial South Africa Tour of 1970 (London: Pitch Publishing, 2020).

43 Bundy, 'On a Sticky Wicket', paragraph based on J. Williams, Cricket and England: A Cultural and Social History of the Interwar Years (London: Frank Cass, 1999), 22–25.

44 This chapter draws largely on A. Odendaal, K. Reddy, C. Merrett and J. Winch, Cricket and Conquest: The History of South African Cricket Retold, vol. 1, 1795–1914 (Cape Town: Best Red,

2016). My thanks to Jonty Winch and Christopher Merrett for permission to use our joint work here. The first section in this chapter is from A. Odendaal, foreword to *Too Black to Wear Whites: The remarkable story of Krom Hendricks, a cricket hero who was rejected by Cecil John Rhodes's empire*, by J. Winch and R. Parry (Cape Town: Penguin Random House, 2020).

45 *Cape Times* report in *The Visit of Mr W. W. Read's 1891–92 English Cricket Team to South Africa*, by B. Bassano and R. Smith (Ewell J. McKenzie, 2007), 173–75; E. Rosenthal, 'The "D'Oliveira" incident of the 1890s', *Cape Times*, undated, André Odendaal Collection.

46 A. E. Knight, 'The Complete Cricketer' (1906), in *The Joy of Cricket*, ed. John Bright-Holmes (London: Martin Secker & Warburg, 1984), 241.

47 *Cape Times*, 11 January 1894.

48 See R. Barker, 'The Demon Against England', in *The Picador Book of Cricket*, ed. R. Guha (London: Picador, 2001), 301–17.

49 *Cape Times*, 2 February 1894.

50 T. Couzens, *Battles of South Africa* (Cape Town: David Philip, 2004); see also battle.blaauwberg.net.

51 D. Oakes, ed., *Reader's Digest Illustrated History of South Africa: The Real Story* (Cape Town: Reader's Digest, 1988), 94.

52 N. van Burgst, *Adventures at the Cape of Good Hope*, 1, 78, quoted in *Playing the Game: The Story of Cape Town Cricket Club*, by L. Moult and P. Hartman (Cape Town: Cape Town CC in association with Western Province Cricket Association, 2012), 13.

53 R. Bowen, *Cricket: A History of Its Growth and Development Throughout the World* (London: Eyre & Spottiswoode, 1970), 85.

54 Odendaal et al, *Cricket and Conquest*, 19–20.

55 On the role of the military in the spread of the game in South Africa, see especially ibid., ch. 1–3, 9–10.

56 For detailed descriptions of the subjection of the various African chiefdoms between 1868 and 1906, see M. Wilson and L. M. Thompson, eds., *The Oxford History of South Africa II* (Oxford: Oxford University Press, 1971), ch. 5; D. Oakes, ed., *Reader's Digest Illustrated History of South Africa: The Real Story* (Cape Town: Reader's Digest, 1988), 176–92.

57 W. D. Hammond-Tooke, *Command or Consensus: The Development of Transkeian Local Government* (Cape Town: Oxford University Press, 1975), 23–24.

58 Quoted in A. Odendaal, 'Liberalism and the African National Congress', paper presented at the conference on 'Liberalism in South Africa', Houw Hoek Inn, 30 June–3 July 1986.

59 Odendaal, 'Liberalism and the African National Congress'.

60 'Canterbury Cricket Week', Wikipedia, last modified 29 October 2019, https://en.wikipedia.org/wiki/Canterbury_Cricket_Week.

61 'The cricket tournament', *Eastern Province Herald*, 7 January 1876, 5.

62 'The cricket matches', *Eastern Province Herald*, 18 January 1876.

63 A. Trollope, *South Africa* (1878; Cape Town: A. A. Balkema, 1973), 156–58, 161–62. With thanks to John Young for this source.

64 W. M. Luckin, *The History of South African Cricket: Including the Full Scores of All Important Matches Since 1878* (Johannesburg: W. I. Horton, 1915), 19, 168.

65 Birley, *The Willow Wand*, 89–90.

66 'Ibala labadlali', *Imvo Zabantsundu*, 15 December 1892.

67 M. Bose, *A History of Indian Cricket* (London: André Deutsch, 2002), 28.

68 Odendaal et al, *Cricket and Conquest*, 271.

69 Ibid., 271

70 Ibid., ch. 9, 27, 29.

71 Ibid., introduction.

72 J. Morris, *The Spectacle of Empire: Style, Effect and the Pax Britannica* (London: Doubleday, 1982), ch. 8.

73 R. Guha, *A Corner of a Foreign Field: The Indian History of a British Game* (London: Picador, 2002), 6.

74 Quoted in Odendaal et al, *Cricket and Conquest*, 120.

75 Ibid., 120.

76 B. Stoddart, 'Sport, Cultural Imperialism and the Colonial Response to the British Empire', *Comparative Studies in Society and History* 30, no. 4, 662.

77 For the full story of Krom Hendricks, see Winch and Parry, *Too Black to Wear Whites*. On discrimination against Jews at the Cape around the turn of the twentieth century see, M. Shain, 'Jewish community's long fight against discrimination', *Cape Times*, 7 September 2016. This article deals interestingly with a delegation to the Cape Attorney General, Thomas Lynedoch Graham, who was a member of the WPCC and one of the organisers with Milton of the first international tour, though none of Graham's views are discussed.

78 K. McCrone, 'Play up! Play up! And play the game! Sport at the late Victorian public school', in *From Fair Sex to Feminism: Sport and the Socialization of Women in the Industrial and Post-Industrial Eras*, ed. J. A. Mangan and R. Park (London: Frank Cass, 1987), 99.

79 Odendaal et al, *Cricket and Conquest*, 402–3. See R. Morrell, *From Boys to Gentlemen: Settler Masculinity in Colonial Natal, 1880–20* (Pretoria: Unisa Press, 2001), 60–61, 65, 79, 85, 95, 96, 101–3.

80 Quoted in F. J. G. van der Merwe, *Sporting Soldiers: South African Troops at Play in World War I* (Stellenbosch: FJG Publikasies, 2012), 41.

81 For details, see A. Odendaal, K. Reddy, and C. Merrett, *Divided Country: The History of South African Cricket Retold*, vol. 2, *1914–60* (Cape Town: Best Red,

2018), ch. 1.

82 Ibid., 23.

83 B. Nasson, *Springboks at the Somme: The Making of Dellville Wood, 1916* (Johannesburg: Institute for Advanced Social Research, University of the Witwatersrand, 1996), 4–5, 9–12.

84 J. Bantjies, 'Boys' schools examined afresh', *Cape Times*, 8 July 2015.

85 The basis for this chapter is A. Odendaal, *The Founders: The Origins of the ANC and the Struggle for Democracy in South Africa* (Johannesburg: Jacana Media, 2012); this draws on several histories of nineteenth-century black sport written by the author, such as 'South Africa's Black Victorians' (1988), *The Story of an African Game* (2003) and *Cricket and Conquest* (2016).

86 See B. Willan, 'An African in Kimberley', in *Industrialisation and Social Change in South Africa: African Class Formation, Culture, and Consciousness, 1870–1930*, ed. S. Marks and R. Rathbone (New York: Longman, 1982), 241–42, 248–52.

87 M. Poland to A. Odendaal, 6 November 2019, with her piece on 'The Anglican Institution' attached; 'Ibala labadlali', *Imvo*, 8 October 1891.

88 'Umdlalo we krikiti', *Isigidimi Sama-Xosa*, 15 March 1884.

89 Paper read by Elijah Makiwane to the United Missionary Conference, *Imvo*, 19 July 1888.

90 See A. Odendaal, *The Story of an African Game: Black Cricketers and the Unmasking of One of South Africa's Greatest Myths, 1850–2003* (Cape Town: David Philip, 2003), ch. 3–5; and Odendaal et al, *Cricket and Conquest*, ch. 4, 11, 12, 21.

91 'Ibola e-Monti', *Isigidimi Sama-Xosa*, 15 October 1883.

92 'King William's Town NCC vs. E. London NCC', *Isigidimi Sama-Xosa*, 16 January 1884.

93 'Ibala le cricket', *Imvo*, 19 January 1885.

94 Luckin, *The History of South African Cricket* (1915), 19; 'Cricket tournament',

Cape Mercury, 3 January 1885. The four teams participating were Port Elizabeth, King William's Town, Kimberley and Cape Town.

95 'Amangesi nabantsundu', *Imvo,* 2 March 1885.

96 Editorial notes, *Imvo,* 2 March 1885.

97 Editorial notes, *Imvo,* 16 February 1885; 'Ibola e Komani', *Imvo,* 9 December1885. 'Ibala labadlali', *Imvo,* 21 December 1887.

98 Quoted in 'Imvo Zabantsundu', *Imvo,* 22 December 1884. Please note that the K-word is quoted on limited occasions to document the hatefulness of its usage.

99 Quoted in Imvo Zabantsundu, *Imvo,* 9 March 1885.

100 'Cricket', *Cape Mercury,* 24 March 1885; 'Amangesi nabantsundu', *Imvo,* 23 March 1885.

101 'Natives and cricket', *Imvo,* 9 March 1885.

102 'Editorial notes', *Imvo,* 3 November 1884.

103 See, for example, 'Ibali laba dlali', *Imvo,* 23 November 1887.

104 'Ixesha le bhola, 1889', *Imvo,* 17 October 1889.

105 'Eze bola', *Isigidimi Sama-Xosa,* 15 August 1884'.

106 'Kubadlali bola', *Isigidimi Sama-Xosa,* 1 November 1884.

107 Editorial notes, *Imvo,* 28 February 1889.

108 Marks and Rathbone, *Industrialisation and social change,* 248–49.

109 'A sound mind in a sound body', African Political Organisation, 15 January 1910.

110 See, for example, 'Ibala labadlali', *Imvo,* 26 March 1886; 'Ibala labadlali' and 'Ukuzigcobisa', *Imvo,* 26 September 1889 and 21 September 1889; 'Ibala labadlali', *Imvo,* 18 February 1897; 'Intenetya e Qonce', *Imvo,* 18 December 1897; 'Ukuzigcobisa', *Imvo,* 21 August 1898 and 11 September 1899.

111 'Ibala labadlali – I Jabavu Cup', *Imvo,* 16 December 1897.

112 Reports of Frontier CC meetings, *Imvo,* 13 October 1892, 17 October 1894, 29 August 1895, 10 September 1896 and 21 September 1898.

113 'Editorial notes', *Tsala ea Becoana,* 16 December 1911.

114 Paper read by Elijah Makiwane to the United Missionary Conference, *Imvo,* 19 July 1888. See *Imvo Zabatsundu,* 12 April 1888; 'Izimiselo ze Kroki', *Isigidimi Sama-Xosa,* 16 June 1884.

115 'Union Football Club', *Imvo,* 7 May 1891.

116 See 'Rugby in the eastern Cape', *Work in Progress,* no. 17 (1981).

117 J. Peires, '"Facta non verba"', *Work in Progress,* no. 17 (1981), 1; Dobson, *Rugby in South Africa,* 201.

118 B. Ngozi, 'Port Elizabeth black rugby', 'Black rugby in Port Elizabeth, 'Orientals Rugby Football Club' and 'History of Spring Rose Rugby Football Club', compilation of writings and cuttings, n.p.

119 'Ibala labadlali', *Imvo,* 18 January 1888.

120 'Ibala labadlali', *Imvo,* 13 January 1898.

121 'Ibala labadlali', *Imvo,* 7 January 1897.

122 A. Desai, V. Padayachee, K. Reddy and G. Vahed, *Blacks in Whites: A Century of Black Cricket in KwaZulu-Natal* (Pietrmaritzburg: University of KwaZulu-Natal Press, 2003), 127–29. Don Mtimkulu, who had a master's degree from Fort Hare and studied at Harvard, and the former (white) West Indian captain, George Copeland Grant, who played twelve tests in the 1930s and later became a teacher and promoter of cricket at Adams, were responsible for this. See Desai et al, 126, quoting Gordon Mears.

123 'Match report', *Inkanyiso Yase Natal,* 5 January 1894.

124 'Imidlalo', *Izwi Labantu,* 22 October 1907.

125 National Archives, Pretoria, 1/33 N.A. 765 Correspondence files F130 1907–11: Resident Magistrate Bethulie, OFS, to acting secretary for Native Affairs, 16 February 1911.

126 'Colour and sports', *Tsala ea Becoana,* 19 August 1911.

127 KZNCU Archives: Krish Reddy Collection, Durban District Indian Cricket Union report/meetings, 1912/13, SA Coloured Cricket Board – rules etc.

128 N. Mostert, *Frontiers: The Epic of South Africa's Creation and the Tragedy of the Xhosa People* (London: Pimlico, 1992), 1247.

129 S. Gordon to A. Odendaal, 13 October 2015, with newspaper cutting by D. Whitfield, 'Tory stake . . . 1 in 4 Tory MPs have investments in South Africa', *Morning Star*, undated.

130 See R. D. Mandell, *The Nazi Olympics* (London: Souvenir Press, 1972), an invaluable source.

131 *Schutzstaffel*, the paramilitary Nazi Party group transformed by Hitler into a state terror agency.

132 See J. Holmes, *Olympiad 1936: Blaze of Glory for Hitler's Reich* (New York: Ballantine Books, 1971).

133 See O. Hilmes, *Berlin 1936* (London: Bodley Head 2018), another invaluable source.

134 Ibid., 246.

135 See Bell, *In Apartheid's Shadow*, 134.

136 See B. Willan, '"One of the most gentlemanly players that ever donned a jersey": The English Rugby Career of Richard Msimang (1907–1912)', *Quarterly Bulletin of the National Library of South Africa* 66, no. 3 (July–September 2012); Odendaal, *The Story of an African Game*, ch. 1. Bob Edgar provided the reference and photograph of Mantenga and Mzimba. The details about quarterbacks in the United States are from D. Gartland, 'The First Black Quarterback to Start for Each NFL Team', *Sports Illustrated*, 22 September 2016, https://www.si.com/nfl/list-first-black-starting-quarterback-every-team, accessed 15 February 2020.

137 'The kaffir football team', *Pastimes*, 7 October 1899. Our thanks to Bob Edgar for this reference.

138 On the 1899 tour see, A. Odendaal, 'Sport and liberation: The unfinished business of the past', in *Sport and Liberation in South Africa*, ed. C. Thomas (Alice: National Heritage and Cultural Studies Centre, University of Fort Hare/Pretoria: Department of Sport and Recreation, 2006), 18–21; Odendaal, *The Founders*, 174–75; C. Bolsmann, 'The Orange Free State football Team Tour of Europe: "Race", Imperial Loyalty and Sporting Contest', in *Sport Past and Present in South Africa: (Trans)forming the Nation*, ed. S. Cornelissen and A. Grundlingh (London: Routledge, 2012), 80–95.

139 R. Hauman, *Century of the Marathon, 1896–96* (Cape Town: Human & Rousseau, 1996), 121.

140 C. Greyvenstein, *The Fighters: A Pictorial History of SA Boxing Since 1881* (Cape Town: Signma Motor Corporation, 1981), ch. 4.

141 'A Question of Racial Supremacy: Jack Johnson vs. Jim Jeffries, 1910', *Sports in Black and White*, 2 November 2012, http://www.sportsinblackandwhite.com/2012/11/02/a-question-of-racial-supremacy-jack-johnson-vs-jim-jeffries-1910, accessed 24 January 2020.

142 Odendaal et al, *Divided Country*, 28.

143 S. Carmichael, ed., *112 Years of Springbok Rugby, Tests and Heroes, 1891–2003* (Cape Town: South African Rugby Football Union, 2003), 58–59.

144 C. de Broglio, introduction to *South Africa: Racism in Sport* (London: International Defence and Aid Fund, 1970).

145 Greyvenstein, *The Fighters*, 416–17.

146 De Broglio, *South Africa*, 6; P. Melling and T. Collins, eds., *The Glory of Their Times: Crossing the Colour Line in Rugby League* (Skipton: Vertical Editions, 2004), 198–99.

147 This section is a reworking of A. Odendaal, 'Girls and Boys: Looking Back at Cricket's Strange History', in *CSA Girls U19 Cricket Week*, brochure, 4–9 December 2013, 7–12. For more in-depth narratives of women's cricket history, see Odendaal et al, *Cricket and Conquest*, ch. 31–32; Odendaal et al, *Divided Country*, ch. 10, 23, 32; A. Odendaal, '"Neither

Cricketers nor Ladies": Towards a History of Women's Cricket in South Africa, 1860s–2000s', in Cornelissen and Grundlingh, *Sport Past and Present*, 114–35.

148 T. McGirck, 'Neither Cricketers nor Ladies', in *The Boundary Book: Second Innings*, ed. L. Frewin (London: Spring Books, 1986), 196. For a comprehensive explanation of the inferior position accorded to women in nineteenth-century sport, see Mangan and Park, *From Fair Sex to Feminism*, especially the contributions by Hargreaves, McCone, Crawford, King and Fletcher.

149 R. Holt, *Sport and the British: A Modern History* (Oxford: Clarendon Press, 1989), 129.

150 Holt, *Sport and the British*, 214.

151 M. Williams, ed., *Double Century: Cricket in The Times*, vol. 1, *1785–1934* (London: The Pavilion Library, 1989), 22–23.

152 Frewin, *The Boundary Book* (London: Spring Books, 1986), 214–15.

153 McGirck, 'Neither Cricketers nor Ladies', 196.

154 K. A. P. Sandiford, *Cricket and the Victorians* (Aldershot: Scholar Press, 1994), 1–2, 29.

155 McCrone, 'Play up!', 99.

156 Ibid., 104.

157 Odendaal, '"Neither Cricketers nor Ladies"', quoting Jennifer Hargreaves.

158 J. Hargreaves, 'Victorian Familism and the Formative Years of Female Sport', in Mangan and Park, *From Fair Sex to Feminism*, 134–35, 137, 141.

159 On the educational reformers and school sports, see McCrone, 'Play up!', 103–22.

160 See S. Fletcher, 'The Making and Breaking of Female Tradition: Women's Physical Training in England, 1880–1980', in Mangan and Park, *From Fair Sex to Feminism*, ch. 6. The quote is from Hargreaves, 'Victorian Familism', 139.

161 See Sandiford, *Cricket and the Victorians*, 43–48.

162 Williams, *Double Century*, 100.

163 Holt, *Sport and the British*, 128.

164 McCrone, 'Play up!', 119–20.

165 See, for example, H. Colleton, 'Sonnet on the Mistresses v. Girls cricket match', *African Roedean* (April 1911), 14.

166 'Cricket', *African Roedean* (May 1910), 7, 23.

167 See Odendaal et al, *Cricket and Conquest*, 296–98.

168 Ibid., 298–99.

169 E. Kingswell, 'Women at the wicket', *South African Ladies Pictorial* (May 1934), 29.

170 Interview with Milase Majola, New Brighton, 19 October 2002.

171 D. Behrens, 'S.A. vroue raak dol oor krieket', *Die Huisgenoot*, 27 February 1957, 56–57.

172 Private collection: H. Butler, *Cape Times*, undated newspaper cutting; undated handwritten profile.

173 For details of SASA and its campaigns, we refer to T. August, *Dennis Brutus: The South African Years* (Cape Town: Best Red in association with African Lives, forthcoming), MS, 146–50.

174 The material for this section on the emergence of SANROC and the life and death of John Harris comes from the original correspondence of John Harris, researched by Katie Clark from papers held by John Harris's son, David Wolfe; Peter's autobiography *Outside In* (London: Biteback Publishing, 2012); his biography of his parents, *Ad & Wal: Values, Duty, Sacrifice in Apartheid South Africa* (London: Biteback Publishing, 2014); and August, *Dennis Brutus*.

175 The details of this address are from the John Harris private papers and are used with the permission of his family.

176 Like Basil D'Oliveira, McKenzie was forced to move to Britain, which he represented on numerous occasions including the 1968 Mexico Olympics and the Commonwealth Games in 1966, 1970 and 1974, setting new Commonwealth records.

177 For other accounts of John Harris's life see, C. J. 'Jonty' Driver, *The Man with the Suitcase* (Cape Town: Crane River, 2015); D. Beresford, *Truth Is a Strange Fruit: A Personal Journey Through the Apartheid War* (Johannesburg: Jacana Media, 2011); and the documentary *The Good Terrorist*, produced by Simon Finch (Channel Four, 2016).

178 G. Winter, *Inside Boss: South Africa's Secret Police* (London: Allen Lane, 1981), 96–97.

179 A. Odendaal, 'Robben Island – Bridgehead for Democracy', paper presented to Mayibuye Centre Winter School, Celebrating Democracy Festival, University of the Western Cape, 15 July 1994, 1. See also I. Naidoo, *Island in Chains: Ten Years on Robben Island* (Johannesburg: Penguin Books, 1982), 65–66.

180 Odendaal, 'Robben Island – Bridgehead for democracy', 1–2.

181 For example, N. Mandela, *Long Walk to Freedom* (London: Abacus, 1996), 560–61, 587–88.

182 This quote and details on Dennis Brutus's imprisonment on Robben Island in this section are from August, *Dennis Brutus*, ch. 5.

183 D. Brutus, '"You've come to Hell Island": A Political Prisoner Under Apartheid, Autobiographical Notes, 1974', in L. Sustar and A. Karim, *Poetry and Protest: A Dennis Brutus Reader* (Chicago: Haymarket books/University of KwaZulu-Natal Press, 2006), 75; quoted in August, *Dennis Brutus*, 234.

184 Ibid., 75–76, quoted in August, *Dennis Brutus*, 233.

185 Sustar and Karim, *Poetry and Protest*, 76.

186 August, *Dennis Brutus*, 235.

187 Naidoo, *Island in Chains*, 87.

188 Ibid., 104

189 Brutus, *Stubborn Hope* (1978), 28, quoted in August, *Dennis Brutus*, 237.

190 On cricket and representations of beauty, and for the stories about the Group Areas Act, see A. Odendaal, 'Newlands Cricket Ground and the Roots of Apartheid in South African Cricket', in *The Cambridge Companion to Cricket*, ed. A. Bateman and J. Hill (Cambridge: Cambridge University Press, 2011).

191 Quoted in Birley, *The Willow Wand*, 223. This next section of the chapter is based on Odendaal, 'Robben Island – Bridgehead for Democracy' and '"Maintain the Human and Social Within You": Reflecting on Robben Island, Sport and Change in South Africa'; and keynote address to the conference on 'Sport and the Struggles for Social Justice', Robben Island Museum and Department of Sports Science, Stellenbosch University, 10 October 2019. See also printed exhibition brochure, *The Power of the Dream: From Robben Island to Rio, An Exhibition on South Africa and the Olympic Games, 1896–2016* (Cape Town: Western Cape Government Department of Cultural Affairs and Sport, ICESSD/UWC-RIM Mayibuye Archives, 2016), for which André Odendaal was the lead writer.

192 C. Roberts, *Sport in Chains* (Cape Town: Township Publishing Co-operative, 1994), 25.

193 B. Hutton, *Robben Island: Symbol of Resistance* (Cape Town: Mayibuye Books/Sached Books, 1994), 55; Odendaal, 'Robben Island – Bridgehead for Democracy', 3. See also Murphy Morobe and Solomon Musi quoted in M. Keim and L. Bouah, 'Sport and Recreation on Robben Island', *The International Journal of the History of Sport* 30, no. 16 (2013), 12.

194 Roberts, *Sport in Chains*, 2.

195 Ibid., 45, 53.

196 Ibid., 25.

197 Quoted in Keim and Bouah, 'Sport and Recreation on Robben Island', 20.

198 Ibid.

199 C. Korr and M. Close, *More Than Just a Game: Football v Apartheid* (London, HarperCollins, 2008).

200 Hain, *Ad and Wal*, 234.

201 A. Kathrada, 'Opening Address' (26 May 1993), in *Esiqithini: The Robben Island Exhibition* (Cape Town: South African Museum/Mayibuye Books, University of the Western Cape, 1996).

202 A. Odendaal, K. Reddy and A. Samson, *The Blue Book: A History of Western Province Cricket, 1890–2011* (Cape Town: Fanele, 2012), 15.

203 A. Brink, *A Fork in the Road: A Memoir* (London: Harvill Secker, 2009), 183.

204 See Hain, *Ad & Wal*, 227–37.

205 O. Lewis, 'Little Pyongyang', *The Spectator*, 31 March 2012.

206 T. Huddleston, *Naught for Your Comfort* (New York: Doubleday & Company, 1956).

207 See A. Steel, 'Sport Leads the Way', *Africa South* 4, no. 1 (October–December 1959), 114–15.

208 An excellent booklet on much of this period is G. Brown and C. Høgsbjerg, *Apartheid Is Not a Game: Remembering the Stop The Seventy Tour Campaign* (London: Redwords, 2020).

209 For an inside account, see de Broglio, *South Africa*.

210 Fellow South African exiles Wilfred Brutus, Omar Cassem, Isaiah Stein were part of SANROC's delegation in Amsterdam with Chris de Broglio and Dennis Brutus.

211 H. Edwards, *The Revolt of the Black Athlete* (New York: Collier-MacMillan, 1969).

212 J. M. Coetzee, 'Playing total (arian) Rugby', *Suid-Afrikaan*, 4–6 August 1988, 4.

213 'Inside Job', *Guardian*, 23 October 2002.

214 Winter, *Inside Boss*.

215 For an account of the case, see D. Humphry, ed., *The Cricket Conspiracy* (London: National Council for Civil Liberties, 1973).

216 See P. Hain, *Mistaken Identity* (London: Quartet, 1976).

217 For an analysis, see former BBC journalists, B. Penrose and R. Courtiour, *The Pencourt File* (London: Secker & Warburg, 1978).

218 See P. Hain, *A Putney Plot?* (Nottingham: Spokesman, 1987).

219 See especially S. Dorril and R. Ramsay, *Smear!* (London: Fourth Estate, 1991).

220 K. Jeffrey and P. Hennessy, *States of Emergency* (London: Routledge & Kegan Paul, 1983), 235.

221 See P. Wright, *Spycatcher* (Australia: Heinemann, 1987).

222 Gurney, 'In the Heart of the Beast'.

223 Quoted in C. Bundy, 'South Africa on the switchback', *New Society*, 3 January 1986, 7–12.

224 Gurney, 'In the Heart of the Beast'.

225 T. G. Karis and G. M. Gerhart, *From Protest to Challenge: A Documentary History of African Politics in South Africa, 1882–1990*, vol. 5 (Bloomington: Indiana University Press, 1997), 98.

226 Ibid., 98–99.

227 Bundy, 'South Africa on the switchback'.

228 For the growth of the black trade unions, see S. Friedman, *Building Tomorrow Today: African Workers in Trade Unions, 1970–1984* (Ravan Press: Johannesburg, 1987). This overview of political changes in the 1960s and 1970s draws directly on A. Odendaal, 'The liberation struggle in South Africa, 1948–1994', in Y. N. Seleti, ed., *Africa Since 1990* (Cape Town: New Africa Education, 2004), 167–71.

229 Minutes of the SACOS founding conference, Durban, 17–18 March 1973, in South African Council on Sport, [*First*] *Biennial Conference* (Durban: SACOS, 1975), 12–20. For memories of George Singh, see A. Kathrada, *Memoirs* (Cape Town: Zebra Press, 2004), 46, 166.

230 C. Roberts, *No Normal Sport in an Abnormal Society. Struggle for Non-Racial Sport in South Africa: From Apartheid to Sport's Unity* (Cape Town: Havana Media, 2011), 55–56.

231 Minutes of the SACOS founding conference in South African Council

on Sport, 1975, 15.

232 'United Nations', in South African Council on Sport, 1975, 23.

233 SACOS, *Biennial Conference*, 63–64.

234 'The South African Non-Racial Olympic Committee', in South African Council on Sport, *Third Biennial Conference* (Durban: SACOS, 1979), 128–32.

235 C. Chivers, 'Isaiah Stein: Activist who played a significant role in the overthrowing of apartheid', *The Independent*, 7 February 2011, https://www.independent.co.uk/news/obituaries/isaiah-stein-activist-who-played-a-significant-role-in-the-overthrowing-of-apartheid-2206210.html, accessed 1 December 2019.

236 See 'Davis Cup Group Bars So. Africa', *New York Times*, 15 April 1972, https://www.nytimes.com/1972/04/15/archives/davis-cup-group-bars-so-africa-early-decision-is-reversed-way.html, accessed 1 December 2019.

237 Sustar and Karim, *Poetry and Protest*, 144; see also 140–41, 143 for Brutus's description of the later acrimonious fallout between him and Ramsamy.

238 The delegates to the first SACOS conference were: SASF – S. K. Chetty, Charles M. Pillay, R. Bijou, Geo Singh; SACBOC – Hassan Howa, Pat Naidoo; SALTU – M. K. Naidoo, E. Osman, A. Y. Mulla, S. S. Singh; SAASF – S. K. Naidoo, D. Nair, D. K. Singh, L. Fabre; SATTB – Cassim M. Bassa, A. S. Tayob, A. G. M. Randeree, I. G. H. Patel; SAAWBBF – A. Rasool, A. S. Robert, Billy J. Naidoo, T. G. Govender; SAA&CBOC – D. Naidoo, S. J. Reddy, S. Narain, R. Hemraj; SASSSA – N. Rathinasamy, D. Soma.

239 South African Council on Sport, *Sixth Biennial General Meeting* (Durban: SACOS, 1985), 178.

240 For the Aurora CC history, see C. Nicholson and M. Hickson, *The Level Playing Field: How the Aurora Cricket Club Stumped Apartheid* (Pietermaritzburg: KwaZulu-Natal

Cricket Union/Cricket South Africa, 2015).

241 'Rugby in the Eastern Cape: A History', *Work in Progress*, no. 17 (April 1981), 2–3.

242 See, for example, *Eastern Province Herald*, 17 January 1973.

243 Interview with Khaya Majola, Johannesburg, 3 July 2000.

244 Interview with Dan Qeqe, New Brighton, 29 October 2002.

245 Ibid.

246 Personal communication, Ebrahim Rasool, 2001.

247 See J. Burgess, *The Great White Hoax: South Africa's International Propaganda Machine* (London: Africa Bureau, 1977).

248 See, for example, 'Howa gives some straight answers', *Drum*, 8 March 1973.

249 Ramsamy, *Reflections*, 28.

250 'Mixed cricket', *Daily Dispatch*, 19 January 1976; A. Odendaal, *Cricket in Isolation: The Politics of Race and Cricket in South Africa* (Cape Town: André Odendaal, 1977), 41–43.

251 See Odendaal, *Cricket in Isolation*, ch. 3.

252 Ibid., ch. 4.

253 Ibid., 59.

254 'Bravo's in the fold', *Cape Herald*, 15 November 1977.

255 'Varachia lays it on the line', *Cape Herald*, 12 December 1977.

256 For details of this tumultuous year in football, see G. Venter, 'Discord in the Dressing Room: The Ideological Complexities Within Non-Racial Football During the Late 1970s', in *Exploring Decolonising Themes in SA Sport History: Issues and Challenges*, ed. F. J. Cleophas (Stellenbosch: Sun Press, 2018), 55–65. See also P. Alegi, 'The Era of Change', in *Laduma! Soccer, Politics and Society in South Africa, from Its Origins to 2010* (Scottsville: University of KwaZulu-Natal Press, 2010), ch. 9.

257 See A. Odendaal, 'Resistance, Reform and Repression in South Africa in the 1980s', in *Beyond the Barricades: Popular Resistance in South Africa in the 1980s*

(London: Kliptown Books, 1989), 127.

258 See C. Roberts, *SACOS 1971–1988: 15 Years of Sports Resistance* (Durban: 1988), 21–22.

259 M. Mamabolo, 'Terror was an "inspiration for black boxers"', *Cape Times*, 20 January 2020.

260 'Seven quit PECU clubs', *Cape Herald*, 17 January 1978.

261 See, for example, 'More SACOS men on "New Brighton" charges', *SACOS Bulletin* 1, no. 6 (September–October 1983), 1.

262 'The role of the non-racial sportsperson', *SACOS Bulletin*, 3–5.

263 N. Goodall, 'Opposing Apartheid Through Sport: The Role of SACOS in South African Sport, 1982–1992' (MA thesis, Wits University, 2016), 45.

264 Roberts, *SACOS 1971–1988*, 30.

265 'New cricket body formed', *Cape Herald*, 15 November 1977; Mogamad Allie, *More Than a Game: History of the Western Province Cricket Board 1959–1991* (Cape Town: Cape Argus/WPCA, 2000), 143–44.

266 Minutes of the third biennial conference of SACOS, Cape Town, 1 September 1979, in South African Council on Sport, *Fourth Biennial Conference* (Durban: SACOS, 1981), 12–14, 22–23, 29.

267 J. C. Ganga to president of SACOS, 'c/o SAN-ROC', 10 May 1978, in SACOS, *Third Biennial Conference*, 136.

268 Quoted in letter from M. F. Johnson to T. Feetwood, president of the American Darts Organisation, in SACOS, *Third Biennial Conference*, 80.

269 Roberts, *SACOS 1971–1988*, 31.

270 Ibid., 26.

271 Ibid., 33–34.

272 Quoted in G. Venter, 'Discord in the Dressing Room', 59.

273 Ramsamy, *Reflections*, 73–75.

274 Gurney, 'In the Heart of the Beast'.

275 For an authoritative account see T. Richards, *Dancing on Our Bones: New Zealand, South Africa, Racism and Rugby* (Wellington: Bridget Williams Books,

1999).

276 R. Archer and A. Bouillon, *The South African Game, Sport and Racism* (London: Zed Press 1982), 296.

277 For a fascinating account of Māori involvement see T. Richards, 'Neither forgotten nor forgiven', *E-Tangeta*, 9 November 2019, https://e-tangata.co.nz/history/neither-forgotten-nor-forgiven/.

278 Richards, Dancing on Our Bones, 3.

279 F. van Zyl Slabbert, 'The dynamics of reform and revolt in South Africa', *IDASA Occasional Papers*, no. 8 (1987), 3; H. Giliomee, introduction to *The Parting of the Ways: South African Politics, 1976–82* (Cape Town: David Philip, 1982).

280 K. Williamson, *Brothers to Us: The Story of a Remarkable Family's Fight Against Apartheid*, 2nd ed. (Ringwood, Australia: Penguin Books, 1998), 32–34.

281 Ibid., 37–40.

282 Ibid., 44.

283 See Odendaal, 'Resistance, Reform and Repression in South Africa in the 1980s', 137.

284 Interview with Dan Qeqe, New Brighton, 29 October 2002.

285 The references to KWARU here are from A. Odendaal, *The Story of an African Game*, 245–46.

286 J. Froman, *Papa Joe: 80 Not Out* (UK: Jody Froman, 2011), 79.

287 A. Odendaal, 'Stop Padding Up to Apartheid' (unpublished article, 1989); for some background and context, see also A. Odendaal, ed., *'The Gate': Commemorating SA Sport's June 16 Moment and the Non-Racial Struggles that Led to Cricket Unity* (Cape Town: Cricket South Africa, 2014), 13–15.

288 H. van Vuuren, *Apartheid Guns and Money* (London: Hurst & Co, 2018)

289 T. Smith, 'Once more the ghosts of apartheid's horrors will arise, haunting the inquest into Neil Aggett's death', *Sunday Times*, 19 January 2020.

290 R. S. Roberts, 'Hillela and the Whale', in *A Writing Life: Celebrating Nadine Gordimer*, ed. A. Olifant (London: Viking, 1998), 54–55.

291 A. Odendaal, 'Analysis and Action', address to annual research conference for staff at Leeds Metropolitan University, 2008.

292 Letter from A. Odendaal to A. Mangera, 3 October 1984.

293 See the details in Nicholson and Hickson, *The Level Playing Field*, especially ch. 10–17.

294 Quoted in South African Bishops Conference report, 'Police conduct during the township protests, August–November 1984' (Pretoria: 1985).

295 See, for example, *Weekly Mail*, 20 May 1988.

296 Message from M. Naidoo, president, South African Council on Sport, *SACOS Sport Festival '82* (Cape Town: SACOS, 1982), 1.

297 See 'Sports festival', in SACOS, *Fifth Biennial Report* (Cape Town: SACOS, 1983), 147–54.

298 SACOS, *Sixth Biennial General Meeting*, 35. Allan Zinn drew attention to the intersecting political perspectives of the SACOS leadership in the 1980s; telephone conversation with A. Odendaal, 18 February 2020.

299 South African Council on Sport, *Seventh Biennial Conference* (Johannesburg: SACOS, 1987), 131.

300 Roberts, *SACOS 1973–1988*, 59–60. See 'Cheryl Roberts Championing Women's Sport', *Gsport*, https://gsport.co.za/cheryl-roberts-championing-womens-sport/, accessed 12 February 2020.

301 *Seventh Biennial Conference*, 130–33.

302 'Message from the president of SACOS', in *SACOS Sportsperson of the Year Award, 1984*, 3; Minutes of the SACOS general meeting, Kimberley, 8–9 September 1984, in SACOS, *Sixth Biennial General Meeting*, 9–10.

303 'SACOS Sport and Liberation Conference',

in SACOS, *Sixth Biennial General Meeting*, 148–51.

304 See *SACOS Bulletin*.

305 'Meetings between SACOS and other progressive people's organisations', in SACOS, *Sixth Biennial General Meeting*, 71–72.

306 A detailed description of this turn to progressive constitutional options going alongside an intensifying 'four-pillar' struggle, which took place before the 'unbannings', between 1985 and February 1990, and which has not properly been described until now, will be provided in André's forthcoming book dealing with the first steps in the making of South Africa's constitution. The provisional title is *Dear Comrade President*.

307 'A chronology of meetings between South Africans and the ANC in exile 1983–2000 by Michael Savage', South African History Online, https://www.sahistory.org.za/archive/chronology-meetings-between-south-africans-and-anc-exile-1983-2000-michael-savage, accessed 8 February 2019.

308 L. Callinicos, *Oliver Tambo: Beyond the Ngele Mountains* (Cape Town: David Philip, 2015), 571.

309 S. Ramsamy, *Reflections on a Life in Sport* (Cape Town: Greenhouse, 2004), 100.

310 Roberts, *SACOS 1973–1988*, 52.

311 See K. Naidoo, *Krish: Struggle Lawyer* (Crown Mines: Krish Naidoo, 2019), 148–49.

312 Ibid., 154–56.

313 E. Groenink, *Incorruptible: The Story of the Murders of Dulcie September, Anton Lubowski and Chris Hani* (Cape Town: Evelyn Groenink, 2018), 11–12.

314 For details see W. Campschreur and J. Divendal, *Culture in Another South Africa* (London: Zed Books, 1989). Kier Schuringa provided the original programme and a list of participants.

315 Campschreur and Divendal, *Culture in Another South Africa*, 259–65.

316 Naidoo, *Krish,* 196–200.

317 Ramsamy, *Reflections*, 100.
318 T. Bedford, personal communication with A. Odendaal, and talk to Wynberg Boys' High old boys on thirtieth anniversary of Dakar conference, Cape Town, July 2017.
319 For the report, see 'Rugby', in South African Council on Sport, *Eighth Biennial Meeting* (Cape Town: SACOS, 1989), 107–8.
320 For an insider account of these meetings, see A. Pahad, *Insurgent Diplomat: Civil Talks or Civil War?* (Johannesburg: Penguin Books, 2014). The film *Endgame* (UK, 2009) – based on R. Harvey, *The Fall of Apartheid: The Inside Story from Smuts to Mbeki* (London: Palgrave Macmillan, 2001) – provides a rather shallow version of the discussions.
321 J. Gerwel, 'Towards a disciplined, healthy sports movement in preparation for post-apartheid South Africa', in C. Roberts, ed., *Sport and Transformation: Contemporary Debates in South African Sport* (Cape Town: Township Publishing Co-operative, 1989), ch. 9.
322 Ibid., 64.
323 Ibid.
324 A. Desai, 'Tales of a Devil Child' (unpublished article, 2020).
325 H. Willemse, 'The Duality of Belonging and Rejection: Attending UWC in the 1970s' (unpublished article, 2020).
326 Ramsamy, *Reflections*, 101.
327 SACOS, *Eighth Biennial Meeting*, 72–77; Roberts, *SACOS 1973–1988*, 77.
328 Roberts, *SACOS 1973–1988*, 72.
329 The sources used in this section include: 'The meeting between the South African Amateur Athletics Board and the African National Congress', in SACOS, *Eighth Biennial Meeting*, 87–88; Naidoo, *Krish,* 157–59, 163; and B. Brown, 'The Destruction of Non-Racial Sport: A Consequence of the Negotiated Political Settlement', in Thomas, *Sport and Liberation*, 138–50.
330 A. Jeffery, *People's War: New Light on the Struggle for South Africa* (Johannesburg:

331 P. May, *The Rebel Tours: Cricket's Crisis of Conscience* (Cheltenham: SportsBooks, 2009), 270.
332 M. Bose, *Sporting Colours, Sport and Politics in South Africa* (London: Robson Books, 1994), 202–3; Jeffery, *People's War,* 222–23.
333 J. Foster, 'Critics leave Bacher room to recant and retreat', *The Independent*, undated; Odendaal, 'The Gate', 15.
334 This section, on the decision to form the NSC and militantly oppose the treble tour, is based on Naidoo, *Krish*, 177–79 and Ramsamy, *Reflections*, ch. 8.
335 M. Engel, 'Wise counsel needed in SA talks about tour', *Guardian*, 8 November 1989.
336 'First rebel test for Newlands', *Cape Times*, 7 November 1989.
337 Africa Fund, 'Re: Conference for a Democratic Future Held in South Africa on December 9th 1989', http://psimg.jstor.org/fsi/img/pdf/t0/10.5555/al.sff.document.af000258_final.pdf, accessed 27 January 2020.
338 Jeffery, *People's War*, 230–31; 'CDF calls for end of rebel tours' and 'Resolution on sports boycott and rebel tours to South Africa', *City Press*, 17 December 1989; 'Rebel tour is on CDF agenda', *Weekly Mail*, 8 December 1989.
339 'The National Sports Congress Anti-Tour Committee', *South*, 22 February 1990. The reports on the rebel tour that follow come from the André Odendaal Collection, Box B.8, Sports activism: P. Hain, the Gatting rebel tour and the launch of the National Sports Congress, 1989–90.
340 R. Houwing, 'City rally urged to disrupt Gatting's tour', *The Argus*, 17 January 1989; R. du Preez and C. du Plessis, 'Rebels not welcome – NSC', *Sunday Times* (*Extra*), 21 January 1989; 'Vandale beskadig oefenblaaie', *Die Burger*, December 1989.
341 'Hani: ANC bombed Avendale clubhouse',

Cape Times, 17 January 1990, 3; 'Rebel tour linked to blast?', *Weekend Argus*, 6 January 1990.

342 See S. Gunn and S. Haricharan, eds., *Voices from the Underground: Eighteen Life Stories from Umkhonto we Sizwe's Ashley Kriel Detachment* (Cape Town: Penguin Random House, 2019), 35, 81, 117, 150, 269.

343 A. Odendaal, 'Die rebelletoer: Nee!' and J. Cook, 'Maar Cook se: Ja, beslis!', *Vrye Weekblad*, 12 January 1990.

344 G. Abrahams, 'Crosstalk: So whose the one wearing blinkers?', *South*, 7 December 1989; 'Tour should go on says Woolmer', *London Evening Standard*, 17 January 1990.

345 *Cape Times*, 26 January 1990

346 *Cape Times*, 16 January 1990

347 *Cape Times*, 24 January 1990.

348 Odendaal, ed., *'The Gate'*, 1, 14.

349 Odendaal, *'The Gate'*, 19.

350 Ramsamy, *Reflections*, 106.

351 'Tour starts, Stormy send-off for UK cricket rebels', *Cape Times*, 19 January 1990; 'Polisie tree op by lughawe. Betoging faal teen toerspan', *Die Burger*, 20 January 1990; 'PAM wil nie vra om te betoog', *Die Burger*, 23 January 1990.

352 *The Argus*, 25 January 1989, front page.

353 E. Jacobs, 'It was riot cops in their full regalia', in Odendaal, *'The Gate'*, 33–34. Quotations when not attributed are also from this article.

354 See André Odendaal Collection: 'Tour demo ends in township riot', *Cape Times*, undated; see also Odendaal, *'The Gate'*.

355 'Mayhem as police break up anti-tour meeting', *The Argus*, 30 January 1990; 'More protests planned at today's Bloem march', *The Argus*, 31 January 1990; 'Krieket-betogers se stormloop gestuit', *Die Burger*, 2 February 1990; 'Wonde van man gewys aan Gatting', *Die Burger*, 2 February 1990; 'Tour violence, Black club withdraws', *Cape Times*, 2 February 1990.

356 Quoted in *The Argus*, 30 January 1990. For the Pietermaritzburg protests, see

Nicholson and Hickson, *The Level Playing Field*, ch. 19; K. Chetty, 'Political activists bounce white cricket out of SA', *Sunday Tribune*, 27 October 2019.

357 'OFS next stop for demos', *City Press*, 28 January 1990; Gatting pitches in as eatery staff walk out', *Sunday Times*, 28 January 1990.

358 'Government worried protests could derail reform', *Cape Times*, 29 January 1990.

359 W. Estherhuyse, *Endgame: Secret Talks and the End of Apartheid* (Cape Town: Tafelberg, 2012), 261–64; Pahad, *Insurgent Diplomat*, 200.

360 Naidoo, *Krish*, 183–85; Ramsamy, *Reflections*, 107–9.

361 Gunn and Haricharan, *Voices from the Underground*, 34–35.

362 Odendaal, *'The Gate'*, 28–29.

363 Ramsamy, *Reflections*, 109.

364 Ibid., 114–22.

365 Ibid., 120–21.

366 Gurney, 'In the Heart of the Beast'.

367 André Odendaal Collection, Box B.8: 'The Sports Movement of the future! The background, emergence and policy of the National Olympic and Sports Congress (NOSC)' (NOSC Western Cape, November 1990), 13–14.

368 For the unfolding negotiations process, see H. Ebrahim, *The Making of the Constitution: The Story of South Africa's Constitutional Assembly* (Cape Town: Churchill Murray, 1997). This chapter draws extensively on this work.

369 For the timeline, see Ebrahim, ibid. See also Jeffery, *People's War*, 244–45, 254–55, 270–72.

370 A. Sparks, *Tomorrow Is Another Country* (Johannesburg: Jonathan Ball, 2003), 130.

371 These details are from Ramsamy, *Reflections*, ch. 10.

372 Sparks, *Another Country*, 194–95.

373 Brown, 'The Destruction of Non-Racial Sport', 138.

374 Ibid., 149.

375 See Dougie Oakes's comments in Roberts,

No Normal Sport, 107.

376 See A. Desai, *Reverse Sweep: A Story of South African Cricket Since Apartheid* (Johannesburg: Jacana Media, 2016).

377 See J. Carlin, *Playing the Enemy* (London: Atlantic Books, 2008).

378 Ibid.

379 See I. Hawkey and L. Alfred, *Vuvuzela Dawn* (London: Pan Macmillan, 2019).

380 See P. Hain, *Back to the Future of Socialism* (Bristol: Policy Press, 2015).

381 J. Liew, 'Broadcast rights trump human rights in Premiere League's Newcastle battleground', *Guardian*, 22 April 2020, https://www.theguardian.com/football/2020/apr/22/broadcast-rights-trump-human-rights-in-premier-leagues-newcastle-battleground.

382 J. Liew, 'It's not just Bury and Bolton', *New Statesman*, 4 September 2019.

383 This section is based on an unpublished article that *Leadership South Africa* commissioned André to write for a proposed sports edition, which did not materialise: 'Reflecting on year one of a cricket revolution' (2007).

384 See, for example, G. Phelps, ed., *Arlott and Trueman on Cricket* (London: British Broadcasting Corporation, 1977), 55–56, 108–10; and K. Booth, *George Lohmann: Pioneer Professional* (London: SportsBooks, 2007), 55.

385 Odendaal, 'Reflecting on year one of a cricket revolution'.

386 André Odendaal CEO report, in *Western Province Cricket Association Annual Report, 2013/2014* (Cape Town: Formsxpress, 2014).

387 See P. Canoville, *Black and Blue* (London: Headline, 2007).

388 Yolanthe Fawehinmi, 'Paul Canoville: Forgiving Chelsea, Overcoming Racial Abuse and Mastering the Art of Bringing Culture into Sport', *Daily Telegraph*, 5 February 2020, https://www.telegraph.co.uk/football/2020/02/05/paul-canoville-forgiving-chelsea-overcoming-racial-abuse-mastering/;

Samuel Lovett, '"It's coming back": Paul Canoville, Chelsea's first black player, on a career being racially abused and why it's never gone away', *The Independent*, 11 December 2018, https://www.independent.co.uk/sport/football/premier-league/paul-canoville-chelsea-fc-racism-raheem-sterling-abuse-message-a8677821.html.

389 'The ugly spectre of racism in football on the rise across Europe', *Guardian*, 16 December 2018, https://www.theguardian.com/football/2018/dec/16/racism-on-the-rise-across-europe-football-raheem-sterling-chelsea.

390 For her story, see *E. Aluko, They Don't Teach This (London: Yellow Jersey Press, 2019)*.

391 André Odendaal Collection: A. Diesel 'How to define a woman', *City Press*, undated; O. de Villiers, 'Semenya looking to go out with a bang in Doha', *Cape Times*, 3 May 2019.

392 'A freedom fighter of her time', *City Press*, 22 December 2019.

393 'Mokgadi Caster Semenya', South African History Online, 15 August 2017, https://www.sahistory.org.za/people/mokgadi-caster-semenya. See also P. de Vos, 'Stereotyping's stale stench', *Sunday World*, 21 August 2016.

394 O. Yaniv, 'Caster Semenya, forced to take gender test, is a woman . . . and a man', *New York Daily News*, 10 September 2009.

395 Yaniv, 'Caster Semenya'.

396 'Caster Semenya', Wikipedia, https://en.wikipedia.org/wiki/Caster_Semenya, accessed 10 January 2019.

397 N. Daniels, 'Medical journal shines spotlight on Semenya', *Weekend Argus*, 7 August 2019.

398 'Mokgadi Caster Semenya', South African History Online.

399 'Caster Semenya/IAAF timeline', *City Press*, 22 December 2019.

400 Yaniv, 'Caster Semenya'.

401 M. Siluma, 'Of Semenya, Saartjie and the

IAAF', *City Press*, 24 February 2019.

402 See R. Holmes, *The Hottentot Venus: The Life and Death of Saartjie Baartman* (Johannesburg: Jonathan Ball Publishers, 2007); Clifton Crais and Pamela Scully, *Sara Baartman and the Hottentot Venus: A Ghost Story and a Biography* (Johannesburg: Wits University Press, 2009).

403 N. Daniels, 'Medical journal shines spotlight on Semenya', *Weekend Argus*, 7 August 2019.

404 'Mokgadi Caster Semenya', South African History Online; 'Caster Semenya', Wikipedia.

405 S. Camporesi, 'Why Caster Semenya and Dutee Chand deserve to compete (and win) at Rio 2016', *The Conversation*, 19 April 2016.

406 De Vos, 'Stereotyping's stale stench'.

407 N. Arendse to A. Odendaal, 10 January 2020, forwarding N. Arendse to J. Kelly, 22 March 2019, with attachment, 'United Nations adopts resolution to support Semenya, 22 March 2019'. With thanks to Norman Arendse for these Court of Arbitration documents.

408 L. Isaacs, 'Physicians urged to defy IAAF rule on female athletes', *Cape Times*, 3 May 2019.

409 N. Daniels, 'Medical journal shines spotlight on Semenya', *Weekend Argus*, 7 August 2019.

410 Interview, *CNN World Sport* (CNN International), 20 September 2019.

411 See also O. de Villiers, 'The Caster I have got to know over 10 years: An in-depth interview with her lawyer Greg Nott', *Cape Times,* 15 November 2019.

412 M. Ziegler, 'Women's track star is "biological male"', *The Times*, 24 February 2019, 3.

413 R. Calland, L. Naidoo and A. Whaley, *The Vuvuzela Revolution: Anatomy of South Africa's World Cup* (Johannesburg: Jacana Media, 2010).

414 See, for example, C. S. Herzenberg, ed., *Player and Referee: Conflicting interests and the 2010 FIFA World Cup* (Tshwane: Institute for Security Studies, 2010).

415 A. Makinana, 'If this is not corruption then what is it – AG', *Sunday Times*, 5 July 2020.

416 M. Marqusee, 'Sport and Stereotype: From Role Model to Muhammad Ali', *Race and Class* 36, no. 4 (1995), 5; quoted in A. Desai, ed., *The Race to Transform: Sport in Post-Apartheid South Africa* (Cape Town: HSRC Press, 2010), 1.

417 E. Makhaya, 'Coronavirus: The impact on PSL and South African football', *Goal*, 24 March 2020, https://www.goal.com/en-gb/news/coronavirus-the-impact-on-psl-and-south-african-football/ztnyf628lhly1a5rk2tllpbjw.

418 See K. Mitchell, 'Cricket has lost the role it had in 1939 but it's still far more than a game', *Observer*, 22 March 2020, https://www.theguardian.com/sport/blog/2020/mar/22/cricket-has-lost-the-role-it-had-in-1939-but-its-still-far-more-than-a-game.

419 For an account of cricket in the Second World War see E. Midwinter, *The Lost Seasons: Cricket in Wartime 1939–45* (London: Methuen 1987).

420 'The impact of Covid-19 on sport, physical activity and well-being and its effects on social development', United Nations, 15 May 2020, https://www.un.org/development/desa/dspd/2020/05/covid-19-sport/.

421 Welsh Parliament – Culture, Welsh Language and Communications Committee, 'Impact of the Covid-19 Outbreak on Sport', June 2020, https://senedd.wales/laid%20documents/cr-ld13267/cr-ld13267%20-e.pdf.

422 K. Badenhausen, 'The World's 50 Most Valuable Sports Teams 2019', Forbes, 22 July 2019, https://www.forbes.com/sites/kurtbadenhausen/2019/07/22/the-worlds-50-most-valuable-sports-teams-2019/#697c7d36283d.

423 We thank Nadia Odendaal for her

research assistance in this section.

424 Christine Brennan, CNN Sport, 13 July 2020 (00:21 South African Standard Time).

425 'CEO Sporting Equals Statement: Equality of Opportunity in the Sport Sector', Sporting Equals, http://www.sportingequals.org.uk/news-and-blogs/ceo-sporting-equals-statement-equality-of-opportunity-in-the-sport-sector.html, accessed 11 July 2020.

426 D. McRay, 'Michael Emenalo: "The narrative that white is good has to change"', *Guardian*, 19 July 2020, https://www.theguardian.com/football/2020/jul/19/michael-emenalo-the-narrative-that-white-is-good-has-to-change?.

427 R. Broadbent, 'Exiled, rejected, defunded – the price of making a stand against racism', *The Times*, 7 July 2020, https://www.thetimes.co.uk/article/exiled-rejected-defunded-the-price-of-making-a-stand-against-racism-6kc70c0dl#top.

428 'Lungi Ngidi comes under fire from ex-South African cricketers for Black Lives Matter stand', *Indian Express*, 10 July 2020, https://www.google.co.za/amp/s/indianexpress.com/article/sports/cricket/lungi-ngidi-under-fire-south-africa-black-lives-matter-stand-6498120/lite/.

429 'Statement by former South African cricketers and senior coaches on #BlackLivesMatter, 14 July 2020'.

430 Makhaya Ntini interview, SABC Morning Live, 17 July 2020, https://www.youtube.com/watch?v=KasKB02Vt_E, accessed 11 July 2020.

431 L. del Carme, 'Black rugby coaches and former players throw their weight behind Black Lives Matter and Lungi Ngidi', Sowetan Live, 15 July 2020, https://www.sowetanlive.co.za/sport/rugby/2020-07-15-black-rugby-coaches-and-former-players-throw-their-weight-behind-black-lives-matter-and-lungi-ngidi/; H. Schenk, '"A vital first step" – SA sportswomen join hands in support of Black Lives Matter', News24, 17 July 2020, https://www.news24.com/sport/othersport/south-africa/a-vital-first-step-sa-sportswomen-join-hands-in-support-of-black-lives-matter-20200717.

432 U. Nkanjeni, '"I will speak, even if it costs me my place": Siya Kolisi adds his voice to Black Lives Matter', *Times Live*, 20 July 2020, https://www.timeslive.co.za/sport/rugby/2020-07-20-i-will-speak-even-if-it-costs-me-my-place-siya-kolisi-adds-his-voice-to-black-lives-matter/.

433 'Study reveals racial bias in English football commentary', *Network Fare*, 30 June 2020, https://www.farenet.org/news/study-reveals-racial-bias-in-english-football-commentary/; A. Kajuma, 'Commentators racially biased?', *Cape Times*, 1 July 2020; Sachin Nakrani, 'Groundbreaking report reveals racial bias in english football commentary', *Guardian*, 29 June 2020, https://www.theguardian.com/football/2020/jun/29/groundbreaking-report-reveals-racial-bias-in-english-football-commentary.

434 B. Okri, *Mental Fight* (London: Rider, 2012).

Index

Photo credits

225 top: © PA Images
225 bottom: © UPI
226 top: Courtesy of the Marx Memorial Library & Workers' School, London
© *Morning Star*
226 bottom left: © AAM Archives Committee
226 bottom right: © *Cricket Monthly/The Cricketer*
227 top left: Courtesy of the AAM Archives © AAM Archives Committee
227 top right: © Central Press/Hulton Archive via Getty Images
227 bottom: © TopFoto
228 top: © Leonard Burt/Hulton Archive via Getty Images
228 bottom: © *The Guardian*
229 top: © Stop The Seventy Tour Committee
229 bottom left: © PA Photos/TopFoto
229 bottom right: © News Ltd/Newspix
230 top left: Courtesy of the Western Province Cricket Association Archives
230 top right: © Mr Derrick S. Hubbard
230 bottom: Courtesy of Cory Library, Rhodes University/Africa Media Online
231 top left: © Bella Forsyth, Port Elizabeth. Courtesy of Jonty Winch, Richard Parry and
Penguin/Random House, 2020
231 top right: Courtesy of Lincoln University, Pennsylvania
231 bottom: Courtesy of The National Archives, Kew (ref. COPY 1/442)
232 top left: Courtesy of Creative Commons
232 top right: Courtesy of Missouri History Museum, St Louis, Missouri
232 bottom left: Courtesy of the Majola family collection, with thanks to Gerald Majola
232 bottom right: © SACBOC
233 top: © Noel Syers
233 bottom: © Keystone Press/Alamy Stock Photo
234 top: © SARWCA
234 bottom: © HMP (unknown)
235 top: Courtesy of Cory Library, Rhodes University/Africa Media Online
235 bottom: Courtesy of the Majola family collection, with thanks to Gerald Majola
236 top left: Courtesy of the De Broglio family collection
236 top right: Photographer unknown
236 bottom: © Abe Berry collection, UWC/RIM Mayibuye Archives
237 top left: Photographer unknown
237 top right: Courtesy of the De Broglio family collection
237 bottom: © UWC/RIM Mayibuye Archives
238 top left: © International Defence and Aid Fund for Southern Africa
238 top right: © UWC/RIM Mayibuye Archives
238 bottom: © UWC/RIM Mayibuye Archives
239 top: © UWC/RIM Mayibuye Archives
239 bottom: Courtesy of Derek Carelse
240 top left: © Frank Black, *The Star*
240 top right: *Drum* magazine
240 bottom: Courtesy of the Dan Qeqe family collection